THE MEMOIRS AND SPEECHES OF
JAMES, 2nd EARL WALDEGRAVE,
1742–1763

The House of Lords at the end of the session of 1741–2, a year after the 2nd Earl Waldegrave had succeeded to his title. George II, enthroned, is flanked by the bishops on the left of the engraving, the peers on the right. The Commons are in attendance on the floor of the House, led by their Speaker, Arthur Onslow

THE MEMOIRS AND SPEECHES OF JAMES, 2nd EARL WALDEGRAVE, 1742–1763

Edited with an introduction by
J. C. D. CLARK

CAMBRIDGE UNIVERSITY PRESS

Cambridge
New York   New Rochelle
Melbourne   Sydney

Published by the Press Syndicate of the University of Cambridge
The Pitt Building, Trumpington Street, Cambridge CB2 1RP
32 East 57th Street, New York, NY 10022, USA
10 Stamford Road, Oakleigh, Melbourne 3166, Australia

© Cambridge University Press 1988

First published 1988

Printed in Great Britain at
the University Press, Cambridge

British Library cataloguing in publication data

Waldegrave, James Waldegrave, Earl, 1715–1763
The memoirs and speeches of James, 2nd Earl Waldegrave, 1742–1763
1. Great Britain. Politics. Waldegrave, James Waldegrave, Earl 1715–1763
I. Title II. Clark, J.C.D. (Jonathan Charles Douglas)
941.07′092′4

Library of Congress cataloguing in publication data

Waldegrave, James Waldegrave, Earl, 1715–1763.
The memoirs and speeches of James, 2nd Earl Waldegrave, 1742–1763
Includes index
1. Waldegrave, James Waldegrave, Earl, 1715–1763
2. Great Britain – Court and courtiers – Biography
3. Politicians – Great Britain – Biography
4. Great Britain – History – George II, 1727–1760
5. Great Britain – Politics and government – 1727–1760
I. Clark, J.C.D. II. Title
DA501.W14A3   1988   941.07′2′0924   [B]   88–5014

ISBN 0 521 36111 7

CE

CONTENTS

List of illustrations page	vii
Preface	ix
List of abbreviations	x
Textual conventions	xii

INTRODUCTION

The Court Society	1
The Family Background	21
The Political Career of James, 2nd Earl Waldegrave, 1741–1763	33
The launching of a career	33
The Waldegraves' social milieu	41
Leicester House and the Court, 1750–1755	48
The outbreak of the Seven Years' War, 1751–1756	64
The loss of Leicester House, 1755–1757	72
The last years, 1757–1763	85
The Publication of the Memoirs	101
The Historical Influence of the Memoirs	112
The Text of the Memoirs	134

1	Memoirs of the Leicester House Years, 1752–1756	143
2	Memoirs of 1754–1757	146
3	Memoirs of the Seven Years' War	212
4	Memoirs of the Accession of George III	213
5	Reflections on the New Reign: 'A Parallel'	218
6	An Allegory of Leicester House	226
7	A Satire on Bute's Ministerial Power, late 1762	238
8	Speeches in the House of Lords, 1742–1763	242
9	Notes from Plutarch	315

10	Notes from Montaigne	316
11	Notes from Montesquieu	318
12	Notes on Constitutional Law	323
13	Notes on the Constitution	326
14	Notes on English History	329

Index 333

ILLUSTRATIONS

The House of Lords in 1741–2. Engraving by John Pine.
(By courtesy of the House of Lords Record Office)　　*frontispiece*

James, 2nd Earl Waldegrave by Sir Joshua Reynolds, at Chewton.
(By courtesy of the Paul Mellon Centre for Studies in British Art)　　141

Maria, Countess Waldegrave by Sir Joshua Reynolds, at Chewton.
(By courtesy of the Paul Mellon Centre for Studies in British Art)　　142

PREFACE

The *Memoirs* of James, 2nd Earl Waldegrave are one of the most often used, but least accurately understood, of the basic texts for the history of eighteenth-century England. For an invitation to prepare a new edition in the light of modern scholarship I am indebted to the present Earl and Countess Waldegrave. Their hospitality and encouragement have added to my pleasure in tracing the career of their able but unfortunate ancestor. Lady Waldegrave's own researches into her family's history, as yet unpublished, were a valuable introduction to my subject and his background; I am grateful for the opportunity to take Lady Waldegrave's *History* as my starting point.

I happily acknowledge the generous support for my research provided, on different occasions, by the British Academy, the Political Science Fund of the University of Cambridge, and my college.

All Souls College, Oxford
July 1987

ABBREVIATIONS

Add MSS	Additional Manuscripts, British Library.
Bedford Correspondence	Lord John Russell (ed.), *Correspondence of John, Fourth Duke of Bedford* (3 vols., London, 1842–6).
Bedford MSS	Bedford Manuscripts, Bedford Estate Office, 29A Montagu Street, London, WC1.
Brooke, *George III*	John Brooke, *King George III* (London, 1972).
C	The Chewton ms. of the *Memoirs*.
Chesterfield, *Letters*	Bonamy Dobrée (ed.), *The Letters of Philip Dormer Stanhope, 4th Earl of Chesterfield* (6 vols., London, 1932).
Clark, *Dynamics of Change*	J.C.D. Clark, *The Dynamics of Change: The Crisis of the 1750s and English Party Systems* (Cambridge, 1982).
Coxe, *Pelham*	William Coxe, *Memoirs of the Administration of the Right Honourable Henry Pelham* (2 vols., London, 1829).
Coxe, *Walpole*	William Coxe, *Memoirs of the Life and Administration of Sir Robert Walpole, Earl of Orford* (3 vols., London, 1798)
DNB	*Dictionary of National Biography*
Dodington, *Diary*	John Carswell and L.A. Dralle (eds.), *The Political Journal of George Bubb Dodington* (Oxford, 1965).
EHR	*English Historical Review*
Fitzmaurice, *Shelburne*	Lord Fitzmaurice, *Life of William Earl of Shelburne* (2nd edn., 2 vols., London, 1912).
HJ	*Historical Journal*.

Harcourt Papers	E.W. Harcourt (ed.), *The Harcourt Papers* (7 vols., privately printed, Oxford [1880–1905]).
Hervey, *Memoirs*	John, Lord Hervey, *Some Materials Towards Memoirs of the Reign of King George II*, ed. Romney Sedgwick, (3 vols., London, 1931).
HMC	Historical Manuscripts Commission.
JMP	John Murray Papers, in the possession of the publishers John Murray, 60 Albemarle Street, London.
nf	not foliated.
M	The Murray ms. of the *Memoirs*.
Memoirs	[Lord Holland, ed.] *Memoirs from 1754 to 1758 by James, Earl Waldegrave, KG* (London, 1821).
Namier and Brooke	Sir Lewis Namier and John Brooke (eds.), *The History of Parliament: The House of Commons, 1754–1790* (3 vols., London, 1964).
Parl. Hist.	*The Parliamentary History of England, from the Earliest Period to the Year 1803*, ed. W. Cobbett (36 vols., London, 1806–20).
PRO	Public Record Office.
Sainty and Dewar, *Divisions*	J.C. Sainty and D. Dewar, *Divisions in the House of Lords: An Analytical List 1685 to 1857* (London, 1976).
Sedgwick	R.R. Sedgwick (ed.), *The History of Parliament: The House of Commons, 1715–1754* (2 vols., London, 1970).
Walpole, *George II*	Horace Walpole, *Memoirs of King George II*, ed. John Brooke (3 vols., New Haven and London, 1985).
Walpole, *George III*	Horace Walpole, *Memoirs of the Reign of King George the Third*, ed. G.F. Russell Barker (4 vols., London, 1894).
Walpole, *Letters*	*The Yale Edition of Horace Walpole's Correspondence*, ed. W.S. Lewis *et al.*, (48 vols., London, 1937–83).
Yorke, *Hardwicke*	Philip C. Yorke, *The Life and Correspondence of Philip Yorke Earl of Hardwicke* (3 vols., Cambridge, 1913).

TEXTUAL CONVENTIONS

The object of this edition has been to present a text which is both authentic and readable. To that end, emendations have been kept to a minimum. The original spelling, punctuation and paragraphs have been retained, with the exceptions set out here. Accidental duplications of words have been silently deleted, and capitals have been given to the first words of sentences where these were lacking. Maria Waldegrave sometimes spelt Leicester House as 'Liecester': this has been standardised. Finally, a number of obvious abbreviations have been silently expanded in the text of the *Memoirs* and speeches. Majy, P and B are printed as Majesty, Prince and Bishop; D, Ld, and Sr as Duke, Lord and Sir; wch, wd and shd become which, would and should. In other respects the text is unchanged, and the wilful prose of the eighteenth century has not been reproved by the frequent use of *sic*.

The 2nd Earl's name was sometimes written by contemporaries as 'Waldgrave' or even 'Walgrave'. These variants have been retained as evidence of pronunciation.

INTRODUCTION

THE COURT SOCIETY

It is only comparatively recently that English historiography has reluctantly abandoned its old self sufficiency – the idea that England's constitutional development pursued a path so different from that of her continental neighbours that a peculiarly insular *genre*, constitutional history, was necessary to explain its precedents, broadening down, or its teleology, urging it forwards to 'modernity'. In 1905, the foremost continental historian of mid-eighteenth-century England entered a protest against this scheme of interpretation:

> The opinion is widely and generally entertained, that the English state is the purest form of constitutional government, and that it was impressed with this form at a very early date. While other states were labouring under great uncertainty or entire confusion of constitutional form, or were burdened by the weight of despotism, England is supposed to have secured a careful delimitation of spheres of influence and a balance of power between co-existing forces ... I cannot think that things were greatly different in other countries, least of all in Germany ... Utterly false is the opinion that there was at any time in England an equilibrium of different forces with constitutional right above them as a final court of appeal.[1]

Eighteenth-century rhetoric about checks and balances needs to be interpreted, not merely read as a neutral description of a stable and widely accepted regime. The state structure which Whigs defended with this rhetoric proves, on closer inspection, to be very different from that rule-bound, clearly defined system of limited monarchy and cabinet government which we have been too ready to see through the categories

---

[1] Albert von Ruville, *William Pitt Earl of Chatham* (1905; trans. H. J. Chaytor, 3 vols., London, 1907), vol. 1, pp. 1–3. Sir Herbert Butterfield, in *George III and the Historians* (London, 1957), pp. 172–3, praised von Ruville: 'Since he was a continental historian, he was able to envisage the England of the elder Pitt as an example of the *ancien régime*.'

of Walter Bagehot's *The English Constitution* (1867).[2] Waldegrave's *Memoirs* belong rather to the world of Saint-Simon and Montesquieu, Clarendon and Lord Hervey. Its practical politics revolved around King and nobility; its scale of values was moulded by the theoretical claims of monarchy and aristocracy. These characteristics, shared by many European states in this period, have invited a common label: the Court society.

The Court society has been proposed by one sociologist as a unique formation, intermediate in Europe between feudal society and industrial society.[3] France gave one particular expression to this model by the periodic importance of Versailles as the sole focus of social attention. In England, the same society was divided in its focus between St James's, Kensington and the royal palace of Westminster. In France, Court etiquette was deliberately built up and exploited by one monarch, Louis XIV; in England, a succession of dynasties meant a frequently changing role for the immediate circle of the King within the wider society which revolved around him. Nevertheless, London's dominance within Britain meant that its Court ranked with Paris, Vienna and Madrid as cultural capitals of ancien regime societies. This membership of an international order was affirmed in the abstract by doctrine, in practice by a certain style. Court ceremonial reached its apogee in England in the early and mid-eighteenth century. 'It is impossible for me to make you understand and imagine the pomp and magnificence of this solemn procession,' wrote a foreign observer of the coronation of George II. 'Persons of an advanced age, who have seen the coronations of King James II, of William III and Mary, of Queen Anne, and of King George I, are all agreed that the magnificence of the present coronation has far surpassed that of the preceding.'[4]

This deliberate and ceremonially accentuated focus on the Court did not shield it from criticism. Indeed, the political ills of a Court society could be blamed on its monarch. In 1733, Lord Hervey deplored the growing breach between George II and Frederick, Prince of Wales, and hinted at the worst conceivable outcome, a Stuart restoration: 'this House divided against itself could not stand'. Hervey claimed he said:

People who make their fortunes under a Prince will submit to be snubbed and ill used; and people who are caressed by a Prince, cajoled with good words, and treated with kindness, will serve him without great hire. But our Master endeav-

---

[2] For an attempt to differentiate Victorian values from all that went before, and to offer a model which allows England to be seen more clearly in its European setting, see J.C.D. Clark, *Revolution and Rebellion: State and Society in England in the Seventeenth and Eighteenth Centuries* (Cambridge, 1986)

[3] Norbert Elias, *The Court Society* (trans. Edmund Jephcott, Oxford, 1983).

[4] M. van Muyden (ed.), *A Foreign View of England in the Reigns of George I & George II: The Letters of Monsieur César de Saussure to his Family* (London, 1902), p. 257.

ours by neither of these ways to attach people to his interest; he has not address enough to win them by flattery, nor has he liberality enough to gain by interest. For in no Court was there ever less to be got, though in no Court was there ever more to be done; never was greater attendance expected, nor ever fewer rewards distributed, and though the servants of no King were ever more punctually paid, yet none were ever less satisfied, nobody making a fortune under him, or getting more than just what defrayed the annual expenses of birthday clothes and the other necessary expenses incurred by dangling after a Court. The true state therefore of his case is (as you very well know) that as he cares for nobody, nobody cares for him; and that even his favours are so awkwardly bestowed that he gives without obliging, is served without being respected, and obeyed without being loved.[5]

The Hanoverian experience was very often of a Court divided between St James's and Leicester House; but this very division acted to emphasise, not to diminish, its courtly characteristics. Its most famous division occasioned the *Memoirs* of James, 2nd Earl Waldegrave.

Waldegrave's *Memoirs*, then, record the politics of a society focussed on the Court. Lord Holland, writing an introduction for the 1821 edition, recognised this characteristic but sought to place it in a disparaging perspective; he wrote dismissively of the post of Lord of the Bedchamber, which the 2nd Earl obtained in 1743. John Wilson Croker, reviewing the volume in the *Quarterly*, challenged this interpretation, quoting their editor:

'Such offices were then held in high estimation; they often led to favour and greatness. It was in the spirit of those times to be more greedy of imaginary honours, than obsequious to real power. Noblemen of the first rank sought with avidity employments which their descendants regard with indifference, or reject with disdain, as badges of dependence, rather than marks of distinction or importance.' – *Introduction*, p. viii.

This observation of the editor is very just; and it is not uninteresting, nor foreign from our subject, to examine what may be the cause of such a change – for we do not believe that men, high or low, are more disinterested or less ambitious now than they were a reign or two ago. We are aware that the alteration is attributed *exclusively* to a *spirit of independence*; and that a philosophical indifference to court-favour is considered as one of the results of 'the force of public opinion.' There is some truth in this: the motives and actions of public men, and particularly of those who may be connected with the government, are liable to such misrepresentations – and on the other hand – those who oppose the Court and reject its honours are so naturally the objects of popular applause, that the same vanity which formerly courted the smiles of kings now flatters a more noisy but not a more discriminating or honourable patron.

But there is also another circumstance which has still more tended to lower the rate of such offices as Lords of the Bedchamber – we mean the alteration in the modes of the private life of our sovereigns:- such places gave, as the editor says, in the reign of George II, access to the king's presence and opportunities of intercourse and of influence; but his late Majesty's domestic taste and habits (and probably the

---

[5] Hervey, *Memoirs*, vol. 1, pp. 205, 208.

general influence of the age co-operating with those tastes and habits) induced him to get rid, as much as he could, of the irksome ostentation of his rank, and to live, as far as he might, as a *private gentleman*. One by one, the pride, pomp and circumstances of the *court*, (as it was understood in the times of our grandfathers,) vanished – the royal circle became matter of personal selection rather than of official designation; Lords of the Bedchamber became in fact sinecurists, and they have now no more share in the personal society of the sovereign, and little more access to his person, than any other noblemen: if, 'the descendants of nobleman of the first rank' now despise or reject what their ancestors sought with so much eagerness, it is not, we believe, that they are less vain, or less interested, or less ambitious, but because the places themselves, in the present state of society, can no longer contribute either to vanity, interest or ambition. If the Court of England should ever be re-established on its old principles, and if some future monarch should condemn himself to live the life of a *king*, and to find amongst his *official* servants all the pleasures of his *private society*, we do not doubt that we should see these now disregarded offices rise again into the same kind of request and consideration in which they were held in the time of George II and his predecessors.[6]

The increasing distinction in England between the personal and the public life of the sovereign had already begun in the reign of Charles II; it did not correspond with any widely perceived decline in the role of the Crown after the Hanoverian accession. Certain aspects of English Court etiquette appear indeed to have become more formalised as the century progressed. Although George I abandoned the custom of being dressed by his Bedchamber servants, George II reintroduced it. Ceremonial in the assemblies known as 'drawing rooms' became steadily less informal.[7] Lord Hervey too was struck by the coronation of George II, 'performed with all the pomp and magnificence that could be contrived; the present King differing so much from the last, that all the pageantry and splendour, badges and trappings of royalty, were as pleasing to the son as they were irksome to the father.'[8] The most politically powerful Court office of the century was to be that of Lord Bute, who as Groom of the Stole to the Prince of Wales in 1756–60 and to George III in 1760–1 demonstrated the lasting importance of access to the King.[9] Because the monarch remained the active head of the executive, closely involved in the formulation of policy and the choice of ministers, 'The court was still at the centre of the political world.'[10]

[6] *The Quarterly Review* 25 (1821), pp. 392–3.
[7] John M. Beattie, *The English Court in the Reign of George I* (Cambridge, 1967), pp. 11, 14, 54–5.
[8] Hervey, *Memoirs*, vol. 1, p. 66.
[9] Precedents for Bute's non-accountable position as 'minister behind the curtain' are explored by S.B. Baxter, 'The Age of Personal Monarchy in England', in Peter Gay (ed.), *Eighteenth Century Studies presented to Arthur M. Wilson* (New York, 1972), pp. 3–11.
[10] Beattie, *English Court*, p. 217.

Introduction

In one symptomatic respect the accession of the House of Hanover strengthened a characteristic which St James's shared with other European courts. Fluency in languages was increasingly at a premium. Above all, command of French was an essential qualification in circles which made little distinction between social and political success. French was not the principal language spoken at St James's, as it was at some European courts; but many English courtiers could switch easily and naturally into French in a way which affirmed their membership of international princely society. Thus George I, knowing little English, often spoke French with his son, mistresses and courtiers;[11] George II did the same, corresponded with Frederick Prince of Wales in French, and (at a moment of high emotion and unconscious humour) resorted to that language at the bedside of the dying Queen Caroline.[12] Language and the cultural ramifications of language, like dress, marked off the members of the Court with considerable clarity from those who failed so to qualify.

If the Court enhanced society's already hierarchical orientation, and if most courtiers were peers or their kin, the third estate was slow to develop institutions to give expression to self-consciously different values. The House of Commons was not yet defined against the House of Lords, as two embodiments of separate and antagonistic interests. In personnel as in values, the links between the two were, as yet, far stronger than their rivalries. Consequently, eighteenth-century Englishmen did not share later historians' preoccupation with the lower House.[13] The power of the peers, collectively and severally, was daily in evidence. Against this power, the House of Commons failed to provide an effective counterpoise partly because it seldom sought to do so. In the short term, only a more independent monarchy seemed to offer such a hope. After the Duke of Devonshire's ignominious exit from his post of Lord Chamberlain in October 1762, Horace Walpole wrote:

> It is very amusing to me to see the House of Lords humbled. I have long beheld their increasing power with concern, and though not at all wishing to see the higher scale proponderating, I am convinced nothing but the Crown can reduce the exorbitance of the peers – and perhaps it will be able; for I believe half those who are proud of twenty thousand pounds a year, will bear anything for a thousand more.[14]

---

[11] *Diary of Mary Countess Cowper, Lady of the Bedchamber to the Princess of Wales 1714–1720* (London, 1864), pp. 9–10, 28, 142, 145, 150, 161, 191–2.

[12] Cf. Hervey, *Memoirs*, vol. 1, pp. 271–2; vol. 2, pp. 471, 560, 603, 611–12; vol. 3, pp. 776–84, 802–6, 896, 917. For an impression of this polyglot society in action, see Lord Hervey's miniature dialogue, vol. 2, pp. 585–96.

[13] It seems likely that only the mischance of the deaths of the two peers who dominated politics in the early years of George I's reign (James, 1st Earl Stanhope in 1721; Charles, 3rd Earl of Sunderland in 1722) permitted the domination of the scene by a commoner, Sir Robert Walpole, in subsequent decades.

[14] Walpole to Mann, 9 Nov. 1762: Walpole, *Letters*, vol. 22, p. 95.

The political controversies of early eighteenth-century France are often explained in terms of a rivalry between a *thèse royale*, which stressed the need for a strong monarchical government, and a *thèse nobiliaire* which emphasised the necessity for the checks on that central power which only the aristocracy and the institutions it staffed could provide. In practical terms, this rivalry between crown and nobility was largely played out at Court. In England too, the noisy life of the House of Commons did not greatly reduce the importance of political conflict between a monarchical executive and a legislative dominated by the patrician elite. In France, the Physiocrats evolved a plan for a competitive, free-market society (eliminating feudal rights and restrictions) which could only be held together by an absolute monarch; in England too, the growing professional and commercial sectors of society found themselves largely in alliance with the Court before 1832.

Louis de Rouvroy, Duc de Saint-Simon, the Walter Bagehot of the Court society, was born in 1675 and died in the same year as Montesquieu, 1755. Montesquieu spoke for the professional *noblesse de robe*, Saint-Simon for the warrior *noblesse d'épée*; yet as in England, the code of values to which the men of affairs and the landed elite appealed was virtually identical.[15] This code, which was Waldegrave's, can be reconstructed from the voluminous writings which that society produced. Its most characteristic literary *genre* was the Court memoir. Often written out of revenge by the unsuccessful courtier, driven to redress on paper and in private the thousand slights and humiliations of his public career, this *genre* brought the sensibility of the age to its highest pitch. Thus Saint-Simon became a model for the prose of Marcel Proust, and Horace Walpole exercised an influence on the development of the English novel out of proportion to his impact on the politics of his own day. Indeed, the best memoirs were commonly written by figures of the second rank. As Hervey acknowledged,

> I very freely declare that my part in this drama was only that of the Chorus's in the ancient tragedies, who, by constantly being on the stage, saw everything that was done, and made their own comments upon the scene, without mixing in the action or making any considerable figure in the performance.[16]

Never reaching the highest ranks, never reaping the major rewards, the ordinary courtier was trapped in a world which he found at once fascinating, repulsive, and inescapable. The satirist and minor courtier La Bruyère (1645–96) recognised the dependence which Court life imposed on its followers: 'Nobody is a greater slave than an assiduous courtier, unless it be a courtier who is more assiduous'. His biting irony was directed against

---

[15] See, especially, Duc de Saint-Simon, *Historical Memoirs* ed. and trans. Lucy Norton (3 vols., London, 1967–72).
[16] Hervey, *Memoirs*, vol. 1, p. 3.

precisely those characteristics of court life which their admirers had found so compelling. Yet even this bitter critic was forced to admit the centrality of the institution for which he felt such distaste: 'Whoever has seen the court has seen the most handsome, the best-looking, and the most decked-out part of the world. He who despises the court after having seen it, despises the world.'[17] He died at Versailles.

La Bruyère's satires were still current, for the world he described survived. Like Saint-Simon, Lord Hervey

> applied to his political life the maxim which he enunciates of his physical one, that existence on any terms is preferable to no existence at all ... The most painful scenes took place when it became necessary for George II to insist, with the utmost kindness and consideration, on his surrendering his office, and to explain that it was impossible to grant his entreaties to be given some compensation, however small, even if it were only a Lordship of the Bedchamber.[18]

Hervey and Saint-Simon were natural and eager courtiers: they pursued every scrap of status, every minor advantage, and were embittered by their loss of position. Waldegrave was a natural but reluctant courtier: drawn to seek a political career through Court rather than party channels, he found the stresses of court life more repulsive than addictive. Nevertheless, Waldegrave too felt the same keen disappointment at the loss of office, and it was this passion which drove him, like them, to justify himself to posterity.

Waldegrave's *Memoirs* end in disillusion: 'I have been too long behind the Scenes, I have had too near a View of the machinery of a Court, to envy [any] Man either the power of a Minister, or the Favor of Princes'. But disillusion did not mean the end of his political career. He continued to attend at Court; before death intervened in 1763, it had seemed that a new chapter was about to open, and that the highest honours were at last to be his. Like most courtiers, Waldegrave was sceptical of those around him; again like most courtiers, he was unable to free himself from the compelling fascination of the Court.

One reason for his inability to escape was that he lacked an alternative power base in the organisation of a political party. In 1757, Waldegrave warned the King of his unsuitability for the place of First Lord of the Treasury: 'a Minister must expect few Followers, who had never cultivated political Friendships, and had always abhor'd Party Violence'. Impor-

---

[17] Jean de La Bruyère, *Les Caractères* (1688; trans. H. van Laun, London, 1963), pp. 133, 139–40.
[18] Romney Sedgwick, Introduction, in Hervey, *Memoirs*, p. lv. Hervey seems to have begun his memoirs in 1733; he died in 1743. Saint-Simon retired from Court life in 1723 and had completed a large part of his manuscript by 1743 (*Memoirs*, vol. 3, p. 493); he died in 1755. The *Memoirs* of Thomas, Earl of Ailesbury (2 vols., Roxburghe Club, London, 1890) were written in 1728–9.

tantly, he disclaimed personal ambition: 'I had no Conception how a reasonable Man, who was not necessitous, could have any Inducement to undergo the Fatigue, and anxiety of a Ministerial Employment, unless he was animated with a probable Expectation, of rendering his King and Country some important Services, and of being afterwards rewarded with that general Approbation, which such Services merited.' The values of the Court society commended disinterested public service and the pursuit of personal honour, not bureaucratic drudgery or political self-aggrandisement. The fount of honour was the Crown. Waldegrave wrote in the *Memoirs* that he 'esteem'd' access to the King 'the only valuable part of a Ministerial Employment'. He exaggerated, and later amended 'only' to 'most'; but he still spoke as a courtier, not a man of business.

What was it that courtiers sought? Lord Hervey was driven to a string of synonyms by contemplating the 'Court interest, power, profit, favour, and preferment' that Sir Robert Walpole almost lost, then regained, at the accession of George II. Success would go to 'those few alert courtiers who, like cautious and skilful sailors, see every cloud as soon as it rises and watch every wind as fast as it changes', so that they could 'set their sails in such a manner as should enable them to shift to the gale that was most favourable, and put them in a readiness to pursue the course they were in or tack about, just as the weather should require, and to that point of the compass where sunshine was most likely to appear.'[19] Waldegrave's career, like Hervey's, illustrates the extreme difficulty of this task in practice.

Waldegrave's self-justification takes its underlying values for granted: the values of the man of honour. In monarchical governments, according to Montesquieu, honour took the place which political virtue filled in republics. *De L'Esprit des Lois* is a sustained eulogy of the nobleman's code of conduct. It was a code

> not taught in colleges or academies. It commences, in some measure, at our setting out in the world; for this is the school of what we call honour, that universal preceptor which ought everywhere to be our guide . . . the education of monarchies requires a certain politeness of behaviour . . . a person that would break through the rules of decency, so as to shock those he conversed with, would lose the public esteem, and become incapable of doing any good . . . Politeness, in monarchies, is naturalised at court. One man excessively great renders everybody else little. Hence that regard which is paid to our fellow-subjects; hence that politeness, equally pleasing to those by whom, as to those towards whom, it is practiced, because it gives people to understand that a person actually belongs, or deserves to belong, to the court . . . There is nothing so strongly inculcated in monarchies, by the laws, by religion and honour, as submission to the prince's will; but this very

[19] Hervey, *Memoirs*, vol. 1, pp. 68, 80.

honour tells us that the prince never ought to command a dishonourable action, because this would render us incapable of serving him.[20]

Essentially the same account was given by Montesquieu's and Waldegrave's friend the 4th Earl of Chesterfield (1694–1773), whose private letters to his son of *c.* 1747–51 proved hugely popular when collected and published in 1774. It was then discovered that he had explicitly recognised the relevance of Montesquieu's description to the English monarchy, despite obvious constitutional differences which Chesterfield even sought to stress. In 1750, Chesterfield thought the similarities sufficiently important to transcribe for his son a long passage from Book 4, chapter 2 of Montesquieu's great work. He explained its importance:

> The President Montesquieu (whom you will be acquainted with at Paris) after having laid down, in his book *de l'Esprit des Lois*, the nature and principles of the three different kinds of government, viz. the democratical, the monarchical, and the despotic, treats of the education necessary for each respective form. His chapter upon the education proper for the monarchical I thought worth transcribing, and sending to you. You will observe that the monarchy which he has in his eye is France ... Though our government differs considerably from the French, inasmuch as we have fixed laws, and constitutional barriers, for the security of our liberties and properties;[21] yet the President's observations hold pretty near as true in England as in France ... the same maxims and manners almost in all Courts; voluptuousness and profusion encouraged, the one to sink the people into indolence, the other into poverty, consequently into dependency. The Court is called the world here, as well as at Paris; and nothing more is meant, by saying that a man knows the world, than that he knows Courts. In all Courts you must expect to meet with connections without friendship, enmities without hatred, honour without virtue, appearances saved, and realities sacrificed; good manners, with bad morals; and all vice and virtue so disguised, that whoever has only reasoned upon both, would know neither, when he first met them at Court. It is well that you should know the map of that country, that when you come to travel in it, you may do it with greater safety.[22]

Chesterfield's tireless insistence to his son on the graces of civilised manners had a specific practical application: they would be essential 'when you go to Courts'. An appropriate reading list (in French) included the *Mémoires* of Cardinal de Retz ('You will there see what Courts and courtiers really are'), La Rochefoucauld's *Les Réflexions Morales* and La Bruyère's *Les Caractères*. Philip Stanhope's itinerary was carefully planned: 'You will

---

[20] Baron de Montesquieu, *The Spirit of the Laws* (trans. Thomas Nugent, ed. Franz Neumann, New York, 1949), Book 3, chapter 6; Book 4, chapter 2.
[21] Chesterfield had been deeply influenced by the Deism and quasi-republicanism of the 1720s; his writings abound with stock phrases in contempt of 'popery' and 'arbitrary rule'. This blocked a deeper understanding of the similarities between the French and English governments, despite his grasp of the other features which those societies shared.
[22] Chesterfield, *Letters*, vol. 4, p. 1553.

now, in the course of a few months, have been rubbed at three of the considerable Courts of Europe – Berlin, Dresden and Vienna; so that I hope you will arrive at Turin tolerably smooth, and fit for the last polish.'[23]

In England as on the continent, the Court sustained its own style and its own preoccupations:

> There is a sort of chit-chat, or *small-talk*, which is the general run of conversation at Courts, and in most mixed companies. It is a sort of middling conversation, neither silly nor edifying; but, however, very necessary for you to be master of. It turns upon the public events of Europe, and then is at its best; very often upon the number, the goodness, or badness, the discipline, or the clothing of the troops of different princes; sometimes upon the families, the marriages, the relations of princes, and considerable people; and sometimes, *sur la bonne chère*, the magnificence of public entertainments, balls, masquerades etc.

Mastery of these subjects was insufficient without a certain manner:

> more people have made great figures and great fortunes in Courts by their exterior accomplishments than by their interior qualifications. Their engaging address, the politeness of their manners, their air, their turn, has almost always paved the way for their superior abilities, if they have such, to exert themselves. They have been favourites before they have been ministers.

The detailed instructions to which Philip Stanhope was subjected were universally applicable: 'With these qualifications . . . I will answer for your success, not only at Hanover, but at any Court in Europe.'[24]

Montesquieu's account of the principles of monarchy owed much to the greater priority he ascribed to the nobility. James, 2nd Earl Waldegrave, a Hanoverian loyalist from a lately Jacobite family, took especial note of Book 26, chapter 16 of *De l'Esprit des Lois* in which the philosopher implicitly rejected the claim of the Stuart family to the English throne.[25] Both the 1st and 2nd Earls were principally attached to the service of the Crown rather than to a political party; but this attachment stemmed from the ethic of nobility, not from the doctrine of *indefeasible* hereditary right.

If the ideological significance of George III's notion of kingship was unduly dramatised by Victorian writers, it may have been drained of too much of its historical meaning by more recent scholars. John Brooke relegated the issue to a footnote: Horace Walpole's 'belief that George III was educated by disciples of Bolingbroke in arbitrary principles of government is a theme which runs throughout his memoirs, and is entirely imaginary'.[26] In a literal sense, the idea that a Hanoverian heir to the

---

[23] Chesterfield, *Letters*, vol. 3, pp. 1171, 1202, 1207; vol. 4, pp. 1312, 1408, 1645.
[24] Chesterfield, *Letters*, vol. 4, p. 1758; vol. 5, pp. 1831, 1909; vol. 5, pp. 1998–2005.
[25] Waldegrave's notes from Montesquieu, section 11 below.
[26] Walpole, *George II*, vol. 1, p. 193. The same interpretation is classically to be found in the Introduction to Romney Sedgwick (ed.), *Letters from George III to Lord Bute 1756–1766*

Introduction

throne was indoctrinated with Stuart doctrines is indeed untrue; but to appreciate the still-vivid nature of these charges, we must recreate a world in which the Jacobite option was only recently still alive, and in which political ideology and daily politics still revolved to a significant degree around dynastic questions.

In 1822 the *Edinburgh Review*, reviewing Waldegrave's *Memoirs* and Walpole's *George II*, sketched the political background:

The accession of the House of Hanover divided England into two parties – the Whigs, or friends of the new establishment; and the Tories and Jacobites, its secret or avowed opponents. The Tories, bigoted to the notion of indefeasible right in the succession to the Crown, but apprehensive for their religion if a Papist should mount the Throne, were distracted between their scruples about the validity of a Parliamentary settlement, and their fears, lest, in subverting it, they might restore, or pave the way for the restoration of, the Catholic church. Though deterred by their religious fears from embarking decidedly in the cause of the Pretender, they kept on terms with his friends, and were not unwilling to disturb, though they hesitated to overturn, a government they disliked, because it was founded on principles they abhorred. The Jacobites, though most of them were zealous members of the Church of England, had a stronger infusion of bigotry in their composition, and were ready to restore a Popish family, and submit to a Popish Sovereign, rather than own a government founded on a Parliamentary title. It was impossible that either Tories or Jacobites should have the confidence of the Hanoverian Princes; and therefore, while those divisions subsisted, all places of power and profit were in the hands of the Whigs.

Of these two parties, the Tories and Jacobites were the most numerous. They included a certain number of the ancient nobility, and comprehended a very large proportion of the landed interest; and, what gave them in those days a prodigious influence over the common people, a vast majority of the parochial clergy. The University of Oxford was at that time, as it was long after termed by Lord Chatham, a seminary of treason; and its members, dispersed over the kingdom in their different capacities of squires and parsons, retained in their several destinations the zeal and bigotry they had imbibed from their nurse. It may appear surprising, that a party so formidable by its numbers, its influence and its property, should have failed of success. The true solution of the enigma is perhaps given by Lord Orford in his character of Lord Elibank and his brother. 'Both were such active Jacobites, that if the Pretender had succeeded, they could have produced many witnesses to testify their zeal for him; both so cautious, that no witnesses of actual treason could be produced by the government against them; the very sort of Jacobitism that has kept the cause alive, and kept it from succeeding.' If treasonable toasts, drunken bouts, election brawls, mobbing of Dissenters, and idle correspondence, could have brought back the Pretender, the Stuarts would have been restored. But, as the views of the party were irrational, so the zeal of its adherents had more of bluster than firmness in its ingredients. When their spirit was tried by the bold attempt from Scotland to establish their cause by arms, the

(London, 1939) and Ian R. Christie, 'Was there a "New Toryism" in the Earlier Part of George III's Reign?', *Journal of British Studies*, 5 (1965–6), 60–76.

success of the rebels only showed the incapacity of the rival government, and the prudence or faint-heartedness of their English friends.[27]

Recent scholarship has confirmed Horace Walpole's account of the party alignment.

> The opposition to the House of Brunswic was composed partly of principled Jacobites, of Tories, who either knew not what their own principles were, or dissembled them to themselves; and of Whigs, who from hatred of the Minister both acted in concert with the Jacobites, and rejoiced in their assistance.[28]

Lord Holland, editing Walpole's *Memoirs*, commended their subject matter as 'not undeserving our curiosity as it forms the transition from the expiring struggles of Jacobitism to the more important contests that have since engaged, and still occupy our attention'.[29] These dynastic themes, which preoccupied the 1st and 2nd Earls, give a significance to these *Memoirs* which the inadequacy of Lord Holland's edition of 1821 has obscured.

In such a world, the characters of princes assumed a heightened public significance. That of Frederick, Prince of Wales, excited widespread alarm: 'The King's great natural probity and aversion to falsehood, caused him to be greatly disgusted with the mean and insincere temper of the Prince. His little regard to veracity and honor was too early and too much a matter of public notoriety'.[30] With so much at stake, the upbringing of heirs to the throne was inevitably a political issue. The result was predictable: 'Princes have long had the exclusive privilege of being worse educated than all the rest of mankind', quipped Chesterfield.[31] This was not for want of forethought; rather for excess of it. If one literary *genre* produced in ancien regime societies was the Court memoir, another was the manual of instruction for the education of royal pupils. Louis XIV's preceptor was

---

[27] *The Edinburgh Review* 37 (1822), p. 21.
[28] Paget Toynbee (ed.), *Reminiscences Written by Mr Horace Walpole in 1788* (Oxford, 1924), p. 86.
[29] Horace Walpole, *Memoires of the Last Ten Years of the Reign of George the Second* (ed. Lord Holland, 2 vols., London, 1822), vol. 1, pp. xxvi–xxvii.
[30] Henry Etough, 'Free and Impartial Reflexions on the Character, Life, and Death of Frederick Prince of Wales,' *Miscellanies of the Philobiblon Society* 7 (1862–3), p. 9. Frederick's character reflected a childhood distorted, like that of so many princes, by reason of state. George I, on his accession in 1714, compelled his son George, now Prince of Wales, to reside in England but to leave his son Frederick to be educated as a German prince in Hanover, thereby paving the way for a separation of the two states. Frederick did not see his parents again until after George I's death.
[31] Chesterfield, *Letters*, vol. 5, p. 1982. On this neglected theme, see H.R.H. Prince Chula Chakrabongse of Siam, *The Education of the Enlightened Despots: A Review of the Youth of Louis XV of France, Frederick II of Prussia, Joseph II of Austria, and Catherine II of Russia* (London, 1948); Edward Gregg, 'The Education of Princes: Queen Anne and her Contemporaries' in J.D. Browning (ed.), *Education in the 18th Century* (New York, 1979), pp. 78–97; Derek Beales, *Joseph II*, vol. 1 (Cambridge, 1987).

Introduction

Hardouin de Beaumont de Péréfixe (1605–70), Archbishop of Paris, who caused a posthumous crisis when his writings found their way into the hands of Prince George and Prince Edward at Leicester House in the 1750s.[32] Louis XIV dictated his own manual of instruction, its declared aim being to extend his care for his subjects 'beyond us by handing down all our insights to our successor'.[33]

French writings on this theme enjoyed some currency in England, not least thanks to the efforts of the exiled Jacobite Andrew Michael Ramsay, follower and promoter of Archbishop Fénélon. His text was a series of unexceptionable injunctions to piety, justice, sound administration, the choice of wise advisers, morality at Court, frugality and the avoidance of unnecessary wars. All turned, as Fénélon ealised, on the person of the monarch: 'Courtiers are servile imitators, and take a pride in having all the faults of their Prince'.[34] The same moral was endorsed by Ramsay himself. Like Bolingbroke, he premised political regeneration on the person of the monarch. Constitutions were liable to decline from their primitive integrity, Ramsay argued, and fall into corruption;

> The true method of preventing such corruptions, is by the education of young princes. All other methods may stop the effects, for a time, but they can't alter the cause, nor dry up the source; and this was what induc'd the great Mons. de Fénélon, Archbishop of Cambray, to write his Telemachus. Some superficial minds look upon his maxims as impracticable and chimerical, tho' they really inspired them into a young prince,[35] who gave all reasons to believe, that he would have followed 'em, had he lived.[36]

In Waldegrave's bitter satire against Leicester House, printed as section 6 below, the youthful Prince of Wales appears under a thin disguise as 'Telemachus'.

Of the education of Prince George and Prince Edward before the appointment of Lord Bute, little is known. The elaborate syllabi drawn up for some continental Courts were not for them. Thomas Hayter, Bishop of Norwich, their Preceptor (whose resignation with Lord Harcourt in December 1752 was to plunge Waldegrave into public life) drew up a perfunctory account of his timetable for George II:

---

[32] Dodington, *Diary*, 8 February 1753.
[33] Louis XIV, *Mémoires for the Instruction of the Dauphin*, ed. Paul Sonnino (New York, 1970), p. 22. In England, even Defoe turned his hand to the *genre*, drafting in 1728–9 'a colleccion of examples from history and the best informacion of the miserable consequences of the want of education in princes and men of the first rank in former times': Daniel Defoe, *Of Royal Educacion*, ed. Karl Bülbring (London, 1895), p. 14. The editor suggests that the extreme political sensitivity of the issue in 1728–9 deterred Defoe from completing it.
[34] François de Salignac de la Mothe Fénélon, *Proper Heads of Self-Examination for a King. Drawn up for the Use of the late Dauphin of France, Father to his present Majesty K. Lewis XV whilst Duke of Burgundy* (London, 1747), p. 22.
[35] The Duc de Bourgogne (d. 1712), Louis XIV's eldest grandson.
[36] A.M. Ramsay, *A Plan of Education for a Young Prince* (London, 1732), p. xv.

A plan of instruction for their Royal Highnesses, during the ensuing winter, laid before his Majesty and approved by him, September 25th 1751.

It is proposed, that their Royal Highnesses do rise at seven o'clock, and translate such parts of Caesar's Commentaries as they had before read till half past eight, at which hour breakfast, allowing until nine as a sufficient length of time for that purpose; at which time will be Lectures in History and Geography.

As soon as their Royal Highnesses shall have acquired the necessary knowledge, they will be taught Geometry.

At ten the translations from Caesar are to be reviewed and corrected, and new parts of that author read by their Royal Highnesses and explained to them.

At eleven, writing, arithmetic, and dancing three times a week, and the French Master the other three days.

Their Royal Highnesses will also be instructed in the principles of Fortification.

From twelve o'clock, riding and other exercises, &c. until dinner, which is proposed to be at three o'clock.

After dinner the Princes usually visit her Royal Highness the Princess at Leicester House; where Mr Young attends them three days in the week to improve them in the German language and History; and Mr Desnoyer attends them the remaining three days.

It is proposed that the hours from seven to nine in the evening be spent in reading some useful and entertaining books, such as Addison's works, and particularly his political papers published in the year 1715; and that in general a view be had to give their Royal Highnesses a true notion of the nature of the constitution of this Country, its interests, and the present state of its connection with Foreign powers.

Every Sunday morning after breakfast the Bishop of Norwich reads to their Royal Highnesses a practical explanation of the principles of the Christian religion, and recapitulates the substance of the preceding Lectures; and the utmost attention has been, and will be had to explain and inculcate to their Royal Highnesses, the great duties of Religion and Morality, and particularly those that more immediately concern their Royal Highnesses from their high rank and station.[37]

More can be reconstructed of the content and tone of this course of instruction from the sermons with which Hayter had established his political orthodoxy and recommended himself to the authorities.[38] In 1746, as Archdeacon of York, he took the opportunity of an invitation to preach before the Commons to argue that 'good Princes in general are the principal instruments in the hand of Providence, by which Blessings are dispensed to Societies . . . That God doth, in a peculiar manner, bless and protect good Princes.' This mattered, since Princes

[37] Printed in William Harding, *The History of Tiverton, in the County of Devon* (2 vols., London, 1845–7), vol. 2, book iv, p. 115.
[38] For the continued currency of Anglican political theology, and the substantial area of agreement between Whig orthodoxies and Jacobite orthodoxies, see J.C.D. Clark, *English Society 1688–1832: Ideology, Social Structure and Political Practice during the Ancien Regime* (Cambridge, 1985).

Introduction

stand at the head of their respective societies, reaching out the benefits of an equal government to all the members of the community, in a manner that bears some analogy to God himself . . . In this sense it is that Kings are the *Vicegerents of God*, because they are *his ministers to us for good*.

Hayter argued both that 'All power is derived from God', and also that power may be misapplied by men. Kings need 'the aid of just and known laws'.

Bad kings undoubtedly want this restraint; and *good* kings rejoice in it. For *they* have no desire to do, what the laws of a well-instituted government prohibit. *They* know themselves not to be infinite in perfection; and therefore they have no inclination to be, or to be thought to be, absolute in power. *Their* power is indeed, in another and better sense, absolute; Not because it cannot, or must not, upon any account, be resisted *merely* as it is *their* power; not because obedience to the lawful Sovereign, is bound upon the Subjects, by the strongest and most sacred ties of human and divine laws; not because Nothing can free them from those ties, but a case of extreme necessity, which will always explain itself when it comes; but neither can, nor ought to be precisely pointed out, and defined beforehand: But it is, in effect, an absolute power, because it is so exercised, as not to afford the subjects the least motive or temptation to resist it. For who would resist a power, that is perpetually exercised, in securing and promoting his own happiness? If any one can be so ungrateful, so lost to all sense of his own and the Public Good, as to resist his Sovereign under those circumstances; he most undeniably *resisteth the ordinance of God*, with every possible aggravation of guilt. He will suffer punishment from men here, unpitied; and, if he doth not sincerely repent of the great wickedness he hath committed, *will receive to himself* from God, *who can kill both body and soul, damnation* hereafter.

For Hayter as for many others, such doctrine generated the orthodox Whig ideal of a just king:

guided by no interest, but the public welfare; governed by no principle, that does not spring from the fear of God, and tend to promote the honour of God, in the encouragement of true religion, the support and practice of real virtue, and the discountenancing vice and profaneness; governs his subjects, with the affection of a parent, the kindness of a benefactor, and the fidelity of a friend. By this means, he raises in them a conscientious love and awe of himself, as their ruler; a veneration for the laws, by which he rules them with so much mildness and equity; and insensibly forms them, in their several ranks and stations, to an imitation of himself.

This paragon of political and religious virtue could only have two enemies: infidelity and Popery. Both, according to Hayter, had been to blame for the rebellion of 1745:

Had not *Infidelity*, the natural product of licentiousness, by an avowed ridicule of whatever is held most sacred, nearly brought us to be indifferent, what Religion we professed, or whether we professed any Religion at all? Did not *Popery*, a dark active mischief, lurking within the bowels of the Kingdom, with a restless assiduity, all the while corrupt the Faith, and poison the Allegiance of deluded Multitudes?[39]

These somewhat impassioned sentiments were delivered in the immediate aftermath of rebellion and civil war. In 1750, after his elevation to the see of Norwich, Hayter gave expression to the same doctrine in a more tranquil idiom:

> To honour the King, is to obey him with that awful Sense of the Regal Character, which the Majesty of it impresses upon our Mind. By Parity of Reason, and upon the same Principle, that we *submit to the King as supreme*; we are required to pay a suitable Submission to all who are appointed by him to bear any Share in the great Work of Government. The Supreme Power thus diffused, and operating thro' the whole Extent of a Community, creates that public Authority, which is necessary to maintain general Peace and Order; and which constitutes the real internal Strength of every Government. All the Obligations to Obedience which are laid upon us, as Subjects, are calculated to secure a proper Deference to public Authority: But all those Obligations, however enforced by the joint Power of Civil Society, are ultimately render'd effectual, by the Sanctions of Religion; and can obtain their full Operation and Effect, from the Motives of Religion only. The Influence of Religion therefore, in the last Resort, is the fundamental support of every Government.

There was now no danger from 'arbitrary Exertions of the Prerogative'. Rather,

> The Danger now arises from a contrary Cause; from a profligate Abuse of those very Blessings of which the Revolution gave us full Possession, *civil* and *religious* Liberty. And to such Lengths hath this Abuse been carried, as hath produced an open Disregard to all Authority, both divine and human.[40]

Due partly to the underpinning of such an ideology, partly to the quantifiable limits to the distribution of authority and of information, the world of Westminster, Whitehall, St James's, and Kensington, of Parliament, clubland and Court, was self-sufficient and self-referential to a degree impossible to reconcile with Victorian assumptions of constitutional propriety or twentieth-century egalitarian ideals of the strength of democratic pressure. This pattern changed little in the eighteenth century, and was fairly captured by the denunciations of an early nineteenth-century Benthamite radical:

---

[39] Thomas Hayter, *A Sermon Preached before the Honourable House of Commons, at St Margaret's Westminster, On Wednesday, June 11, 1746. Being the Anniversary of his Majesty's Happy Accession to the Throne* (London, 1746), pp. 10–14, 22.

[40] Thomas Hayter, *A Sermon Preached before the Right Honourable the Lords Spiritual and Temporal in Parliament Assembled, in the Abbey-Church Westminster, On Tuesday, January 30, 1749–50. Being the Day appointed to be observed as the Day of the Martyrdom of King Charles I.* (London, 1750), pp. 2, 6.

Introduction

Political parties in England, and among them the Whigs, know generally very little of the popular opinions. Political men are accustomed to live in separate, exclusive and narrow coteries. They form a society for themselves; their own set is to them, the world; and the opinions of that set, they fancy the reigning opinions. Of the silent working of discussion during late years, the Whigs were profoundly ignorant, and fancied that the people out of doors were like the House of Commons.[41]

It was not that Whigs ignored public opinion, though at times they disparaged it. On the contrary, their political rhetoric was heavily weighted with adulatory references to 'the people'. Rather, their perception of public opinion was profoundly influenced both by their perspective on society and by their tactical purposes. On 27 April 1744, in the Lords' debate on the Bill to make treasonable any correspondence with the sons of the Stuart King James III, the Duke of Bedford rebuked the Marquess of Tweeddale:

> I am persuaded his Lordship said nothing but what he thought and believed to be true; but it is very difficult to judge of the voice of the people without doors; for I have always observed, that every man judges of it from the company he keeps, and if they generally approve, or disapprove of any measure, he concludes accordingly, and says, that such a measure was approved of, or disapproved of by the general voice of the people without doors.[42]

Conventional formularies about the positive advantages of a mixed and balanced constitution rested importantly on a negative condemnation of the inherent vices of the three components which, ideally, were to be held in balance. The popular interest, in particular, had the greatest scope to overturn a system based on its substantial exclusion. Talk of 'balance' was therefore something of a euphemism, as Horace Walpole unwittingly revealed:

> For the people, they are not capable of Government, and do more harm in an hour, when heated by popular incendiaries than a king can do in a year. It is a government like ours, in which all the three parts seeks augmentation of their separate powers, and in which King, Lords, and Commons, are a watch and a check upon the other two, that best ensures the general happiness.[43]

The role of 'the people' in politics was more a rhetorical convention than a verifiable and recognised force. 'People talk of public opinion,' reflected Shelburne, 'and what creates or constitutes public opinion? Numbers certainly do not.' Orators who claimed to stand for 'the people' promised more than they could deliver: 'Lord Chatham told me that he could never

---

[41] John Arthur Roebuck, *History of the Whig Ministry of 1830, to the Passing of the Reform Bill* (2 vols., London, 1852), vol. 1, p. 347.
[42] *Parl. Hist.*, vol. 13, col. 780. [43] Walpole, *George III*, vol. 3, p. 123.

be sure of the Publick passions, that all that he could do was to watch, and be the first to follow them.'[44]

It is often pointed out, quite correctly, that eighteenth-century London witnessed the proliferation of a print culture. This much is true, but a conclusion is too easily drawn: that newspapers, pamphlets, cartoons, satires and ballads in bewildering diversity rocked high society, galvanised public opinion, and compelled the accountability of the elite to the wider world. There is occasional truth in this picture, but a better acquaintance with the Court and the Lords qualifies it severely. More striking than the vitality of this print culture is its shallowness, its constricted scope, its lack of real information, its general inability to penetrate behind the ostensible surface of events.[45] In such a world, rumour and paranoia assumed an inordinately large place. But in terms of personnel and policies, such handicaps meant that much public business and many prominent figures escaped scrutiny altogether.

Waldegrave is a salutary example of the obscurity even of politicians of considerable consequence. Despite a career of twenty years close to the centre of power, it appears that he never featured in a satirical cartoon and was never the subject of a political pamphlet.[46] Waldegrave sought power, and would have exercised it, largely outside that spotlight of publicity and accountability which lends, in retrospect, such apparent importance to so many less significant Members of the House of Commons. Waldegrave belonged to the same closed world as the man who replaced him, the 3rd Earl of Bute.

This closed world had its structures of authority, its code of conduct, and its attitude to the evolution of the wider society of which it was part. In its own perception, the Court society carried with it a characteristic pattern of historical causation: a pattern often reflected upon by contemporaries, and generally ignored as uncongenial by later commentators. In November

---

[44] 'A Chapter of Autobiography' in Fitzmaurice, *Shelburne*, vol. 1, pp. 24, 36.
[45] These characteristics are rightly emphasised by Jeremy Black, *The English Press in the Eighteenth Century* (London, 1987).
[46] The provisional nature of this claim must be stressed. Where so much ephemeral evidence has been lost, it is more than ordinarily difficult to prove a negative. This claim rests on the absence of evidence in the following sources where it might have been expected. (a) F.G. Stephens's *Catalogue of Prints and Drawings in the British Museum. Division I: Political and Personal Satires* (4 vols., London, 1870–83) lacks an index. But a close reading of vol. 3 part 1 (1734–50), vol. 3 part 2 (1751–60) and vol. 4 (1761–70) has failed to reveal the appearance of the 2nd Earl Waldegrave in the political caricatures there described. This is confirmed by the comprehensively indexed collection of prints in the Lewis Walpole Library, in which, again, Waldegrave does not feature. For that collection, see W.S. Lewis, *Rescuing Horace Walpole* (New Haven, Conn., 1978), p. 8. (b) The pamphlets listed in Clark, *Dynamics of Change*, pp. 569–93 for 1753–7 do not attend to the 2nd Earl. Nor to those for 1760–3 listed in John Brewer, *Party Ideology and Popular Politics at the Accession of George III* (Cambridge, 1976), pp. 340–7.

Introduction

1753, in the debate on the repeal of the Jewish Nationalisation Bill, Henry Pelham began his speech: 'it is an old observation which almost every day's experience confirms, that great events often spring from trivial causes'.[47] Power was focussed within a small arena: distance and ignorance no longer isolated the provinces, as in former centuries, yet the diffusion of information was not yet sufficient to diffuse power also. Within that small arena, the subordination of criteria for success to the criteria of social acceptability acted to formalise the rules of action. These influences conspired to personalise politics, and to highlight as prominent causes the details of personal character and conduct.[48]

Such characteristics gave a particular value to the Court memoir as the only *genre* capable of lifting the veil on the arcana of events. A particular importance therefore attached to the men in a position to write them. With false modesty, Horace Walpole apologised for 'the necessity I am under of unfolding the secret springs of many events in which I was unwillingly a considerable actor'. He had a unique advantage, he believed:

> No man is acquainted with the whole plot; as no man knows all the secret springs of the actions of others ... Yet, partial as the narratives of the actors must be, they will certainly approach nearer to truth than those of spectators, who, beholding nothing but events, pretend to account for them from causes which they can but suppose, and which frequently never existed ...
> It is my part to explain, as far as I could know them, the leading motives of actions and events; and, though the secret springs are often unfathomable, I had acquaintance enough with the actors to judge with better probability than the common of mankind.[49]

Equally, he criticized the historian Mrs Macaulay, whose republican commitments had blinded her to these aspects of the real nature of events:

> Too prejudiced to dive into causes, she imputes everything to tyrannic views, nothing to passions, weakness, error, prejudice, and still less to what operates oftenest, and her ignorance of which qualified her yet less for a historian, – to accident and little motives.[50]

'Grave issues are often decided by chance', agreed Saint-Simon, emphasising the inside knowledge which allowed him to write with authority.[51] 'The most weighty affairs are determin'd by the slightest reasons', echoed Fénélon.[52]

---

[47] *Parl. Hist.*, vol. 15, col. 142.
[48] 'What we think of as "external", as "formalism", is nothing other than an expression of the primacy of the relationship of all things and events to the status or power of the *person* involved in relation to others': Elias, *Court Society*, p. 109.
[49] Walpole, *George III*, vol. 1, pp. 1–2, 162.   [50] Walpole, *George III*, vol. 3, pp. 121–2.
[51] Saint-Simon, *Historical Memoirs*, vol. 3, pp. 218, 484–7.
[52] Fénélon, *Proper Heads of Self-Examination*, p. 71.

Lord Hervey drew the same inference from the very centralisation of authority in the sovereign:

> For my own part, I have the conduct of princes in so little veneration, that I believe they act yet oftener without design than other people, and are insensibly drawn into both good and bad situations without knowing how they came there. Those authors and commentators, then, must oftener than any others lose their time and their labour who will always be looking out for great causes to great events. By neglecting trifles they overlook truth and by continual refinements what they seek.

Sir Robert Walpole's estrangement from Lord Townshend had just such an origin in the superior grandeur of Walpole's new house at Houghton:

> those who fancy the passions of princes, the quarrels of heroes, and wrangles of great men, are not often at first stirred by as mean engines and lighted by as small sparks as the dissensions of their most obscure inferiors; must have been little conversant with such people, or conversed with them (if knowing them be the end of conversing with them) to very little purpose.[53]

Sir Nathaniel Wraxall similarly commended his own *Memoirs*: 'between 1780 and 1794, during all which period I sat in Parliament, I possessed many means and opportunities of knowing various facts from high authority, and, in some instances, of ascertaining their secret causes or springs'.[54]

Nor were such insights the conventional formulae of literary men only. They continued to be expressed by active politicians for as long as the ancien regime survived in England. One MP, writing in 1819–20 of the reign of George III, was moved to reflect 'how often important events depend on little circumstances'.[55] These characteristics of daily politics encouraged participators to adopt a certain view of history. Shelburne thus echoed Thucydides:

> It is common with most men to attribute all events to some one cause. It suits the pedantry of the historians, who are for making everything into a system, and it saves others the great trouble of combining and thinking. But no great river arises from one source, but on examination will be found to come from the accidental junction of a number of small streams. Besides I am convinced that there are two classes of causes, one ostensible and plausible, calculated to meet the publick eye and mind: the other from private and bye motives, which men scarcely dare to own to themselves. How few actions in life are there which cannot be traced to motives of the latter sort.[56]

---

[53] Hervey, *Memoirs*, vol. 1, pp. 45–6, 84.
[54] Henry B. Wheatley (ed.), *The Historical and the Posthumous Memoirs of Sir Nathaniel William Wraxall 1772–1784* (5 vols., London, 1884), vol. 1, p. 4.
[55] John Nicholls, *Recollections and Reflections, Personal and Political, as Connected with Public Affairs, during the Reign of George III* (London, 1820), p. 31.
[56] 'A Chapter of Autobiography' in Fitzmaurice, *Shelburne*, vol. 1, p. 79.

Such reflections were eventually to evolve into what we now understand as the historical method, via a rejection of reductionism and of answers known in advance of enquiry. As Sir Herbert Butterfield observed in a similar context, 'Historical research may lead us to a scientific discovery when it forces us to see that some apparently unimportant event is the tiny pivot on which the larger course of history turns'.[57] For such reasons, Waldegrave's *Memoirs* are both particularly deserving of attention, and particularly in need of interpretation. As an insight into a closed world, their value was appreciated at the time of their first publication. The *New Edinburgh Review* made this a leading point of its notice: the book was 'highly interesting, as it lays open to the profane view of the vulgar, those secret springs which set in motion the state machinery of courts and cabinets'.[58] The *British Critic* was equally enthusiastic about 'such details as profess to penetrate into the springs by which the counsels of nations were moved and guided; which draw aside the veil from the privacy of public life; and exhibit, in all their nakedness, the inclinations, the plans, and the motives which have governed the governors of mankind'.[59] It was a just assessment.

THE FAMILY BACKGROUND

The Waldegraves were a long-established Catholic gentry family whose estates at Navestock in Essex and Chewton in Somerset were owed to grants from Queen Mary in the 1550s. Loyal service to Charles I added a baronetcy in 1643; but thanks partly to their recusancy, their local prominence was, for a century, not followed by any tradition of political service at national level. All this seemed about to change on the accession of James II: the hour of the Waldegraves, as of many Catholic gentry families, seemed at last to have come.[60] Their barony was one of only ten peerages

---

[57] Butterfield, *George III and the Historians*, p. 298.
[58] *The New Edinburgh Review* 1 (July–Oct. 1821), p. 1.
[59] *The British Critic* 16 (August 1821), p. 163.
[60] Another to find favour in this reign was Sir William Waldegrave (1618–?), one of the cadet branch of Borley in Essex; they figured prominently in the admissions registers of Douai and St Omer in the seventeenth century, and although Sir William's name has not been located there, it is possible that he was an alumnus. Graduating as Doctor of Medicine at Padua, he became physician to James II's queen, Mary of Modena, and witnessed the birth of the future Stuart James III on 10 June 1688. Waldegrave's testimony to the authenticity of the birth was a vital part of the official report which assembled such evidence: *At the Council-Chamber in Whitehall, Monday the 22. of October, 1688* (London, 1688). Following the Revolution, this document became a central text of Jacobite propaganda and continued to be reprinted, under the title *The Several Declarations, Together with the Several Depositions made in Council On Monday, the 22d of October, 1688* (henceforth without printer or date). The Waldegrave name was thereby given a notoriety most unwelcome after the 2nd Baron's conversion to the Hanoverian cause.

created by that king before his exile in 1688: it was conferred in January 1685/6 on Sir Henry Waldegrave, 4th Bt. (1661–1689/90), who in 1683 had married Henrietta Fitzjames, his sovereign's illegitimate daughter.[61]

So close an allegiance was not to be broken by the Revolution of 1688. The 1st Baron Waldegrave was sent as James II's envoy to the French court in November of that year, and his wife and family soon followed him into exile in France.[62] Henry had been appointed Comptroller of the Household in February 1686/7 and retained the same post in the Stuart court at St Germain until his death there, at the age of 28, in January 1689/90.

The title then devolved on his infant son James, 2nd Baron (1684–1741), the father of the author of these *Memoirs*. His minority, and the early return of his mother to England, preserved the family estates from forfeiture. Nevertheless, James, 2nd Baron, was brought up in France as a Roman Catholic, in the family and with the children of his uncle James Fitzjames, Duke of Berwick (1670–1734). A determined attempt was made to commit the young man to the Roman religion, both at the great Jesuit college of La Flèche in Anjou,[63] and during a two years' residence at the Medici court in Florence from 1704 to 1706. Such an education, and observation of the unsavoury entourage of Grand Duke Cosimo III (reigned 1670–1723), may eventually have produced a reaction. In the short run, however, he continued to move in the same circles. May 1714 saw his marriage to Mary Webb, second daughter of Sir John Webb, Catholic, Gloucestershire baronet, nonjuror and Jacobite. For his daughter, Sir John provided a handsome dowry of £12,000; to the Stuart cause during the rebellion of 1715 he contributed a more modest £500.[64] But his allegiances, like Waldegrave's, were not in question.

In consequence, the 2nd Baron was obliged to declare himself by a hostile piece of Whig legislation, 1 Geo. I, c. 55, 'An Act to oblige Papists to register their names, and Real Estates'. Under its provisions, he registered his income from three properties. The Navestock estate, after deduction of his mother's jointure of £600 p.a., was held to be worth £278 15s 4d p.a.

[61] After the 1st Baron's death, she may have married again, in mysterious circumstances, Piers Butler, 3rd Viscount Galmoye, but remained within the Waldegrave family circle. She died in 1730 and was buried at Navestock.

[62] Sir William Waldegrave likewise accompanied his sovereign to France, becoming chief physician to James II (HMC *Stuart*, vol. 1, p. 103) and a trustee of the estate of the infant James, 2nd Baron Waldegrave, after the 1st Baron's death.

[63] This famous school was the alma mater of René Descartes; in 1735–7, David Hume was to live in the town, using the Jesuits' library, while composing his *Treatise of Human Nature*. For Waldegrave's stay, see the Diary of Thomas Marwood, *Miscellanea VI* (Catholic Record Society, vol. 7, 1909), pp. 44–160.

[64] Duke of Berwick to James III, 7 May 1714, 21 June 1715: HMC *Stuart* vol. 1, pp. 321, 370. 'I am sorry he gives so little', apologised Berwick, 'but he excus'd himself upon having marryd lately two of his daughters'.

Introduction

The Hever estate, also charged with a £600 p.a. annuity to his mother, produced an additional £439 6s 8d; and the manor of Chewton added £410 13s 10¾d. Waldegrave's income was therefore modest;[65] as a Catholic, he was subject both to a double land tax, and to threats of expropriation. His family was also exposed to highly unwelcome publicity: the list of those who had registered under the Act of 1714–15 was reprinted in 1745, and the Catholic, Jacobite antecedents of the 2nd Earl brought once more before the nation.[66]

England's legacy of bitterness and division, the consequence of 1688, was only compounded by the Hanoverian accession and the rebellion of 1715. The 2nd Baron evidently viewed with dismay the prospect of being trapped within this impasse; he took a leading part in an initiative begun in 1716 by one section of the Catholic nobility and gentry to reach a negotiated settlement with the new regime, and 'to establish the Englishness of English Catholic hearts'.[67] The initiative culminated in June 1719 with a conference at the Duke of Norfolk's London house; Waldegrave attended as one of the Catholic delegates, to be faced with a series of conditions set out by James Craggs, Secretary of State. Waldegrave was eager to pursue a compromise and find an acceptable formula;[68] but, as a later co-religionist recorded, 'The committee of Catholics, appointed to conduct the business, disagreed amongst themselves; the affair sunk, and was heard of no more ... there was a narrowness in the minds of Catholics, Laity as well as Clergy, which little less than miraculous powers could have enlarged'.[69] A second conference under the same roof in December 1719 (this time including Waldegrave's father-in-law Sir John Webb among the representatives of the gentry) confirmed the disagreement.[70]

For the Catholic community, the future seemed to promise only repression and proscription. Rebellion was the logical consequence, but one that Waldegrave shunned. Added to this, his wife died in childbed in January 1718/19: his Jacobite family ties were suddenly if tragically weakened. The failure of negotiations for Catholic reconciliation, and the death of his wife,

---

[65] Philip Waldegrave of Borley in Essex, the cadet branch, registered estates worth £505 8s 4d. p.a.. At his death in February 1721 these estates were left to the 2nd Baron. E.E. Estcourt and J.O. Payne, *The English Catholic Nonjurors of 1715* (London, [1886]), pp. 60, 64, 88, 230.

[66] John Cosin, *A List of the Names of Roman Catholics, Nonjurors and Others who refused to take the oaths to his late Majesty King George* (London, 1745).

[67] Eamon Duffy, '"Englishmen in Vaine": Roman Catholic Allegiance to George I', in S. Mews (ed.), *Studies in Church History* 18 (Oxford, 1982), pp. 345–65; DOM Basil Hemphill, *The Early Vicars Apostolic of England 1685-1750* (London, 1954), pp. 105–17.

[68] Duffy, *loc. cit.*, p. 358.

[69] [Joseph Berington], *The State and Behaviour of the English Catholics, from the Reformation to the Year 1780* (London, 1780), p. 90.

[70] Duffy, *loc. cit.*, p. 360.

were decisive. On 12 February 1721/2, Waldegrave took his seat in the House of Lords, swearing the oaths of allegiance, supremacy and abjuration, and making the declaration against transubstantiation, as required by law. Faced by a choice between his political career and his religious allegiance, Waldegrave, at least temporarily, chose the former. With what feelings he took this step can only be conjectured; the sole piece of evidence, relating to 1741, is moving but ambiguous and not necessarily reliable.[71]

Despite a spate of conversions in James II's reign, the proportion of peers who were Roman Catholics had been steadily eroded since the early seventeenth century. So had their calibre.[72] In 1641, a fifth of the 121 peers are estimated to have professed that allegiance;[73] by *c*. 1700 only 19 Catholic peers remained out of a total of 173. Of these nineteen, during the course of the eighteenth century, two were attainted for Jacobitism, five titles became extinct, and the holders of seven renounced their Roman Catholicism: Cardigan (1709), Waldegrave (1721), Fauconberg (1737), Audley (1740), Montagu (1767), and Teynham (1781).[74] No new creations added to the Catholic ranks, and to such a small community each secession was a major blow. To the Whig-Anglican establishment, by contrast, each conversion was a useful propaganda victory, and the converts were welcomed with enthusiasm: both the 1st Earl Waldegrave and the 4th Baron Fauconberg quickly became Lords of the Bedchamber.[75]

Waldegrave clearly envisaged a political career for himself. In the 1720s he acquired an essential accessory for such a role, selling the Hever estate and building a substantial house in the Palladian style on his property at Navestock, within easy reach of London.[76] Friendship with Lord Townshend, ally of that rising figure Sir Robert Walpole, brought Waldegrave his first office: in June 1723 he was appointed a Lord of the Bedchamber to George I. Reappointed in that office to George II in 1730, Waldegrave was to hold it until his death in 1741, and his son was soon to succeed him in it. More important than the £1000 p.a. salary was the crucial advantage it brought in a 'court society': access to the King. Both the 1st and 2nd Earls were to owe almost everything to their personal relationship with successive monarchs.

[71] P. 28 below.
[72] John Miller, *Popery and Politics in England 1660–1688* (Cambridge, 1973), pp. 14–15, 65, 219, 221.
[73] Lawrence Stone, *The Crisis of the Aristocracy 1558–1641* (Oxford, 1965), p. 742.
[74] John Cannon, *Aristocratic Century: The Peerage of Eighteenth-Century England* (Cambridge, 1984), pp. 60–1.
[75] Thomas Belasyse, 4th Baron Fauconberg (1699–1774); took the oaths February 1736/7; a Lord of the Bedchamber from 1738; created in 1756 Earl Fauconberg.
[76] For the history of the family in that county, see [P. Muilman], *A New and Complete History of Essex ... By a Gentleman* (6 vols., Chelmsford, 1769–72), vol. 4, pp. 47–53; Thomas Wright, *The History and Topography of the County of Essex* (2 vols., London, 1831–5), vol. 2, pp. 416–20.

Introduction

The 2nd Baron's extensive if unusual European experience made him a particularly valuable recruit. Townshend soon drew him into diplomatic activity, first as Envoy Extraordinary to Paris in September-October 1725, and again from December 1727 to April 1728; then as Ambassador at Vienna in 1728–30; and finally as Ambassador in Paris from 1730 to 1740. For these services he received a reward, and a mark of Whig acceptance, being created in September 1729 Viscount Chewton and Earl Waldegrave. The Order of the Garter followed in February 1737/8. In addition to this diplomatic record, George II had a particular though exceedingly private reason for gratitude to the 1st Earl: Waldegrave had collaborated in the suppression of George I's will. Horace Walpole discovered this in 1760. On the morning after George II's death, the Duke of Cumberland explained to the 2nd Earl Waldegrave his expectations of the King his father's bequests:

Lord Waldegrave in return showed his Royal Highness an *extraordinary* piece; it was endorsed, *very private paper*, and was a letter from the Duke of Newcastle to the first Earl of Waldegrave, in which his grace informed the Earl, that he had received by the messenger the copy of the will and codicil of George the First; that he had delivered it to His Majesty, who put it into the fire without opening it – 'So', adds the Duke, 'we do not know whether it confirms the other or not.' And he proceeds to say, 'I despatch a messenger to the Duke of Wolfenbüttel with the treaty, in which is granted all he desires; and we expect by return of the messenger the original will from him.'

George I left one copy of his will with William Wake, Archbishop of Canterbury; George II obtained possession of it without its contents being known. 'The letter I have quoted above', added Horace Walpole, 'shows what was the fate of the other copy: the honest Duke of Wolfenbüttel sold it for a subsidy!'[77] It was a good bargain, for the will had threatened a diplomatic revolution of major proportions. In it, George I had attempted to provide for the dissolution of the personal union of Britain and Hanover after his son's death. George II's ability to pass on his beloved Electorate in the British succession was owed not least to the tactful collaboration of the 1st Earl Waldegrave.[78] A measure of his tact is that he kept the knowledge of the will's contents from his son, Viscount Chewton, despite their close co-operation in the work of the Paris embassy during the 1730s.

The 1st Earl's extensive diplomatic correspondence, surviving at Chewton, in the British Library and the Public Record Office, has won the respect of historians who have worked on it. In 1798 Archdeacon Coxe echoed the standards of the age: 'His letters are written with great spirit,

[77] Walpole, *George II*, vol. 3, pp. 120–1. Walpole, like the 2nd Earl, was evidently unaware of the most important bequest; he presumed that George II's avarice had led him to avoid paying certain monetary legacies.
[78] On the plan to dissolve the union see Ragnhild Hatton, *George I: Elector and King* (London, 1978), pp. 165–9.

perspicuity, and good sense ... They do honour to his diplomatic talents, and prove sound sense, an insinuating address, and elegant manners'.[79] The suggestion has been made, but not proved, that the Earl failed to discern Fleury's design to engineer a major war to check British power. Whether the War of the Austrian Succession could have been averted by a British ambassador in Paris is beyond the scope of this introduction to speculate. Less hypothetical is Waldegrave's good standing in the eyes of both Walpole and two sovereigns.

George II prided himself on his knowledge of European affairs, and deplored the English amateurishness which accepted the promotion to high diplomatic offices of men who had not been trained to fill them. In late 1756 he complained of the custom. '"What a strange country", said he to Fox, "is this! I have never known but two or three men in it who understood foreign affairs: you do not study them – and yet here comes one man (Pitt) and says he has not so much as read Wicquefort, has all to learn, and demands to be Secretary of State!"'[80] This was not true of the 1st Earl Waldegrave; his copy of Abraham van Wicquefort's classic *L'Ambassadeur* (La Haye, 1681) remains in the library at Chewton to this day.

Other senior Whig statesmen beside Townshend recognised the value of the 1st Earl's contacts in the enemy camp. In 1731 the Duke of Newcastle, long-serving Secretary of State for the Southern Department, needed only to allude to these advantages: 'It is certain the Jacobites begin to conceive hopes of France, & therefore the greatest Attention imaginable should be given to that. You have *a way* of knowing what Foundation there is for it, and whether France is playing us any such Trick or no.'[81] The ambassador was convinced of the reality of the Jacobite threat, despite the years of peace built on the Anglo-French alliance; in 1739 he warned Newcastle:

> I do not believe the Cardinal [Fleury], unless we were at open war with France, would give into all the trifling Jacobite schemes the Court of Spain might be proposing to him, but I am firmly of opinion that nobody would go greater lengths to help the Pretender than the Cardinal, were he satisfied of a probability of success in an undertaking of this nature.[82]

It was a situation which was to come about in the mid 1740s, after the deaths of both Fleury and the 1st Earl.

No evidence survives to cast doubt on the 1st Earl's commitment either to the Protestant religion or to the House of Hanover. His Jacobite contacts offered, rather, the hope of revelations of conspiracies. Yet the greatest chance of this sort was unluckily missed: when the exiled Jacobite Francis

---

[79] Coxe, *Walpole*, vol. 1, p. 350. [80] Walpole, *George II*, vol. 2, p. 187.
[81] Newcastle to Waldegrave, 'Private', 1 April 1731: Waldegrave MSS, Chewton.
[82] Waldegrave to Newcastle, 5 June 1739 (NS): quoted in Jeremy Black, *British Foreign Policy in the Age of Walpole* (Edinburgh, 1985), p. 153.

Atterbury, Bishop of Rochester, died in Paris on 4 March 1732, his compromising papers were seized by order of Cardinal Fleury and quickly 'weeded' of sensitive material.[83] To Waldegrave, however, must go the credit of recruiting to the British secret service an agent who was to have an important influence on the outcome of the dynastic question. François de Bussy, first a secretary to the French ambassador in Vienna from 1728, then an official in the French foreign ministry from 1733, became Minister Plenipotentiary in London in 1740. From 1735, he had been selling information regularly to Waldegrave; the English ministry were eager to preserve the association. In February 1744, Bussy betrayed the vital French plans for an invasion aimed at overthrowing the settlement of 1714.[84] The real Jacobite threat was the armada of '44; after this was frustrated, the unaided rising of '45 stood little chance. James, 1st Earl, had died in 1741; posthumously, he made as large a contribution as any diplomat to the defeat of the last credible attempt at a Stuart restoration.

During his embassy in France, the 1st Earl's change of religion demanded considerable tact to carry off in a deeply Catholic state. The following anecdote, from an unknown source, survived:

Some time after the late Lord Waldegrave abjured the catholic religion, he was sent ambassador to France, where he resided several years. Being one day at an entertainment where his cousin the Duke of Berwick, and many other noblemen, were present, the Duke wanting to mortify him on the score of religion, asked his Lordship, whether the *ministers* of state, or the *ministers* of the gospel, had the greatest share in his conversation? – "I am astonished, my lord Duke," says Waldegrave, "how you can ask me such a question! Do not you know, that when I quitted the Roman Catholic religion, *I left off confession.*"[85]

The 1st Earl was used to taunts on his political origins, and responded with tact and good humour. Horace Walpole noted an anecdote which he very probably derived from his friend the 2nd Earl:

When Lord Waldegrave was Ambassador at Paris, among other English he invited to dinner on the King's birthday, Alderman Parsons' wife, a noted Jacobite. After dinner she filled a bumper and nodding very significantly to the Ambassador, drank *the* King's health, showing she meant the Pretender's. He replied with

---

[83] G.V. Bennett, *The Tory Crisis in Church and State 1688–1730: The Career of Francis Atterbury Bishop of Rochester* (Oxford, 1975), pp. 304–6. Dr. Bennett blamed Waldegrave's and Whitehall's prevarication for failing to secure the Atterbury papers. Whether the ambassador could have carried them off in the face of French ministers' determination to possess them is open to debate.

[84] Eveline Cruickshanks, '101 Secret Agent', *History Today* (April 1969), pp. 273–6.

[85] Rev. John Adams, *Anecdotes, Bon-Mots, and Characteristic Traits of the Greatest Princes, Politicians, Philosophers, Orators and Wits of Modern Times* (London, 1789), p. 141. In 1821, the 6th Earl suggested this anecdote to Lord Holland for inclusion in the latter's edition (Waldegrave to Holland, 'Monday', Add MSS 51598, n.f.); but the anticlerical editor did not dwell on the religious dimension of the *Memoirs*.

admirable quickness, 'Madam, since you have not named what King you mean, we will drink *the best* in Christendom'.[86]

English Catholics, their numbers diminished by proscription and worse penalties, were less relaxed: they neither forgave nor forgot the defection of the 1st Earl. A cautionary tale was preserved in Catholic circles: that Waldegrave had

> abjured the religion of his forefathers about the year 1723, and in consequence was loaded with perishable honours and titles, of which death stripped him 11th April, 1741, at Navestock, Essex. On his death-bed, alluding to his taking the oaths of supremacy and abjuration, he put his hand to his tongue, and, to the terror of the bystanders, made use of this exclamation: 'This bit of red rag has been my damnation.' This anecdote I have repeatedly heard from the late Thomas Taunton, Esq., a gentleman of most retentive memory and unimpeachable veracity. He had received it from his aunt, Ann Taunton, who died in 1783, aet. eighty-seven, and whose sister, Grace Taunton, died in 1760, aet. eighty-two, and was wife to Mr. Dillon, then his lordship's steward.[87]

The main problem of the 1st and 2nd Earls, however, was their vulnerability to the stratagems of rival Whigs, not the reproaches of former co-religionists. The Jacobite antecedents of other recent converts were not forgotten. William Murray, lawyer and rising MP, found himself accurately identified in satirical verse in 1745:

> This new-fangl'd *Scot*, who was brought up at Home,
> In the very same School as his Brother at *Rome*,
> Kneel'd, conscious, as tho' his old Comrades might urge,
> He had formerly drank to the *King* before George.[88]

In Murray's case it was true, and his successful career within the Whig establishment could at any time have been destroyed by hard evidence of his youthful indiscretion; no evidence emerged.

One episode in every man's life which was likely to leave formal evidence was his schooling. Into the early eighteenth century, education at one of the great Catholic colleges in exile, especially those of the Benedictines at Douai and the Jesuits at St Omer, retained unmistakable political implications. As a Catholic priest admitted in 1780, 'It was in these seminaries

---

[86] W.S. Lewis (ed.), *Memoranda Walpoliana* (Farmington, Conn., 1937), p. 7. For the Jacobite loyalty of Humphry Parsons, MP (c. 1676–1741) and his wife, see Sedgwick, vol. 2, pp. 326–7.
[87] Very Rev. George Oliver, *Collections, Illustrating the History of the Catholic Religion in the Counties of Cornwall, Devon, Dorset, Somerset, Wilts and Gloucester* (London, 1857), pp. 69–70. (The 2nd Baron's conversion must be dated before 12 Feb. 1721/2, when he took his seat in the House of Lords.) It has been suggested that this anecdote is to be read as evidence of Waldegrave's deathbed repentance: J.O. Payne, *Records of the English Catholics of 1715* (London, 1889), pp. 56–7.
[88] Porcupinus Pelagius [i.e. M. Morgan], *The Processionade* (London, 1745), p. 7.

Introduction

that was chiefly kept alive that Jacobitical folly, which, like an *ignis fatuus*, led the Catholics of England almost to the brink of ruin.'[89] The association of the Waldegrave family with both institutions had been a strong one. The practice of Catholic gentry sending their sons to be educated at St Omer or Douai 'got really under way in the early 1590s, when St Omer was founded, and had probably become the norm by about 1620';[90] thereafter, the lists of both schools contain the names of many seventeenth-century Waldegraves from several branches of the family. The last name so to appear seems to be that of Sir Charles Waldegrave, 3rd Bt. (d. 1684); but although the place of education of his son Henry, 1st Baron, is not recorded, it seems unlikely that it was not at a Catholic institution. Neither the 1st nor 2nd Earls are listed as alumni of Douai or St Omer;[91] but the 1st Earl, possibly to escape the connotations of those two establishments in exile, was sent to the French Jesuit college of La Flèche, and the same may have been true of his father Henry. Despite the care taken over the 2nd Earl's education, who was sent in turn to *both* of England's leading Protestant schools, the memory of this association remained, and could be exploited by the Waldegraves' enemies. One such now appeared under the ambassador's own roof.

When the 1st Earl moved to Paris he was provided with an unwelcome Secretary to the Embassy by the Duke of Newcastle, Secretary of State for the Southern Department. Thomas Pelham junior (c. 1705–43) had been found a parliamentary seat in 1728 and had already been launched on a diplomatic career by the Pelham clan. Early in 1732, in London for the parliamentary session, he took an opportunity to undermine his ambassador's position. The 1st Earl had just withdrawn his two sons from Eton, meaning to complete their education in Paris. Now a rumour spread that they were to be educated as Roman Catholics; Thomas Pelham criticised his ambassador's handling of business; back in Paris that summer, he implied that he was about to succeed Waldegrave in the embassy. His senior protested indignantly to Charles Delafaye, Newcastle's Under Secretary of State:

I can't help owning to you that I am under the greatest uneasiness and anxiety imaginable to think that any friends of mine could give in to the belief of so absurd a thing as my proposing to breed up my sons Papists. Whoever could imagine such a thing must think me fitter for Bedlam than for the place I have, and perhaps an eye

---

[89] [Berington], *State and Behaviour of the English Catholics*, p. 178.
[90] John Bossy, *The English Catholic Community 1570–1850* (London, 1975), p. 165.
[91] E.H. Burton and E. Nolan (eds.), *The Douay College Diaries: The Seventh Diary 1715–1778* (Catholic Record Society, vol. 28, 1928); Hubert Chadwick, *St Omers to Stonyhurst* (London, 1962); P.R. Harris (ed.), *Douai College Documents 1639–1794* (Catholic Record Society, vol. 63, 1972), pp. 17, 24; G. Holt (ed.), *St Omers and Bruges Colleges, 1593–1773* (Catholic Record Society, vol. 69, 1979), p. 274.

towards it may have made some folks more ready to pretend to believe me capable of so extravagant an Imagination . . .

I did not imagine I should ever have been under the necessity of troubling you or any body else upon so disagreeable a subject as that I am to write upon, for its with the utmost concern that [I] think it my being oblige[d] to justifie my self from a Suspicion I should have hoped my conduct in every Respect ever since I embraced the Religion of my country would have kept me free. I need not tell you how great a misfortune it is to anybody to have been educated in different principles from those establisht in ones Country, and it is never too Late to return to the Right when one has been in the wrong . . . My reason for sending for my children over, was that my Eldest was full old for to remain at school, and that my youngest would never be a scholar, that I was willing to see them before I took any resolution about the kind of business I should put them to, that my intention before I sent for them was to have my son Chewton go to Geneva, and to sound my youngest son's dispositions whether for the Sea or Land service, and put him out of hand to his business if I found him strong enough to begin, if not to have him go for a twelve month to Geneva with his brother and learn mathematicks or anything else that should be usefull to him in a military way. That before I sent for my sons from Eaton I got Mr Saladin his Majesty's resident here who is of Geneva to write there and to get me an account of the Place, and of the expence, and that he, Mr Saladin having at the same time recommended to me a young minister of Geneva[92] as a proper person to be my sons' tutor, I desired he might be sent for. I had been so cautious about them as to get a protestant valet-de-chambre for them, and that they should have none but such servants about them. I submit it to you or any body if this looks like a design to breed up my children Papists . . . P[elham] at his arrival here, told several people in confidence that my sending for my Children had given great offence in England, that his Majesty was so offended at it that I was likely to be recalled . . . this very gentleman hires a Country house for three years, furnishes it new, makes a magnificent Chariot, and seems to dispose his matters as if he was not only to stay here three years, but three to that . . . told me that by a letter he had writ, he believed I might stay here two or three months longer. This you will allow was talking more like a Secretary of State than like a Secretary of the Embassy to his Ambassador . . .

I was brought out of my Native Country at three years old, Educated in the Religion of my Parents, when I was my own master, and had satisfied myself of the Stupidity of the principles [93] in which I was educated, I changed its line and such a change ought not to be thrown in an honest man's face, by men who profess that Religion I changed to, if they are of the same.[94]

[92] This proved to be Pierre Clément, who later acquired a reputation as a minor Enlightenment literary figure: see below, pp. 46–7.
[93] This phrase is open to interpretation: the 1st Earl may mean political rather than theological principles.
[94] 1st Earl Waldegrave to Mr Delafaye, nd [April 1732]: reconstructed from several drafts in the Waldegrave MSS at Chewton. The letter does not survive in the ambassador's official correspondence, PRO SP 78/199–205; but Delafaye's retirement in August 1734 establishes the latest likely date of this episode. Since at least some of the correspondence between the two men was destroyed (SP 78/199 f. 93), it seems probable that the prudent Under Secretary did not file this most sensitive letter with the ordinary despatches. Nevertheless, Waldegrave also asked his deputy to relay his complaint and his valid excuse

Introduction

Too much was public knowledge. Horace Walpole recalled perfectly well the ancestry of the family. 'I was school-fellow of the last two [2nd and 3rd] Earls of Waldegrave, and used to go to play with them in the holidays when I was about twelve years old. They lived with their grandmother, natural daughter of James II. One evening while I was there, came in her mother Mrs Godfrey, that King's mistress – ancient in truth, and so superannuated that she scarce seemed to know where she was'.[95] In the 2nd Earl's time, too, Horace Walpole often stayed at the house, and described it as it was just after his host's marriage in 1759.

> I came this morning in all this torrent of heat from Lord Waldegrave's at Navestock. It is a dull place though it does not want prospect backward. The garden is small consisting of two French *allées* of old limes that are comfortable, two groves that are not so, and a green canal; there is besides a paddock. The house was built by his father and ill-finished, but an air seigneurial in the furniture; French glasses in quantities, handsome commodes, tables, screens etc. goodish pictures in rich frames, and a great deal of noblesse *à la St Germain*. James II, Charles II, the Duke of Berwick, her Grace of Buckingham, the Queen Dowager in the dress she visited Madame Maintenon, her daughter the Princess Louisa, a Lady Gerard that died at Joppa returning from a pilgrimage to Jerusalem, and above all *la Godfrey*, and not at all ugly, though she does not show her thighs. All this is a little leavened with the late King, the present King, and Queen Caroline . . .[96]

It was a thoroughly Jacobite collection, reminiscent of the exiled Court at St Germain en Laye. The Duke of Berwick, the 2nd Earl's great-uncle, was James Fitzjames (1670–1734), son of James II by Arabella Churchill. The Duchess of Buckingham was another daughter of that monarch, Lady Catherine Darnley (?1682–1743), this time by the Countess of Dorchester. The Queen Dowager was Mary of Modena (1658–1718), James II's Queen; the Princess Louisa (1692–1712) was his youngest daughter. *La Godfrey* was Arabella Churchill (1648–1730) herself, wife of Colonel Charles Godfrey and mistress of James II. It was her daughter by that King, Henrietta, whose marriage to Sir Henry Waldegrave, later 1st Baron Waldegrave, cemented the family's relations with the Stuart dynasty. Horace Walpole, who toyed with Deism and flirted with an ineffectual republicanism, could hardly have been more out of place; but his liking for his old schoolfriend overrode politics.

These family associations survived to embarrass a politician of the 1750s. The 1st Earl's sister Arabella was a nun in a convent near Paris. Henrietta, the 1st Earl's mother, was in charge of the education of her son's

---

to London. Thomas Pelham duly sent a perfectly neutral account of both to Newcastle, seemingly without trying to profit from his ambassador's embarrassment. T. Pelham to Newcastle, Paris, 23 April 1732 NS: Add MSS 32776 f. 427.
[95] Walpole to Mann, 8 April 1785: Walpole, *Letters*, vol. 25, p. 570.
[96] Walpole to Montagu, 26 July 1759: Walpole, *Letters*, vol. 9, p. 243.

three children.[97] She remained a Catholic; after her death in 1730, the 1st Earl's Catholic parents-in-law, Sir John and Lady Webb, took his daughter Harriet into their family. The two sons alone, later 2nd and 3rd Earls, received a Protestant education. The month after their grandmother's demise died Mrs. Arabella Godfrey, a remarkable survival from an age long past. The associations continued in the Paris of the 1730s. The 1st Earl was still on friendly terms with his uncle the Duke of Berwick. In 1734, the Ambassador was reported as organising a lodge of freemasons at the house of the aged Louise de Kerouaille, Duchess of Portsmouth, sometime mistress of Charles II.[98] The English government had no doubts of Waldegrave's loyalty; but the circumstantial evidence was considerable.

Rumours like those launched by Thomas Pelham could have a remarkable currency within the closed world of the Court society. Even in the mid 1750s, the 2nd Earl found it necessary to draft a speech (no. 6 below) indignantly repudiating the whispers that he had been 'educated a Papist by the Jesuites at St Omers'. The reports were, of course, untrue, although Waldegrave's school career is hidden by the informal and incomplete nature of eighteenth-century records. By his own evidence (speech no. 6 below, confirmed by bills in the Waldegrave papers), it appears that he was first at Westminster, then at Eton in the years 1725–32. More is known of his contemporaries: John Stuart, later 3rd Earl of Bute (1713–92) was at Eton in 1720–8; William Pitt, later 1st Earl of Chatham (1708–78) in 1718–26; Horace Walpole (1717–97), Waldegrave's lifelong friend, in 1727–34.[99] Here, at least, was an alibi. Yet even at Eton, the two brothers continued to move in their grandmother's social circles – in the early 1730s including Mrs Fermor, Lady Petre and the outspokenly Jacobite Duchess of Buckingham.

In Paris with their father from 1732, the two boys often visited Chateau Fitzjames, seat of their great-uncle the Duke of Berwick. None of this seems to have lured either brother from their allegiance to the Church of England and the Hanoverian dynasty, however. The elder was soon trusted by his father the ambassador in the role of confidential secretary. His brother John, who had (on even his father's admission) acquired no reputation for scholarship at school, received a commission as Ensign in the 1st regiment of Footguards in 1735 and embarked on the military career that was to take

[97] In the 1760s, the 2nd Earl's satire against Lord Bute and the Dowager Princess of Wales (printed as section 6 below) displayed an unusual knowledge of the Spanish Jesuit theologians Thomas Sanchez, Luis de Molina and Antonio Escobar y Mendoza. It may be that the 1st Earl was not able to shield his son from all the influences of a Catholic family.
[98] *Whitehall Evening Post*, 5–7 Sept. 1734.
[99] R.A. Austen-Leigh, *The Eton College Register 1698–1752* (Eton, 1927), pp. 57, 271, 353, 356. The *Register* records the early deaths from smallpox of a number of the 2nd Earl Waldegrave's cohort.

him to the battles of Fontenoy in 1745 and Minden in 1759. James meanwhile laid the foundations of political and diplomatic knowledge which were to carry him to the centre of state affairs. It was to be needed all too soon.

THE POLITICAL CAREER OF JAMES, 2ND EARL WALDEGRAVE, 1741–1763

The launching of a career

The 1st Earl died of 'Dropsy and Jaundice' at Navestock on 11 April 1741, aged only 57, six months after his return from the Paris embassy. His elder son, the author of these memoirs, succeeded to his father's title and estates at the age of 26, and took his seat in the Lords on 24 April. It was not the easiest of entrances into the political world. He was, to begin with, too young. Together with his father's untimely death, which deprived him of his only Whig kinsman, the 2nd Earl's residence abroad for much of the 1730s had prevented the accumulation of contacts and allies. His father, succeeding to his Barony in 1690 at the age of six, had had no experience of the House of Commons, and there is no evidence that either of the 1st Earl's two sons were being prepared to contest seats at the general election of 1741. Despite his diplomatic experience, the young 2nd Earl carried, as yet, no weight at Westminster. Others of his cohort had already established themselves in the public arena.

Who were his contemporaries? Their dates of birth (Table 1) reveal the head start enjoyed by the group of men who were to achieve prominence in politics during the two decades of Waldegrave's public life.

When the 2nd Earl succeeded to his title, politics was still dominated by a much older set of men, who often left the stage in the late 1750s and 1760s: 1st Lord Anson (1697–1762), 3rd Duke of Argyll (1682–1761), 1st Earl of Bath (1684–1764), 1st Earl Granville (1690–1763), 3rd Duke of Devonshire (1698–1755), 2nd Duke of Grafton (1683–1757), 1st Earl of Hardwicke (1690–1764), 1st Duke of Newcastle (1693–1768); plus, of course, the Stuart King James III (1688–1766) and the Hanoverian King George II (1683–1760). An important aspect of the politics of the 1740s and 50s was the attempt of the cohort of Pitt and Fox to break the stranglehold of the generation of Newcastle and Hardwicke. Into this scenario the 2nd Earl Waldegrave did not fit easily or naturally. Fox and Pitt had left him behind in the race for power; but Waldegrave was too young to be of much value to Newcastle's generation. Not until the 1760s did the 2nd Earl find his political opportunities opening up.

Parliament was dissolved on 25 April 1741, the day after the 2nd Earl

Table 1 *Waldegrave's Cohort: dates of birth*

1705	Henry Fox
1708	William Pitt
1709	Sir George Lyttelton
1710	4th Duke of Bedford; 2nd Baron Talbot
1711	2nd Duke of Dorset; 2nd Earl of Egmont; 2nd Earl Temple
1712	George Grenville
1713	3rd Earl of Bute
1714	1st Earl Harcourt; Charles Pratt
1715	2nd Earl Waldegrave
1716	2nd Earl of Halifax; Lord George Sackville
1717	2nd Viscount Barrington
1718	4th Earl of Sandwich; 4th Earl of Holdernesse; 3rd Earl of Lichfield; 2nd Viscount Hillsborough
1720	4th Duke of Devonshire
1721	Duke of Cumberland; 2nd Earl Gower
1722	Richard Rigby; Charles Yorke

took his seat, and did not reassemble until 1 December. In the ensuing session, which lasted until July 1742, Waldegrave was present on 31 business days, the highest attendance of any session in which he sat in the Lords. His record during his years in the upper house is set out in Table 2, together with comparable figures for four of his contemporaries. None of them is offered as a 'typical peer'; nor would average attendances for the whole House be meaningful. Individuals differed markedly in their willingness to shoulder the burdens of Lords' business, both as against their colleagues and over different sessions; Waldegrave's career is therefore compared with four specific instances, each different in its pattern. George Montagu Dunk, 2nd Earl of Halifax (1716–71), represents a successful Pelhamite man of business. Succeeding to his title in 1739, he passed from being a Lord of the Bedchamber to the Prince of Wales in 1742–4 to the position of First Lord of Trade in 1748, a post he filled with industry and success until 1761. In George III's reign he was to progress to the more exalted offices of Lord Lieutenant of Ireland (1761–3), First Lord of the Admiralty (June-October 1762), Secretary of State (1762–3, 1763–5, 1771) and Lord Privy Seal (1770–1). In his case, regular attendance in the 1750s was rewarded with a distinguished career in the 1760s.

John Montagu, 4th Earl of Sandwich (1718–92) illustrates a similar career interrupted. Succeeding early to his title in 1729, service in the army led him to politics and the early reward of a seat at the Admiralty Board in 1744–6; appointed (rather than Waldegrave) Minister Plenipotentiary at the conferences of Breda in 1746, and Aix la Chapelle in 1748,[100] he followed this with a period as Minister at The Hague in 1746–9; briefly out of London politics, he returned as First Lord of the Admiralty in 1749–51. Thereafter his alliance with the Duke of Bedford took him into opposition during the 1750s, wasted years not redeemed by a lucrative sinecure post. Sandwich's career only regained momentum with his return as First Lord of the Admiralty in 1763; after Secretaryships of State in 1763–5 and 1770–1, his finest hour was again at the Admiralty, during the American war, from 1771 to 1782. Sandwich illustrates recovery from an early setback.

John West, 7th Baron Delawar (1693–1766), illustrates a career of consistent loyalty and regular drudgery. Succeeding in 1723, an early army career, a Lordship of the Bedchamber in 1725–7 and the Treasurership of the Household in 1731–7 were never followed by high office or distinguished achievements. Delawar held the sinecure post of Governor of Guernsey from 1752 to his death; he attended regularly in the House, spoke often on the government side, and frequently acted as Teller. His reward in the new reign was honorific: on 18 March 1761 he was created Viscount Cantelupe and Earl Delawar.

Halifax, Sandwich and Delawar all attended the House more often than Waldegrave, generally in that order of frequency; but Waldegrave progressively outpaced a fourth contemporary, whose career illustrates an emptiness only highlighted by its final reward. William Talbot, 2nd Baron Talbot (1710–82), succeeded his father in 1737 and soon attached himself to Frederick Prince of Wales. His initial zeal for politics and service as an opposition Teller was never followed up; his career languished, and when in March 1761 he was created Earl Talbot, his new dignity and post of Lord Steward excited only surprise. Delawar and Talbot illustrate two patterns of political failure.

This frenetic activity at the outset of the 2nd Earl Waldegrave's career was not surprising. The session of 1741–2 saw the toppling of Sir Robert Walpole, the destruction of his ministry, and the greatest political crisis for a generation. Once deposed, the fallen minister was hounded by a revengeful opposition. Waldegrave was at once drawn in: the articles of impeachment against Sir Robert included the charge that he had appointed as Ambassador in Paris a near relation of the Pretender – Waldegrave's father. The 2nd Earl drew up a speech (no. 1 below) in his father's defence; but a decisive vote in the Lords on 25 May revealed to an enraged opposition that they would not command a majority to pass an

---

[100] For the value of these opportunities at the outset of his career, see James M. Haas, 'The Pursuit of Political Success in Eighteenth-Century England: Sandwich, 1740–71', *Bulletin of the Institute of Historical Research*, 49 (1970), 56–77.

Table 2 *House of Lords Attendances 1741–1763*

Session dates, N.S.	Business Days*	2nd Earl Waldegrave Days	(%age)	2nd Earl of Halifax Days	(%age)	4th Earl of Sandwich Days	(%age)	7th Baron Delawar Days	(%age)	2nd Baron Talbot Days	(%age)	Divisions
April 1741†	2	1	(50)	0	(0)	0	(0)	1	(50)	2	(100)	—
Dec. 1741–July 1742	85	31	(36.5)	35	(41.2)	55	(64.7)	45	(52.9)	19	(22.4)	14
Nov. 1742–Apr. 1743	60	6	(10.0)	13	(21.7)	43	(71.7)	18	(30.0)	8	(13.3)	11
Dec. 1743–May 1744	80	17	(21.3)	26	(32.5)	43	(53.8)	26	(32.5)	14	(17.5)	3
Nov. 1744–May 1745	68	9	(13.2)	12	(17.6)	20	(29.4)	14	(20.6)	6	(8.8)	0
Oct. 1745–Aug. 1746	118	19	(16.1)	32	(27.1)	24	(20.3)	34	(28.8)	11	(9.3)	1
Nov. 1746–June 1747	85	21	(24.7)	37	(43.5)	0	(0)	23	(27.0)	21	(24.7)	1
Nov. 1747–May 1748	74	7	(9.5)	18	(24.3)	0	(0)	25	(33.8)	2	(2.7)	8
Nov. 1748–June 1749	85	11	(12.9)	48	(56.6)	31	(36.5)	23	(27.1)	7	(8.2)	3
Nov. 1749–Apr. 1750	65	17	(26.2)	21	(32.3)	18	(27.7)	25	(38.5)	0	(0)	1
Jan.–June 1751	79	23	(29.1)	45	(57.0)	30	(38.0)	30	(38.0)	5	(6.3)	2
Nov. 1751–Mar. 1752	65	14	(21.5)	31	(47.7)	4	(6.2)	13	(20.0)	1	(1.5)	1
Jan.–June 1753	81	10	(12.3)	53	(65.4)	9	(11.1)	15	(18.5)	2	(2.50)	3
Nov. 1753–Apr. 1754	66	6	(9.1)	14	(21.2)	11	(16.7)	20	(30.3)	1	(1.5)	1
May–June 1754	5	0	(0)	1	(20.0)	1	(20.0)	1	(20.0)	0	(0)	0
Nov. 1754–Apr. 1755	77	12	(15.6)	41	(53.2)	34	(44.2)	16	(20.8)	5	(6.5)	3
Nov. 1755–May 1756	98	18	(18.4)	51	(52.0)	27	(27.6)	26	(26.5)	21	(21.4)	6
Dec. 1756–July 1757	105	25	(23.8)	49	(46.7)	33	(31.4)	28	(26.7)	12	(11.4)	5
Dec. 1757–June 1758	97	24	(24.7)	27	(27.8)	32	(33.0)	22	(22.7)	23	(23.7)	6
Nov. 1758–June 1759	88	2	(2.3)	14	(15.9)	9	(10.2)	2	(2.3)	4	(4.5)	2
Nov. 1759–May 1760	86	16	(18.6)	24	(27.9)	18	(20.9)	31	(36.0)	6	(7.0)	1
Nov. 1760–Mar. 1761	55	0	(0)	6	(10.9)	3	(5.5)	7	(12.7)	8	(14.5)	0
Nov. 1761–June 1762	92	13	(14.1)	3	(3.3)	16	(17.4)	28	(30.4)	13	(14.1)	2
Nov. 1762–Apr. 1763‡	57	7	(12.3)	23	(40.4)	15	(26.3)	16	(28.1)	14	(24.6)	3

* Excluding days when the house adjourned early, transacting no important business and with very few peers having attended. This occurred on the State fasts or festivals of 30 January (Charles I's martyrdom), 29 May (Charles II's restoration), 11 June (George II's accession), in 1745 only on 5 November (Gunpowder Plot); on days when the king was presented with an Address from the House; on days appointed by royal proclamation for a general fast, or of thanksgiving for military victory.
† Waldegrave took his seat on 24 April; Parliament was dissolved on 25th. Only the last two days of the session are included here.
‡ Waldegrave was taken ill on 30 March and died on 8 April; Parliament was prorogued on 19 April. Counting 30 March, Waldegrave thus missed nine business days at the end of the session. During this period the attendances of the peers here listed were: Halifax 2; Sandwich 3; Delawar 3; Talbot 4.

Introduction

impeachment, and Waldegrave's defence of his father's memory was never heard in the House.

The 2nd Earl later acquired a reputation for equanimity; but his initiation was into a world of bitter conflict and sharply defined polarities, very often of a dynastic and religious nature. His loyalty to his father's memory and to his father's political associates made his choice of allegiance a foregone conclusion. His success was not; and the first step on the ladder was to take two years. Only in 1743 did Waldegrave become a Lord of the Bedchamber to George II, a post worth £1000 p.a.; his career as a courtier was launched, but without *éclat*. The young Earl's promotion was entirely due to the King. Newcastle apologised to a disappointed patron:

> I waited on His Majesty this day for the first time since th G[o]v[ernmen]t Lord Carteret was in with me. The King began addressing Himself to Lord Carteret. 'What! the Duke of Roxborough, won't take Lord of the Bechamber'; & then turned to me & said, 'I will make my Lord Waldegrave'; upon which I said, I had last night received a Letter from your Grace requesting it, for Lord Berkeley. He said, He would give it to Lord Waldegrave, and as there could be no objection to Him, & ye King was determined, I said no more ... I didn't know yt any body has named Waldegrave to ye King. It looks as if it was His Majesty's own doing.[101]

Waldegrave thus entered the political arena without the support (indeed, despite the mild disapproval) of the Pelhams. With this handicap, his advance was to be slow. Nevertheless, he possessed one advantage of supreme importance: access to the King. A Bedchamber post was not nominal: George II required the personal attendance of his Lords of the Bedchamber at his dressing and at a morning *levée*.[102] Holders of that fairly onerous office served for a week in turn, and although Waldegrave's full-time appointment to the household of the Prince of Wales obliged him to relinquish his Bedchamber post in 1752, his brother had acquired the only slightly less influential position of Groom of the Bedchamber in 1747. The Waldegrave family presence did not disappear.

The detailed arrangements of Courts are apt to distract attention from the momentous issues which were conducted through those highly formalised channels. It is easy enough to find evidence for a picture of Walpolian England as tranquil, somnolent, unmindful of great issues and geopolitical conflict. Such evidence can, of course, be found in all ages, even ones of turmoil; and more significant is its flat contradiction by the

---

[101] Newcastle to Duke of Richmond, 14 Dec. 1743: Timothy J. McCann (ed.), *The Correspondence of the Dukes of Richmond and Newcastle 1724–1750*, Sussex Record Society, vol. 73 (Lewes, 1984), p. 131.

[102] John M. Beattie, *The English Court in the Reign of George I* (Cambridge, 1967), p. 59.

repeated testimony of political leaders.[103] The 2nd Earl of Hardwicke recalled his father's perception of Sir Robert Walpole:

> Sir Robert was averse to War from opinion, from interest, and from fear of the Pretender. He told Mr O[nslo]w (the late Speaker) that he was not cut out to carry the truncheon; that, if there was a war, the King's crown would be fought for on this land; which happened to be the case in 1745 and 6, at Preston Pans, Falkirk and Culloden ... In fact, his fears of Invasions and of Jacobitism were real; though his enemies affected to say they were state artifices.[104]

It was the widespread indifference towards the Hanoverian regime, as much as positive Jacobitism, which most alarmed Henry Pelham. In the summer of 1745, he wrote:

> I am not so apprehensive of the strength or zeal of the enemy, as I am fearful of the inability or languidness, of our friends. I see, the contagion spreads in all parts; and, if your Grace was here, you would scarce, in common conversation, meet with one man who thinks there is any danger from, scarce truth in an invasion, at this time. For my part, I have long dreaded it; and am now as much convinced as my late friend lord Orford was, that this country will be fought for some time before this year is over.[105]

Prince Charles Edward's standard had been raised at Glenfinnan the day before.

The progress and military suppression of the rebellion is familiar territory. During the '45, it was essential for the 2nd Earl to make public his Hanoverian loyalty. His seat at Navestock made him a leader in Essex society, and an expression of county solidarity was naturally forthcoming from the Quarter Sessions at Chelmsford. An (evidently impecunious) observer wrote:

> We have just now signed here a most loyal Address with an offer of our Lives and Fortunes which you will say is no great Compliment from me and an Association, and tho' late we are come pretty Hearty. We had the Lords FitzWalter[106] and Waldegrave and the greatest Appearance I ever saw at Sess[ions] and almost Assizes.[107]

To most historians, the defeat of the Stuart cause at the battle of Culloden in April 1746 has seemed the end of an age, the inevitable (indeed, too-long-delayed) closing of a chapter. The best informed of contemporaries showed no such premonition, however. Cumberland had been appalled at what he found in Scotland, reporting to London:

---

[103] For Sir Robert Walpole's preoccupations, see especially Paul S. Fritz, *The English Ministers and Jacobitism between the Rebellions of 1715 and 1745* (Toronto, 1975).

[104] [Philip Yorke, 2nd Earl of Hardwicke], *Walpoliana* (London, 1781), pp. 7, 9.

[105] H. Pelham to Duke of Argyll, 20 Aug 1745: Coxe, *Pelham*, vol. 1, p. 258.

[106] Benjamin Mildmay, 19th Baron FitzWalter (1672–1756), created in 1730 Earl Fitz-Walter; Lord Lieutenant of Essex 1741-d.

[107] Champion Bramfill to Sir Thomas Drury, 9 Oct 1745: HMC *Lothian*, p. 151.

Introduction

> I really think the *éclat* of it [the rebellion] over, but believe there will be left such seed, that God knows how soon it may break out again, if a care and caution, unusual in this island, be not, on this occasion, kept. All in this country are almost to a man Jacobites; and mild measures will not do ... I am sorry to say, that, though all in this country are as ill inclined as possible, and though their spirit for rebellion is extremely great, yet the managers of this part of the kingdom have made it, if possible, worse, by putting the power of the Crown into the most disaffected hands, for the sake of elections.[108]

Even after Culloden, he added:

> I am sorry to leave this country, in the condition it is in; for, all the good that we have done has been a little bloodletting, which has only weakened the madness, but not at all cured; and I tremble for fear that this vile spot may still be the ruin of this island, and of our family ...[109]

The Whig establishment responded with a programme of social reform the centrepiece of which was the Heritable Jurisdictions Bill. Waldegrave supported the measure during its passage through the Lords in May 1747; his forthright eulogy of 'Revolution Principles' and endorsement of a measure of the Lord Chancellor, Hardwicke, aligned him firmly with the ministry and against both the Tories and Prince Frederick's Leicester House opposition (speech no. 3 below).[110] Even so, this measure did not produce an immediate solution to the problem. As the war in Europe dragged on, the strategic danger of a disaffected Scotland posed the same, unchanging, threat. Cumberland, once more in command of the British forces in Germany, was reminded of the continuing danger:

> Many of the troops allotted for the defence of England and Scotland, have been sent abroad; and I doubt, we do not find the latter mended in their affection, or subdued in their power; for I hear, the Jacobites are more insolent than ever. The former has, indeed, shewn great zeal for the King, and chosen a good parliament; but the lurking Jacobite spirit begins to shew itself. Many insolences and petty riots have broken out; and those who, in open rebellion, thought it best not to appear, begin now to pull off the mask.[111]

It was hardly possible to explain to Cumberland that the next stage in the succession question might turn not on a positive affirmation of the Stuarts but a negative rejection of the family of Brunswick. George II's advancing age brought into steadily greater prominence the egregious and erratic heir to the throne, Frederick Prince of Wales. The disastrous unsuitability of this candidate weighed heavily on the minds of the

---

[108] Cumberland to Newcastle, 4 April 1746: Coxe, *Pelham*, vol. 1, p. 299.
[109] Cumberland to Newcastle, 17 July 1746: Coxe, *Pelham*, vol. 1, p. 303.
[110] Any favour thereby curried was probably offset by Waldegrave's opposition to another ministerial measure, the Buckingham Assizes Bill, in March-April 1748: see speech no. 4 below.
[111] Henry Pelham to Duke of Cumberland, 8 Sept 1747: Coxe, *Pelham*, vol. 1, p. 373.

Pelhams. Frederick's brother Cumberland had already acquired the nickname 'The Butcher', and a sinister reputation for unconstitutional designs on the throne. Prince Charles Edward's expulsion from France only made things worse: he took up residence, instead, in Switzerland. Henry Pelham confided his fears to his brother:

> You desire my opinion, whether it might not be proper for lord Sandwich to make his instances, for removing the Pretender's son farther from France, than Switzerland. I heartily wish they could get him back to Rome; but I doubt they will not be able to do it. I cannot say, but I have my fears of ill consequences from his residence in Switzerland; not from its vicinity to France, but from its distance from Rome. I hope and trust in God, no change will happen in our time; but if *this young gentleman* should declare himself a Protestant, and another [Frederick, Prince of Wales] should not act suitable to the great and good examples he has had before him, the Lord knows how matters may end.[112]

A rumour had long circulated that Queen Caroline 'wished to set aside Frederic Prince of Wales, and place William Duke of Cumberland on the throne'[113] after her husband's death; in the event, Cumberland's growing political weight sustained the rumour after his mother's demise in 1737. Within England, allegiance to the exiled dynasty was in steep decline by the late 1740s. But the Jacobite issue did not immediately disappear; it survived into the next decade as an option within European diplomacy. Newcastle feared that France's predominance and system of alliances might 'reduce Britain to a state of dependency or even by another Jacobite rising overturn the constitution'.[114] Henry Pelham agreed that the outbreak of another European war would be followed by another Jacobite rebellion. He pointed out the danger of war among the Baltic states:

> I am every day more convinced of the necessity of keeping things quiet there; for, besides the natural consequence, being a general war, which neither we nor our allies are yet in a condition to carry on, I am satisfied, any disturbance there, would immediately be followed by domestic troubles here. I have reason to think the Jacobites expect it, even depend upon it; and I fear this country is not so well disposed to some branches of our royal family, as they were upon the late rebellion. The eldest [Frederick, Prince of Wales] loses esteem and confidence, more and more, every day; and the youngest [the Duke of Cumberland] does not conduct himself so prudently, with regard to the temper of this country, and constitution, as to be able to make up for the unfortunate turn of the other. Our whole dependence, at present, is upon the king; and, as I am a well-wisher to all of them, I pray God

---

[112] Henry Pelham to Duke of Newcastle, 29 July/9 Aug 1748: Coxe, *Pelham*, vol. 1, p. 461.
[113] John Nicholls, *Recollections and Reflections, Personal and Political, as connected with Public Affairs during the Reign of George III* (London, 1820), p. 367.
[114] D.B. Horn, 'The Cabinet Controversy on Subsidy Treaties in Time of Peace, 1749–50', *EHR* 45 (1930), 463–6, a paraphrase interpolated into the text of Newcastle to Hardwicke, 25 August 1749: Add MSS 35410 f 126.

Introduction 41

things may mend, before Nature calls him from us. I trust in God, that fatal event will not be in my time; for, whenever it comes, I see a melancholy prospect.[115]

The Waldegraves' social milieu

The marriages of the two brothers were soon talked about, the younger first. In 1751, it was 'generally believed that Lady Betty Leveson is married privately to Colonel Waldegrave'; and so, sensationally, she was. Horace Walpole later noted that 'by the intrigues of the Earl of Sandwich, Colonel John Waldegrave stole Lord Gower's daughter, and the marriage was performed at Lord Sandwich's at the Admiralty'.[116] More importantly, she was the Duchess of Bedford's sister, and a connection with the Bedford clan was to be an important aspect of the Waldegraves' fortunes. Attention now turned to the 2nd Earl. 'I really think he continues to preserve all his good qualities in the midst of the filth and dirt of the Court, and the corruption of the ministers', added Lady Townshend.[117] Soon Lord Waldegrave was reported to be on the verge of matrimony with Miss Harriet Drax, daughter of Prince Frederick's secretary;[118] Horace Walpole believed so, and, knowing something of the lady, consoled George Montagu: 'you will be sorry when I tell you that Lord Walgrave certainly dis-Solomons himself with the Drax'.[119] The match 'I hear is declared', wrote Lady Harcourt to her son Lord Nuneham; 'and I am told a person representing to him the flaw there was in that Lady's character, his Lordsp replyed that nothing was worthy of consideration in a woman but her beauty; are not these glorious principles, and is not he a proper person to form the mind of a young Prince[?]'[120] But whatever the accuracy of the report, the match did not take place. By the autumn of 1755 it was a Miss Townshend who was spoken of for that role.[121] Yet this possibility likewise evaporated, and political cares were steadily drawing Waldegrave away from domestic happiness.

The career of the 2nd Earl's brother was progressing more successfully. A professional army officer with a distinguished record of active service in

---

[115] Pelham to Newcastle, 1/12 June 1750: Coxe, *Pelham*, vol. 2, p. 342.
[116] Edward Jeffery (ed.), *The Works, of the Right Honourable Sir Charles Hanbury Williams, KB* (3 vols., London, 1822), vol. 1, p. 184.
[117] Lady Townshend to Countess of Denbigh, 21 Feb [1751]: HMC *Denbigh*, vol. 5, pp. 270–1. Lady Elizabeth Leveson-Gower, daughter of Earl Gower, married Colonel John Waldegrave on 7 May 1751.
[118] W.F. Hamilton to Earl of Huntingdon, 13 Dec. 1754: HMC *Hastings*, vol. 3, p. 89.
[119] Walpole to Montagu, 16 Nov 1754: Walpole, *Letters*, vol. 9, p. 165. William Pitt and Lady Hesther Grenville, just espoused, were dubbed Solomon and Hesther by Lady Townshend.
[120] Lady Harcourt to Lord Nuneham, 16 Sept 1754: *Harcourt Papers*, vol. 3, p. 63.
[121] Rev. T. Lindsey to Earl of Huntingdon, 16 Nov. 1755: HMC *Hastings*, vol. 3, p. 108.

the War of the Austrian Succession (and more to come in the Seven Years' War), he was made aide-de-camp to the Duke of Cumberland in 1747.[122] In the same year he was brought into Parliament on the ministerial interest, and held a seat in the Commons until he succeeded his brother in 1763; in 1747, too, John Waldegrave became a Groom of the Bedchamber to George II, a post which he held (with a salary of £500 p.a.), again, until 1763.

Meanwhile, the Earl and his brother Colonel Waldegrave continued to move in London society; but the soldier was not as happy in the political world of Dublin, where his regiment was posted. In 1751 George Stone, the highly politicized Archbishop of Armagh and key figure in the Dublin administration, wrote to Lord George Sackville:

> I expect Col. Waldegrave to dinner ... To tell you the truth, the Colonel does not shine upon new ground, and as the ideas and language of White's (in which I conclude him supreme), are not current here, he seems entirely devoid of any other, so that, in the eyes of us unpolished people, he appears rather simple and ignorant. This is only the first impression, and perhaps I am quite mistaken.[123]

By 1755, Colonel Waldegrave had had enough of Ireland, and was on the point of returning to England without leave; only Lady Betty Waldegrave's intervention with Cumberland via Princess Amelia avoided an embarrassing situation.[124] It is difficult to avoid the conclusion that the preferred milieu of both brothers was not Westminster, but White's.

White's was the most distinguished of the London clubs; until the 1760s it had few rivals, and its membership list reads like a roll-call of the most powerful men in England.[125] At unknown dates were elected Henry Pelham and William Pulteney, Horatio Walpole and George Bubb Dodington, the 1st Duke of Newcastle and the 3rd Dukes of Devonshire and Marlborough. The dates of election are recorded for many more: in 1736 the 2nd Earl of Albemarle, the 4th Earl of Chesterfield and Sir Robert Walpole; in 1737 the 2nd Duke of Grafton; in 1740 the 1st Duke of Dorset; in 1742 the 4th Earl of Holdernesse and Lord Hartington, later 4th Duke of Devonshire; in 1743 the 1st Earls of Harcourt and Ilchester, the 2nd Earls of Egremont and Ashburnham, Lord George Sackville, Henry Fox, and Newcastle's two Under Secretaries of State, Andrew Stone and James

---

[122] His ranks were: Ensign 1735; Captain 1739; Major 1748; Colonel 1748; Major-General 1757; Lieutenant-General 1759; General 1772.
[123] Primate to Lord George Sackville, 2 July 1751: HMC *Stopford-Sackville*, vol. 1, p. 173.
[124] Lady Betty Waldegrave to Bedford, 30 June 1755: Bedford MSS vol. 31, f. 56.
[125] From 1744 until 1781 there were two clubs meeting in the same premises; the Young Club was a wilder version of the Old Club, and a probationary stage in admission to the senior body. We may assume that several young men-about-town elected in the mid 1740s were members first of the Young Club: Horace Walpole, George Selwyn, the 2nd Earl Waldegrave. In 1755, 120 members were listed for the Old Club, 230 for the Young Club.

West; in 1744 the 4th Duke of Argyll, the 1st Earl of Egmont, General Conway, George Grenville, Horace Walpole and Admiral Anson; in 1745 the Earl of Kildare and Colonel George Townshend; in 1747 Charles Townshend and the 1st Earl Gower; in 1748, the 4th Earl of Sandwich, the 2nd Viscount Barrington, and G.B. Rodney; in 1751 the 2nd Marquis of Rockingham and 3rd Earl of Albemarle; in 1753 the 6th Baron Digby and in 1754 H.B. Legge. From this catalogue, and from this social world, two men above all held aloof: William Pitt was not elected until some date in the 1760s; the Earl of Bute was evidently never a member. By contrast the Waldegraves entered in an easy progression: the 1st Earl in 1738, the 2nd in 1743, the 3rd in 1746, the 4th in 1773. This choice of club had a certain significance: although the membership was relatively wide, the orientation was distinctly pro-ministerial. George Dodington, a senior adviser of Frederick, Prince of Wales, hardly visited his club during the years of that Prince's open opposition;[126] when Dodington sought again to ingratiate himself with the Pelhams, White's became a regular port of call.

The social life into which the Waldegraves entered was often less than high minded. The club's historian records that 'the reputation for high play which distinguished White's from the first, reached its zenith during the last ten years of the reign of George II'. This was, indeed, the period in which the gambling mania among the elite, like gin drinking among the masses, reached the scale of a social problem. The depredations which it wrought in the estates of the nobility and gentry was a growing complaint. Sir George Lyttelton complained to the Dissenting minister Philip Doddridge:

I join with you in sorrow for the poor Dryads of Boughton, and thank you for the regard and concern you express for those of Hagley. They are at present pretty secure, but I sometimes tremble to think that the rattling of a dice-box, at *White's*, may one day or other (if my son should be a member of that noble academy), shake down all our fine oaks. It is dreadful to see not only there, but almost in every house in town, what devastations are made by that destructive fury, the spirit of Play! The time, the fortunes, the honour, and the consciences of our nobility and gentry, both male and female, are all falling a prey to it, and what is still worse, the force of the laws has been tried against it, and proves ineffectual. Those laws are openly broke every day by the legislators themselves; we are now trying what sermons can do, but I fear this one vice will be too hard for all our preachers, assisted by yours, and three or four earthquakes besides.[127]

---

[126] Dodington, *Diary*, 13 June 1751.
[127] Sir George Lyttelton to Philip Doddridge, April 1750: R. Phillimore (ed.), *Memoirs and Correspondence of George, Lord Lyttelton, from 1734 to 1773* (2 vols., London, 1845), vol. 1, p. 420. Hagley was Lyttelton's seat; Boughton was then owned by George, 4th Earl of Cardigan, created 3rd Duke of Montague in 1766. Minor earthquakes in February and March 1750 had provoked a religious panic.

44 *Introduction*

Undeterred by a thunderbolt which (according to Hogarth's engraving) struck the club in 1733, the members of White's took an irreverent interest in the workings of Providence, and recorded it in the Betting Book. On 18 November 1743 Waldegrave bet Lord Lincoln and Lord Coke 50 guineas each 'that Mr Fazackerley outlives Mr Paul Foley'. On 29 September 1744, 'Ld Waldegrave betts Ld Hallifax and Sr Wm. Stanhope Fifty guineas each, that Fourteen Members of the House of Commons dont Die before the 29 Septr 1745'. Colonel Waldegrave's bets are in the same idiom.[128]

In this, Waldegrave was only echoing the scale of values of his social circle. Within it, politics occupied a strictly subordinate priority. The astonishingly beautiful Gunning sisters 'and a late extravagant dinner at White's are twenty times more the subject of conversation than the two [Pelham] brothers, and Lord Granville', noted Walpole;

> The dinner was a folly of seven young men, who bespoke it to the utmost extent of expense; one article was a tart made of dukecherries from a hot house; and another that they tasted but one glass out of each bottle of champagne. The bill of fare is got into print, and with good people has produced the apprehension of another earthquake. Your friend St Leger was at the head of these luxurious heroes – he is the hero of all fashion.[129]

Presumably the organisers had their menu printed to immortalise the occasion. In due course, the *Gentleman's Magazine* reprinted it (in uncertain French):[130]

A LATE BILL OF FARE

Some Gentlemen* of Distinction a few weeks ago having agreed to dine together, the following is handed about as their Bill of Fare

	£	s	d
Bread and beer	0	4	0
Potage de Tortue	0	16	6
Calipash	1	1	0
Calipees	0	16	0
Un Pate de Jambon de Bayone	2	10	0
Potage Julien verd	1	12	0
Two turbots to remove the soops	2	0	0
Haunch of venison	2	12	0
Palaits de mouton	0	6	0
Selle de mouton	0	6	0
Salade	0	4	0
Saucisses aux ecreoisses	0	18	0
Boucin blanc a la reine	0	18	0

[128] [W.B. Boulton], *The History of White's* (2 vols., privately printed, London, 1892); vol. 1, pp. 94, 125–6; vol. 2, pt. 1 reprints the Betting Book.
[129] Walpole to Mann, 18 June 1751: Walpole, *Letters*, vol. 20, p. 258.
[130] *The Gentleman's Magazine*, 21 (1751), p. 280.

	£	s	d
Petits pates a l'Espaniol	1	10	0
Coteletts a la cardinal	0	16	0
Selle d'agneau glace aux cocomtres	0	18	0
Saumon a la chambord	1	11	0
Fillets de saules royales	1	10	0
Une bisque de lait de maqueraux	1	15	0
Un lambert aux innocents	1	10	0
Des perdrix sauce vin de champaign	1	10	0
Poulets a le Russiene	0	10	6
Ris de veau en arlequin	0	18	0
Quee d'agneau a la Montaban	0	10	6
Dix cailles	2	2	0
Un lapreau	0	10	6
Un phesant	0	12	0
Dix ortolens	7	4	0
Une toarte de cerises	1	1	0
Artichaux a le provensalle	0	16	0
Choufleurs au flour	0	16	6
Cretes de cocq en bonets	0	10	6
Amorte de Jesuits	0	12	6
Salade	0	4	6
Chicken	0	2	6
Ice cream and fruits	5	5	0
Fruits of various sorts forced	16	16	0
Fruit from market	2	10	0
Butter and cheese	0	2	0
Claret	1	10	0
Champaign	7	10	0
Burgundy	0	6	0
Hock	0	12	0
White-wine	0	2	0
Madeira	0	1	6
Sack	0	1	6
Cape	2	0	0
Cyprus	0	3	0
Neuilly	0	10	6
Usquebaugh	0	10	0
Spa and *Bristol* waters	0	6	0
Oranges and lemons	0	5	0
Coffee and tea	0	10	6
Lemonade	0	16	0
Total	81	11	0

* W---d---e, S---s--x, C---k--e, B--l--d, D---ne, M.S. L--g--r, C. V----n, C. C---.

The *Gentleman's Magazine* supplied (for the cognoscenti) clues to the names of eight participants. Among them we may recognise Waldegrave; and Lords Sussex and Downe, newly appointed Lords of the Bedchamber to Prince George.[131] Presumably they were celebrating their new posts, and did so in style: the cost of their entertainment represented the annual income of a Page of the Bedchamber, a naval lieutenant, or the incumbent of an ordinary living. Eyebrows were raised; Richard Rigby reported:

> The town is grown extremely thin within this week, though White's continues numerous enough with young people only, for Mr St. Leger's vivacity, and the idea the old ones have of it, prevent the great chairs at the old club from being filled with their proper drowsy proprietors.[132]

Politics often seemed less than serious within such a milieu. In 1752, Colonel Sir Richard Lyttelton, a member, penned a satire on his club's more authentic reaction to George II's return from Hanover:

> THE GAMESTERS' ADDRESS TO THE KING
> MOST RIGHTEOUS SOVEREIGN,
> May it please your Majesty, we, the Lords, Knights, etc., of the Society of White's, beg leave to throw ourselves at your Majesty's feet (our honours and consciences lying under the table and our fortunes being ever at stake), and congratulate your Majesty's happy return to these kingdoms, which assembles us together to the great advantage of some, the ruin of others, and the unspeakable satisfaction of all, both us, our wives and children. We beg leave to acknowledge your Majesty's great goodness and lenity in allowing us to break those laws which we ourselves have made, and you have sanctified and confirmed, while your Majesty alone religiously observes and regards them. And we beg leave to assure your Majesty of our most unfeigned loyalty and attachment to your sacred person, and that next to the Kings of Diamonds, Clubs, Spades and Hearts, we love, honour and adore you.

Lyttelton supplied the King's reply:

> MY LORDS AND GENTLEMEN,
> I return you thanks for your loyal address, but while I have such rivals in your affections as you tell me of, I can neither think it worth preserving or regarding. I look upon yourselves as a pack of cards, and shall deal with you accordingly.[133]

Although a man of pleasure, the 2nd Earl had a lively interest in the arts, in literary fashion and philosophical debate. In the 1730s, the 1st Earl had employed as tutor to his sons one Pierre Clément (1707–67), a Calvinist minister from Geneva who, once in Paris, had left the ministry for the more congenial occupations of playwright, man-about-town and literary commentator. In the 1740s, the latter vocation bore fruit in the form of a

---

[131] Other diners, with their dates of election, might be: Lord Bellfield, later 1st Earl Belvedere (1744); Matthew St Ledger (1751); Charles Churchill (1743; not the poet, but the soldier and sinecurist, c. 1720–1815, who married Sir Robert Walpole's illegitimate daughter Lady Maria Walpole).
[132] Rigby to Bedford, 2 July 1751: *Bedford Correspondence*, vol. 2, p. 99.
[133] [Boulton], *The History of White's*, vol. 1, pp. 96–7.

distinguished periodical surveying the intellectual life of Enlightenment Europe. Clément evidently visited his old pupil; one issue, dated from London on 1 January 1752 remarked on the pleasures of Waldegrave's favourite haunt: 'moi j'y passerois des journées entières aussi délicieuses qu'au Caffé de *White*'. Earlier, on 1 February 1751, he had shared Waldegrave's enthusiasm for Montesquieu, writing from Paris:

> On pense ici de *l'Esprit des Loix* à peu près ce qu'on en pense à Londres; c'est-à-dire qu'on le regarde comme un des meilleurs Livres de ce Siècle, par l'abondance & l'élévation des pensées; par l'étendue, le choix, & l' *à propos* de l'érudition ... mais imparfait dans la partie systmatique ...

Clément's periodical took the form of letters mostly addressed to an unnamed Englishman, evidently Waldegrave. They represent one half of a correspondence in which the Earl and his former tutor evidently exchanged views. In 1754, when Clément assembled these pieces in book form, the unnamed dedicatee was probably, and naturally, the 2nd Earl. If so, it would explain much about the remarkably large number of Englishmen in the subscription list, including Lords Ashburnham and Barrington, the Earls of Bath and Chesterfield, the Duke of Dorset, Lords Downe and Fane, the Duke of Grafton, the Marquess of Hartington, Lord Hillsborough, the Earls of Holdernesse and Lincoln, Sir George Lyttelton, the Duke of Marlborough, William Pitt, Lord Pulteney, Sir Thomas Robinson, Earls Stanhope and Temple, Colonel Waldegrave, and – subscribing for ten copies, the highest number of any subscriber – the 2nd Earl Waldegrave himself. The subscription list reads like a roll-call of White's, and it seems likely that the 2nd Earl had done his best to promote the book among his fellow members.[134]

Social and literary life rather than political manoeuvre or administration were evidently Waldegrave's *métier*. He was at his most happy on occasions like that in the summer of 1752, accompanying the Duke of Cumberland on a tour of Suffolk and Norfolk, visiting the Duke of Grafton at Euston and the Earl of Leicester at Holkham. His own seat at Navestock served the same function. 'In humble Imitation of all these great Partys', he reported to Newcastle, 'I have also had a Whites Party with me in Essex which lasted three or four days. Ld Hartington, Ld Ashburnham, Ld Downe, Mr Watson, Mr O'Brien, Mr Edgcumbe, and six or seven more of Yr Grace's humble Servants honoured me with their Company.' Boredom was evidently the great enemy. 'Since Mr Pelham and the Young Lords sett out for the North Whites has been quite desolate', he added sadly.[135] The same

---

[134] Pierre Clément, *Les Cinq Années Littéraires ... Des Années 1748 ... 1752* (4 vols., La Haye, 1754); Charles I. Rosenberg, 'A Critical Analysis of Pierre Clément's *Les Cinq Années Littéraires*' (Ph.D. dissertation, Northwestern University, 1959).
[135] Waldegrave to Newcastle, 6 Aug. 1752: Add MSS 32729 f. 34.

year found him at the races, though with a less adventurous friend: 'I was last week at Newmarket and as London was very empty and very dull I seduced the Earl of Ashburnham to go with me. For those who are very imprudent Newmarket is not the safest Place in the World but Yr Grace will easily imagine that his Lordship did not run any great Risque.'[136]

Not even Waldegrave was able to disregard politics for much longer, however. His post at Leicester House drew him inexorably into the mainstream of events. In 1754, he was obliged to withdraw from an engagement to visit Newcastle at Claremont, pleading a prior engagement with a still more important host, Cumberland: 'When I was last at the Duke's, his Royal Highness proposed going to Maidenhead races. But as I do not at present think quite so much about those Diversions as I did two or three years ago, the Engagement went entirely out of my Head, nor did I recollect it till his Royal Highness reminded me of it this Morning in the Drawing Room.'[137]

Leicester House and the Court, 1750–1755

George II's liking for the young Earl Waldegrave was no secret in Court circles. During his summer residence in Hanover in 1750, he confided these ambitions to Newcastle. The King

> ran out into great encomiums of my lord Waldegrave; that he should be more than he was (in which I entirely agreed); that he would have sent Waldegrave to Aix la Chapelle, when I prevailed upon him to send Sandwich; that he yielded to it, out of regard to my lord Waldegrave, thinking it a very difficult, and hazardous commission; and I thought a great while, that he meant Waldegrave, either for Secretary of State, or Master of the Horse.

Later in the conversation, he returned to the same theme:

> And then, says the King, 'Albemarle shall come to England; and Waldegrave go embassador to France; and then he will be qualified to be Secretary of State.' And his Majesty hinted to me, that if I had let him send Waldegrave to Aix la Chapelle, he might have been Secretary of State now.

Newcastle objected to recalling Albemarle, and added his own guess as to the outcome: 'If the Duke of Bedford accepts the President [i.e. the post of Lord President], as the King would have him, there is only the Master of the Horse, and that the King will certainly dispose of himself; I do not know to whom. If Waldegrave does not go to Paris, I believe he will give it him . . .'[138]

---

[136] Waldegrave to Newcastle, 13 Oct. 1752: Add MSS 32730 f. 100.
[137] Waldegrave to Newcastle, 8 Sept. 1754: Add MSS 32736 f. 468.
[138] Newcastle to Pelham, Hanover, 2/13 Sept. 1750: Coxe, *Pelham*, vol. 2, p. 383.

Introduction

It was not to be. Henry Pelham, First Lord of the Treasury, thought Waldegrave quite unsuitable to succeed Bedford as Secretary of State; the 2nd Earl, thought Pelham, was 'as good-natured, worthy, and sensible a man as any in the kingdom, but totally surrendered to his pleasures; and I believe that mankind, and no one more so than himself, would be surprised to see him in such an office'.[139] Such a verdict was damaging. The Pelhams, whatever their demerits, were men of business and prided themselves on their industry. Edmund Burke acknowledged this quality in the elder brother:

I know and feel what an irksome task the writing of Long Letters is; and there was nothing I was so much surprised at in the Late Duke of Newcastle, as that immense and almost incredible Ease with which he was able to dispatch such an infinite Number of Letters. That employment seemed to be a sort of recreation to him.[140]

Waldegrave's reputation as a man of pleasure did him little good in the world of affairs. In the round of appointments made in June 1751, the new Lord President of the Council was Earl Granville; when Bedford resigned his Secretaryship of State, he was replaced by the Pelhams' ally the 4th Earl of Holdernesse, like Sandwich Waldegrave's junior by three years. The new Master of the Horse proved to be Lord Hartington, heir to the dukedom of Devonshire, and five years younger than Waldegrave.

The King continued to seek a way of providing for the young Earl. To a marked degree Waldegrave already enjoyed his sovereign's confidence. In 1751,

It is told about town that one day the last week the Prince of Wales [Frederick] had been taking the air and in returning back over the new bridge he saw a coach coming on at the other end. He ordered the guards to go and turn it back. When they came up to it, the King was come incognito in it to see the bridge. It was Lord Waldegrave's. It is said His Majesty was extremely pleased with it.[141]

Or at Court:

Upon his Majesty's birthday an uncommon number of ladies and gentlemen had French clothes. This his Majesty took notice of with some concern, but more particularly to Lord Walgrave. From this it is to be hoped none of his attendance will encourage so very pernicious a traffic.[142]

The death of Frederick, Prince of Wales, raised the threat of a minority, and the ministry moved to anticipate such a misfortune. The Regency Act of 1751[143] made provision for four Regents out of the total of fourteen to be

---

[139] Pelham to Newcastle, *Bedford Correspondence*, vol. 2, p. 84.
[140] Burke to Rockingham, 2 July [1769]: L.S. Sutherland (ed.), *The Correspondence of Edmund Burke* vol. 2 (Cambridge, 1960), p. 40.
[141] M. Cutts to Viscount Irwin, 9 May 1751: HMC *Various*, vol. 8, p. 174.
[142] Henry Lowther to Viscount Irwin, 16 Dec. 1752: HMC *Various*, vol. 8, p. 176.
[143] See speech no. 5 below.

nominated by the King; the Regency Council would govern in the event of George II's demise before his grandson reached the age of majority on 4 June 1756. Again, the monarch's favour was believed secretly to have distinguished Waldegrave. Horace Walpole recorded:

> It was thought that the four persons on whom the late King had fixed, were the Duke of Grafton, the then Duke of Devonshire, who had retired from business, the Earl of Waldegrave, and Dr Butler, Bishop of Durham. On the majority of the successor, it was supposed that the late King had burned that designation; but his present Majesty told Lord Mansfield that he had found the paper, though he would not disclose who had been the persons specified.[144]

This was a high mark of royal favour; but the distinction did not carry a salary.

After Frederick's death the Dowager Princess of Wales 'determined to have nothing to do with her husband's party', to the horror of Lord Egmont, an Irish peer, who had taken a leading part in it. 'I heard that at White's they affected mightily to pity me,' he minuted; 'an insolent kind of compassion.' One of his informants 'said that they were full of jokes at White's about our Party, said they saw the ghosts of Peers that were to have been walking about the streets etc'.[145] As the *habitués* of White's realised, the patronage powers of the junior Court now passed into the hands of the ministry. At last, the King was able to do something substantial for his young courtier. Much of the income of Frederick Prince of Wales had derived from the considerable estates of the Duchy of Cornwall, administered by the Lord Warden of the Stannaries.[146] But the dukedom of Cornwall was automatically inherited only by the eldest son of a sovereign; on Frederick's death it reverted to the Crown. George II reserved to himself the title and the revenues, naming a new Lord Warden. It was to this post (worth £450 p.a. in salary) that Waldegrave was appointed in 1751, kissing hands on 18 April. 'Lord Waldegrave, long a personal favourite of the King, who has now got a little interest at his own Court, is warden of the stannaries in the room of Tom Pitt', reported Walpole.[147]

---

[144] Walpole, *George III*, vol. 2, p. 73.
[145] Aubrey Newman (ed.), 'Leicester House Politics, 1750–60, from the Papers of John, Second Earl of Egmont', in *Camden Miscellany*, Camden 4th series, vol. 7 (London, 1969), pp. 206–7.
[146] For the political and economic aspects of the tin industry and its political regulation, see Thomas Pearce, *The Laws and Customs of the Stannaries in the Counties of Cornwall and Devon* (London, 1725); Dodington, *Diary*, 22 April 1750, and Eveline Cruickshanks, 'The Convocation of the Stannaries of Cornwall: The Parliament of Tinners 1703–1752', *Parliaments, Estates and Representation*, 6 (1986), 59–67. In 1743, a Stuart agent, sent to report on the prospects for an invasion to restore the exiled dynasty, reported of Cornwall: 'Cette Province, distinguée par le grand nombre du mineurs qui s'y trouvent, a toujours été attachée à son roi naturel': Eveline Cruickshanks, *Political Untouchables: The Tories and the '45* (London, 1979), p. 116.
[147] Walpole to Mann, 22 April 1751: Walpole, *Letters*, vol. 20, p. 244.

Introduction

Thomas Pitt had held that office since 1742; using its influence, he had been Prince Frederick's election manager for Cornwall, a vital county by virtue of its 44 MPs.[148] This role now passed into the hands of the ministry. Waldegrave thereby became the administrator of the Duchy of Cornwall's considerable patronage powers, and was soon at work dispensing jobs at Newcastle's behest.[149] Ever tactful, however, he did not neglect the Duke of Bedford, who had suddenly resigned his Secretaryship of State in June 1751 after the dismissal of his ally Sandwich;[150] and his willingness to help Bedford with minor Stannary offices extended to 1754 at least.[151]

The chief though irregular responsibility of the Warden of the Stannaries was the holding of a Convocation, colloquially called a Parliament of Tinners. Revived in 1750, under the auspices of Prince Frederick, the result was political conflict and deadlock. A petition for the regulation of recent abuses in the tin trade, presented to the King in January 1751, occasioned the calling of a further Parliament (after the Prince's death) in August 1752 to enact remedial legislation. Waldegrave knew that his task was to ensure that its activities went no further, that the Parliament did not break free from ministerial control and become an instrument for opposition protest. But Henry Pelham advised that the Convocation be held in person by the Vice Warden, since 'in the present Case there are no Contracts to be made, no Transactions wherein the Kings Interest is any Ways concerned, all they have to do relating entirely to the settling their own private Affairs'.[152]

Waldegrave made no difficulty about agreeing. At Ascot races, he was evidently too busy to accept a last-minute invitation from Cumberland to visit Cranbourne, but soon after was able to fulfil his duties. Rigby reported that Waldegrave

> entertained me with shewing me his speech to the Stannary parliament, as Lord Warden; as good a one at least as I think they deserve; he does not go himself, but leaves it to his Vice Warden to deliver, though the latest precedent of the absence of a Lord Warden at the opening of their convention, is in James the First's time; but I think he preserves his dignity at the same time that he confesses his ignorance (of tin matters I mean), as well as it is possible; you will see it hereafter in the newspapers.[153]

---

[148] Thomas Pitt was furious at being displaced, 'talked of pointing out the way to the Duke of Bedford to gain half Cornwall, did not know but they might make him a Jacobite at last, that he was very popular among the tinners and [in] times of trouble could do a great deal': Newman (ed.), 'Leicester House Politics', p. 209.
[149] Waldegrave to Newcastle, 17 June 1751: Add MSS 32724 f. 376.
[150] Waldegrave to Bedford, [c. 2 July 1751]: Bedford MSS, vol. 27, f. 83.
[151] Bedford to Waldegrave, 16 June 1754; Waldegrave to Bedford, 22 June 1754: Bedford MSS, vol. 30, ff. 60, 66.
[152] Waldegrave to Newcastle, 6 Aug. 1752: Add MSS 32729 f. 32.
[153] Rigby to Bedford, 13 Aug 1752: *Bedford Correspondence*, vol. 2, p. 110.

Pelham's confidence was not misplaced, and Waldegrave could later report that 'the Gentlemen of the Convocation went thro their business with great Unanimity and good Humour. Their quick dispatch was owing to their having prepared most of the Laws some time ago when the Quarrel with the late Warden put a stop to their Proceedings'.[154] They never met again: patronage rather than political management henceforth comprised the Warden's duties.

Other reshuffles were inevitable at Leicester House in April 1751. Prince George was created Prince of Wales in succession to his father, and a new Household selected for him by the King.[155] The old Household had been chosen by Prince Frederick without consulting his father. Henry Pelham was concerned: he had had no hand, he protested, in the appointment of Lord North in November 1750 as Treasurer of the Household and Governor, or the appointment of the mathematician George Lewis Scott as Sub-Preceptor. Scott was 'recommended, as I understand, by Lord Bolingbroke, I suppose thro' the Channel of Lord Bathurst'. Nevertheless, 'I hear an exceeding good character of this man from all quarters, and as he sets aside Askew [sc. Ayscough], I should hope the young Prince will gain by it'.[156] Now, after the Prince's death, Lord North was replaced by Lord Harcourt, characterised by Walpole as 'a creature of the Pelhams'. Andrew Stone, Newcastle's secretary, was given the more laborious post of Sub-Governor. The education of the princes was chiefly in the hands of Thomas Hayter, Bishop of Norwich, who became Preceptor, seconded by George Lewis Scott, continued as Sub Preceptor.

In November 1804, George III reminisced to George Rose, MP, about his education:

> his Majesty told me that most serious inconvenience had arisen from disagreements and intrigues amongst those who were entrusted with the care of his education; mentioning Dr Thomas, afterwards Bishop of Winchester, and Mr George Scott, afterwards a Commissioner of Excise, as men of unexceptionable characters (preceptor and sub-preceptor). But he considered Dr Hayter, Bishop of Norwich, as an intriguing unworthy man, more fitted to be a Jesuit than an English Bishop; and as influenced in his conduct by the disappointment he met with in failing to get the archbishopric of Canterbury [in 1747]. His Majesty added that his Lordship was the author of the gross and wicked calumny on George Scott; accusing him, a man of the purest mind, and most innocent conduct, of having attempted to poison

---

[154] Waldegrave to Newcastle, 13 Oct. 1752: Add MSS 32730 f. 100. Newcastle was spending the summer with the King in Hanover.

[155] For the problems at Leicester House in 1752–6, see especially Romney Sedgwick (ed.), *Letters from George III to Lord Bute 1756–1766* (London, 1939), Introduction. Sedgwick believed only that 'Lord Waldegrave's account, though correct as far as it goes, requires amplification' (p. xxiv).

[156] Pelham to Newcastle, 16 Oct. 1750: Add MSS 32723 f. 159. The rumour was not accurate: Scott was Ayscough's assistant, not his replacement.

Introduction 53

his wife. The King then spoke of Lord Waldegrave and Lord Harcourt (both I believe his governors, they were certainly both about him), the first as a depraved worthless man,[157] the other as well-intentioned, but wholly unfit for the situation in which he was placed.

Rose added his own impression of George Scott:

I knew this gentleman long and very intimately: and I can aver, with the sincerest truth, I never knew a man more *entirely blameless* in all the relations of life; amiable, honourable, temperate, and one of the sweetest dispositions I ever knew.[158]

In private, Horace Walpole accepted the merits of the young princes' other instructors in order to condemn Bute alone:

A few pedantic examples were the sum of Lord Bute's knowledge; yet his partisans affected to celebrate the care he had taken of the King's education. A well-founded panegyric on a man who was deficient in the orthography of his own language! The King had had able preceptors; the Bishop of Norwich was a scholar; the Bishop of Salisbury not deficient. Stone and Scott had taste and knowledge. Lord Waldegrave, for forming a King, was not to be matched. It proved, indeed, that his Majesty had learned nothing, but what a man, who knew nothing, could teach him.[159]

Letters written to Lord Harcourt by Prince George and Prince Edward between June 1751 (when the Prince of Wales was 13) and October 1752 suggest a harmonious relationship between the Governor and his royal charges despite the unavoidable formalism; but a rather cooler princely regard for the Bishop of Norwich, then 'very low spirited' and in ill health.[160] This was noticed: Princess Augusta said 'that she was afraid the Bishop of Norwich had sometimes carried it with too high a hand, which sometimes might have occasioned a coolness, if not an indifference towards

---

[157] See below, p. 79.
[158] Rev. Leveson Vernon Harcourt (ed.), *The Diaries and Correspondence of the Right Hon. George Rose* (2 vols., London, 1860), vol. 2, pp. 187–8. It was Bute who, in 1758, obtained the post of Commissioner of Excise for Scott: J.L. McKelvey, *George III and Lord Bute: The Leicester House Years* (Durham, North Carolina, 1973), p. 67.
[159] Walpole, *George III*, vol. 1, p. 42. Walpole elsewhere added his interpretation of Scott, writing of the formation of the household of the new Prince of Wales in October 1756: 'The fate of one man was singular: the Prince of Wales himself condescended to desire Mr Stone to prevent Scott, his sub-preceptor, from being continued in any employment about him – and it was granted. Scott has been mentioned in the civil wars of the tutorhood as attached to Stone: the reason given for his exclusion was, his having talked with contempt of the Prince's understanding, and with freedom of the Princess's conduct. The truth was, Scott was a frank man, of no courtly depth, and had indiscreetly disputed with Lord Bute, who affected a character of learning': Walpole, *George II*, vol. 2, p. 182.
[160] *Harcourt Papers*, vol. 3, pp., 40–54. The fortunes of Harcourt and Hayter after the accession of George III do not suggest any lasting resentment. Both were rehabilitated through Lord Talbot's intercession, Harcourt being sent to escort the new Queen from Harwich in September 1761, and Hayter being translated to the see of London in October: Walpole, *George III*, vol. 1, pp. 55, 57.

him'.¹⁶¹ The following month, William Murray pointed out the shortcomings of both Harcourt and Hayter:

> Levity on the one hand & Austerity on the other, from a Jealousy & Consciousnesss of having lost their Esteem & Affection; has so alienated the 2 Pr[inces] from our Friend the Bp, that it is difficult to keep them easy. They have shewn the Contempt they have, before their Aunt [Princess Amelia]; & have, I believe, to a Degree trusted her with their Complaints.¹⁶²

It was a situation ripe for exploitation by skilful politicians.

The King had few illusions about the prudence and tactical skill of the Dowager Princess. According to Horace Walpole, George II

> told Mr Pelham soon after [Frederick] Prince of Wales's death; "You none of you know this woman, and you none of you will know her till I am dead." Lord Cobham told L[ady] S[uffolk] he had studied her [Princess Augusta] but could not find her out. "All I know is," said he, "that those she is most civil to, she hates the most."¹⁶³

Shelburne, too, painted a similarly unflattering picture of the Dowager Princess,

> left to herself, neglected by her husband, kept down by Lady Archibald [Hamilton, Frederick's mistress], and suffering all the mortifications attendant upon great and insignificant situations in all Courts. Naturally given to dissimulation and intrigue, she had both time and opportunity to improve these important qualifications; she was surrounded with nothing else, and the perpetual mortifications she submitted to pressed and obliged her to exert both.¹⁶⁴

She was to have ample opportunity in the years which followed Frederick's death.

Waldegrave had no time to settle into his new role as Warden of the Stannaries before that most sensitive of issues was aired once more. The immediate cause was the Ministry's programme of social reconstruction in the Highlands in the aftermath of the '45. In February 1752 a Bill was introduced into the Commons (later passed as 25 Geo. II, c. 41) 'to empower the government to purchase . . . the estates in Scotland forfeited by the late rebellion, and which the King was to cede to the public, in order to have colonies settled on them, especially of foreign Protestants'. Tories fought the Bill as unnecessary; Whigs urged it with evidence of Scots disaffection; the Duke of Cumberland was silently opposed to it as too generous to a disaffected enemy. In the Lords in March, Bedford was induced to oppose the Bill by arguing that its payments to Scots lords made another rebellion *more* likely, and added the charge that 'favour' and

---

¹⁶¹ Harcourt to Newcastle, 4 May 1752: Add MSS 32727 f. 76.
¹⁶² W. Murray to Newcastle, 12 June 1752: Add MSS 32727 f. 393.
¹⁶³ W.S. Lewis (ed.), *Memoranda Walpoliana* (Farmington, Conn., 1937), p. 15.
¹⁶⁴ 'A Chapter of Autobiography' in Fitzmaurice, *Shelburne*, vol. 1, p. 49.

Introduction 55

'rewards' had already been inadvertently conferred on many 'rebels' by the ministry.[165]

Cumberland himself then exploited these embarrassments by presenting George II with 'a list of sixty Jacobites, who had been preferred in Scotland since the rebellion'.[166] From March to July 1752, the Pelhams were in consternation; an inquisition duly turned up a few disaffected individuals, but what was far more damaging to the ministry was the implication that it was willing to turn a blind eye to men of unreliable backgrounds and suspected principles. These issues were soon to be raised within the confines of the junior Court. In March, Thomas Hayter, the Preceptor, issued an ominous warning in a sermon before the King. Religious warnings were proper, he argued:

> To illustrate this by a familiar Instance; – Suppose a Traveller passing through a strange Country, the Inhabitants of which are no less insidious than agreeable;[167] and that, whilst he is walking on in the midst of Perils, with full Security, he meets a faithful Friend, who, with the unfeigned zeal of Friendship, points out the Snares with which he is encompassed, and the Destruction that hangs over him. Would our Traveller take it unkindly of his Friend, that he had alarmed him with Apprehensions from which he was before free, and treat his honest Monitor in such a Manner, as if he had brought him into the Danger from which he meant to deliver him? Would he not rather embrace him with all the Warmth of Gratitude due to a Deliverer?[168]

By July 1752, Walpole could report: 'The tutorhood at Kew is split into factions; the Bishop of Norwich and Lord Harcourt openly at war with Stone and Scott, who are supported by Cresset, and countenanced by the Princess and Murray – so my Lord Bolingbroke dead will govern, which he never could living!'[169] The 'explosion' came after the King's return from his summer in Hanover on 18 November: 'the instant he came, it was pretty plain that he was prepared for the grievances he was to hear – not very impartially it seems, for he would not speak to Lord Harcourt'.[170] Eventually, when admitted to the Closet on 21 November, Harcourt made his sensational charge against Stone, Cresset and Scott.

According to Waldegrave, 'The Crimes objected against them were Jacobite Connections, instilling Tory Principles and Scott was moreover pronounced an Atheist on the presumptive Evidence of being a Philoso-

---

[165] Walpole, *George II*, vol. 1, pp. 175–86. [166] Walpole, *George II*, vol. 1, p. 186.
[167] The Bodleian's copy has a ms. note in a contemporary hand: 'This was written with a View to Cresset &c. Persons about ye Pr. of Wales, as ye Bp himself informed me.'
[168] Thomas Hayter, *A Sermon Preached before the King. On Sunday, March 22, 1752. Drawn up for the Use of their Royal Highnesses George Prince of Wales, and Prince Edward* (London, 1752), pp. 22–3.
[169] Walpole to Mann, 27 July 1752: Walpole, *Letters*, vol. 20, p. 321.
[170] Walpole to Mann, 11 Dec. 1752: Walpole, *Letters*, vol. 20, p. 342.

pher and a Mathematician'.[171] Not succeeding in their complaint, Harcourt and the Bishop had no honourable course but to resign. On 5 and 6 December 1752, they did so. This did not end the matter. Waldegrave treated it as a bid for power by Harcourt and Hayter – 'that they as Governor and Preceptor must be the sole Directors of the young Prince' but saw that they were also 'artfully made use of to raise ... a Clamor'.[172]

The 'Clamor', inconveniently for Waldegrave, centred on the alleged Jacobite infiltration of the ministry and the junior Court.[173]

The first occasion of uneasiness, was the Bishop's finding the Prince of Wales reading the *Revolutions of England*, written by Père d'Orléans to vindicate James II and approved by that prince.[174] Stone at first peremptorily denied having seen that book these thirty years, and offered to rest his whole justification upon the truth or falsehood of this story. However, it is now confessed that the Prince was reading that book, but it is qualified with Prince Edward's borrowing it of Lady Augusta [his eldest sister]. Scott, the under-preceptor, put in by Lord Bolingbroke, and of no very orthodox odour, was another complaint.[175]

William Murray, the Solicitor General, was reported to have put pressure on the Bishop of Norwich to give Stone a greater share in the princes' education; the ministry was rumoured to be planning to replace Hayter with James Johnson, newly created Bishop of Gloucester – 'of Stone's and Murray's year, and certainly of their principles – to be sure, that is, Whig – but the Whigs don't seem to think so'.[176]

Who would replace Hayter and Harcourt? 'As yet no successors are named,' added Walpole; 'the Duke of Leeds, Lord Cardigan, Lord Waldegrave, Lord Hertford, Lord Bathurst and Lord Ashburnham are talked of for governor. The two first are said to have refused, the third dreads it; the next I hope will not have it; the Princess is inclined to the

---

[171] Waldegrave's *Memoirs*, section 1 below.
[172] *Ibid*. Waldegrave's low view of Harcourt and Hayter was essentially the same as that of the Dowager Princess of Wales: cf. Dodington, *Diary*, 28 Dec. 1752.
[173] This was deeply ironic if, as Dodington suggested (*loc. cit.*), Harcourt's father had been 'till the last years of his life always reckon'd a thorough Jacobite'.
[174] F.J. D'Orléans, *The History of the Revolutions in England under the Family of the Stuarts, From the Year 1603, to 1690*. (Paris, 1689; trans. 2nd edn., London, 1722). The translation contained an enthusiastic preface dated 8 May 1711 in which the irreproachably Whig historian Laurence Echard commended the work for its merits and treated its mild partisanship as of secondary importance.
[175] Walpole to Mann, 11 Dec. 1752: Walpole, *Letters*, vol. 20, p. 342. The Dowager Princess said 'that the stories about the History of the Père d'Orélans was false; the only little dispute between the Bishop [of Norwich] and Prince Edward was about le Père Péréfixe's history of Henry IV, and that was nothing at all to produce such an event. That there must be politicks at the bottom ... ': Dodington, *Diary*, 8 Feb. 1753.
[176] Walpole to Mann, 11 Dec. 1752: Walpole, *Letters*, vol. 20, p. 342. James Johnson (1705–74), Bishop of Gloucester 1751, of Worcester 1759; ed. at Westminster School 1717–24, with Andrew Stone 1717–22 and William Murray c. 1719–23.

Introduction

Table 3 *Posts at the Junior Court*

Governor	Lord North Nov 1750–Apr 1751	Lord Harcourt Apr 1751–5 Dec 1752	Lord Waldegrave 18 Dec 1752–Oct 1756
Sub-Governor	none	Andrew Stone Apr 1751–	Andrew Stone –Oct 1756
Preceptor	Rev. Francis Ayscough 1744–Apr 1751	Thomas Hayter, Bishop of Norwich Apr 1751–6 Dec 1752	John Thomas, Bishop of Peterborough 20 Dec 1752–Oct 1756
Sub-Preceptor	George Lewis Scott Nov 1750–	George Lewis Scott	George Lewis Scott –Oct 1756
Warden of the Stannaries	Thomas Pitt 1742–Mar 1751	Lord Waldegrave Apr 1751–	Lord Waldegrave –1763
Secretary to (Dowager) Princess of Wales	Thomas Potter 1748–Apr 1751	James Cresset Apr 1751–	James Cresset –1772

fifth; and the last I believe eagerly wishes for it'.[177] Six days later, on 17 December, Walpole added a footnote: 'Well! at last we shall have a governor: after meeting with divers refusals, they have forced Lord Waldgrave to take it; and he kisses hands tomorrow. He has all the time declared that nothing but the King's earnest desire should make him accept it – and so they made the King earnestly desire it!'[178] Deferring to this personal request,[179] the young Earl gave up his post as a Lord of the Bedchamber to George II and accepted a position of equal salary but far greater labour and anxiety.

Lord Waldegrave was not the obvious man for the job. Horace Walpole's correspondent, the diplomat Sir Horace Mann, replied from Florence: 'I can't say that I was surprised to hear that the humours in the tutorship were come to a head. They had been too long gathering not to burst, and you had prepared me for it, but not for the nomination of Lord Waldegrave, nor should I have ever guessed him.'[180] Horace Walpole, however, praised his friend:

---

[177] Walpole to Mann, 11 Dec. 1752: *loc. cit.*   [178] *Ibid.*

[179] Waldegrave's own account in the *Memoirs* suggests that he had a little more ambition than Horace Walpole implied. The King's offer was conveyed via Newcastle, 'who told me his Majesty did not chuse to speak to me himself, that I might be at full liberty to either accept or refuse as I liked best'.

[180] Mann to Walpole, 2 Feb. 1753: Walpole, *Letters*, vol. 20, p. 355.

At last, after long waiving it, Lord Waldegrave, at the earnest request of the King, accepted it, and after repeated assurances of the submission and tractability of Stone. The Earl was very averse to it: he was a man of pleasure, understood the court, was firm in the King's favour, easy in his circumstances, and at once undesirous of rising, and afraid to fall. He said to a friend, 'If I dared, I would make this excuse to the King; Sir, I am too young to govern, and too old to be governed' – but he was forced to submit. A man of stricter honour, or of more reasonable sense could not have been selected for the employment; yet as the Whig zeal had caught flame, even this choice was severely criticized: Lord Waldegrave's grandmother was daughter of King James; his family were all Papists, and his father had been but the first convert.[181]

The two new arrivals in the junior Court made a good start. In February 1753, Dodington recorded the impressions of the Dowager Princess:

She began at once by saying she had good news to tell me: that they were very happy in their family; that the new Bishop gave great satisfaction; that he seem'd to take great care, and in a proper manner: that the children took to him, and seemed mightily pleas'd. I said ... she would give me leave to hope that they were all very well pleas'd with the new Governor also, who was my very good friend[182] and for whom I had a very great regard. She said, 'Yes, indeed'; that she was but little acquainted with him but from all she saw she had a very good opinion of him, that he was very well bred, very complaisant, and attentive, &c. and the children liked him extremely. 'But,' says she, 'I look upon a Governor as a sort of pageant, a man of quality for show, &c. I stick to the learning as the chief point. You know how backward they were when we were together[183] and I am sure you don't think they are much improv'd since. May be it is not too late yet to acquire a competence, and that is what I am most solicitous about, and if this man, by his manner, should hit upon the means of giving them that, I shall be mightily pleas'd.[184] The Bishop of Norwich was so confus'd, that one could never tell what he meant, and the children were not at all pleas'd with him.'[185]

The following month, the Princess was more explicit in her complaints of Lord Harcourt's behaviour. Dodington 'said I flatter'd myself that she could find a very different behaviour in Lord Waldegrave. She said, yes indeed, that she very well lik'd all she saw of him.'[186] In his *Memoirs*, Waldegrave confessed: 'sometimes I thought myself almost a Favorite'. It was this fair prospect which disintegrated in the coming years.

Horace Walpole had evidently drawn a lesson from Bedford's tactics in opposing the Forfeited Estates Bill in March 1752. Harcourt and Hayter

---

[181] Walpole, *George II*, vol. 1, pp. 199–200.
[182] This was by no means the case. Dodington was presumably trying to ingratiate himself with the rising figure at Leicester House.
[183] I.e. when Dodington was part of Prince Frederick's Leicester House opposition.
[184] It seems probable that Waldegrave set about his task conscientiously. For his notes on the constitution and on English history, which may have formed part of the Princes' education, see sections 12–14 below.
[185] Dodington, *Diary*, 8 Feb. 1753.   [186] Dodington, *Diary*, 3 March 1753.

Introduction 59

resigned on 5 and 6 December respectively; on 20 December an anonymous and sensational memorandum was sent through the post to General Hawley and Lord Ravensworth. Through their channel, copies at once reached the Duke of Cumberland (and therefore the King) and the Duke of Newcastle.

This 'Memorial of several noblemen and gentlemen of the first rank and fortune'[187] was in fact written by Horace Walpole himself. Its object was to cause the maximum embarrassment at a moment of extreme delicacy, and Walpole evidently despatched it without regard for its impact on the position of his young friend.[188] The 'Memorial' vindicated the innocence of Harcourt and Hayter, and pointed an accusation at 'three or four low, dark, suspected persons' who were left in their posts. Through such men, Prince George was being, implied the Memorial, 'early initiated in maxims of arbitrary power'. Why had there been no inquiry? Men could only infer the 'worst designs' in the ministers who supported such 'low and suspected persons'.

George II lacked no confidence in his ministers in this respect at least: Walpole's conspiracy theory was as wide of the mark as possible. Yet his Memorial had an unexpected consequence, and succeeded far better than he could have hoped: 'In the beginning of February Lord Ravensworth came to town, and acquainted Mr Pelham that he had strong evidence of Jacobitism to produce against Stone, Murray the Solicitor-General, and Dr Johnson, Bishop of Gloucester'.[189] The key witness, Christopher Fawcett, a Durham attorney, broke down under questioning before the Cabinet in a series of sittings in February 1753, and nothing came of Walpole's *canard*. It was not for want of trying, however: Waldegrave was present when on 22 March Bedford moved in the Lords that the papers relating to the enquiry be laid before the House. Waldegrave evidently drafted two speeches for use on the occasion (nos. 6 and 7 below): a long defence of his own background, political principles and personal integrity; and a short statement of his confidence in his colleague, Andrew Stone.

Would Bedford seek to involve Waldegrave in the insinuations being made against the junior Court? In fact he took the opposite course, praising the King's personal choice of Waldegrave in order to call in question the Pelhams' choice of other courtiers.[190] Waldegrave was safe, at least for the moment; he delivered his short speech instead. A connection with the Bedford interest had its advantages: when his brother John (later 3rd Earl

---

[187] Printed in Walpole, *George II*, vol. 1, pp. 204–6.
[188] There is no evidence that Waldegrave ever discovered the author. That Walpole should have so acted, regardless of friendship, is another instance of his disloyalty and malice.
[189] Walpole, *George II*, vol. 1, p. 207.   [190] Walpole, *George II*, vol. 1, p. 216.

Waldegrave) married in 1751 the sister of the Duchess of Bedford, a crucial alliance had been cemented. The 2nd Earl had already obliged Bedford over the disposition of minor Stannary posts; he was to do more in the coming months for Bedford's ally Henry Fox.

By surviving the crisis unscathed, Waldegrave preserved his value in the eyes of the ministry. In private, he kept a speech of self-justification (no. 10 below) drafted and revised in case a similar problem recurred. It did not. Superior ministerial intelligence frustrated the last plan for a rising in Scotland, the 'Elibank Plot'; with the arrest on 12 March 1753 of a leading organiser, Dr Archibald Cameron, the secrecy of the conspiracy was compromised. The preparations were 'far more complete than they had been on the eve of the Forty-Five',[191] but Cameron's examination in April and execution on 7 June made it impossible to put these preparations into effect. Moreover, Cameron was executed under his old attainder of 1746: the Pelhams preferred not to stage a new trial and thereby reveal the extent of ministerial knowledge of Stuart conspiracies. The Jacobite issue was not reawakened in English domestic politics.

Waldegrave meanwhile was making the transition from a life of pleasure to one of business, and doing his best not to lose touch with his former friends. One reported:

> We dined at Lord Waldegrave's; half a dozen from White's, and as many of his own family, as unlike each other, I trust, as his present from his former way of life. We found cards indeed before dinner; but no card table. After dinner they were our match, for at eating and drinking I never saw their superiors, particularly Mr Scott, whom I had never seen before: he seems shrewd and cunning; but though I have no great faith in countenances, I would not trust him with untold gold, nor, for Lord Waldegrave's sake, with any thing but what I would wish to have told. He affects the jolly fellow however, and so gets to these dinners, to let his graver patron know what is said at them.[192]

Waldegrave was skating on thin ice. Yet the Jacobite problem did not obviously surface in the general election of 1754. Essex had last been contested in 1734, and was thereafter represented by two Tories; no contest now materialised. There is no evidence that Waldegrave worked to build up an electoral interest around his seat at Navestock; his value to the ministry was of a different sort.

Henry Pelham's death on 6 March 1754 transferred power to his brother, the Duke of Newcastle. From Newcastle, Waldegrave received an important invitation in October:

---

[191] Sir Charles Petrie, *The Jacobite Movement: The Last Phase 1716–1807* (London, 1950), p. 154; 'The Elibank Plot, 1752–3', *Transactions of the Royal Historical Society*, 4th series, 14 (1931), pp. 175–196.
[192] Rigby to Bedford, 3 Aug. 1753: *Bedford Correspondence*, vol. 2, p. 129.

Introduction

My Dear Lord.

The long Experience, which I have had of your Friendship, and Goodness to Me, & My Dependance upon it, as Well as My certain Knowledge, that what I am going to ask, is in Every Respect, for the King's Service, encourages Me to ask the Favor of Your Lordship to propose Our Address to the King. You must allow, that the present Conjuncture is very particular in many Considerations; The opening of the New Parliament; The Beginning of an Administration, weaken'd in the greatest Degree by unavoidable Misfortunes, opposed from different Quarters by private Views, Not in the power of the Administration to Satisfy. In such a Situation, Where Can One so Materially involved in the Success of the King's Measures, as I am, apply, but to Those, Whose Friendship, Abilities, & Reputation, can & must give Him the greatest Support; And if you will look round the House of Lords, I could almost appeal to your own Candour, & Judgement that there is No One, who can in All Circumstances, answer this Description, but Yourself. I know the Moving of an Address, is generally looked upon, As A Thing of Course, & of little Consequence; It is The person, That moves, That makes it so, or not, at all Times; But this, as I have observed is a very particular Conjuncture, Every Body's Attention will be had to The First Day of the Session; the Ability & Consequence of Those, Who appear upon that occasion, will greatly contribute to give Countenance, & Stability to our future Measures, and make a Good, or Bad Impression, in favor of the Administration, & Their Success. There is also another Consideration of a publick Nature, which immediately affects the King's Service. The Conjunction is very delicate, with regard to What should, & should not be said, & No Man in the House of Lords, will execute that difficult part, so properly, so prudently as yourself. The Encroachments, I may say the Hostilities of the French in North America, have made the Measures the King is taking there, absolutely necessary for our own Defence; But there will be Nicety in the Manner of Treating, or talking upon Those Measures in Parliament; That may be right & necessary to do, which It may not be prudent to brag of. The Speech will probably point out the Method, and to a Judicious Man, may be so explain'd, as to avoid these Difficulties. But Spirit, & popularity, make such strong Impressions upon ordinary Minds, that the most Injudicious Speech upon this occasion, may be thought Meritorious, & a mark of Zeal. And there are not many, whom I would trust with my Thoughts as to the Caution to be observed upon this occasion. It would be very unfortunate, if these necessary Measures against the Encroachments of the French in N America, should produce a War with France in Europe; and Nothing is so likely to prevent *That*, as a Cautious and prudent Speech from the Throne, answer'd in the same cautious and prudent Manner by Both Houses. You see My Dear Lord, That I don't represent the Favor I am asking, as Nothing; I state All the Difficulties, & It is on account of those Difficulties, That I ask the Favor; and It is for these reasons, That I flatter Myself you will not upon full Consideration refuse me. The Speech will be finally settled this Week; My Lord Chancelor & Myself, will be ready to give your Lordship, Whatever Lights you may desire; We have full Time for it; and our Question with regard to the Business of The Speech, lies in so Narrow a Compass, That I am sure in one Hour's Time, you will be as fully Master of it, as any of us all. I shall conclude, with observing to you, That I know what I ask, is right for the King, right for Myself, & All His Majesty's Ministers, but I would not ask it, If I did not in

62   *Introduction*

My Conscience think, That It was right for yourself also. I am More Than I can express

Most Affectly & respectfully yours
Holles Newcastle [193]

His freedom of action was somewhat limited, however. Newcastle sent Waldegrave a copy of the King's Speech before George II had seen it, but followed it soon after with the text of the motion which Waldegrave was to move and the Address which the Lords were to vote.[194] Waldegrave's role was confined to supporting the ministry's carefully prepared position. This he did with skill, in the speech printed as no. 8 below. Waldegrave's stock was evidently rising. Perhaps in anticipation of a more active public role, he negotiated to buy a handsome house in Albemarle Street[195] (after his death to become Wildman's Club).[196]

The momentous European events of the mid 1750s distract our attention from the absence of an older preoccupation. Waldegrave's speech of self-exculpation (no. 10 below) was never needed; the Jacobite issue did not resurface. Its last echo was heard on 27 November 1754, when William Pitt scored a major success in the Commons by reawakening the old charge; but he had pointed the finger at his Oxford-educated rival, William Murray. 'Colours, much less words, could not paint the confusion and agitation that worked in Murray's face during this almost apostrophe!' noted Walpole with malice; 'his countenance spoke everything that Fawcett had been terrified to prevaricate away'.[197] Would Waldegrave's name be brought into the debate? It was not to be. William Pitt's developing alliance with Bute and Leicester House in 1755–6 meant that Pitt and the Grenville faction soon had an interest in the Jacobite charge being laid to rest: if resurrected, it would be Bute himself who would suffer most.

It was this lack of a tactical opportunity which doomed to obscurity Thomas Hayter's effort at revenge. Nursing his resentment at his replacement as Preceptor, in 1755 he published, anonymously, a remarkable attack on Newcastle's ministry:

Suppose a Set of Men should insinuate themselves into Power, who are known to be Enemies to the Political Constitution. Suppose them to manifest their Principles in the Course of their Measures, whilst they deny them, at proper Seasons, by the

[193] Newcastle to Waldegrave, 27 Oct. 1754: Add MSS 51380 f. 45.
[194] Newcastle to Waldegrave, n.d. [?Nov. 1754]: Add MSS 51380 f. 47.
[195] Waldegrave to Earl of Strafford, 5 Nov. [1754], 21 Nov. 1754: Add MSS 22254 ff. 66, 68.
[196] Lord Barrington to Earl of Buckingham, 26 Feb. 1764: 'There is an antiministerial club set up in Albemarle Street, at the house where poor Lord Waldegrave lived, on the footing of White's; but I hear no amusement or vice going on there; so I conclude it will be soon abandon'd'. HMC *Lothian*, p. 248. For the club's short-term importance, however, see D.H. Watson, 'The Rise of the Opposition at Wildman's Club', *Bulletin of the Institute of Historical Research*, 44 (1971), 55–77.
[197] Walpole, *George II*, vol. 2, p. 28.

most solemn Professions. Suppose the Characters of these Men, and the Situation of the Public to be such, that no Friend to his Country can act in Concert with them, and preserve his Integrity; will it be called personal Slander, or will any honest Man judge it criminal, to expose the political Characters and Views of such Men? Will it be an Abuse of the Liberty of the Press, to open the Eyes of the Public, or to rouze its Lethargic Friends? Will it not rather be considered, by all disinterested Men, as the original Use and Intent of that Liberty? . . . in Times when Men are as licentious in their political, as in their religious Conduct; when true Patriotism is become ridiculous, and a Coalition of WHIG and TORY, that is, of Light and Darkness, is thought by some Men more natural, than a rigid Perseverance in the Principles of Liberty, which only can secure the Throne, which is founded upon them; in such Times Treason and Jacobitism will break out of their dark Corners, in which they had been lurking. They will venture, upon stamped Paper, to take the Tour of the two Kingdoms, and scatter their diabolical Seed, for a Harvest of Mischief and Confusion . . . When the public Affairs are carried on by the Advice of a private Cabal; when that Cabal consists of Men, who are more popular among the Disaffected, than the Loyal Part of the People; when the Well-affected shrug their Shoulders, and *whisper* the Discontent, which Prudence, or Obligations, or Decency, restrain them from avowing; when Men of known unshaken Zeal for the Service of their King and Country are discountenanced; when Party Distinctions are said to be abolished, whilst the worst Principles, of the most dangerous Party, are insidiously gaining Ground, and the Principles of Liberty, in which the Revolution was founded, decrease in their Value, by not being current; when Men are advanced to high Stations, who stand in Need of Vouchers for so indispensable, presupposed a Qualification as their Loyalty; and, in short, when Considerations of Decency, of Policy, and even of public Peace, are sacrificed to the narrow Views, the Party Prejudices, and the unpopular Support of the Cabal; then a free People will make use of their Eyes to see, of their Tongues to speak, and of their Hands to write; then the Liberty of the Press will be exercised upon its proper Objects, for it will be legally and honourably employed, in the Defence of the Crown, and of the Liberty of the Subject.[198]

But Hayter's embittered charges were not taken up. For the moment, his successors at Leicester House were safe.

Waldegrave's prominence in moving the Address in November 1754 soon won for him a new role, that of honest broker. The ambitions unleashed by the death of Henry Pelham found a dramatic expression in December of that year, when Fox, in a subordinate role, bid for a greater share of power than convention allowed him. It was Waldegrave to whom Newcastle turned in order to reassure Fox and retain him in the government.[199] The King, anxious to pacify Fox, agreed to the use of Waldegrave as an intermediary. It was now that the Earl learned of another reason for the royal favour he enjoyed: that he had refused to enlist in Prince

---

[198] [Thomas Hayter], *An Essay on the Liberty of the Press Chiefly as it respects Personal Slander* (London, [1755]), pp. 12–13, 30–1, 46–7.

[199] Clark, *Dynamics of Change*, pp. 126–30.

Frederick's opposition. Waldegrave evidently told Horace Walpole with some pride what the King had said to him: 'I have obligations to you that I never mentioned; my son (the Prince) tried you, and you would not join him; and yet you made no merit of it to me'.[200] Thanks not least to Waldegrave's diplomatic skill, the pride and ambition of Fox were, for the moment, contained. Yet the tacit understanding which kept the peace between Pitt and Fox was now at an end. Soon, Pitt was to look for support to another quarter, the junior Court; and Bute's rise to power there, in alliance with Pitt, was to signal Waldegrave's eclipse.

The outbreak of the Seven Years' War, 1751–1756

Waldegrave's family antecedents were a major threat to his success in his political career; but the danger was fading by 1755. His misfortune was that this handicap was progressively replaced by another no less severe. For Waldegrave was heir to an early eighteenth century tradition in foreign policy, associated in Anne's reign with the Tories (though by George II's often taken up by opposition Whigs), which insisted that Britain's interests could be sufficiently defended and best promoted by an avoidance of continental involvements and a concentration on naval and colonial warfare.[201] Ironically, this disengagement from European alliances and reliance on naval supremacy was to become an orthodoxy from the early 1760s, with consequences in the late 1770s as yet unforeseen. Had Waldegrave become a chief architect of this policy early in the reign of George III, his reputation for wisdom in affairs of state might not stand so high.[202] But it was Waldegrave's lot to enter a decisive phase in the advancement of his career in the mid 1750s, at a time when colonial conflicts were impelling Britain into involvement with a European conflagration. His antipathy to European alliances influenced his account of events in the *Memoirs* and significantly reduced the realism of his appraisal of the outbreak of war in 1755.

By contrast, Newcastle's foreign policy until mid–1755 was built around

---

[200] Walpole, *George II*, vol. 2, p. 30.
[201] See especially Richard Pares, 'American versus Continental Warfare, 1739–63', *EHR* 51 (1936), 429–65. How unrealistic an antithesis this was is revealed by Max Savelle, 'The American Balance of Power and European Diplomacy, 1713–78', in Richard B. Morris (ed.), *The Era of the American Revolution* (New York, 1939), pp. 140–69. Pamphlets of 1755–63 debating these policy issues are listed in C.W. Eldon, *England's Subsidy Policy towards the Continent during the Seven Years' War* (Philadelphia, 1938), pp. 167–73.
[202] Britain's ministerial instability and vicious political controversies during the 1760s, including the attacks on Bute and the Dowager Princess of Wales which Waldegrave did something to instigate, were widely reported abroad and significantly damaged Britain's credibility as a consistent, reliable or worthwhile ally: M. Roberts, *Splendid Isolation, 1763–1780* (Reading, 1970), pp. 13–15.

the preservation of the Anglo-Austrian alliance, the lynchpin of British strategy in the age of Marlborough, recently reaffirmed by the treaty of Vienna in 1731 and again in the War of the Austrian Succession (1741–48). Yet the insecurity of that co-operation was evident even in the negotiations for the Treaty of Aix la Chapelle. Newcastle sought to bolster the alliance by arranging the election of the Archduke Joseph, heir-apparent to the Austrian throne, as King of the Romans, thereby making him next in succession to the throne of the Holy Roman Empire.[203] By stabilising Austria's position as the dominant power within the Empire, Newcastle hoped to remove her temptation to ally with France. To win the votes of the Imperial Electors for his chosen candidate, Newcastle's bait was a series of subsidy treaties with the lesser German princes: the military defence of Hanover against Prussia and the preservation of the Austrian alliance would thus be promoted together, and a subsidy policy shielded against Henry Pelham's parsimoniousness.

Initially, the Imperial election plan seemed to make progress. Six out of the nine electoral votes were needed, and Newcastle already relied on those of Hanover (George II), Bohemia (Maria Theresa), Mainz and Trier. Bavaria[204] and Cologne were soon added, though the latter was quickly lost. A subsidy agreement signed on 13 September 1751 secured Saxony.[205] Thereafter the impetus was lost. Austria wavered, then refused to proceed to an election in the face of open Franco-Prussian opposition, and the plan languished. Newcastle acknowledged its failure in September 1754. The expiry of the treaties (the Saxon on 29 September 1755 and the Bavarian on 21 July 1756) provoked Waldegrave's ridicule in the *Memoirs*; yet, though the plan itself was a failure, it had perhaps one immensely important

[203] D.B. Horn, 'The Origins of the Proposed Election of a King of the Romans, 1748–50' *EHR* 42 (1927), 361–70, argued that these efforts accelerated the dissolution of the Austrian alliance. Newcastle's policy was defended by Sir Richard Lodge, 'The Continental Policy of Great Britain, 1740–60', *History* 16 (1931–2), 298–304, and Reed Browning, 'The Duke of Newcastle and the Imperial Election Plan, 1749–1754', *Journal of British Studies*, 7 (1967), 28–47. For an unconvincing restatement, see D.B. Horn, 'The Duke of Newcastle and the Origins of the Diplomatic Revolution' in J.H. Elliott and H.G. Koenigsberger (eds.), *The Diversity of History. Essays in Honour of Sir Herbert Butterfield* (London, 1970), pp. 247–68.

[204] The Bavarian treaty was signed at Hanover on 11/22 August 1750, to run for six years from 21 July 1750. Bavaria was to cast its imperial vote in accordance with George II's wishes and continue to maintain 6000 foot (as in the previous treaty of 1746) in return for an annual subsidy of £40,000, half to be paid by Britain, a quarter each by Austria and Holland. It is printed in *Commons Journals*, vol. 26, pp. 24–5.

[205] See D.B. Horn, *Sir Charles Hanbury Williams & European Diplomacy (1747–58)* (London, 1930), pp. 68–100. Saxony's annual subsidy was £48,000, of which £32,000 was paid by Britain, £16,000 by Holland; in return Saxony undertook to furnish 6000 men for England or Holland in any war in which they were engaged, and gave a strong assurance (though not a guarantee) of intention to co-operate with George II in Imperial affairs. The treaty ran for four years from 29 September 1751. It is printed in *Commons Journals*, vol. 26, pp. 371–2.

side-effect: it kept alive the old alignment of powers a little longer, and deferred a Franco-Austrian alliance until the 'Diplomatic Revolution' of 1756–7 made it, in effect, too late.[206]

From Britain's point of view, the chain of events which led to war began in a theatre in which Waldegrave would have welcomed vigorous measures. French expansion south from Canada into the disputed Ohio valley was designed to cut off the expanding British colonies and confine them to the area east of the Allegheny mountains. The defeat in July 1754 of a local force commanded by Major George Washington induced Britain to despatch a substantial reinforcement under Major General Braddock in October 1754. France replied by sending a much larger military reinforcement via her Canadian possessions in early 1755. At this point Waldegrave took up the story in the *Memoirs*.

His intention, writing in 1758 and before the conquest of Canada, was to ascribe the ill success of British strategy in 1755–6 to ministerial indecision and timidity. It is important to bear in mind, however, that his account of these events was not drawn from first-hand knowledge. Waldegrave did not have a seat in the Cabinet, nor was he one of the Lords Justices who administered the kingdom during the King's absence abroad from 28 April to 16 September 1755. Waldegrave's account reflects 'common knowledge', as modified by the prejudices and viewpoint of Henry Fox.

Waldegrave ascribed British circumspection to ministerial timidity. Yet, in his account of the events of 1755, and not questioning in 1758 the inevitability of war, Waldegrave's antipathy to European involvement made him leave out of account the diplomatic context which made that circumspection rational. Newcastle's aim throughout 1755, however, was to confine the fighting to North America and avoid its triggering a European conflict in circumstances unfavourable to Britain.[207] His foreign policy, before the 'Diplomatic Revolution' of 1755–6, was dedicated to sustaining and reviving the triple alliance with Austria and Holland, and to giving effect to the Barrier Treaties of 1713 and 1715, protecting the Austrian Netherlands from French attack by a chain of Dutch-garrisoned fortresses. It was a fragile system, yet some European alliance was essential

[206] The viability of an Anglo-Austrian alliance to 1754 at least is demonstrated by Reed Browning, 'The British Orientation of Austrian Foreign Policy, 1749–1754', *Central European History*, 1 (1968), 299–323.

[207] Newcastle was committed to a hawkish policy in resisting French encroachments in North America, but sought to limit British operations there to measures which seemed least likely to provoke a general war. It was Cumberland and Fox who finally 'transformed Braddock's expedition from that limited removal of French encroachments in successive stages of which Newcastle had approved, into an aggressive attack on the French in America on four fronts simultaneously': T.R. Clayton, 'The Duke of Newcastle, the Earl of Halifax, and the American Origins of the Seven Years' War', *HJ* 24 (1981), 571–603, at 595. In March 1755 Newcastle still did not expect an early war in Europe: *ibid.*, p. 600.

Introduction 67

while a connection between Britain and Hanover remained. If the Electorate were lost, any British gains in America would have to be bargained away at the final peace conference.

Hanover was vulnerable, moreover, not only to French attack but also to Prussian intervention. In 1755, therefore, George II's summer residence in his electorate was marked by frantic diplomatic activity designed to secure its defence by a series of subsidy treaties. All would be lost if Britain were seen to be the aggressor in Europe. Holland could then refuse to stand by her treaty obligations. Austria seemed only too willing to abandon a disadvantageous British alliance in favour of links with France, but there were still hopes of Austrian loyalty. The British minister in Madrid, Sir Benjamin Keene, seemed on the brink of detaching Spain from her Bourbon alliance partner through his influence with General Wall, Spain's Anglophil chief minister. Finally, from early 1755 there were hopes of a Russian alliance that would neutralise the Prussian threat to Hanover more effectively than anything else. All these possibilities would be blighted if Britain were seen to be the aggressor.

It was exceedingly difficult to avoid this role, however. Braddock's reinforcement for the threatened American colonists was designed to be sent quietly: it was Fox who, without authorisation, gave dramatic publicity to the preparations in an attempt to hurry forward the outbreak of war. Waldegrave was obviously unaware that his ally, Fox, had given this twist to events.[208] In early January 1755 Mirepoix, the French *chargé d'affaires* in London, somehow obtained a copy of Braddock's instructions. A massive French reinforcement then became certain.[209] On 10 March Mirepoix advised his government that an accommodation of colonial disputes with Britain would be hopeless.[210] On 25 March the King's message was presented to Parliament requesting an augmentation of forces. The question was not whether a colonial war could be avoided but whether Britain would be cast in the role of an aggressor, and whether a war in North America could be prevented from spreading to Europe. Waldegrave's claim that Braddock's reinforcement made a European *as well as* an American war 'inevitable' at least misses the point of ministerial policy.

Equally, Waldegrave's claim of a transition from resolution in late 1754 to timidity in early 1755 is not justified. The 'resolution' was Fox's unauthorised attempt to drive matters forward. The 'timidity' was Newcastle's natural attention to the European implications of American events

[208] T.W. Riker, 'The Politics Behind Braddock's Expedition', *American Historical Review*, 13 (1907–8), 742–52; Clark, *Dynamics of Change*, pp. 99–105.
[209] Julian S. Corbett, *England in the Seven Years' War* (2 vols., London, 1907), vol. 1, p. 31.
[210] *Ibid.*, vol. 1, p. 40.

at a time, from September 1754 onwards, when he realised that his plan for the election of a King of the Romans had definitely failed, and that Austria was slipping away from its ancient alliance with Britain. By December 1754, Newcastle saw that 'the great system is on the point of being dissolved . . . The conduct of Vienna is astonishing. They act as if they had no occasion for us.'[211] But dissolution still did not finally materialise: by February 1755, Newcastle was more sanguine of Austrian co-operation. If time could be bought, it was still well worth buying.

Also doubtful is Waldegrave's implication that the ministry was indecisive in giving Boscawen orders to fight only in American waters. It was the case that, as Waldegrave recorded, 'the French sail'd unmolested'; but the object of Boscawen's expedition, departing on 21 April 1755 with 10 ships of the line, and of a reinforcement of 6 ships under Holburne sent after him on 11 May, was to bring to action the whole French fleet off Louisbourg. A pre-emptive strike was to be justified by the scale of the damage inflicted. A major French reverse in America would deter her from launching a war in Europe.[212] This plan miscarried tactically: Boscawen was too late to intercept the main French force, which had already passed into the St. Lawrence. By engaging an isolated French detachment of three ships, and capturing two, Boscawen did some strategic damage to the British position without corresponding tactical gain. But he incurred no censure from the ministry; 'He had obeyed his orders literally'.[213]

Newcastle sent Waldegrave, for the information of Leicester House, the earliest news of Admiral Boscawen's capture of the French warships *Alcide* and *Lys* off Louisbourg.[214] Waldegrave replied to this momentous news with ominous brevity: 'As to myself, I am really at a Loss how to express myself, whether I should congratulate Yr Grace on the Success of his Majesty's Fleet, or whether I should lament our ill Fortune that Hostilities are now begun without that considerable Advantage, which might animate his Majesty's Subjects, and dishearten the Enemy'.[215] Waldegrave had clearly not been party to the ministry's thinking up to this point, and something was now done to remedy this. Copies of a number of diplomatic despatches were circulated to him, with the evident intention of briefing the junior Court. During the King's summer residence in Hanover, these briefings continued, and Waldegrave prepared careful abstracts of the diplomatic letters he was shown by Newcastle. Waldegrave was fully aware

[211] Newcastle to Bentinck, 17 Dec. 1754: Add MSS 32851 f. 325: Clayton, 'Seven Years' War', p. 598.
[212] Newcastle to Holdernesse, 23 May 1755: 32855 f. 112; Newcastle to Hartington, 17 May 1755: 32855 f. 35. Clayton, *loc. cit.*, p. 601.
[213] Corbett, *Seven Years' War*, vol. 1, p. 58.
[214] Newcastle to Waldegrave, [15 July 1755]: Add MSS 51380 f. 51.
[215] Waldegrave to Newcastle, [15 July 1755]: Add MSS 32857 f. 113.

Introduction

of the King's unwillingness to allow Hawke, commanding the Channel squadron, to attack the French fleet or merchant marine 'whilst the Negotiation is still depending'. Waldegrave realised that Newcastle's 'Opinion that the whole Fleet should put to sea without hostile Orders' went beyond this royal reluctance, and left scope for such hostile orders swiftly to be issued. But the revelation of differing opinions within the Regency evidently struck Waldegrave, not a great admirer of Newcastle, as proof of indecision rather than as a series of difficult reactions to a still-fluid situation.[216]

The same issue of strategic principle now recurred. Waldegrave admitted, in the *Memoirs*, the problem of manning the fleet at short notice. The rapid despatch of 16 ships of the line to North America meant that it was not until mid-July 1755 that Sir Edward Hawke, commander in chief at Portsmouth, was ready to put to sea with the remainder. What were to be his orders? Waldegrave's account in the *Memoirs* again neglects the diplomatic imperatives, still as strong as when Boscawen sailed in April, and paints a Foxite picture of a bellicose Cumberland frustrated by a pusillanimous Newcastle, afraid to strike and finally compromising by ordering Hawke to confine himself to commerce raiding.

By June 1755, however, negotiations with Austria had collapsed, this time finally.[217] Newcastle's reticence was to be explained rather by the need to avoid being the first to begin those hostilities in Europe which were now unavoidable. Boscawen's ill-success was known in London on 14 July, and the principle had been grasped that only a decisive blow would justify Hawke in acting first. In July, Newcastle insisted that he was 'of the Opinion I always was; that the Orders should depend upon the Nature & Considerableness, of the Object; that Hawke should be directed to attack any Number of Men of War, or Merchantmen; But that he should not begin Hostilities in Europe, for the Sake of a Single Ship'.[218] When Hawke's orders were signed on 22 July, Newcastle justified the decision to take no merchantmen at the outset, rather than

> to take every little insignificant French ship, that should be met, whereby we might actually be charg'd with Beginning Hostilities in Europe, for Nothing. The same Reason inclin'd Many of His Majesty's Servants to confine (as is done) the seizing of Men of War, to ships of the Line; or, otherwise, the War might be, most probably, begun here, in these Seas, *by us*, within 48 hours.[219]

---

[216] Waldegrave's abstracts are in Add MSS 51380 ff. 80–2.
[217] Newcastle to Holdernesse, 6 June 1755: Add MSS 32855 f. 352: Clayton p. 601; Eldon *Subsidy Policy*, pp. 15–21.
[218] Newcastle to Holdernesse, 15 July 1755: Add MSS 32857 f. 109.
[219] Newcastle to Holdernesse, 22 July 1755: Add MSS 32857 f. 295; cf Corbett, *Seven Years' War*, vol. 1, pp. 59–61.

Waldegrave's account of differences in the Cabinet over Hawke's orders reflects a Foxite perspective. It represents the outcome as a compromise forced by Newcastle's timidity: 'that Hawke should sail with hostile orders; but War was not to be declared'. Yet this decision embodied a rational strategy. Hawke's instructions, dated 22 July, were received by him the next day at Spithead, where he was detained by adverse winds; he sailed on the 24th. The instructions, citing French aggression in North America as justification, ordered him to intercept the main French fleet under Du Guay, just sailed from Brest for the Spanish coast. Those secret orders were of course the subject of much political speculation at home. Observers could only infer their content from Hawke's actions. It was, however, additional orders dated 6 August which extended the Channel fleet's activities to a war against French commerce. This did not modify Hawke's chief aim, and after his return he credited himself with 'never once losing sight of the principal object of my cruise'. Only through missing Du Guay was a major fleet action fortuitously avoided. Hawke stayed out until on 23 September he received intelligence that the French fleet had succeeded in returning to Brest and Rochefort, only then retiring to Portsmouth. The commerce war in the Channel had meanwhile mopped up some 6000 French sailors and officers plus 1500 soldiers.[220] France's diplomatic response was ineffectual: unprepared militarily and without alliances, she clung to peace. Not until Austrian support had been assured could France take the offensive, with an invasion of the British-held island of Minorca, in April 1756. With France now revealed as the aggressor, a British declaration of war against her followed on 17 May 1756. In 1755, however, it is difficult to see how British policy could have been better framed to delay a European war, consistent with taking effective counter-measures against French reinforcements to North America. Waldegrave's insistence in the *Memoirs* that war might have been further delayed does not appear to be well founded. Throughout the summer of 1755, Newcastle had sought to avoid a war on the continent; even Cumberland had agreed.[221] The strategy had succeeded. War followed that realignment of European affairs known to historians as the 'Diplomatic Revolution'; it did not cause it.

After a summer spent in his Electorate, George II returned to Kensington Palace on 16 September 1755; on 19/30 September an Anglo-Russian treaty was signed which was to transform the diplomatic landscape.[222] A subsidy treaty with the Landgrave of Hesse Cassel had already been signed

---

[220] Ruddock F. Mackay, *Admiral Hawke* (Oxford, 1965), pp. 115–33 for the naval events of 1755.
[221] Cf Walpole, *George II*, vol. 2, pp. 56–7, n. 3.
[222] See D.B. Horn, *Sir Charles Hanbury Williams & European Diplomacy (1747–58)* (London, 1930), pp. 178–293.

Introduction

at Hanover on 18 June.[223] In the *Memoirs*, Waldegrave is sceptical of the value of these treaties. When they were presented to Parliament for ratification, however, he supported them, though with reservations, in the Lords' debate of 10 December 1755, carefully drafting his speech (no. 12 below). It seems that his account in the *Memoirs* takes some advantage of hindsight; at the time, the merits and successes of the ministry's policy were more evident.

In one respect, the effect of the Russian treaty was immediate. Frederick the Great, fearing an Austrian revenge attack on Silesia, seized by Prussia in 1740, now sought an English alliance as a way of maintaining the peace in Germany; the Convention of Westminster was signed on 16 January 1756. If this treaty finally led Prussia into a pre-emptive strike against Austria, it provided Britain with a continental ally, tied inescapably to her British alliance. In such a situation America could be conquered in Germany, Prussia paying most of the price.

The Convention of Westminster deprived France of her major European ally; war in Europe was thereby delayed again. The First Treaty of Versailles, a French defensive alliance with Austria, followed on 1 May 1756. Frederick of Prussia, imagining a tripartite conspiracy assembling against him, launched his pre-emptive invasion of Saxony on 29 August 1756. This destroyed the Anglo-Russian alliance. Austria reached agreement on military co-operation with Russia on 2 February 1757; France responded with the Second Treaty of Versailles on 1 May 1757, allying her with Austria and Russia, and committing her to the recovery of Silesia. Sweden and Saxony joined this alliance, and the alignments of the Seven Years' War were complete. For Britain it was the best outcome that could have been envisaged. Newcastle's intricate and unpopular schemes of continental involvement set the scene for an unparalleled series of naval and colonial triumphs in the Seven Years' War. Waldegrave and others like him could either not see or not admit the dependence of the second on the first.

Waldegrave remained the ministry's inevitable channel to Leicester House. Newcastle, however, placed too much reliance on the Earl's influence:

Tho' I can't pretend to give advice, I would submit it to your Lordship's Consideration; Whether, as our Treaty with the King of Prussia is no secret, Your Lordship might not take an opportunity to acquaint the Prince of Wales this morning with it, *in form*; When You may Observe that it is the certain Consequence of our Treaty with Russia; & That you know to your knowledge, That use was always designed to be made of our Treaty with Russia. I would also submit, Whether you might not add Some Insinuations of the Impropriety of the opposition

---

[223] For their terms, see p. 166 below.

to the Prussian Treaty; and the Injustice of the Reflections cast upon it; Which now so soon are proved to be without the least foundation.[224]

It was too much to ask. Waldegrave's heart was not in the ministry's policy, and Leicester House was already anticipating a radically different stance.

The loss of Leicester House, 1755–1757

Waldegrave was irreversibly associated with the ministry by moving the address in the Lords in November 1754, and his role as mediator during that autumn identified him more specifically still with Fox and Cumberland. Fox's promotion within the ministry, and Cumberland's elevation as one of the Lords Justices on the King's departure for Hanover in April 1755, now triggered a development of lasting importance. The Dowager Princess of Wales turned for advice to Lord Bute;[225] Bute soon began to put out feelers to William Pitt. Secret negotiations ensued. One public result was the encounter between Pitt and Fox on 9 May at which Pitt announced that their co-operation against Newcastle was over. Speculation about the launch of a new opposition now gathered momentum.

Waldegrave was among the first to pick up the signs of a changing climate at Leicester House, and passed the news to Fox. In July 1755, Fox duly relayed it to Dodington:

he told me that he was sure that Mr Pitt had made up with the Princess; had it in mind, when he declar'd off with him [on 9 May]. That he [Fox] had long cultivated (above 6 months) an acquaintance with one [Waldegrave],[226] no way connected with D[uke] of N[ewcastle], with whom he had had the first confidential conference since he saw me. That in talking of things of that court [Leicester House], I think he call'd it 'his court', to that person, he said that he had heard that Stone was not so well as usual there, what could be the reason of it? The person [Waldegrave] answer'd, 'Shall I tell you? I fear you will not like it, but as you command me I will. I take it to be from thinking him [Stone] too much in your [Fox's] interest'. The same person told him (who, he says, some times converses with Cresset) that Mr Pitt was better at that court than usual: to what degree, or by what means he did not know; but that he found Cresset spoke more favourably of him than he us'd to do: He then (Fox) went on to say that Lord Egmont was thought to have the chief management there: and that the Prince was much fonder of *him*, than of any other man living.[227]

---

[224] Newcastle to Waldegrave, [? Jan 1756]: Add MSS 51380 f. 54.
[225] For a full study of this episode, see James Lee McKelvey, *George III and Lord Bute: The Leicester House Years* (Durham, North Carolina, 1973).
[226] Horace Walpole's attribution, in a note to his copy of the 1784 edition of Dodington's *Diary*.
[227] Dodington, *Diary*, 21 July 1755.

Introduction

It was not Egmont, however, but Bute who was destined to win Prince George's confidence, and Pitt who was to provide the focus of a parliamentary opposition serious enough to enable Leicester House to go into open opposition to St James's.

The Prince's instructors had evidently still failed to penetrate his youthful reserve. In August, the Dowager Princess admitted that her son's

> education had given her much pain. His book-learning she was no judge of, suppos'd it small, or useless, but hop'd he might have been instructed in the general course of things. That she did not know Lord Waldegrave: and for Mr Stone, if she were to live 40 years in the house with him, she should never be better acquainted with him, than she was: she, once, desir'd him to inform the Prince about the Constitution; but he declin'd it, to avoid giving jealousy to the Bishop [of Norwich].[228]

Whatever the Governor's relations with his pupils, his relations with their mother had evidently not progressed beyond the merely formal.

By the autumn, a rumour of the insecurity of Waldegrave's position reached the press. From Florence, Sir Horace Mann asked for confirmation:

> The German gazette which is famous for lies, even to a proverb, *il ment comme une gazette allemande*, says this week 'that Lord Waldgrave has on a sudden been removed from the Prince of Wales, which was the more extraordinary, as he was a personal favourite of the King and the Duke of Newcastle'.[229]

Such a rumour was premature; but after Parliament met, hostilities became open. The set-piece issue was the ministry's subsidy policy: when the treaties were laid before Parliament, the new chiefs of the Leicester House opposition fought them in both Houses. In the Lords, there was no division; in the Commons, the ministry triumphed on 13 November by 311 to 105, and a week later Pitt, Legge and Grenville were dismissed.

Waldegrave now found himself caught up in a full-scale conflict between the two Courts. In the ministerial reshuffle which followed the dismissal of Bute's allies, Waldegrave was not relieved of his duties: on the contrary, he became more valuable to the ministry as his situation became more disagreeable to himself. Horace Walpole reported his friend's reaction to the rearrangement of posts: 'Lord Waldegrave last night hearing them talk over these histories, said with a melancholy tone, alas! they talk so much of giving places for life, I wish they don't give me mine for life!'[230] His personal predicament, an unwelcome individual in a vital Household post, was made worse by his public opposition to key items of Leicester House

---

[228] Dodington, *Diary*, 18 August 1755.
[229] Mann to Walpole, 25 Oct. 1755: Walpole, *Letters*, vol. 20, p. 504.
[230] Walpole to Thomas Gray, 25 Dec. 1755: Walpole, *Letters*, vol. 14 p. 86.

policy: his support for the subsidy treaties on 10 December 1755; his backing for the Lords' Address commending the summoning of Hessian troops on 23 March 1756; his opposition to George Townshend's Militia Bill on 24 May (speeches nos. 13, 14, 17 below).

If the attempt to win Leicester House's support for the ministry's foreign policy made Waldegrave's uneasy position difficult, the next turn of the screw was to bring events to a crisis. Prince George would be legally of age at his eighteenth birthday on 4 June 1756, and a separate Establishment required to maintain his due dignity. From Waldegrave, Newcastle procured a report on the current state of the Prince's household and on those formerly maintained by Prince Frederick, the first when he had been allowed £50,000 p.a. and the second after an additional £50,000 had been granted in 1742.[231] In February 1756 Waldegrave asked of Newcastle a Household post for a friend; evidently he did not anticipate the full extent of the Leicester House rebellion.[232] Nor did Fox, who in May solicited a Household post for his ally Lord Digby.[233]

Other experienced observers agreed. In May, the Earl of Chesterfield reported, via Newcastle, the disposition of employments in the new Household to a young aspirant: that the King had 'absolutely fixed Lord Waldegrave for Groom of the Stole and the Marquess of Rockingham for Master of the Horse'.[234] Clearly, it was intended that the 2nd Earl should make the transition from the Prince's Governor to the new King's First Minister. George II could scarcely have given a clearer indication of his confidence, and Waldegrave must have seen the greatest political prize well within his grasp. His hopes were soon to be dashed.

The King's official notification of his intention to create a separate Establishment for Prince George was conveyed through Waldegrave on 30 May: it provided for an ungenerous allowance of £40,000 p.a., and for the removal of the two princes from their mother's charge to their own apartments at Kensington and St James's.[235] Prince George's formal reply was returned at once via the same route: refusing, in effect, to leave his mother and implicitly demanding a veto over appointments in his household.[236] The result was consternation and frenzied political activity.[237]

[231] Newcastle's memorandum for Waldegrave, 22 Feb. 1756: Add MSS 51380 f. 55.
[232] Waldegrave to Newcastle, 24 Feb. 1756: Add MSS 32863 f. 85.
[233] Fox to Waldegrave, 15 May 1756: Add MSS 51380 f. 6.
[234] Chesterfield to Lord Huntingdon, 19 May 1756: Chesterfield, *Letters*, vol. 5, p. 2190.
[235] This had not been done after the death of Prince Frederick in 1751, evidently because of the Pelhams' fear that the young princes would thereby fall under the control of the Duke of Cumberland and Henry Fox: Walpole, *George II*, vol. 1, p. 71, n. 1.
[236] George II to Prince of Wales, [30 May 1756]; Prince of Wales to George II [30 May 1756]: Royal Archives, 211, 212.
[237] Undated letters between Andrew Stone, Waldegrave and Newcastle: Add MSS 51380 ff. 58–72.

Introduction

This was quickly noticed. A Scots MP reported to his patron: 'I know no other news but suspect something is on the anvil about the Prince of Wales as Lord Waldegrave was at the Duke of Newcastle's this morning in close consultation first with the Duke of Newcastle and then with the Attorney General'.[238] But the forcible removal of the Princes was inconceivable. Soon he wrote again:

As to the Prince of Wales I don't know who governs but the conduct is like what you hear. A list of those intended to have places was sent, and first he said he desir'd not to be taken from his mother, to which Lord Waldegrave said, You mistake, it is not meant to take you from your mother but from the nursery. After it was said, Lord Waldegrave, who was put down as Groom of the Stole, had some hard things said to him for which as reported he desires to resign and the Prince of Wales desires Bute may be Groom of the Stole. Upon that pin all is said now to hang.[239]

It was too true. On 14 June, Waldegrave had written to Newcastle, putting on paper his oral request for the King's permission to resign from the household of the Prince, and in terms which could hardly be refused:

I do not presume to claim the least Merit from the Slavery I have undergone for some Years past, nor from my constant Attention and Zeal for his Majesty's Service. If I had done less I should not have perform'd my Duty.

But the Circumstances of the last Winter have been such, that no Temper not absolutely callous, could remain unmoved. Such things have been said to me which I can never forget. And I have made such answers as they can never forgive.

Not to trouble Yr Grace with trifling Reasons, I am clear in my Opinion that as things now are, it would be impossible for me to continue in his RH's Service, and to act a Part, becoming a Man who his Majesty had honour'd with the Title of Governor to the Prince of Wales. Nor am I less certain that in this new Employment even my best Services would be of very little Use.[240]

His release was not immediate, however. Even in September, Waldegrave was kept at his post, an essential intermediary, but still demurring: others would be of more use, he insisted to Newcastle. 'My Lord Waldegrave is of opinion, That They would not be so likely to Shuffle with my Lord Chancellor, and my Lord President, as They would with Him'.[241]

At last, however, the King bowed to the inevitable, and rewarded his remarkably loyal servant with unusual generosity.

The late governor, Lord Waldegrave, was offered a pension on Ireland, and refused it: they then gave him the reversion of a Teller's place; and one cannot tell which was most rejoiced at the separation, he or the Princess, who had been suspicious enough to take for a spy, a man, who would even have scorned to employ one.[242]

---

[238] Hume Campbell to Earl of Marchmont, 3 June 1756: HMC *Polwarth*, vol. 5, p. 317.
[239] Hume Campbell to Earl of Marchmont, 12 July 1756: HMC *Polwarth*, vol. 5, p. 320.
[240] Waldegrave to Newcastle, 14 June 1756: Add MSS 32865 f. 302.
[241] Newcastle, 'Memorandum with Lord Waldegrave', 16 Sept. 1756: Add MSS 32867 f. 335.
[242] Walpole, *George II*, vol. 2, p. 182.

Waldegrave, who later chose to ascribe this to the King alone, gave at the time a share of the credit to Newcastle:

> Mr Stone has acquainted me with his Majesty's great Goodness towards me. I am also thoroughly sensible how much I am indebted to Your Grace's Friendship and good Offices.
>
> Making me entirely easy in my Circumstances, as long as I live, is an Obligation of so high a Nature; that my Satisfaction would have been mix'd with some Uneasiness, had it not been the Gift of a King who I love and honour, or had it been owing to the Assistance of any Minister except Yr Grace.

He added a note of the final, unsatisfactory, resolution of the crisis over the Prince's household:

> I was this morning at Kensington with Letters from the P[rince] and [Dowager] Princess of Wales. I red them in the Closset and think both full as well as could be expected. The Prince of Wales's is more explicit than I expected. Both make the strongest Professions. And his Majesty tho he doubts their Sincerity, seems, upon the whole to be very well satisfied.[243]

Waldegrave had to wait only a few months before his reversion fell in, with the death of Lord Walpole of Wolterton on 5 February 1757. 'I certainly did not expect to be so soon in Possession', he told Newcastle. 'But had I waited many Years, I should never have forgot that I only named the Reversion to Yr Grace, and by his Majesty's Favor, and Yr Grace's Friendship it was immediately granted.'[244]

It only remained for Waldegrave to take his revenge on the two individuals who, as he must have thought, had blighted his political career. Rumours of an illicit relationship between Bute and the Dowager Princess of Wales were widely current from the late 1750s, but reliable evidence was lacking and failed to appear.[245] This in itself raised doubts. When Waldegrave's *Memoirs* were published in 1821, one reviewer entered a caution:

> It should be remembered that unauthorised whispers are not a safe foundation for the superstructure of history; and that the annalist, who builds his fame upon no more solid basis than *La Cour d'Auguste*, *Les Amours des Gaules*, or the endless *Secret Histories* which every reign produces, would attain the reputation, and deserve the fate of Sir Nathaniel Wraxall.[246]

[243] Waldegrave to Newcastle, 18 Sept 1756: Add MSS 32867 f. 321.

[244] Waldegrave to Newcastle, 5 Feb. 1757: Add MSS 32870 f. 150. Waldegrave made careful notes on the duties of a Teller of the Exchequer, Add MSS 51380 ff. 236–7, and evidently approached his new duties, largely nominal though they were, with his habitual scrupulousness.

[245] Circumstantial evidence against the probability of any such liaison is marshalled by Brooke, *George III*, pp. 48–9.

[246] *The British Critic*, 16 (1821), p. 166. Sir Nathaniel Wraxall (1751–1831), author of *Historical Memoirs of My Own Time* (2 vols., London, 1815). For a libel contained in that work, Wraxall spent three months in jail and paid a fine of £500. This, and hostile reviews in both the *Edinburgh* and *Quarterly*, combined to discredit Wraxall's veracity.

Introduction

In 1822, the reviewer in the *Edinburgh* sought to place as favourable an interpretation as possible on Waldegrave's role at Leicester House in order to disparage the role of the Dowager Princess of Wales and bolster the thesis that a new royal absolutism was to be traced to the doctrines which she and Lord Bute impressed on Prince George in the 1750s.

> We cannot conclude our remarks on these *Memoirs*, without stating as our opinion, after a careful, and, we trust, impartial consideration of the conduct of Lord Waldegrave, that he appears to us to have behaved in the most fair and honourable manner to his pupil and to the Princess Dowager. While they were disposed to remain on friendly terms with the King, he did them all the good offices in his power. When they leagued themselves with persons in opposition to his Majesty's government, he still endeavoured to do as little harm as possible, and made use of every opportunity to soften and alleviate what appeared amiss. But he owed a superior duty to the King; and, having been intrusted by his Royal Master with the charge of his grandson, it was his duty, when required, to give information to his Majesty of what passed at Leicester-house; and, to use his own words, if 'it had been his intention to deceive the King, even in that case it would have been absurd to have denied those things which might be seen at every drawingroom, and were the subject of conversation at every coffeehouse.' When the Princess Dowager engaged her son, a boy of seventeen, to set his grandfather at defiance, it was natural she should wish to remove from her household a person whose perspicacity she could not blind, and whose fidelity she could not shake. But it would be unjust to blame Lord Waldegrave for doing his duty to his Sovereign, and keeping aloof from intrigues of which he could not participate or approve.
>
> Lord Waldegrave has certainly alluded to the rumours then generally prevalent about Lord Bute and the Princess Dowager. Whether the suspicions then current were founded or not, we have neither curiosity to inquire, nor means to ascertain. That they afterwards gave occasion to much gross and popular ribaldry, is undoubted; but, long before they descended to the rabble, they had been the topic of conversation among their superiors. They are mentioned by Lord Orford in still plainer language than by Lord Waldegrave; and allusions to them, we venture to say, will be found in the private correspondence of all the distinguished politicians of that time. They may have been false, but they appear to have been universally credited.[247]

Denials were current even at the time, however. On 24 March 1772, James Boswell recorded a conversation with the Court physician and eminent scientist Sir John Pringle:[248]

> He said he was now come to give little faith to history, because he knew for certain that the Princess Dowager of Wales had for these many years taken no share in politicks, and never had any improper connection with Lord Bute; and yet she would go down to posterity as having managed all the affairs of this nation till her

---

[247] *The Edinburgh Review* 37 (June-Nov. 1822), pp. 18–19.
[248] Sir John Pringle (1707–82). Physician; professor in Edinburgh; physician-general to the forces in Flanders; 1749 physician-in-ordinary to Duke of Cumberland; in 1761 to the Queen; in 1774 physician to the King.

death, and been concerned in a criminal intercourse with Lord Bute. He said it would not be proper for him to mention them; but that his situation about the Royal Family gave him an opportunity of knowing circumstances that made it certain that the Princess was altogether free of both these concerns. He said that when it was imagined there would be a long minority, the late King being very old and his Grandson very young, a party of the great people about court, apprehending that Lord Bute's intimacy with Frederick Prince of Wales might give him a great ascendancy over this King, formed the plan to raise a report of scandal between the Princess Dowager and Lord Bute, and he would do Mr. Fox, afterwards Lord Holland, the justice to say that he alone struck out against it. It was however put in execution, and was asserted with such effrontery that many, who had occasion to know better, believed it. He therefore could not regard history farther than just as Chronology and relating certain facts which could admit of no falsifying, such as that a King reigned so long, a battle was fought, or such things. But as to accounts of characters, or the secret springs and motives of actions and events, he could not credit historians. This was really a good evening with my father's old friend.[249]

Horace Walpole added his authority to the historiographical tradition. In a collection of extracts from his writings published in 1799, the curious could read: 'The King had quarrelled with Bute before he came to the throne; it was his mother, the princess dowager, who forced her son to employ that nobleman. I am as much convinced of an amorous connexion between B. and the P.D. as if I had seen them together'.[250] This conviction was duly transferred to Walpole's *Memoirs*, transmuted into fact, and backed by suggestive anecdotes and innuendoes.[251] But Walpole failed to record his source: the 2nd Earl Waldegrave. The latter's motive for denigrating his supplanter is already clear. So too is the timing of the rumours: only after Waldegrave's eclipse did Walpole show any interest in Bute's role at Leicester House.

Prince George's aversion to Waldegrave may have crystallised in a short period. In June 1756, the Prince of Wales still wrote to Lord Bute in terms which suggested relations of courtesy and respect with his Governor:

I have spoken very openly to Lord W[aldegrave] telling him the regard I had for him; but I hop'd he would decline coming into my family and at the same time desir'd him to excuse himself with the K[ing] in such a manner that I might not appear in it, that in doing that he wou'd oblige me and which I never wou'd forget; he answer'd to this with great civility that it was very good of me to let him know my thoughts, and at the same time said that he had been with the D[uke] of

---

[249] G. Scott and F.A. Pottle (eds.), *Private Papers of James Boswell from Malahide Castle* (18 vols., privately printed, 1928–34), vol. 9, pp. 34–5.
[250] *Walpoliana* (2 vols., London, [1799]), vol. 1, p. 64.
[251] Walpole, *George II*, vol. 2, pp. 151–2. Remarkably, Walpole tried to blame the rumour on Hardwicke, 'who having been slighted and frowned on by the Princess in the winter, was determined to be revenged; and the gentle method he took was to embroil the Royal Family, and blast the reputation of the mother of the heir apparent' (*ibid.*, pp. 160–1). No evidence has been found to support this claim.

N[ewcastle] to whom he had told that he wou'd not at present accept nor would he refuse till he saw how things turn'd out.[252]

The Prince can have had no motive for concealing any aversion to Waldegrave from Bute, who already possessed his confidence. Within a month, however, Prince George's mood changed totally. He had been told of the nature of the rumours concerning Bute's relations with the Princess Dowager. These the son blamed unequivocally on 'the Ministers', and made a commitment to which he resolutely adhered:

> I look upon myself as engag'd in honor and justice to defend these my two friends [his mother and Bute] as long as I draw breath. I do therefore here in the presence of Our Almighty Lord promiss, that I will ever remember the insults done to my mother, and never will forgive anyone who shall offer to speak disrespectfully of her.[253]

It seems likely that, in the eyes of the Prince of Wales, Lord Waldegrave carried a share (perhaps even a large share) of the responsibility for the reports of his mother's adultery. If so, George III's verdict in 1804 that his late Governor had been 'a depraved worthless man'[254] would need no further explanation. But the evidence is not conclusive.

Newcastle had decided to resign on 26 October 1756, immediately after the formation of the Prince's new Household. Waldegrave shared with that Duke and his allies their exile from office during the winter of 1756–7. Neither of them relapsed into political obscurity: Waldegrave drafted a carefully phrased speech for the debate on the Address in reply to the King's Speech, 2 December 1756, setting out his position at length (speech no. 19 below). The 2nd Earl's efforts to remain on good terms with Newcastle bore fruit in the spring: with George II seeking an opportunity of being rid of the Pitt-Devonshire administration, and with Newcastle waiting in the wings for an acceptable opportunity to return to power, Waldegrave was an obvious intermediary. Such a scheme depended on timing. In March, Newcastle 'begs to represent to My Lord Waldegrave how unadvisable It would be, to make any Alteration in the present Administration, till the Supplies are rais'd, And the Enquiry dispos'd of, some Way, or other'. Waldegrave carried Newcastle's memorandum to the King, and brought back the royal approval of the scheme of ministry which it contained.[255] From Fox, Waldegrave received a rival scheme and presented it to the King similarly.[256]

---

[252] Prince of Wales to Bute, n.d. [? 9 June 1756]: Sedgwick (ed.), *Letters of George III to Lord Bute*, p. 1.
[253] Prince George to Bute, 'June 31st, 1756' [sic], Sedgwick, *loc. cit.*, p. 2.
[254] Above, p. 53.
[255] Newcastle, 'Memds with Lord Waldegrave', 1 March 1757: Add MSS 32870 f. 230.
[256] Fox, memorandum, n.d. [? 19 March 1757]: Add MSS 51430 f. 67: Fox to Waldegrave, 19 March 1757: Add MSS 51380 f. 7.

Waldegrave performed these conflicting duties impartially, relaying to Fox the King's objections to the terms asked. The King also hoped that Parliament would bring down the ministry, sparing him the trouble of dismissing them; but Waldegrave 'told him many would be against them [the ministers] when turn'd out, who would not chuse to attack them whilst they continued in his service. Besides Ministers being routed by Parliament might be a bad Precedent. The last Reason seem'd to make some Impression'.[257] Fox in turned showed Waldegrave's reply to Cumberland,[258] and it was on the latter's prompting that the ministers were ultimately dismissed in early April.

If the ministers were removed, what would Newcastle do? Waldegrave carried this question from the King, and brought back Newcastle's answer: that the vacated offices should be left unfilled until the end of the session.[259] This was indeed to be the outcome, but mainly because of the impossibility of devising a ministerial system which would tempt its personnel to accept. Meanwhile, in the midst of a major war, the country experienced a bizarre 'interministerium'. In this crisis it was Waldegrave who took the lead in the House of Lords, moving on 18 May the Address in reply to the King's request of £1,000,000 for the war and defending the sum against Lord Temple's attempt to reduce it to £300,000, restricted to English purposes.[260] In these negotiations Waldegrave was, remarkably, able to retain the good opinion of both the parties to the dispute. Fox complained of the effects of Devonshire's interventions:

a Fatality has attended ev'ry thing His Grace has undertaken to manage for me. I will call it by no other Name. A very contrary Event has succeeded whatever Your Lordship has had the goodness to interpose in, I will impute that to its true causes, your Friendship, & your feeling in points of honour for a Man you honour with your good opinion, as you do for yourself.[261]

It was not least thanks to Waldegrave's diplomacy that Fox was eventually accommodated in the Newcastle-Pitt ministry as Paymaster.[262]

When Newcastle finally told the King on June 8 that he would not resume office without the support and inclusion of Leicester House, George II turned in desperation to Fox.

Mr Fox went to Court and consented to undertake the whole – but it is madness! Lord Waldegrave, a worthy man as ever was born and sensible,[263] is to be the first

[257] Waldegrave to Fox, [? 19 March 1757]: Add MSS 51380 f. 9.
[258] Fox to Waldegrave, 20 March 1757: Add MSS 51380 f. 10.
[259] Newcastle, memoranda, 25 March 1757: Add MSS 32870 ff. 335, 341.
[260] Walpole, *George II*, vol. 2, p. 257.
[261] Fox to Waldegrave, 31 May 1757: Add MSS 51380 f. 16.
[262] Waldegrave to Newcastle, [6 June 1757]: Add MSS 32871 f. 228.
[263] Walpole here deleted a passage, possibly reflecting on Waldegrave's personal uncleanliness.

Lord of his Treasury. Who is to be his anything else I don't know, for by tomorrow it will rain resignations as it did in the year '46 ... I grieve for Mr Fox and have told him so; I see how desperate his game is ... What is certain, great clamour and I fear great confusion will follow.[264]

Walpole reflected:

In this distress the King (probably by the suggestion of Mr Fox) sent for Lord Waldegrave and commanded him to accept that high and dangerous post. The public was not more astonished at that designation, than the Earl himself. Though no man knew the secrets of government better, no man knew the manoeuvre of business less. He was no speaker in Parliament, had no interest there, and though universally beloved and respected where known, was by no means familiarized to the eyes of the nation. He declined as long as modestly became him; engaged with spirit, the moment he felt the abandoned state in which his master and benefactor stood.[265]

Waldegrave accepted the King's commission on 8 June, as he wrote in the *Memoirs*, 'partly moved by his Distress, partly yielding to his Persuasion, or perhaps fired by some latent Spark of Pride or Ambition'. The following day began the mass resignation of Newcastle's followers which (as in 1746) was to make unworkable a ministry undertaken without the sanction of the main body of Whigs. Waldegrave's ministry was impractical, and was never properly launched. Horace Walpole, covertly disloyal as ever to his friend, and driven as always by animosity towards Newcastle, was not above trying a similar expedient in which the Duke of Dorset would be a token First Lord of the Treasury; but this scheme, too, had no chance of success.[266] Waldegrave was asked to assure the King 'that, as some Resignations have happened, and others may, possibly, take place ... the Duke of Newcastle hopes, that His Majesty will have the goodness, not to impute them to Him; But to the General Opinion, which the Duke of Newcastle has humbly represented to the King, would prevail, upon the present Occasion'.[267] Newcastle's professions of innocence were not believed. Faced by this willingness to subvert the ministry, Fox's nerve failed; and on 11 June the King, on Mansfield's advice, decided not to proceed with a Waldegrave-Fox ministry. Formally, they had never taken office; Devonshire had remained First Lord of the Treasury.[268] In an

---

[264] Walpole to Mann, 9 June 1757: Walpole, *Letters*, vol. 21, p. 97.
[265] Walpole, *George II*, vol. 2, p. 262.
[266] Walpole, *George II*, vol. 2, p. 264.
[267] Newcastle, 'Paper laid before the King, by Lord Waldegrave', 11 June 1757: Add MSS 32871 f. 272.
[268] No warrant for a Treasury Board was issued between Devonshire's, on 15 November 1756, and Newcastle's, on 2 July 1757. Waldegrave never held the office of First Lord of the Treasury: cf J.C. Sainty, *Office-Holders in Modern Britain*, vol. 1, *Treasury Officials 1660–1870* (London, 1972), p. 20.

audience that day, Waldegrave advised George II to compromise with Pitt; after protracted negotiation, the celebrated Newcastle-Pitt coalition was launched in an atmosphere of bitterness and recrimination.[269]

Once the manoeuvres were at an end, Waldegrave (evidently on George II's command) sent an appreciation of the outcome to the Duke of Cumberland, then commanding the British army in Germany:

> I did not presume to write some weeks ago, because I was certain that in all material Affairs yr R H had the most early and the best Intelligence. At present it should seem still more improper to take up a Moment of yr R H's time. As the Transactions of a Month ago are now of little Consequence, and as conjectures of what may happen are of too uncertain a Nature to be much depended on. But however improper this letter may be either as to time, or Substance, I am not without hopes it will meet with yr R H Indulgence. Having received Encouragement where even a Hint must be equal to a Command. From the Moment that Plan of Administration was form'd wherein it was the King's Pleasure that I should be a Part, to have been deter'd by any personal Doubts and Difficulties would have been highly criminal as well as dishonourable. It was certain that in the Execution of his Majesty's Commands, we should do nothing for which we could legally be call'd to account, and we should have been Cowards indeed had we apprehended any considerable Danger merely for having done our Duty.
>
> At the same time I was very glad this Plan was not carried into Execution, because I was clear in my Opinion, it would not have answer'd his Majesty's Expectations. Pitt and his Friends had at that time entirely recover'd their Popularity. To our Shame to be spoken, the D[uke] of N[ewcastle] had at that time not only a Majority in the House of Commons, but what is almost incredible a Majority even of the King's own Servants, some of them Men of Quality near his Majesty's Person who were under the greatest personal Obligations.
>
> Besides it was unfortunately the general Opinion that this System could not last and consequently it would not have met with support even from those who consider'd singly their immediate Interest, any more than from them who look'd farther into Futurity. The part the D[uke] of N[ewcastle] acted in all these transactions is perhaps without a Parallel, however he had been tolerably well imitated by his Pupil Holdernesse. [Deleted: The Folly as well as the duplicity and Ingratitude of the D of N passes all] The latter indeed was of too little Consequence to hurt anybody but himself. And as for the Duke of Newcastle, he may ['will' deleted] soon find that when he overturn'd the King's Plan, he at the same time put himself ['entirely' deleted] more than he was aware of in his Majesty's Power. For he has given so much Strength to Pitt and his Friends, that unless he meets with Favor in the Closet he must soon become as insignificant, as many think he deserves. It is therefore most probable that tho underhand he will make great Professions and Promises at Leicester House. Yet upon the whole as far as he is able he will endeavour to please the King, and to atone for past Offences.
>
> As to Pit it seems s[t]ill doubtful what part he will act whether he will dare to resist Faction, by doing that which in his own Judgement he must know to be right, or whether he will court false popularity by pursuing such Measures as must in the

[269] Clark, *Dynamics of Change*, pp. 413–25.

Introduction

end destroy this country. This will greatly depend on the Treatment he meets with. Should the popular Clamor and his Tory Friends turn against him. He certainly would abuse them in his Turn, and would probably do well. But on the other hand, should he find himself quite desperate in the Closet his Pride and Resentment would make him do every thing in his Power to regain Popularity by starving the War in Germany, and throwing Affairs into Confusion at Home.

Upon the whole it seems most probable that affairs may go on for some time in a kind of middle State, on all sides there will be great Mistrust and Jealousy but no open Quarrel. Leicester House will never be quite satisfied, yet will not have spirit or pretence to appear quite Angry. The Duke of Newcastle will endeavour to undermine Pit at Leicester House but will not succeed, because they fear Pit and do not fear his Grace on the other hand I should wish that Pit would endeavour to undermine the D[uke] of New[castle] at St James's, not that I have much concern at which of them prevails, but whilst they are running a Race for favor, the King would probably find both more tractable.

[Deleted: The Duke of Devonshire will always act like himself, as I named him I could not say less. And in that case tho too much time has been lost there might still be some hopes that the War would not be starved or carried on in that Middle State I have been mentioning. But that we should exert our Strength with such Vigor and Spirit as might bring it to a speedy and happy Conclusion, which is not only the most honourable, but would in the end be the best economy.] And though it would be blindness not to see the dangers which every where surround us yet whenever the Strength of this Country is properly exerted, with Yr RH commanding his Majesty's Forces, and properly supported I can never think our Affairs quite desparate.

For this End I very sincerely wish that the present Administration may continue, and if I may presume to say it, that his Majesty may condescend to treat them better than they deserve. For we are in such a Situation that nothing less than our whole united Force can be sufficient. And many will cooperate with these Gentlemen to save the whole, who have no great personal Veneration for them. Whereas on their side they have given a very sufficient Proof that they mean to overturn everything that they had rather this country was ruined than that any administration should be formed of which themselves are not the most considerable Part and it is our misfortune that at present they have the Power as well as the Inclination.

However on the other hand; tho they have this Power, they cannot be ignorant that a prudent Use of it, and a decent Behaviour are the most probable means of preserving it. For there still are many who can give them a good deal of Uneasiness should they either neglect the King's Affairs, or should they dare to misbehave towards his Majesty in the manner the[y] have formerly attempted.

As to the Duke [of] Dev[onshire] the D[uke] of Bed[ford] Mr Fox and others who were to have form'd the late Administration, Yr RH is so well inform'd of their Behaviour, that I shall only say that if at last there was some Difference of Opinion, it is not to be wonder'd at, as some tempers are more sanguine than others but it was a very friendly difference, every one meaning the King's Service, every one meaning well to each other.

As to myself I really thought I had acted on a Principle of Duty and of Zeal for his Majesty's Service. But when I find that either as to honours or Circumstances, his Majesty's goodness has left me nothing to wish for, I must not flatter myself that I have been disinterested. I can only hope I shall never be ungrateful.

I really think these Gentlemen themselves are sensible of it. They also know that tho their Endeavours to mislead the People has succeeded in some particulars; yet in general the King is lov'd and respected. That their own Popularity is now become precarious [alternative: 'of a very uncertain Tenure'], and that Leicester House has no popularity to lose.

I cannot conclude without begging Pardon for the great Liberty I have taken, but as I said before I was encouraged to write, and I should never forgive myself if I had wrote to Yr RH and had not spoke my real Sentiments.[270]

Waldegrave's reward was less tangible; but it signalled his high favour in the King's eyes. 'The first mortification to Lord Holdernesse has been, that having been promised a Garter as well as Lord Waldegrave, and but one being vacant, that one, contrary to custom, has been given to the latter, with peculiar marks of grace.'[271] The Garter 'by this time I believe has got fifty spots', added Walpole; his friend 'was apt to be dirty', he confided to a footnote.[272] Cumberland too was delighted, and sent his congratulations via Fox:

I rejoice with you at the Garter being so properly given. I would actually myself write to old Wall., if I did not know how much he hates a letter; but you will do me pleasure to lett him know, what I hope he does not doubt, how much I love and esteem him, and consequently how glad I am that he is not Minister, but that he has the Garter.[273]

Dissension did not suddenly subside with the formation of the coalition. Waldegrave's investiture with the Garter was itself controversial: 'I hear Mr Pitt or his friends say it is hitting them a slap in the face at the first outset, and a bad omen for their administration', reported Rigby; 'The Duke of Newcastle and his friends, though they like it no better, are, however, silent upon it'.[274] Nevertheless, it closed a chapter in Waldegrave's career. Writing to the Duke of Devonshire to fix a date for his installation, he observed: 'As to Politicks I have at present the Satisfaction to know very little. The King's Mind seems tolerably easy. And the Administration hitherto agree better than most People expected. I most heartily wish both may continue'.[275]

---

[270] Waldegrave to Cumberland, n.d. [July 1757]: draft, Add MSS 51380 f. 87.
[271] Walpole to Mann, 3 July 1757: Walpole, *Letters*, vol. 21, p. 108.
[272] Walpole to Earl of Strafford, 4 July 1757: Walpole, *Letters* vol. 35, p. 281.
[273] Cumberland to Fox, July 1757: Earl of Ilchester (ed.), *Letters to Henry Fox Lord Holland* (Roxburghe Club, London, 1915), p. 116. Cumberland offers a clue to the scarcity of the 2nd Earl's correspondence.
[274] Rigby to Bedford, 28 June 1757: *Bedford Correspondence*, vol. 2, p. 254.
[275] Waldegrave to Devonshire, 19 July 1757: Devonshire MSS, Chatsworth, 393/1.

Introduction

The last years, 1757–1763

Social life reclaimed Waldegrave. In August 1757 he was dining at Strawberry Hill with Lady Rochford, Lady Townshend and a Miss Bland, and was entertained by Horace Walpole with a sight of his private printing press in operation.[276] The following year he was Devonshire's guest at a Chatsworth house-party with Fox, Rigby and others.[277] He did not abandon the Court, however. Waldegrave was at Kensington to see the King 'more dejected, and more depress'd than I had ever known him' at the news of the Convention of Klosterseven. Waldegrave was evidently concerned to defend and vindicate the disgraced Duke of Cumberland. 'The D. of New[castle] talk'd a great deal of his good Offices, how much he had endeavour'd to soften and to appease, but of late, my Faith in his Grace's Professions is somewhat abated'. Yet although Cumberland's position was 'very delicate', Waldegrave added: 'I do not find the public Clamor to be strong against him'.[278]

Fox knew better. 'I was stunn'd with your Lordship's letter', he replied. The disgrace of Cumberland had changed the political balance radically, and that Duke was never to recover the influence he held before 1757. Moreover, Fox had a better understanding of the political scene as a whole than the courtier: 'I fear, My Lord, from the Letters I have receiv'd that yr Lordship is not well inform'd as to the publick & that they blame the D[uke of Cumberland] as much as the King do's'.[279] Cumberland's reputation indeed stood higher in London clubland than in the world outside. Lady Elizabeth Waldegrave reported: 'I have heard no one speak disrespectfully of him upon this occasion & Mr Waldegrave says that Arthur's,[280] which you look upon, at least as the better part of the Town; universally acknowledge this Loss'.[281]

It was the 2nd Earl's brother who had a more prominent role mapped out for him by the war. The unsuccessful military expedition against Rochefort produced another round of recrimination, and an inquiry on which Colonel Waldegrave sat with the Duke of Marlborough and Lord George Sackville. Their findings were leaked to relevant parties:

Mr Waldegrave has order'd me to inclose you, a copy of their report ... He flatters himself if your Grace had been an Enquirer you cou'd have given no other opinion ... Lord Anson is very angry the court of Enquiry has been so severe, upon the Sea & says Sr E[dward] H[awke] will defend himself in parliament. Mr W[aldegrave]

---

[276] Walpole to George Montagu, 25 Aug. 1757: Walpole, *Letters*, vol. 9, p. 215.
[277] Lady Caroline Fox to Countess of Kildare, 10 July [? 1758]: B. Fitzgerald (ed.), *Correspondence of Emily, Duchess of Leinster* (3 vols., Dublin, 1949–57), vol. 1, p. 169.
[278] Waldegrave to Fox, 27 Sept. 1757: Add MSS 51380 f. 22.
[279] Fox to Waldegrave, 2 Oct. 1757: Add MSS 51380 f. 26.
[280] White's was sometimes known as Arthur's, after its early manager, Robert Arthur.
[281] Lady Elizabeth Waldegrave to Lord Trentham, 17 Oct. 1757: PRO 30/29/1/17 f. 969.

answer'd him, that he thought considering their conduct, they had shew'd them a great deal too much lenity. For in his opinion they had behav'd much worse than the Land Officers. There will be great parties arise about this & I don't doubt many will condemn the Generals for the hardness of the Censure. But in the main I think it is approved of.[282]

And in 1759, the 2nd Earl's sister-in-law boasted: 'I can't conclude my letter, without exposing my vanity, in letting you know that Majr. Burton says Mr Waldegrave is not only ador'd by the Army, but by all the Country, wherever he has anything to do'.[283] To these administrative services, John Waldegrave added a distinguished record in battle. His conduct at Minden drew the King's commendation, and his brother did not cease to remind Newcastle of the appropriateness of the King's 'Intention of adding new Favors to the many which had been bestow'd' on the younger brother.[284] The 2nd Earl was not wholly absent from Westminster, drafting speeches for the Seamen's Wages Act in March-April 1758 and in reply to the King's Speech, 13 November 1759 (nos. 25 and 26 below); but the focus of his interests was now more often elsewhere.

Disappointments in the early 1750s, and his duties at the junior Court, had left Waldegrave unmarried. His friend Horace Walpole now intervened, and in April 1759 announced with delight:

in short, I have married, that is, am marrying my niece Maria, my brother's second daughter, to Lord Waldgrave – What say you? A month ago I was told he liked her – Does he? – I jumbled them together, and he has already proposed. For character and credit, he is the first match in England – for beauty, I think she is. She has not a fault in her face or person, and the detail is charming. A warm complexion tending to brown, fine eyes, brown hair, fine teeth, and infinite wit, and vivacity. Two things are odd in this match; he seems to have been doomed to a Maria Walpole – if his father had lived, he had married my sister: and this is the second of my brother's daughters that has married into the house of Stuart – Mr Keppel comes from Charles; Lord Waldgrave from James II. My brother has luckily been tractable, and left the whole management to me – My family don't lose any rank or advantage, when they let me dispose of them – a Knight of the Garter[285] for my niece; £150,000 for my Lord Orford if he would have taken her;[286] these are not trifling establishments.[287]

---

[282] Lady Elizabeth Waldegrave to Duke of Bedford, 26 Nov. 1757: Bedford MSS, vol. 35, f. 78.
[283] Lady Elizabeth Waldegrave to Bedford, [4 Aug. 1759]: Bedford MSS, vol. 40, f. 28.
[284] Waldegrave to Newcastle, 16 March 1760: Add MSS 32903 f. 318; Newcastle to Waldegrave, 16 March 1760: *ibid.*, f. 320.
[285] I.e. Waldegrave.
[286] Walpole referred to the well-endowed Miss Nichols (later married to the Marquess of Carnarvon) who might have been the bride of the 2nd Earl of Orford.
[287] Walpole to Mann, 11 April 1759: Walpole, *Letters*, vol. 21, p. 284.

Before Miss Drax, it seems, had come Sir Robert Walpole's natural daughter Lady Maria Walpole!²⁸⁸ Her marriage in 1746 to Col. Charles Churchill terminated any such possibility. Now, at the fourth attempt, on 15 May 1759, Waldegrave made what proved to be a happy marriage.

Eyebrows were perhaps raised at the disparity in their ages: the 2nd Earl was 44; Maria Walpole was 22. Other eyebrows may have been raised at her family background. Maria's later marriage to the Duke of Gloucester, brother of George III, awakened jealousies and made enemies among high society gossips. One rival, Lady Mary Coke, Bute's daughter, wrote:

> Lady Waldegrave was a most lovely woman; not of much sense, but blameless in character and conduct. She had the manners of the high society in which she had always moved; she was the widow of a distinguished man of quality; but – there was no disguising it – the illegitimate daughter of Sir Edward Walpole, by a mistress whom, if report spoke truth, the keeper of some infamous house, descrying her uncommon beauty, had fairly beckoned in from the top of a cinder-cart.²⁸⁹

True, family pressures had prevented Sir Edward Walpole from formalising an unequal match; but his lifelong mistress, Dorothy Clement, had been a milliner training in a Pall Mall shop at the time of their meeting. Lady Mary Coke's anecdote was mere slander.

At Court, by contrast, Waldegrave's choice was accepted: 'He notified his marriage to the monarch last Saturday, and it was received civilly'.²⁹⁰ 'It was as sensible a wedding as ever was', recorded Walpole: 'there was neither form, nor indecency, both which generally meet on such occasions ... on Sunday she is to be presented ... '²⁹¹ To his *Memoirs*, Walpole confided his private opinion that his friend was 'an excellent man, but as old again as she was, and of no agreeable figure. Her passions were ambition and expense: she accepted his hand with pleasure, and by an effort less common, proved a meritorious wife'.²⁹² The house at Navestock became once more a scene of domestic happiness. Three daughters followed in quick succession: Elizabeth Laura in 1760, Charlotte Maria in

---

²⁸⁸ (c. 1725–1801); see speech no. 4 below.
²⁸⁹ 'Memoir by Lady Louisa Stuart' in J.A. Home (ed.), *The Letters and Journals of Lady Mary Coke* (4 vols., Edinburgh, 1889–96), vol. 1, p. xcv.
²⁹⁰ Walpole to Montagu, 26 April 1759, addendum of 1 May: Walpole, *Letters*, vol. 9, p. 231.
²⁹¹ Walpole to Montagu, 16 May 1759: Walpole, *Letters*, vol. 9, p. 234.
²⁹² Walpole, *George III*, vol. 3, p. 268. Maria's character was later shown to less advantage, after the 2nd Earl's death. In 1766 she was secretly married to the King's younger brother William Henry, Duke of Gloucester. The marriage was not a success. And when made public in 1772, the King refused to recognise a 'wife whom I can never think of placing in a situation to answer her extreme pride and vanity': George III to Lord North, 16 Jan. 1775: Sir John Fortescue (ed.), *The Correspondence of King George the Third from 1760 to December 1783* (6 vols., London, 1927–8), vol. 3, p. 164. By 1787 their marriage had broken down, and the Duke of Gloucester confessed to the King: 'I am indeed severely punished for my juvenile indiscretion by the very ungrateful return I receive at home': Brooke, *George III*, p. 281.

1761, Anne Horatia in 1762. Navestock was convenient, too, for Newmarket. Within days of George III's coronation in September 1761, the 2nd Earl was again enjoying the pleasures of the turf. A German visitor recorded:

> On the day of our visit, the first race was run on the long course between seven geldings, amongst which was a horse of the Duke of Cumberland's; each owner of these seven horses had subscribed 200 guineas as sweepstakes, so that my Lord Waldegrave won 1400 guineas, the Duke of Cumberland's horse coming in last.[293]

It was a temporary reprieve from political entanglements; and the 2nd Earl was lucky to retain Cumberland's friendship.

George II's long-awaited but sudden and unexpected death on the morning of 25 October 1760 had found Waldegrave in London, and at once attending at Court. The new sovereign did not obviously harbour a grudge against his former Governor, and the advantages of a close acquaintance with a young monarch who knew few other politicians were soon apparent. All eyes were on the sovereign during his first public appearances, especially at the Privy Council meeting on the day of his accession. Walpole noted: 'At that first council the King spoke to nobody in particular but his former governor, Lord Waldegrave'.[294]

Waldegrave's familiar haunt, White's Club, proved a hotbed of gossip. On 30 October Lord Egmont, an ally of Frederick Prince of Wales and an aspirant in the new reign, noted:

> being at Arthur's this evening Lord W[aldegrave] told me things were drawing towards a settlement. That the Duke of Newcastle had consented to continue, on consideration that he might chuse the Parliament, but complained of the extravagance of the expense. That *Pitt* had likewise engaged to continue, professing he only desired to stand as he did in the late reign not as the Minister, and what favours he should ask should be through the channel of the Duke of Newcastle, but he hoped *that there might be some ostensible measure, that the war was to be continued, and the same system pursued.*

On 2 November, Egmont continued:

> A vast Court for the 1st time at St James's ... Lord Waldegrave told me he heard I was to be a peer ... said he heard there were to be 3 viz. Lord Mountsteward son to Lord Bute, myself and Sir William Irby. In the morning it was asserted by those who are thought most intelligent that Lord Huntingdon was to be Master of the Horse, and Lord Gower removed. Lord Waldegrave seemed to think it would be so, but that Lord Gower was assured he should soon have a place of equal rank. At

---

[293] Count Frederick Kielmansegge, *Diary of a Journey to England in the Years 1761–1762* (trans. Countess Kielmansegge, London, 1902), p. 49. In March 1762, Cumberland 'again played a game of quinze for just as high stakes as he had played some time before at my lord Waldegrave's; but what he won or lost this time I cannot say. On a previous occasion he had lost 1000 guineas by twelve o'clock': *ibid.*, pp. 282–3.
[294] Walpole, *George III*, vol. 1, p. 6.

Arthur's in the evening Charles Townshend assured me that on the contrary Lord Gower was to keep his post . . . Lord Waldegrave said that Sir Harry Erskine who is Surveyor of the King's Roads, *was to have a regiment*, in order that . . .

and so the manoeuvres went on. On 5 November

Mr Charles was with me and said he heard the peers to be made were Lord Mountstewart Lord Bute's son, myself, Sir William Irby and Lord Downe. Lord Waldegrave again at Arthur's this day also said he heard the same. He told me Lord Gower was at last to be Master of the Wardrobe and a Cabinet Councilor, with such additional salary as the Cabinet Council should think proper to make up for the loss of his place of Master of the Horse which Lord Huntingdon was to keep.

With so much to attend to, it is less surprising that George II's funeral on 11 November was 'Not well attended by the peers nor even the King's old servants'.[295] Waldegrave excused himself: 'A slight Fever, and a bad Cold prevented my having the melancholy Satisfaction of performing my last Duty at my late Master's Funeral. At present I have no Fever, and the Cold is so much better, that under the Protection of a great Coat, I have ventured to go as far as White's', a short step from Albemarle Street; but he declined an invitation to Newcastle's, more distant in Lincoln's Inn Fields.[296] Soon, however, the political consequences of the King's demise drew Waldegrave back into active politics. The general election called for some difficult negotiation as Waldegrave and Fox hammered out a compromise with Newcastle over the seats at Midhurst, where all three had an interest.[297]

Waldegrave was still a regular attender at Court. On 8 July 1761 he was present at the Privy Council meeting summoned 'to hear H.M. declare his intended marriage with Miss Charlotte of Mecklenburgh'; to the despair of Henry Fox, who had expected the royal choice to fall on his sister-in-law Lady Sarah Lennox. The King 'seem'd confused when he made his Declaration in Council', insisted Fox, '& more so as he came by me in going away: a remark which Lord Albemarle & Lord Waldegrave made before I own'd I had made the same'.[298] For the moment, power lay not with Fox but with one whose hold on the new King's confidence was more secure. The new reign meant the triumph of the man who had supplanted

---

[295] Newman (ed.), 'Leicester House Politics', pp. 220–5.
[296] Waldegrave to Newcastle, 17 Nov. 1760: Add MSS 32914 f. 399.
[297] Namier and Brooke, vol. 1, pp. 395–6; Waldegrave to Fox, 10 Dec. 1760: Add MSS 51380 f. 28; Fox to Waldegrave, 12 Dec. 1760: Add MSS 51380 f. 30, and 6 March 1761: *ibid.*, f. 32; Waldegrave to Fox, [? 20 March 1761]: Add MSS 51380 f. 33; Waldegrave to Newcastle, 22 May 1761: Add MSS 32923 f. 220; Newcastle to Waldegrave, 23 May 1761: Add MSS 32923 f. 233.
[298] Henry Fox, 'Memoir on the Events attending the Death of George II and the Accession of George III', in the Countess of Ilchester and Lord Stavordale (eds.), *The Life and Letters of Lady Sarah Lennox 1745–1826* (2 vols., London, 1901), vol. 1, p. 50.

Waldegrave at Leicester House. Bute did not inherit high office at once; but, in stages, the ministry was restructured around him. William Pitt and Earl Temple resigned on 5 October 1761 in the face of Bute's reluctance to extend the war to Spain. Bute had already succeeded Newcastle's nominee Holdernesse as Secretary of State for the Northern Department in March 1761, and by the following year his position was strong enough to allow him to succeed Newcastle as First Lord of the Treasury in May 1762.

If acceptable peace terms were to be negotiated, the temptation precipitately to withdraw the British army from Germany had to be resisted. Bedford's motion in the Lords on 5 February 1762, calling for just such a withdrawal, caused consternation. Newcastle and his friends rallied behind Bute's associates in moving the previous question. Waldegrave drafted a series of speeches on the question (nos. 27–30), some in favour, some against; remarkably, he voted against Bute's 105 supporters in the tiny minority of 16. Bute was furious, and clearly saw that it was Waldegrave's friendship with Bedford and Fox which 'sheltered' him (see speech no. 27).

Bute's tragedy was that he now had to work through the men of whom he most disapproved. The major problem was to steer the controversial peace terms through Parliament after the loss of so much senior support from his cabinet. Bute's solution was one that perhaps shocked the King most: Henry Fox, the arch-manoeuverer, was entrusted with the lead of the Commons and the task of cementing a majority for the Treaties in return for the promise of a peerage. Fox then set about assembling support. Via Bute, potential recruits were vetted by the King. He wrote:

> I have no objection to Lds. Waldegrave and Gower coming to [Cabinet] Council, but wish they were counterballanced by Ch. Townshend (if he can be depended on) and any others that may not be look'd upon as Bedford House men, for else I fear that will be the name the Counsellors will get.[299]

George III had, by 1804, an adverse opinion of Waldegrave's *character*; but at whatever date this judgment was formed, it did not prevent the King from planning to enlist the 2nd Earl's *political* support in the early 1760s. Fox therefore proceded:

> His first application was to the Duke of Cumberland. That haughty and sensible Prince received him with scorn, reproached him warmly with lending himself to support a tottering administration, and bitterly with his former declarations of having given up all ambitious views. The next trial made by Fox was on Lord Waldegrave, to whom he urged that his Lordship had so much ridiculed the Princess and Lord Bute, that they had more to complain of than he had; and he endeavoured to enclose the Earl in his treaty with the Court, by asking him, if it should be proposed to call his Lordship to the Cabinet Council, whether he should

---

[299] George III to Bute, n.d. [16 Oct. 1762]: Sedgwick, *Letters of George III to Bute*, p. 147.

like it? The Earl, who had been bred a courtier, who was of too gentle manners for opposition, was too shrewd not to see that the power of the Crown was predominant, desired time to consider, and went to Windsor to consult the Duke of Cumberland. His Royal Highness acknowledged the attention with many thanks, but would give no advice. The Earl, who wanted not to be told, that not advising him to make his court when he was disposed to it, was advising him against it, was not courtier enough to quit a Prince, his friend, for a Court that he himself despised and hated; and immediately wrote to Fox to desire the proposal might not be made to him.[300]

Fox's attempt to implicate Devonshire in support for the peace terms led that Duke to absent himself from the crucial Cabinet meeting. The King took this evasion as a personal discourtesy and as evidence of an incipient conspiracy within the Cabinet: Devonshire swiftly and dramatically found himself out of office. Waldegrave consoled him, and provided an account of his own conduct:[301]

Tho I foresaw Yr Grace would not continue Lord Chamberlain many Months longer, I was surprised as much as I was concern'd, when I heard the Circumstances of Yr Resignation.

I never had a high Opinion of the Judgment of our great Minister [Bute]. But this Instance of Folly is beyond my Conception. Upon the whole, I am sorry the King has lost a servant who, at least, did Credit to the Court: I am sorry the Nation has lost a Counsellor, who tho he could not do all the Good he wish'd, might have prevented great Mischief. But I rejoice that You have disengaged Yrself from all Difficulties, and have done that which will be most conducive to Yr own Happiness.

I have so often experienced Yr Graces Partiality and Friendship, that I shall trouble You with some Particulars relating to myself. The Day before Mr Fox was call'd to the Cabinet, and declared Minister of the House of Commons, he made me a very friendly Visit. After a long Conversation on the various Branches of foreign and domestic Politics, going out of the Room, he said he would ask a Question, but did not desire an Answer. *Should you like to be call'd to the Cabinet.* We parted. In a day or two, the Question was repeated, and I promised to give an Answer the day following. Early next morning I went to the Lodge, not to lay his R.H. [Cumberland] under Difficulties by asking Advice: but having Doubts, I was unwilling to take a final Resolution till I knew his R Hs Opinion, as to some Particulars.

His R.H. received me with his usual Condescension and Goodness. After a long Conversation, I took Leave without giving the slightest Hint of what I intended. As soon as I arrived in Town, I wrote the following Note to Mr Fox.

Dear Sir.
     Having consider'd Yr most kind and friendly Question, I answer that I had rather the Offer should not be made. Had I been guided by Inclination my Determination might have been different. Such a distinguishing Mark of his Majesty's Favor and Confidence would have made me exceeding happy.

As to the Article of Peace, it appears to me so necessary, that I am convinced

---

[300] Walpole, *George III*, vol. 1, pp. 155–6.
[301] Waldegrave to Devonshire, 2 November 1762: Devonshire MSS, Chatsworth, 393/2.

neither the King nor his Ministers will accept any Terms which I shall not think preferable to the Continuation even of a successful War. As to other Particulars, tho on some Occasions I may have an Opinion of my own, I hate the Peevishness of Opposition, even when it is least violent.

On the other Hand, during the time I either was, or fancied myself ill used, my Language concerning Ministers, was not of the friendly Sort.

Should I change on a sudden, and I cannot do things by Halves, the Turn would be too quick: especially, as I can hope for little Encouragement at a Place where I am under no Engagement, yet where a Disapprobation of my Conduct would give me great Uneasiness.

I am &ra.[302]

When I have the Honor of seeing Yr Grace in Town, I shall acquaint You with other Particulars which in a Letter would be tedious. In the mean time, I shall be very cautious of mentioning the Affair, except to a Particular Friend. Had there really been a Proposal, it would be wrong to publish it: but still more ridiculous to brag of having rejected an Offer which was never made.

Devonshire replied from Chatsworth:

I have receiv'd your very kind Letter & I hope I need not to assure you that this mark of your Friendship & Confidence in me has made me very happy. It is a pleasure that my Friends shou'd approve my conduct, tho' in this instance I had scarse any option, for after the reception I met with it was impossible for any man that had the least spirit or sense of Honour to remain a moment in the Kings service: I feel great satisfaction that we think alike & shall most probably act in concert, as no one values you or loves you more than I do. I lament the part that Mr Fox has taken, it is ill judg'd, & hurts him in the opinion of the world. Yr Lordship may be assured that I shall say nothing to any body in regard to what you mention'd of yourself. Your answer My Lord does you honour it was an honest a wise & a judicious one, & gave our Friend a hint that I wish he wou'd have follow'd; but Ambition has blinded him, & will be his ruin. As the Parliament is put off I intend to stay here till the time of its meeting, I shou'd be glad of some conversation with you as soon as I come to town, my ideas with regard to the Peace & Opposition agree entirely with yours, the difficulty will be how to act conformably to those sentiments & not give stability to the Minister. I was afraid to write by the Post as I have reason to think they are very busy in that Office.[303]

To Cumberland, Waldegrave sent a fuller account:

It is reported, and believed that the Preliminaries of Peace were sign'd at Fontainbleau on Wednesday last, tho the Messenger is not yet arrived.

Should this be the Case, I hope the News will be received in time to prevent Yr R H return to Sea. If Hostilities cease, there can be no Object worthy Yr R Hes

---

[302] A copy of Waldegrave to Fox, 17 Oct. 1762: Add MSS 51380 f. 38. In the original are two minor differences: para. 1, 'might have been' *sc* 'would have been'; para. 2, 'preferable to' *sc* 'more desirable than'.

[303] Devonshire to Waldegrave, 7 November 1762: Add MSS 51380 f. 77. Devonshire implied that his letters were being opened.

Introduction

attention, whatever remains may be executed by Officers of inferior Rank and less Consequence.

The Circumstances of the D[uke] of D[evonshire's] Dismission or Resignation surprised every body. I will acquaint Yr R H with the Particulars, as they are told, whether they be true, or false; The D[uke] of D[evonshire] arrived in Town last Thursday seen night in the Morning, went immediately to Court: desired the Page to acquaint the King *that he was there to pay his Duty*. The Page return'd, told him he had his Majesty's orders to say *that he would not see him*. The D[uke] of D[evonshire] then desired the Page to tell the King that he beg'd to know his Majesty's Pleasure, *to whom he was to deliver his Key* &ra, the Page return'd and told him that the King would send him his orders. Whereupon he went immediately to Ld Egremont's left the Wand and Key with his Lordship and went out of Town either the same day or the Morning following.

On the Wednesday last the King call'd for the Council Book and orderd the D[uke] of D[evonshire's] name to be struck out of the List. This Event gives me great concern, not only on account of my private Friendship for the D[uke] of D[evonshire] but because a Man of such a Family, Rank and Character might have been a useful Servant to the King, in these days of ill humor and faction. On the other hand tho' I am convinced the D[uke] of D[evonshire] did not mean any thing disrespectful, I think his second Message hasty and improper, and that the King had just reason to be offended.

Ld Rockingham resign'd on Wednesday last, he gave his Reasons, which were strongly but decently urged against Ld Bute, the King heard all he had to say and answer'd that he never desired to keep any Person in his Service who chose to quit it. I am told it is intended to make D[uke] of Rutland Chamberlain, that the Duke of Marlborough may be Master of the Horse, the D of Rutland would readily accept, but does not care to give a decisive answer till he has consulted Granby, should the Son object, the Father will be greatly disappointed.

It is now imagined that most of the D[uke] of N[ewcastle's] Friends will resign and go into serious Opposition, this will be very disagreeable to many of them who have been long in Possession, and are no wise ambitious of the Honor of becoming Independent.

As to myself there is no Point concerning which I am more indifferent than whether the first Minister is to be an Earl of Bute or a Duke of Newcastle, my private Friendships, Mr Fox excepted, are chiefly amongst the discontented Party. However I shall not follow them a Step farther than I think right. As to the Peace, without considering whether it might have been better in some particulars, I believe upon the whole that the Terms are such as reasonable People will approve off. And as to Opposition in general, I may oppose measures which I think wrong. But shall never enter into Engagements with any Factions Opposers who presume to dictate to the Crown merely to gratify their Ambition or their Resentment. I flatter myself Yr R H will excuse this very imperfect Sketch of our present political State, and that Yr R H will believe that tho I may be mistaken in many particulars I have represented every thing exactly as it appears to me.[304]

The peace treaty passed through Parliament with substantial majorities, despite Bute's earlier fears. Despite his sympathy for the ousted Devon-

[304] Waldegrave to Cumberland, n.d. [? 5–9 Nov. 1762]: Add MSS 51380 f. 107.

shire, Waldegrave agreed to second the Lords' Address in reply to the King's speech at the opening of the parliamentary session on 25 November 1762 (speeches 33 and 34), and supported the peace preliminaries themselves on 9 December (speech 35). Had Waldegrave been eager for office, this could have been turned to his advantage. Fox took his revenge on those who had refused to support the Court: the 'Massacre of the Pelhamite Innocents' saw a clean sweep of senior office-holders who were identified with Newcastle. Given this immense authority, the balance of power within the ministry tilted in favour of Fox. The newly vacated places opened up promising opportunities for Fox's friends. Rumours soon circulated about the Earl's future role. W.G. Hamilton reported: 'What is most probable, as things are now circumstanced, is that Lord Waldegrave will be Lord Lieutenant [of Ireland] and his brother the General will be the Secretary'.[305] Edmund Burke confirmed the rumour: 'Ld Waldgrave, if it were not for the General, would not be very fond of it; and as it is, I believe will not pursue it with great earnestness'.[306] It was not to be. Waldegrave held aloof.

After the attack on Pelhamite office-holders in January 1763, Walpole recorded, evidently on Waldegrave's testimony:

The Duke of Cumberland, on these harsh proceedings, said to Lord Waldegrave: 'Fox has deceived me grossly – not, as you think, by giving me up; he might be as angry with me for talking to Newcastle and Pitt – but he has deceived me, for I thought him good-natured; but in all these transactions he has shown the bitterest revenge and inhumanity'.[307]

Waldegrave's loyalty to Cumberland was evidently stronger than his wish to profit from Fox's 'Massacre'. For Fox was now clearly the driving force in the early months of 1763. Horace Walpole wrote:

If Lord Bute countenanced these hostilities, it was but consonant to the folly of his character. Fox had boldness and wickedness enough to undertake whatever the Court wished to compass. Fox seemed so apprehensive of treachery, that he cast about to recover his old connections. By Lord Albemarle, Lord Frederic Cavendish, and Lord Waldegrave, he laboured to be reconciled to the Duke of Cumberland and the Duke of Devonshire. He asked Lord Waldegrave if the former was still incensed against him. The other replied, he had not heard the Duke mention him of late, but supposed his Royal Highness could not be ignorant how much he had been abused by Murphy,[308] known to write under Fox's direction.

[305] W.G. Hamilton to John Hely Hutchinson, 4 Dec. 1762: HMC *Twelfth Report, Appendix IX*, p. 241.
[306] Edmund Burke to Charles O'Hara, 30 Dec. 1762: T.W. Copeland (ed.), *The Correspondence of Edmund Burke*, vol. 1 (Cambridge, 1958), p. 161.
[307] Walpole, *George III*, vol. 1, p. 190.
[308] Arthur Murphy (1725–1805): ed. St Omer 1738–44; actor and playwright; wrote *The Test* in 1757, a pro-Fox rival to the Pittite paper *The ConTest*, and *The Auditor* from 10 June 1762 in defence of the Bute-Fox ministry.

Introduction

'Formerly he did so', said Fox, 'but I had not seen him in a year and a half, till *hearing* how violent the "Auditors" were, I sent for him and stopped them' – an excuse too weak *for* a sensible man to make *to* a sensible man *through* a sensible man. Lord Waldegrave suspected that Fox's views went deeper than reconciliation; for shortly after this conversation Rigby came to the Earl, and sounded him whether he would not take the Treasury, Lord Bute, he said, not being able to stand his ground. As Lord Waldegrave had married my niece, I knew all these intrigues from him, and was actually in his house at the time of this overture, of which he immediately told me with an expressive smile, which in him, who never uttered a bitter word, conveyed the essence of sense and satire.[309]

Bute, demoralised and determined to resign, persuaded the King to offer the Treasury to Fox; but, diffident as ever of the highest responsibility, Fox initially proposed an unnamed 'stop-gap' at the Treasury, with a reinforcement of other talent:

> The persons I would put into great places now, and give access to His Majesty that he might observe and know them, are Lord Gower, Lord Shelburne, and, I think, Lord Waldegrave . . . The third is a man of strict honour, will go through what he engages in without any indiscretion, has great firmness, with great gentleness of manner, is by his friends both respected and beloved, has few enemies, and no view to popularity.[310]

The King was not impressed:

> I never saw anything less calculated to cement, and make a firm administration that [*sc* than] the scheme form'd by Mr Fox; the making Ld. Gower and Ld. Shelburne Secretaries of State would in my opinion be taking two men little fitter than Denbigh Ravensworth and Pomfret or Ld. Talbot: as to Ld. Waldegrave I think him in some things better than the two others, but he would fairly be but a chip in the porrige.[311]

Perhaps Fox intended this scheme to provoke an offer of the Treasury to himself; this was now the result. Faced with the prospect of the highest office, however, Fox's nerve failed him (as Bute's resolution had just failed under the weight of odium heaped upon him). Bute's intermediary reported to Shelburne: 'I am sorry Mr Fox is not to be Minister. That would have done. The next best thing would be to give Lord Waldegrave the Treasury. This, I doubt, Lord Bute won't do.'[312] Bute would hardly name so savage a critic as his successor, and Waldegrave's opposition to the Cider Tax in the Lords on 28 March (speeches 36–8) can only have increased Bute's aversion.

---

[309] Walpole, *George III*, vol. 1, pp. 196–7. For Walpole's growing hostility to Fox, however, see Walpole, *Letters*, vol. 30, pp. 336–43, Appendix 7.
[310] Fox to Bute, 11 March 1763: Fitzmaurice, *Shelburne*, vol. 1, pp. 142–3.
[311] George III to Bute, n.d. [11 March 1763]: Sedgwick, *Letters of George III to Bute*, p. 199.
[312] Calcraft to Shelburne, 15 March 1763: Fitzmaurice, *Shelburne*, vol. 1, p. 147.

Possibly some other office could be found as the price of the 2nd Earl's support? Fox proposed him for Lord Lieutenant of Ireland:

> I have not said enough of Lord Waldegrave. He will do the King's business in Ireland better than anybody whatever, *suaviter et fortiter*, and though he will never join Devonshire House, yet the employing him will disarm and cast a damp upon them more than anything.[313]

Whether this suggestion was put to the Earl is not known. It seems, however, that Fox thought he might be won over by an offer of his father's old post at Paris. Waldegrave replied:

> Tuesday Evening
>
> Dear Sir
> Wishing to change my Mind, I have consider'd what You mention'd this Morning, in almost every different Shape: but without Success.
> It is possible I may be wrong in this Particular, but there is another in which I am sure I am right, in thinking myself extremely obliged to Mr Fox for this and many Instances of his good Opinion, and of his Friendship.
> I am ever most sincerely Yours
> Waldegrave[314]

The letter is endorsed: 'Ld Waldegrave March 29 1763. On my offering him from Ld Bute the Embassy to Paris. The next day he sicken'd of the Small Pox, & alas! dy'd of it.'

For Providence now cut across Waldegrave's career in a way which shocked even men used to sudden and incurable disease. Walpole wrote:

> You will pity my distress, when I tell you that Lord Waldegrave has got the smallpox, and a bad sort. This day se'nnight in the evening I met him at Arthur's; he complained to me of the headache, and a sickness in his stomach. I said, 'My dear Lord, why don't you go home and take James's powder, and you will be well in the morning.' He thanked me, said he was glad I had put him in mind of it, and he would take my advice. I sent in the morning; my niece said he had taken the powder, and that James thought he had no fever, but that she found him very low. As he had no fever, I had no apprehension. At eight o'clock on Friday night, I was told abruptly at Arthur's that Lord Waldegrave had the smallpox. I was excessively shocked, not knowing if the powder was good or bad for it. I instantly went to the house – at the door I was met by a servant of Lady Ailesbury, sent to tell me that Mr Conway was arrived. These two opposite strokes of terror and joy overcame me so much, that when I got to Mr Conway's, I could not speak to him, but burst into a flood of tears. The next morning Lord Waldegrave hearing I was there, desired to speak to me alone – I should tell you that the moment he knew it was the smallpox, he signed his will. This has been the unvaried tenor of his behaviour, doing just what is wise and necessary and nothing more. He told me, he knew how great the chance was against his living through that distemper at his age. That to be sure he

---

[313] Fox to Bute, 17 March 1763: Fitzmaurice, *Shelburne*, vol. 1, p. 149.
[314] Waldegrave to Fox, [29 March 1763]: Add MSS 51380 f. 41.

should like to have lived a few years longer, but if he did not, he should submit patiently. That all he had to desire was, that, if he should fail, we would do our utmost to comfort his wife, who he feared was breeding, and who, he added, was the best woman in the world. I told him he could not doubt our attention to her, but that at present all our attention was fixed on him. That the great difference between having the smallpox young, or more advanced in years, consisted in the fears of the latter, but that as I had so often heard him say, and now saw, that he had none of those fears, the danger of age was considerably lessened. Dr Wilmot says, that if anything saves him, it will be this tranquillity. To my comfort I am told that James's powder has probably been a material ingredient towards his recovery. In the meantime the universal anxiety about him is incredible. Dr Barnard the Master of Eton, who is in town for the holidays, says, that from his situation he is naturally invited to houses of all ranks and parties, and that the concern is general in all. I cannot say so much of my Lord, and not do a little justice to my niece too. Her tenderness, fondness, attention and courage are surprising. She has no fears, to become her, nor heroism, for parade. I could not help saying to her, 'My dear child, there never was a nurse of your age had such attention' – she replied, 'There never was a nurse of my age had such an object.' It is this astonishes one, to see so much beauty sincerely devoted to a man so unlovely in his person. But if Adonis was sick, she could not stir seldomer out of his bedchamber. The physicians seem to have little hopes, but as their arguments are not near so strong as their alarms, I own I do not give it up – and yet I look on it in a very dangerous light.

'I know nothing of news and the world,' apologised Walpole, 'for I go to Albemarle Street [Waldegrave's town house] early in the morning, and don't come home till late at night.'[315]

Waldegrave's honours and places – Knight of the Garter, Lord Steward of Cornwall, Lord Warden of the Stannaries, a Teller of the Exchequer – made his illness of more than academic interest. The vultures began to gather. Lord Harcourt, whom Waldegrave had succeeded in 1752, now wrote: 'I hope Lord Bute wont carry his resolution [of retiring] into execution, till he sees what turn Lord Waldegrave's illness takes. Such a disorder as the small pox at his time of day, may very probably be attended with fatal consequences: which may enable Lord Bute to make an ample provision for one of his [Gilbert Elliot's] sons.'[316] It was too true. Soon Horace Walpole wrote again:

Amidst all my own grief, and all the distress which I have this moment left, I cannot forget you, who have so long been my steady and invariable friend. I cannot leave it to newspapers and correspondents to tell you my loss. Lord Waldegrave died today. Last night we had some glimmerings of hope. The most desponding of the faculty flattered us a little. He himself joked with the physicians, and expressed himself in this engaging manner; asking what day of the week it was, they told him Thursday: 'Sure,' said he, 'it is Friday' – 'No, my Lord, indeed it is Thursday' – 'Well!' said he,

[315] Walpole to Montagu, 6 April 1763: Walpole, *Letters*, vol. 10, p. 55.
[316] Lord Harcourt to Charles Jenkinson, 4 April 1763: N.S. Jucker (ed.), *The Jenkinson Papers* (London, 1949), p. 133.

'see what a rogue this distemper makes one; I want to steal nothing but a day.' By the help of opiates, with which for these two or three days they had numbed his sufferings, he rested well. This morning he had no worse symptoms. I told Lady Waldegrave, that as no material alteration was expected before Sunday, I would go and dine at Strawberry Hill, and return in time to meet the physicians in the evening – in truth I was worn out with anxiety and attendance, and wanted an hour or two of fresh air. I left her at twelve, and had ordered dinner at three that I might be back early. I had not risen from table, when I received an express from Lady Betty Waldegrave, to tell me that a sudden change had happened, that they had given him James's powder, but that they feared it was too late, and that he probably would be dead before I could come to my niece, for whose sake she begged I would return immediately. It was indeed too late! too late for everything – late as it was given, the powder vomited him even in the agonies – had I had power to direct, he should never have quitted James – but these are vain regrets! Vain to recollect, how particularly kind he, who was kind to everybody, was to me! I found Lady Waldegrave at my brother's; she weeps without ceasing, and talks of his virtues and goodness to her in a manner that distracts one. My brother bears this mortification with more courage than I could have expected from his warm passions: but nothing struck me more than to see my rough savage Swiss Louis in tears as he opened my chase. I have a bitter scene to come; tomorrow morning I carry my poor Lady Waldegrave to Strawberry – her fall is great, from that adoration and attention that he paid her, from that splendor of fortune, so much of which dies with him, and from that consideration which rebounded to her from the great deference, which the world had for his character – visions perhaps – yet who could expect that they would have passed away even before that fleeting thing, her beauty?[317]

To Mann, who had never met Waldegrave, Walpole explained the circumstances:

His brother and sister were inoculated, but it was early in the practice of that great preservative, which was then devoutly opposed, he was the eldest son and weakly. He never had any fear of it [smallpox], nor ever avoided it. We scarce feel this heavy loss more than it is felt universally. He was one of those few men, whose good nature silenced even ill nature. His strict honour and consummate sense made him reverenced as much as beloved. He died as he lived, the physicians declaring that if anything saved him, it would be his tranquillity: I soon saw by their ignorance and contradictions that they would not.

Ironically, Lord Bute resigned on the same day.

The same day that put an end to Lord Waldegrave's life gave a period too to the administration of Lord Bute, his supplanter, whom he did not love, and yet whom he could hardly hate, for aversion was not in his nature; nor did ever any man who had undertaken such a post as governor to a prince with the utmost reluctance, and who could not have been totally void of the ambition which must have attended such a charge when once accepted, feel less resentment at the disappointment.[318]

---

[317] Walpole to Montagu, [8 April 1763]: Walpole, *Letters*, vol. 10, p. 58.
[318] Walpole to Mann, 10 April 1763: Walpole, *Letters*, vol. 22, p. 126.

Introduction

Both Maria and Horace Walpole 'received innumerable testimones of the regard, that was felt for Lord Waldegrave – I have heard of but one man [George III], who ought to have known his worth, that has shown no concern – but I suppose his childish mind is too much occupied with the loss of his last governor!' The Court, claimed the bitter Walpole,

don't find any recruits repair to their standard. They brag that they should have had Lord Waldegrave; a most notorious falsehood, as he had refused every offer they could invent, the day before he was taken ill – the Duke of Cumberland orders his servants to say that so far from joining them, he believes if Lord Waldegrave could have been foretold of his death, he would have preferred it to an union with Bute and Fox.[319]

In his *Memoirs*, Walpole speculated on his friend's political role in the 1760s, had death not intervened.

The very day on which the Favourite resigned the reins of government died the man who, of all England, would perhaps have rejoiced the most to behold that event ... With unbounded benevolence, and of the most flowing courtesy to all men, Lord Waldegrave, whose penetration no weakness could escape nor art impose upon, though vice he overlooked, and only abstained sometimes from connecting with black and bad men ... Lord Waldegrave died most unseasonably for his own honour. He stood so high in the esteem of mankind for probity, abilities, and temper, that, if any man could, he might have accomplished a coalition of parties, or thrown sense into that party, which, though acting for the cause of liberty, rather wounded than served it, so ill were they formed for counsel or conduct. Had he lived still longer he must, by the deaths of the chiefs, have been placed incontestably at the head of that party himself. Indeed, but just before his illness, he was much looked up to by very different sets. Lord Bute himself had thought of him for a considerable share on his own retreat; and, but the day before Lord Waldegrave was seized with the small-pox, he had been offered the Embassy to France or Lord-Lieutenancy of Ireland, both of which he peremptorily declined. And yet, after his death, the Court boasted they had gained him, – a report much resented and eagerly contradicted by his friend the Duke of Cumberland.[320]

Had he lived, and had he sought a political career, the opportunities might now have been immense. For British politics notoriously lacked the sort of senior, respected, untarnished figure which Waldegrave had become. After Bute's resignation in April 1763, politics was plunged into a period of turmoil and short-lived ministries from which the King was only rescued in 1770. Ironically, the man who healed these divisions was Lord North, son of Prince George's governor in 1750–1.

Some such possibilities were apparent soon after Waldegrave's death. It had its repercussions in the 2nd Earl's circle. Horace Walpole now learned more about his real friends; Henry Fox, just ennobled, was not among

---
[319] Walpole to Montagu, 14 April 1763: Walpole, *Letters*, vol. 10, p. 62.
[320] Walpole, *George III*, vol. 1, pp. 212–3.

them. 'To my great satisfaction the new Lord Holland has not taken the least friendly, or even formal notice of me, on Lord Waldegrave's death. It dispenses me from the least farther connection with him, and saves explanations, which always entertain the world more than satisfy.' Horace was still comforting his niece.

She said to me t'other day, 'They tell me that if my Lord had lived, he might have done great service to this country at this juncture, by the respect all parties had for him – this is very fine; but as he did not live to do those services, it will never be mentioned in history!' I thought this solicitude for his honour, charming. – But he will be known by history: he has left a small volume of memoirs that are a *chef d'oeuvre*. He twice showed them to me, but I kept his secret faithfully. *Now* it is for his glory to divulge it.[321]

Horace was too optimistic. Waldegrave's *Memoirs* remained unpublished until 1821, for reasons discussed below.

Waldegrave's lucrative offices were lost by his death, and his estate produced only a modest £2300 p.a.. Out of his place as Teller of the Exchequer he had saved enough to endow his three daughters with 'about £8000 apiece'; they married well.[322] It remained only to erect a memorial tablet in Navestock Church. Even in that age of extravagant eulogies, Waldegrave's was remarkable. Its author may have been Frederick Keppel:[323]

> Underneath this MONUMENT are the Remains
> OF THE
> Two first earls of **WALDEGRAVE**, Father and Son,
> both of the Name of JAMES,
> Both Servants of that excellent PRINCE
> KING GEORGE the Second,
> Both by him created Knights of the most noble ORDER OF THE GARTER.

JAMES the Father was employed in foreign Embassies to the Courts of Vienna and Versailles by King GEORGE the First, and by King GEORGE the Second; and he did his Court and Country Honour and Service, and was respected wherever his Negotiations made him known. In his private Capacity, the Affability and Benevolence of his Disposition, and the Goodness of his Understanding, made him beloved and esteemed throughout his Life.

The Antiquity of his illustrious and noble Family is equal to that of most that may be named in any Country or Time, and needs not to be here recited.

He died of the Dropsy and Jaundice on the 3d of April,[324] 1741, aged 57.

His eldest Son JAMES before-mentioned, and interred within this Vault, died of the Small-pox, on the 8th of April 1763, aged 48.

[321] Walpole to Montagu, 22 April 1763: Walpole, *Letters*, vol. 10, p. 67.
[322] Walpole to Montagu, 14 April 1763: *loc. cit.*
[323] It was printed, evidently for circulation among family and friends, and is here reproduced from a copy in the Lewis Walpole Library, Farmington, Connecticut.
[324] *Sc.* 11th April. The date is inscribed correctly on the memorial tablet.

Introduction

THESE were his Years in Number; what they were in Wisdom, hardly belongs to Time. The universal Respect paid to him while he lived, and the universal Lamentation at his Death, are ample Testimonies of a Character not easily to be paralleled. He was for many Years the chosen Friend and Favourite of a King, who was a Judge of Men, yet never that King's Minister, though a Man of Business, Knowledge and Learning, beyond most of his Cotemporaries; but Ambition visited him not, and Contentment filled his Hours. Appealed to for his Arbitration by various contending Parties in the State, upon the highest Differences, his Judgment always tempered their Dissentions, while his own Principles, which were the Freedom of the People and the Maintenance of the Laws, remained stedfast and unshaken, and his Influence unimpaired, though exercised through a long series of Struggles, that served as Foils to his disinterested Virtue. The Constancy and Firmness of his Mind were Proof against every Trial but the Distresses of Mankind, and therein he was as a Rock with many Springs, and his Generosity was as the Waters that flow from it nourishing the Plains beneath. He was wise in the first Degree of Wisdom, Master of a powerful and delicate Wit, had as ready a Conception and as quick Parts as any Man that ever lived, and never lost his Wisdom in his Wit, nor his Coolness by Provocation. He smiled at Things that drive other Men to Anger. He was a Stranger to Resentment, not to Injuries; those feared him most that loved him; yet he was revered by all, for he was as true a Friend as ever bore that Name, and as generous an Enemy as ever bad Man tried. He was in all Things undisturbed, modest, placid and humane. To him broad Day-light and the Commerce of the World were as easy as the Night and Solitude. To him the Return of Night and Solitude must have been a Season of ever blest Reflection. To him this now deep Night must through the Merits of his Redeemer Jesus Christ be everlasting Peace and Joy.

O Death, thy Sting is to the Living! O Grave, thy Victory is over the unburied, the Wife---the Child---the Friend that is left behind?

THUS saith the Widow of this incomparable Man, his once most happy Wife, now the faithful Remembrancer of all his Virtues, MARIA Countess Dowager of WALDEGRAVE, who inscribes this Tablet to his beloved Memory.

THE PUBLICATION OF THE MEMOIRS

At the time of their first publication in 1821, only one manuscript version of the *Memoirs* was known to exist.[325] Their editor, Lord Holland, wrote:

> The work is printed from a manuscript in the hand-writing of the author, which was found by his heirs after his death, and has remained ever since that event in the possession of the Waldegrave family. It was communicated to Lord Orford [as Horace Walpole became in 1791], who speaks of it with great praise in his printed correspondence, and shows, by borrowing many remarks and even expressions from it in his Memoires, that he had perused it with diligence and attention.[326]

Maria, subsequently Duchess of Gloucester, wife of the 2nd Earl Waldegrave, died in 1807, bequeathing her books (and presumably her papers) to

---
[325] The Murray Ms, discussed below, pp. 134-40.
[326] [Lord Holland], 'To the Reader', *Memoirs*, pp. xxi-xxii.

her grandson John, 6th Earl Waldegrave. He figures in the family annals as a black sheep, and it seems reasonable to suppose that he did not lavish much effort on exploring the family archive.

Nevertheless, it was via this Earl that the publishing history of the *Memoirs* became caught up in that of Horace Walpole's more voluminous writings. At his death in 1797, Walpole's will was discovered to leave a sealed trunk to the next Earl Waldegrave who should reach the age of 25 years. In 1810 John, 6th Earl Waldegrave attained the required age; the chest was opened, and found to contain the manuscripts of Horace Walpole's own *Memoirs* of the reigns of George II and George III.[327] It was a superb archive, destined to become one of the most important sources for the history of mid-eighteenth-century England. Whatever the reaction of the historian, however, their new owner was 'to my shame be it said ... greatly disappointed that it was not [?stow'd] with silver gold or precious jewels',[328] and the collection was neglected for ten years more.

The 6th Earl was no scholar. Before his seventeenth birthday, in 1802, he had been found a commission as Ensign in the Third Foot Guards, and launched on a career of war, amorous adventure and disastrous financial profligacy which took him from the Mediterranean through policing the Luddite disturbances and the Peninsular campaign to Wellington's staff in 1815. With the arrival of peace his spendthrift existence caught up with him, and the demands of creditors became ever more pressing. In 1811 the family's main seat, Navestock Hall in Essex, built by the 1st Earl, had been demolished for reasons of economy. By the end of the decade the 6th Earl, seeking other means of raising funds, turned to his family archive. He asked the opinion of his distant (and highly literate) kinsman Henry Richard Vassall Fox, 3rd Baron Holland (1773–1840), on the publication both of the Waldegrave and Walpole *Memoirs*. Holland had long been a family friend, had helped Waldegrave to solicit for promotion in the army,[329] and had taken a leading part in trying to rescue the young Earl's tottering finances. Moreover, Lord Holland was obsessed by his family's political record since the early eighteenth century[330] and delighted to be given access to so rich a source. In March 1820 he reported at length to the 6th Earl:

In the first place I must thank you & I do most sincerely, for relieving my gout by a very entertaining occupation & still more for the mark of your confidence in consulting me on the propriety of publishing Ld Orford's curious & interesting MSS. Should this business prevail upon you to come sometimes & talk the matter over with me, & thus procure Lady H. & myself the pleasure of seeing you more

[327] Walpole, *George II*, vol. 1, p. xv.
[328] Waldegrave to Holland, 'Monday' [?13 March 1820]: Add MSS 51598, n.f.
[329] Waldegrave to Holland, 18 Oct 1811: Add MSS 51598, nf.
[330] Leslie Mitchell, *Holland House* (London, 1980).

Introduction

frequently than we have done of late, I shall feel yet more obliged to you for the favor you have conferred.

I have proceeded in a very businesslike, you will perhaps think a very tiresome way – but do not be alarmed at my voluminous enclosures, they are not so long as they look –

There is in the first instance a list of the contents of your box as I received it, for Sr James Mackintosh not having finished his extracts,[331] has still in his custody eleven pieces (viz seven volumes & 4 parcels) which I have not seen & of which I can form no judgment tho' I understand they relate to a more recent period & are in a much more unfinished state than those which I have perused.

Holland's report read:

The memoirs of Lord Waldegrave, marked no. 6 in my list, are well written very entertaining & quite fit for publication – They do him great credit & have no fault but that of being very short & treating of a very limited period. Their value must be considerable – They require nothing but a short notice of the life character & family of the Author. The memoirs of the last nine years of George the 2d . . . are prepared for publication by the Author himself with great care & accuracy. They form a separate & complete work throw great light on history & more on many important Characters of that period, & are too valuable to be withheld from the publick – They might in my judgement be published in the shape in which the Author left them with no alterations & few omissions. One or two disgusting unimportant & ill-authenticated anecdotes might be suppressed & some few coarse epithets not suited to our present taste, & such as probably the Author would himself have discarded, might be softened or omitted – Such omissions should not be left entirely to the discretion of a bookseller but entrusted to some one of judgement & delicacy.

The *Memoirs* of George the 3d . . . tho' neatly transcribed they are not, especially as they advance, completely prepared for publication by the Author. From regard to his memory as well as to the feelings of the friends & families of many mentioned in them some time consideration judgement & diligence should be employed in preparing them for the press – The omission of such parts as are highly discreditable to him, as a man or an author, (and there are such) & the refutation in notes of such misstatements or exaggerations relating to others as can be easily explained, are I think necessary & the suppression of some private scandal yet more so – with such precautions the objections to the publication might be removed & it would certainly contain much entertaining matter & useful information. With respect to particular passages, individuals, especially Mrs Damer[332] should be consulted. I could myself furnish documents to vindicate my Grandfather from some very heavy charges & probably the Duke of Grafton & Lord Buckingham could do the same for the late Duke & Mr George Grenville, for to all of these & indeed to most publick men the author is apt to impute the basest & sometimes the most horrible motives on bare surmise, & yet with so much confidence that the

---

[331] The extracts from Walpole's *Memoirs* 1756–8 are now in the Mackintosh Papers: Add MSS 34523, ff. 10–27. For Mackintosh, see below, pp. 120–1.

[332] Anne Seymour Damer (1749–1828), only daughter of Horace Walpole's close friend Henry Seymour Conway. Walpole patronised her, made her his executrix, and left her a right to a life tenancy of Strawberry Hill. From her the house passed to Earl Waldegrave in 1811.

assertion unless contradicted by some contemporary evidence would carry with it all the authority of an eyewitness of the transactions.

On the whole I think this part of your valuable *MSS* should not be entirely suppressed & cannot be very long withheld from the publick without defeating the intention of the writer & depriving those for whom he collected such a variety of historical anecdotes & so lively a picture of the manners & politicks of the time, of the entertainment & instruction to which they are in some sense entitled. On the other hand, I think, a crude publication of them without comment correction or explanation would be painful to many still alive & in some instances substantially injurious to the cause of truth.[333]

Waldegrave authorised Lord Holland, better experienced in such matters, to negotiate for him; Holland approached John Murray II (1778–1843), publisher of the *Quarterly Review* and intimate of most of the major figures of literary London, including Byron, Canning, Coleridge, Croker, Scott, Southey and Madame de Staël. Bargaining ensued. Holland wrote to Murray:

I wrote a letter to you last week which by some accident Lord Lauderdale who had taken charge of it has mislaid. The object of it was to request you to call here some morning & to let me know the hour by a line by two-penny post. I am authorised to dispose of two historical works, the one a short but admirably written & interesting memoir of the late Ld Waldegrave who was a favourite of George the 2d & governor of George the 3 when Prince of Wales.

The second consists of three close written volumes of Memoirs by Horace Walpole (afterwards Ld Orford) which comprise the last nine years of George the second's reign.

I am anxious to give you the refusal of them as I hear you have already expressed a wish to publish any thing of the kind written by Horace Walpole & had indirectly conveyed that wish to Lord Waldegrave, to whom these and many other MSS. of that lively & laborious writer belong ...

Lord Lauderdale has offered to assist me in adjusting the terms of the agreement & perhaps you will arrange with him, who lives at Warren's Hotel Waterloo Place, where you can make it convenient to meet him. I would meet you there or call at your house but before you can make any specifick offer you will no doubt like to look at the MSS which are here & which (not being mine) I do not like to expose unnecessarily to the risk even of a removal to London & back again.[334]

Murray was insufficiently impressed. Holland wrote again:

It appears I confess to me that you are either not aware of the interesting nature of the MSS which I shewed you or that the indifference produced by the present frenzy about the Queen's business[335] to all literary publications, has discouraged you from an undertaking in which you would otherwise engage most willingly. However to come to the point. I have consulted Ld Waldegrave on the subject & we

---

[333] Holland to Waldegrave, Holland House, 22 March 1820: Waldegrave MSS at Chewton. Drafts: Add MSS 51598 ff. 193–4, 195–7.
[334] Holland to Murray, Holland House [endorsed 'November 1820']: JMP.
[335] The trial of Queen Caroline lasted from August to November 1820.

Introduction

agree that the two works viz his Grandfather Ld Waldegrave's Memoirs – & Horace Walpole's Memoirs of the Last Nine Years of George II should not be sold for less than three thousand guineas. If that sum would meet your ideas or if you have any other offer to make I will thank you to let me know before the second of next month. I am likely to be in the country for the next ten days & I have not hitherto mentioned the subject of these MSS to any publisher or bookseller as both Ld Waldegrave & myself were anxious to give you the refusal. It will however for obvious reasons be inconvenient to me & disadvantageous to Ld Waldegrave not to terminate the negotiations soon you will therefore excuse my pressing you for an answer time enough to enable us (in case of your refusal) to enter into an arrangement with others for publishing the works next Spring.[336]

Three thousand guineas was a high price. Murray asked a reader (probably William Gifford) for an opinion. He evidently wrote of Walpole's work:

This book of yours is a singular thing. It is ill written, deficient in grammar, and often in English; and yet it interests, and even amuses, now the subjects of it are all, I suppose gone "ad plures"; otherwise it would be intolerable. The writer richly deserves a kicking or a cudgelling at every page, and yet I am ashamed to say I have travelled unwearied with him thro' the whole, divided between a grin and a scowl. I never saw nor heard of such an animal, a splenetic, bustling kind of a poco-corante.[337] By the way if you happen to hear of any plan for making me a king, be so good as to say that I am deceased; or tell any other good-natured lie to put the king-makers off their purpose. I really cannot submit to be the only slave in the nation, especially when I have a crossing to sweep within five yards of my door, & may gain my bread with less ill usage than a king is obliged to put up with, if half that is here told be true. Lord H- seems to me to tread on

'ignes
Suppositos cineri doloso'

in retouching any part of the manuscript. He is so perfectly kind and good-natured, that he will feel more than any man the complaints of partiality and injustice etc; and where he is to stop, I see not. There is so much abuse that little is gained by an occasional erasure, while suspicion is excited. He would have consulted his quiet more by leaving the author to bear the blame of his own scandal.

Publisher and editor eventually settled on a price of £2,500, which was paid to Waldegrave, through Lord Holland, by November 1821.[338]

Lord Holland reported to the owner:

I have been more lucky in my negotiation than I expected when I last saw you – Read this letter & return it – I shall give Murray the MSS before Thursday & your first instalment will therefore be due on the 1st of May 1821. If you could discover

---

[336] Holland to Murray, n.d.: JMP.
[337] Poco-curante: one who cares little, is indifferent.
[338] JMP; printed inaccurately in Samuel Smiles, *Memoir and Correspondence of the Late John Murray, with an Account of the Origin and Progress of the House, 1768–1843* (2 vols, London, 1891), vol. 2, pp. 88–90.

the plates of Bentley & Müntch it would be handsome to Murray to make him a present of them & would add to the value of the book.³³⁹

The value of the *Memoirs* soon became a question. The unfriendly reviewer in the *Literary Gazette* complained:

A rivulet of text, flowing through a beautiful broad margin; very thick paper, and a frontispiece of the author's head, apparently of the same kind, are the obvious features of this publication... when noblemen who have manuscripts to sell, either on their own account or on account of their friends, manage the business in the style of Jew brokers, the unavoidable result is, that they must be left in oblivion, or that booksellers, paying an enormous price for them, must re-levy the same upon the public in the shape of expensive volumes. This very book, with hardly matter for a good pamphlet (we could cram some four of its pages into one of our columns), ought not to have exceeded a moderate octavo; but having been, as we have heard, hawked about among *the trade*, till it was bid up to twice as much as it was worth, there was no option but to superadd Davison's skill and Murray's splendour, and charge the whole upon the rich class of buyers, and the unfortunate class of readers.³⁴⁰

The reviewer in the *Quarterly* felt impelled to

make an observation or two on the price of this book. It is a thin 4to of 176 pages, and contains not more letterpress than might fill about fifty pages of our Review, and therefore, although the paper and type are very splendid, the price of twenty-five shillings charged for it may appear enormous, and so we confess it seemed to us till we heard of the enormous sum given for the copyright.

At least, reflected the reviewer, such high prices had 'awakened out of the dust of the family scrutoirs' Horace Walpole's *Memoirs*.³⁴¹ Holland was concerned to vindicate his reputation as an editor from any low commercial considerations, writing to his son Charles in November 1821:

Walpole's Memoir*es*, for so he spells them, will be out in a few weeks – ill written but very entertaining, and from the dearth of all good histories of that period, 1751 to 1760, very readable. The notes signed E are mine, but I shall have nothing to do with the preface. Apropos of Memoirs, I wish you would take every opportunity of contradicting a false impression likely to be produced by the review of Waldegrave's Memoirs in the Quarterly. I edited it, wrote the preface and supplied the Appendix, and I made the bargain with Murray for Ld Waldegrave. But I was in no way interested in the sale myself; and the price given for the work, which the Quarterly states to be exorbitant, included the purchase of Walpole's *Memoires*, a work at least four times as long and relating to a much longer period of history. For Walpole's Memoires and Waldegrave's short work Murray gave 2500£, of which no more than 500£ can be supposed to be given for the smaller book.³⁴²

---

³³⁹ Holland to Waldegrave, Holland House, 30 Oct [1820]: Waldegrave MSS at Chewton.
³⁴⁰ *The Literary Gazette and Journal*, 7 April 1821, p. 211.
³⁴¹ *The Quarterly Review* 25 (1831), pp. 413-4.
³⁴² Quoted in the Earl of Ilchester, *Chronicles of Holland House 1820–1900* (London, 1937), pp. 24–5.

Introduction

Among the attractions of dealing with the firm of Murray was its wide connections in literary London. One of the more flamboyant figures in that world now made an unexpected contribution to the historiography which Lord Holland was helping to formulate. John Murray had seemingly sent his editor a manuscript copy of Byron's blasphemous and seditious attack on the recently deceased George III, 'The Vision of Judgement', which obviously appealed to Lord Holland's anticlerical and republican proclivities.[343] Holland replied:

> Allow me to thank you for your note & enclosure. The latter, which I return, is full of wit & fancy, of satire & gaiety. Perhaps I enjoy it more than those whose reverence for the late King's publick character is greater than my own & who will be shocked at his political delinquencies being made the vehicle for ridiculing an injudicious panegyrist.[344] Your letter is very obliging. The time I have devoted to Walpole's work has been very amusing, & in some measure instructive to me & I should feel very happy if I could believe my labours in any degree contributed to the success of the publication. I wrote a long letter to you yesterday on the subject of the MSS of both memoirs, Waldegrave's & Walpole's. As however the purport of it was to communicate to you Ld Waldegrave's wishes & intentions, of which I am sure you will approve, I enclosed it for his perusal before I sent it to you & he has not hitherto returned it.[345]

When it arrived, John Murray read:

> You were so good as readily to acquiesce in a suggestion of mine to restore to Ld Waldegrave the two bound books of the MS in which the original etchings by Bentley & Müntch were preserved, but as since that period you have very judiciously resolved to annex to the printed work engraved copies of those etchings, I am authorized by Ld Waldegrave to request you to keep the MS & to consider it to all intents & purposes as your own property. He is indeed not only willing but desirous you should do so.[346]

Under the same arrangement (whether by confusion or design is unclear) the manuscript of the Waldegrave *Memoirs* passed into the ownership of John Murray and remained in the firm's hands until 1970. Lord Holland believed Murray made a profit on the venture.[347] Murray's ledgers show

---

[343] Cf. John Murray to Holland, 'Thursday' [late 1821]: Add MSS 51382, n.f.

[344] Robert Southey's 'A Vision of Judgement', a funeral ode for George III, was published on 11 April 1821. Byron's satire of nearly the same title was written in reply between May and October of that year, but reputable booksellers were rightly cautious. When it was eventually published in the first number of John Hunt's journal *The Liberal*, 15 October 1822, a private prosecution for criminal libel followed, and Hunt was duly convicted: cf. W.H. Wickwar, *The Struggle for the Freedom of the Press 1819–1832* (London, 1928), pp. 270–3. Such was the preferred reading matter of the editor of the Waldegrave and Walpole *Memoirs*; the involvement of Holland House with the working out of an anti-royalist historiography is explored below.

[345] Holland to Murray, 21 Dec. 1821: JMP.

[346] Holland to Murray, 21 Dec 1821: JMP; draft, Add MSS 51832, n.f.

[347] Walpole, *George II*, vol. 2, p. xvii, n.3.

the contrary, however, and his firm's rights were sold, after his death, to the publisher Henry Colburn.[348] John Brooke recorded that between 1843 and 1845 the 7th Earl Waldegrave sold to Richard Bentley, the publisher, the manuscripts of Walpole's memoirs and journals, and that Frances, dowager Countess Waldegrave, bought them back in 1856; hence their present location at Chewton House.[349]

Whatever their ownership, however, Lord Holland at once set about editing both works for publication. The Waldegrave *Memoirs* were evidently not in his hands for long: the text was sent to press first, and the editor contented himself with assembling a brief preface and appendix while the main text was with the printer. Most of his attention was devoted instead to the far longer work, Walpole's *George II*. To it Lord Holland added notes defending the conduct of his grandfather Henry Fox, and from the text he omitted those passages which had been physically cut from it, evidently in *c*. 1810–16 by Lady Elizabeth Laura Waldegrave, whose sense of propriety or family loyalty had been offended.[350] But in the case of the Waldegrave *Memoirs*, Holland worked from the 2nd Earl's careful and cautious revision: no such excisions were evidently necessary. Holland wrote:

> The duties of an editor have been very simple and easy. Not a syllable has been suppressed. Neither comment nor emendation have been found necessary. His humble labours have been confined to the correction of the press, and the annexation of a few marginal notes for the convenience of the reader.[351]

Holland added an appendix of letters from Henry Fox, and some extracts from Dodington's *Diary*, designed to vindicate Fox's conduct in the manœuvres of 1754–7 and denigrate that of the Duke of Newcastle, who, in 1754, maintained the editor, 'seems to have entertained the project of engrossing all ministerial power entirely to himself'.[352] Holland's brief and superficial introduction to the volume was an uncritical eulogy of Waldegrave, implying that it was hardly surprising that so virtuous a man should have been perceptively critical of the youthful character of Prince George, and should have found himself in the political wilderness after the accession of his former pupil in 1760.

---

[348] Murray's accounts, JMP, set off the fee of £2,500 against the Walpole *Memoirs* alone; if a sum of £500 is included in the account of the Waldegrave *Memoirs*, it is clear that both publications finally made a small loss.

[349] Walpole, *George II*, vol. 1, pp. xvii-xviii.

[350] Waldegrave allowed Holland to retain these passages. They survive in the Fox papers: Walpole, *George II*, vol. 2, p. xvi, n.2. For the history of erasures and excisions from Horace Walpole's letters to Mann, especially of passages concerning the Waldegrave family, see Walpole, *Letters*, vol. 26, pp. 36–42, Appendix 12. Again, Lady Elizabeth Laura seems to have been responsible.

[351] [Lord Holland], 'To the Reader' in *Memoirs*, pp. xxii–xxiii.   [352] *Ibid.*, p. 145.

Introduction

The reviewer in the *Literary Gazette* had observed: 'There is an address *To the Reader* prefixed to the work, which shows that the custodes of the papers were more competent to sell them well, than to write a good preface to them.' Holland was, indeed, a mediocre editor.[353] To elucidate the text of Waldegrave's *Memoirs* he added just one footnote; and even this was supplied by another. Walpole's *Memoires* were his chief concern, and he found little to say either about the 2nd Earl Waldegrave or his family. His problems were compounded by the shortcomings of the manuscripts' owner. John, 6th Earl Waldegrave combined an indifference to literary matters with an inability to answer his editor's letters requesting information. Lord Holland wrote repeatedly with a string of questions:

Do not forget to procure the dates of your maternal Grandfather's birth, marriage & death – & of his various appointments – If you have any correspondence of his relating to publick affairs or any traditional account of his education travels character or public conduct they may be interesting to the Reader of the Memoirs & help to swell the volume which, I fear will be rather too scanty – Perhaps you have some letters to him from George 2d – or from the Duke of Cumberland – if they are of the same date as the Memoirs, between 1754 & 1758 they will be a valuable addition. Let me know too, as soon as you can, 1) who inherited his papers & MSS 2) where the Memoir has been kept since his death & 3) how & when it descended to you.[354]

The 6th Earl evidently supplied copies of the memorial inscriptions in Navestock church, but little more.[355] Holland wrote:

Many thanks for the copy of epitaphs at Navestock – The points which we wish *just now* most particularly to ascertain are at what school if any, & at what college, if any, James 2d Earl Waldegrave was educated? If he travelled as [a] young man & with whom? & when he returned? In short any particulars about the early part of his life – I think you must have some of his correspondence – & as to his schools colleges & tutors it is not impossible that Ld Radstock[356] or Lady Cardigan[357] might recollect hearing from their father or from your mother something of his early connections.

With respect to the queries relating to Walpole's works there is not at this moment any hurry – but your Grandfather's memoirs together with an appendix

[353] It should be remembered that Lord Holland was an active politician at the centre of public affairs, preoccupied with the trial of Queen Caroline in 1820, with parliamentary business during the winter of 1820–1, and absent in France for 'five or six months' from 5 May 1821, while the *Memoirs* were in the press. See Henry Richard Vassall, Third Lord Holland, *Further Memoirs of the Whig Party 1807–1821* (ed. Lord Stavordale, London, 1905), pp. 276–304; Holland to John Murray, 4 May 1821: draft, Add MSS 51832, n.f.
[354] Holland to Waldegrave, Old Burlington Street [postmarked 17 Nov 1820]: Waldegrave MSS at Chewton.
[355] They were not difficult to discover, having been printed in [P. Muilman], *A New and Complete History of Essex . . . By a Gentleman* (6 vols, Chelmsford, 1769–72), vol. 4, pp. 52–3.
[356] William, 1st Baron Radstock (1753–1825), 2nd son of the 3rd Earl Waldegrave.
[357] Elizabeth (1758–1823), elder daughter of John, 3rd Earl Waldegrave married in 1791 James, 5th Earl of Cardigan.

are actually printed & finished & nothing is wanting to the publication but a short notice of his life – he seems to have been so amiable & so sensible a man that one wishes if possible to know something more about him than the scanty & common-place relations which a Peerage book usually furnishes. There is a print of him from Sir Joshua's picture, engraved in 1762[358] – Is the original of that picture yours? – If you have a good portrait of him & another of George 2d Murray might like to have one or the other engraved & at any rate would like the offer.

Walpole's Memoires are very entertaining but they are occasionally so abusive that I rejoice in not having advised you to part with any subsequent to 1760. Ten years more must pass before even truth can [breaks off].[359]

Lord Holland tried to prompt Waldegrave about the provenance of the manuscript. Was it really in the 2nd Earl's hand?

The Manuscript was left I conclude with all his family papers to his brother, your maternal Grandfather from whom it has descended to you. Was it with the family papers at Navestock – or did your Mother keep it separately – any little Anecdote about it – or about him will be acceptable – for instance when your Mother quoted him as your *sensible* Grandfather what did she quote from him – He was as far as I can collect a very judicious amiable accomplished & slovenly Man. I should like to know something more of him.[360]

It was in vain. Holland's Introduction contained almost no hard information about the 2nd Earl. The 6th Earl evidently pleaded that nothing had survived. Holland replied impatiently, having – too late – discovered the survival of the papers of the 1st Earl.

Why you think that our Excellent Author has transmitted nothing to you I do not understand – you have his fun & a good portion of his sense too if you would use it, but you ought to pray to the Gods for a little more impudence & activity. It seems by Coxe[361] that there is a diary of your Grandfather in existence. I wish I had known this it might have been curious & at any rate would have helped to eke out our scanty but interesting Volume which now waits for one sentence on the place of his Education. I hate being baffled in such a trifle.[362]

But baffled he was. Holland wrote to the Provost of Eton in search of information, but Goodall could not find 'a single List of Eton School within ten Years of the required Date'.[363] At Oxford, the Dean of Christ Church received a similar request. Henry Fox, then an undergraduate at that college, wrote disrespectfully to his father:

---

[358] This print was used for the frontispiece of Holland's edition.
[359] Holland to Waldegrave, Old Burlington Street, 28 Jan 1821: Waldegrave MSS at Chewton; letter incomplete.
[360] Holland to Waldegrave, n.d.: Waldegrave MSS at Chewton.
[361] Coxe, *Walpole*, vol. 1, p. 349; vol. 3, p. 26.
[362] Holland to Waldegrave, 8 Feb 1821: Waldegrave MSS at Chewton.
[363] J. Goodall to Holland, 'Cloisters, Windsor', 26 Feb 1821: Add MSS 51832, n.f.

Introduction

The Dean I suppose called upon you in town about Ld Waldegrave's education which does not seem to have received its last touch here. Are you as industrious as you were before I went about the book[?] Murray will be astounded at the activity of one not distinguished for diligence in general.[364]

Lord Holland admitted defeat, writing in his introduction to the *Memoirs* that the 2nd Earl 'seems at an early period of life to have been well instructed in antient and modern languages; but we have been hitherto unable to ascertain the place of his education, and the names of those entrusted with the care of it'.

Perhaps stung to action by his editor's reproaches, the 6th Earl then discovered a second version of the *Memoirs*, now known as the Chewton manuscript. After the publication of Holland's edition, the editor wrote to John Murray:

I believe I told you that Lord Waldegrave, since the publication of his Grandfather's Memoirs, has discovered another manuscript of them, in which there are some slight variations. This copy is written in a sort of common place book containing a variety of other things some of which are in no way connected with the printed Memoirs, but Ld Waldegrave requests me to say that he will furnish you with a copy of all the variations that you may make the use you think proper of them in any subsequent edition – In the same book is a page & half annexed to the end of [the] memoirs announcing an intention of continuing them which seems never to have been executed – & there are besides thirteen pages in MS entitled 'Anecdotes of the first three days of the new Reign', written in 1760. These last two papers Lord Waldegrave is willing to have copied & delivered to you with full permission to annex them to any future edition ... Whenever such an edition takes place, I should also like to be apprized in time, as I have ascertained some circumstances respecting James Ld Waldegrave which might with propriety be introduced into the preface.[365]

It was too late; the present is the first edition to be based on the Chewton manuscript, though it found its way into Holland's possession. Nor did Holland use the 2nd Earl's speeches, preserved among the Holland House papers and printed below.

This accident in the use of texts was to be of decisive importance in the way the historiography of the subject developed in the decades after 1821. Waldegrave's bitter satires against Bute and the Princess were largely unknown; his speeches, revealing the complexities and failures of his own political career, were likewise unpublished. The Chewton manuscript, in which the author's stresses and resentments found expression, was returned to the archives. Consequently, Waldegrave was depicted as the embodiment of disinterested probity.

---

[364] Henry Fox to Holland [postmarked 27 Feb 1821]: Add MSS 51748, n.f.
[365] Holland to Murray, 21 Dec. 1821: JMP. Draft: Add MSS 51382, n.f.

Lord Waldegrave is described by the editor of these memoirs, as possessing a temper of extreme mildness and serenity, as inclining to quiet and indolence, which led him to avoid the turbulence of political storms, and at the same time tempered those disappointments which he met with even in his comparatively peaceable course. The same character is given of him by his cotemporaries; and it is strikingly evinced, by the mild and placid strain of his observations on transactions and characters with which he was himself deeply involved.[366]

But Waldegrave was not a dispassionate spectator, a Victorian 'authority'. He was passionately involved, an active and fallible participant.

THE HISTORICAL INFLUENCE OF THE MEMOIRS

Like their editor, reviewers too had little to go on apart from the text of the *Memoirs* themselves. As Lord Holland had discovered, few original documents from those years were yet in print[367] beyond the 1784 edition of George Bubb Dodington's *Diary*.[368] Nevertheless, the circumstances of the education, accession and political conduct of George III had long been a matter of the keenest controversy, especially among interested parties.[369] Now the most senior Whig politician of his day, kinsman both of Henry Fox and of Charles James Fox, carried the debate a stage further. Holland's editorial activity was common knowledge. The Waldegrave *Memoirs* were therefore highly newsworthy, and provoked immediate controversy.

The popular *Literary Gazette* pointed out, on 7 April 1821, that the *Memoirs* contained 'a good deal of curious matter', and recognised that 'The period to which that information refers, is also one of so much party and constitutional consequence, that even the mightier events of our own times fail to obliterate its memory or efface its importance'. The *New Monthly Magazine* seized on Waldegrave's character-sketch of Prince George, so unlike the later character of George III, to question the author's impartiality:

[366] *The New Edinburgh Review*, vol. 1 (July-Oct 1821), p. 3.
[367] In 1814, John Murray had published *Memoirs by a Celebrated Literary and Political Character*, which dealt with the years 1742–57, and in detail with 1754–57. Their author, Richard Glover (?1712–85), was an MP with tenuous links with Leicester House; he made some disparaging remarks about George II but said nothing of developments at the junior Court. The work is chiefly concerned with ministerial manoeuvres.
[368] Henry Penruddocke Wyndham (ed.), *The Diary of the Late George Bubb Dodington* (Salisbury, 1784). Wyndham was an ally of Christopher Wyvill and was concerned to promote the cause of parliamentary reform by exposing the electoral practices of the 1750s. His preface disparaged Dodington's venal motives, but said nothing against Leicester House or the education of the future King.
[369] The debate is partly reconstructed in Herbert Butterfield, *George III and the Historians* (London, 1957). But it seems that Sir Herbert overestimated the lasting influence of John Adolphus' *The History of England from the Accession of George III* (1802), a work favourable to that monarch, and underestimated the influence of the hostile historiography devised by the Holland House circle. The debate is brought down to the present in Ian R. Christie, 'George III and the Historians – Thirty Years On', *History* 71 (1986), 205–21.

Introduction

That some change or other operated 'greatly to his Royal Highness's advantage', will, we believe, be acknowledged by most who contrast the activity, the sincerity, the many virtues of our late beloved monarch, with this most unpromising portrait of him when Prince of Wales. It must be remembered, that Lord Waldegrave, notwithstanding the excellence of his character, and the suavity of his manners, was never a favourite with either the Princess of Wales or her son; probably from being the acknowledged one of the King: hence they treated him with a degree of injustice, which it was not in human nature entirely to forgive ... we may ... reasonably suppose his delineation of the Prince of Wales to be one of the few instances, in which private feeling somewhat warped his otherwise dispassionate judgement. That he was not apt to suffer this to be the case, his impartial portraits of the Duke of Newcastle, Mr Fox, the Earl of Bute, and others, whom he politically and almost personally disliked, are sufficient and honourable proofs.[370]

The *British Critic*, in a brief notice, observed that 'The Ex-Governor speaks as ill of his pupil as decency will allow'; its reviewer was convinced of 'the error, and the prejudice of the narrator' after Waldegrave's dismissal from his post, but did not develop the theme.[371]

The *British Review*, in its June 1821 issue, blamed the conflicts at Leicester House on the designs and intrigues of the Dowager Princess, but was chiefly concerned to draw a sceptical moral about the value of conventional history:

We have seen what were the real causes that led to the establishment of Pitt and his associates in ministerial power. They are not of a very dignified order: the irresolution and timidity of some, the treachery of others, the interestedness of many, and especially their unwillingness to exclude themselves from the benign rays of the rising sun, by serving faithfully an aged monarch. Let us however turn to the page of vulgar history, and we shall find the scene wonderfully changed. There, forsooth, we behold Pitt soaring into office on the wings of genius and virtue, borne up by the breath of disinterested patriotism, and of enthusiastic popular favour.[372]

Other reviewers were able to go deeper, however. Among serious journals the *Quarterly Review* was first off the mark, reviewing Waldegrave's *Memoirs* alone in its April-July issue of 1821; the *Edinburgh Review* delayed until June-November 1822 in order to deal with Waldegrave and Horace Walpole's *Memoires of the Last Ten Years of the Reign of George II* together.

John Wilson Croker,[373] writing anonymously in the *Quarterly*, quickly grasped the significance of Waldegrave's evidence. To Croker the crisis of 1754–7 was 'one of the most extraordinary and chaotic negotiations, or rather struggles, which ever occurred between contending statesmen', and

---

[370] *The New Monthly Magazine* 1 (1821), pp. 500–4, at p. 504.
[371] *The British Critic*, 16 (August 1821), pp. 165–6.
[372] *The British Review and London Critical Journal*, 17 (June 1821), pp. 362–80, at p. 379.
[373] John Wilson Croker (1780–1857): ed. Trinity College, Dublin and Lincoln's Inn; MP 1807–32; a founder of *The Quarterly Review*, 1809, to which he contributed prolifically until 1854. Secretary of the Admiralty, 1809–30. For his literary career see M.F. Brightfield, *John Wilson Croker* (Berkeley, 1940); for his politics, Louis J. Jennings (ed.), *The*

important in its bearing on the constitutional issues rehearsed during the early years of George III's reign. But equally the *Memoirs* were important in their bearing on the education of that monarch as Prince of Wales in the 1750s, and on that schoolmasterly superintendance over his use of his prerogative which the Whig aristocracy in the circle of Holland House continued to claim into the 1820s.

It was from internal evidence that Croker had to make his case. Writers of memoirs were not to be accepted as impartial; 'generally speaking, it is only their *admissions against* themselves which can be safely relied on'; caution was especially necessary when, 'as in the *Memoirs* before us, the partiality is so artful and so gentlemanlike as neither to offend our taste, nor to excite our suspicions'. Croker focussed first on Waldegrave's account of the household of the dowager Princess of Wales, 'the want of due authority in the late governor, of backstair-manners and of nursery-influence'. From Waldegrave's own admissions, however, the behaviour of the Princess was exemplary; it was Lord Harcourt and the Bishop of Norwich who had 'attempted to form an interest independent of the mother'. Was it not illegitimate for them to make such an attempt? On Harcourt's resignation, Waldegrave was appointed by the ministry to replace him; but still the Princess and her son, though not consulted, behaved correctly and even warmly towards the new governor until 1755. Waldegrave described what followed in terms of '*intrigue, disobedience*, and *opposition to the King*'; but, objected Croker, 'after a few pages we find that this *sudden change* took place just about the time that the dowager and the young prince thought they could dispense with *Lord Waldegrave's services*!'

Waldegrave had treated his charge's wish to replace his governor as rebellion against the King; but this ignored the Prince's legitimate independence. By Lord Holland's admission, the Earl had failed to win his pupil's confidence. More serious still,

> though he might have scorned to employ a spy, it is not quite so clear that he did not condescend to act a little like one – In the appendix to these Memoirs some confidential letters of Mr. Fox to his political friends are given, from which it is clear that Lord Waldegrave gave intelligence of the proceedings and feelings at Leicester House to Mr. Fox, who, as is well known, was looked upon as the avowed opponent of that party, on account of his devotion to the Duke of Cumberland.
>
> Perhaps these passages in Mr. Fox's letters may not quite justify the calling Lord Waldegrave a *spy*; but surely there is enough to excuse the princess for some little disbelief of his lordship's exclusive attachment to her and his pupil, and to relieve her from all the blame of Horace Walpole and all the insinuations of Lord Waldegrave of her having unjustly suspected the latter. But whether the Princess of

Correspondence and Diaries of the Late Right Honourable John Wilson Croker (2nd edn., 3 vols, London, 1885).

Introduction

115

Wales had reason to take Lord Waldegrave for a spy or not, – whether or not she had reason to be satisfied with his original appointment or conduct, – all the world must confess that a young prince of eighteen, whom they already thought of marrying, and who was of age by law to govern his kingdoms if his grandfather should die, might, without any disobedience or spirit of intrigue, wish to be relieved from the authority of a governor, and to see his household placed on a more manly and respectable footing. So blind is self-interest to every other consideration, that Lord Waldegrave was evidently of a different opinion; and the abolition of his office, – though delayed five months, – though communicated to him with all possible delicacy, – though conducted between him and the prince and princess with great politeness, and though softened to his lordship by the grant of a lucrative sinecure, yet left an impression on his mind, and has communicated a colour to his pages, highly unjust both to the princess-dowager and to his late Majesty; and, therefore, we must receive, with great caution and with much abatement, the characters which he draws of these illustrious persons, and of Lord Bute, to whose increasing influence he chose to attribute the loss of an office which, in fact, had expired by the course of nature.

With these qualifications in mind, Croker examined the text in order to soften Waldegrave's somewhat critical character-sketch of George III and to shift the blame for the political instability of the 1750s from Leicester House intrigues to the incompetence of Newcastle and the ruthless ambition of Fox. 'The real state of the case probably was,' suggested Croker with considerable insight, 'that Fox's precipitate retreat broke up the government [in 1756], and that he continued till the very last moment his intrigues and efforts to obtain his share in the new administration'.

Croker concluded his review with a balanced but favourable judgement.

The facts stated in the Memoirs are not new, with the exception of Lord Waldegrave's own attempt to form a ministry, of which, strange to say, we find no trace in Dodington nor any other contemporary, and which, after all, was an incidental intrigue of no importance; but though the facts were pretty well known, they are related with greater detail – with a more extensive knowledge of all the parts of the transaction, and with a juster appreciation of the characters of the several persons and parties than any other writer has had either the opportunity to collect or the ability to convey. With the abatement of his prejudice against Leicester-House and Mr. Pitt, and a little partiality towards Kensington and Mr. Fox, his lordship is not merely a candid but an enlightened historian – his facts are accurate – his feelings good – and his principles honourable; as a literary man, his work is entitled to all the praise of which such a work is susceptible; his style is unaffected and polite – always clear, often forcible, and sometimes lively; and if his lordship had taken the trifling trouble of *dating* the proceedings as he went along, we should have been inclined to say, that his Memoirs were the best we had ever read, and to have proposed them, as far as our opinion would have any weight, as a model of this species of writing.[374]

---

[374] [J.W. Croker], in *The Quarterly Review*, 25 (1821), pp. 392–414.

Having placed a largely favourable interpretation on Waldegrave, Croker went on, the following year, to dissociate that work in its implications from the newly published Walpole *Memoirs*.[375] In a lengthy and destructive review their evidence was scrutinised and their author's veracity undermined:

> historical events and characters are disfigured and, we are sorry to be obliged to say, *traduced* with all the malignity of political party and of private enmities ... the Memoirs were written, like the letters, in all the heat and blindness of faction, and under all the excitements of party feeling, offended vanity, and personal disgust ... The leading facts and the course of events related are, as we have said, generally correct, and may be found in our ordinary histories; most of the private intrigues are already known to the world by Dodington's Diary, Lord Waldegrave's Memoirs, and some similar publications ... the chief facts are true, the additional circumstances false; the style is clever and striking, and the slander bold, amusing, and atrocious.

On the fall of Sir Robert Walpole, on the charges of Jacobitism against Stone and Murray, and on the trial of Admiral Byng, Croker unravelled the falsities in Horace Walpole's account, so far as the evidence then extant permitted. With some ingenuity (confirmed by later scholarship) the reviewer traced his subject's indignation and resentment against the Pelhams to disappointment in an application for the more secure tenure of a sinecure: 'with the very year [1751] in which Horace met this disappointment, *commence those very Memoirs* in which the characters of Mr Pelham and the chancellor are so candidly and so impartially treated!' This resentment carried over to a *cause célèbre*:

> we must observe that the whole scope and *principle* of Walpole's account of Byng's affair, is shown by the lately published Memoirs of Lord Waldegrave to be erroneous, and, as it appears by his own confession, that Lord Waldegrave had communicated the Memoirs to him, the misstatement by which he lays the blame of Byng's death on the *old* ministers [Newcastle and the Pelhams] instead of the new [Pitt], is a *wilful* misrepresentation.[376]

Croker now took it as his special vocation to correct the misrepresentations of Walpole's writings as they appeared, and a series of lengthy reviews in

---

[375] Other reviewers reacted against Horace Walpole with equal hostility, but without Croker's historical expertise. An anonymous writer in *The British Review* for June 1822 greeted Walpole's *George II*: 'We thought we had done with Horace Walpole, Earl of Orford, the publication of whose vain and vicious correspondence we have treated in a former review, we trust, as it deserved ... In levity, illiberality, conceit and contempt of religion, the coxcombry of profane ridicule, the impertinence of inflated egotism, and the tricks of self-adulation, the author of the work before us stands upon the same "bad eminence" with the French philosopher [Voltaire]; and is as proper a parallel to him as can be selected from among our most enlightened *esprits forts*, or intellectual reformers of the last century'.

[376] [J.W. Croker], review of Horace Walpole, *Memoires of the Last Ten Years of the Reign of King George II* (London, 1822) in *The Quarterly Review* 27 (April-July 1822), pp. 178–215.

Introduction 117

the *Quarterly* over several decades was the result.³⁷⁷

Other reviewers, too, were able to relate Waldegrave's account of the 1750s to a wider theory of the evolution of the constitution in the reign of George III. The writer in the *New Edinburgh Review*³⁷⁸ condoned, by explaining, the process by which the Crown had emancipated itself from the grip of an aristocratic faction. To the orthodox in the 1820s, the just power and independence of the executive were entirely legitimate.

The events of 1757, which Waldegrave so well recorded, were the last of their type, the reviewer maintained. In the crisis of the summer of that year,

The union of the great aristocratical families, supported by the extraordinary talents of the chief parliamentary leaders, and by the influence of the people from without, proved in this instance an overmatch for the power of the crown; and we have no example, in our subsequent history, of such another victory being achieved. Since this period, the crown has not only acquired greater resources for its support, but has become more skilful in the use of them. It has thus succeeded in breaking the union of the aristocracy, and has in general managed so dextrously, that in all subsequent contests, it has had either the aristocracy or the people on its side. It has never quarrelled with both at the same time, and by its union with either of those two great parties, it has always proved an overmatch for either.

By contrast, in the crisis of 1783–4³⁷⁹ the crown successfully appealed to the people against the 'aristocratical confederacy';

the aristocracy alone, supported no doubt by a splendid array of parliamentary talent, acted against both the crown and the people; but, the power of the crown being firmly and skilfully directed, its adversaries were ultimately discomfited by the obvious expedient of a dissolution of parliament: whereas, in the contest maintained by the first Mr. Pitt with George II, the aristocracy and the people were leagued against the king, who, besides, was unskilled in the machinery of the constitution, and was not aware of the valuable weapons contained in the royal armoury for the defence of the prerogative. This was better understood in the succeeding reign, when the influence of the crown was successfully exerted to break the union of the great families; and it is of this that Burke, in his well-known work, 'Observations on the Present Discontents', chiefly complains, when he contrasts that period with the constitutional reign of George II. But it is clear, from Lord Waldegrave's Narrative, that George II was most reluctantly forced into consti-

---

³⁷⁷ See especially, *The Quarterly Review* 74 (June-Oct. 1844), pp. 395–416 and *ibid.* 77 (December 1845-March 1846), pp. 253–298.

³⁷⁸ Its politics were conservative. When the journal was launched in January 1819 as *The Edinburgh Monthly Review*, the Prospectus (p. iii) announced: 'It is not intended to make Politics a regular topic of discussion; but as, from its importance, it will occasionally demand attention, it will be treated, when it does occur, in a spirit of loyalty and patriotism, with a jealous and steady regard to the just authority of the magistrate and the civil rights of the subject, considered as reciprocal and inseparable.' I am grateful to Dr. John Dinwiddy for illuminating this point.

³⁷⁹ See John Cannon, *The Fox-North Coalition: Crisis of the Constitution, 1782–4* (Cambridge, 1969) and John Ehrman, *The Younger Pitt: the Years of Acclaim* (London, 1969).

tutional measures, and that nothing could equal the aversion and the arbitrary temper which he displayed, before submitting to those compliances which were extorted from him. It was to be expected that these struggles between the crown and the aristocracy would gradually develope the full extent of the royal powers; that the crown, by constant practice, would naturally grow more expert in the tactics and discipline of party warfare; that all its resources would be strictly looked after, and called into activity; and that, as all violent use of the prerogative was now to be forborne, its patronage and power would naturally be used gently, to mould to compliance with its views those whom it could no longer compel.[380]

To the *Quarterly*, therefore, the 1750s did not witness the genesis of a future royal absolutism; to the *New Edinburgh*, that decade did reveal the last successful attempt to shackle a royal executive which was, in its normal and legitimate state, both strong and independent.

Thanks not least to such critical scrutinies, neither Waldegrave nor Walpole necessarily dictated a distorted picture to the first historians to use them as sources. Henry Hallam[381] cited both in his balanced account of the early eighteenth-century constitution: the coherence of party after 1714 weakened the power of monarchs, but 'the executive government, though shorn of its lustre, has not lost so much of its real efficacy by the consequences of the Revolution [of 1688] as is often supposed.' Waldegrave had, thought Hallam, rightly recognised George II's Germanic 'prejudices in favour of those governments where the royal authority is under less restraint', but judiciously offset this with an appreciation of that monarch's respect for English liberties and constitutional forms. Although he terminated his *History* in 1760 and professed a wish to avoid more recent controversies, Hallam implied a view of them. Following 1688, there had been 'a systematic diminution of the reigning prince's control' which 'affords a real security against endeavours by the crown to subvert or essentially impair the other parts of our government'.[382] The implication was clear: Whig rhetoric about the dangerous and illegitimate power of the Crown since 1760 was grotesquely exaggerated.

In 1844, Lord Mahon[383] used Waldegrave's and Walpole's *Memoirs* to

---

[380] *The New Edinburgh Review*, vol. 1 (July–October 1821), no. 1, pp. 1–15, at 13–14. The conflict between George, Prince of Wales and George II arose from 'a misunderstanding', thought the reviewer; this led the Prince and the Princess Dowager to look on Waldegrave as 'a sort of honourable spy', but unjustly.

[381] Henry Hallam (1777–1859): ed. Eton and Christ Church, Oxford; barrister; succeeded to father's estates 1812, and held the sinecure office of a Commissioner of Stamps. Private means allowed him to devote himself to historical writing. A Whig, known in the Holland House circle, but an opponent of the 1832 Reform Bill.

[382] Henry Hallam, *The Constitutional History of England from the Accession of Henry VII to the Death of George II* (1827; 8th edn., 3 vols., London, 1855), vol. 3, pp. 291–304.

[383] Philip Henry Stanhope, 5th Earl Stanhope (1805–75), styled Viscount Mahon 1816–55. MP 1830–2, 1835–52. Macaulay called him 'a violent Tory, but a very agreeable companion, and a very good scholar'. T.B. Macaulay to Hannah Macaulay, 30 May

Introduction

ridicule the idea that Prince George had been 'trained in Jacobite principles'. Horace Walpole's personal animosity towards William Murray and Andrew Stone was now sufficiently evident to a sceptical historian. Of Waldegrave's testimony, by contrast, Mahon recorded his opinion that 'there can be none higher'. He took from Waldegrave a generally favourable account of George III's early personality, and, having discounted the myths of Leicester House Jacobitism, he was able to see that the application of the old label 'Tory' to the King's Friends of the early 1760s was a merely terminological revival: it did not prove the establishment of a 'new Toryism'.[384]

Croker, Hallam and Mahon did not, however, represent the mainstream of nineteenth-century historical interpretation. The mainstream derived from a quite different source, the anonymous review article of Waldegrave and Walpole together which appeared in the *Edinburgh Review* for 1822.[385] Its author was Lord Holland's paid retainer John Allen,[386] who resided at Holland House as librarian and propagandist from 1805 until his death. He was powerfully motivated to engage in this form of controversy. It was widely known outside that circle that Allen 'is said to profess bare-faced atheism, and goes by the soubriquet of Lady Holland's Atheist'.[387] Even Macaulay called him 'her Ladyship's Atheist in ordinary',[388] and the 4th Lord Holland recorded privately: 'His violence about kings and priests is almost childish, and does his cause more harm than good. He is fond of prejudice, and when he has none of his own he adopts the prejudices of others . . . '.[389]

Allen's historical knowledge and abilities were considerable, however.[390] They were to lead to his partisan constitutional study *Inquiry into the Rise and*

1831: Thomas Pinney (ed.), *The Letters of Thomas Babington Macaulay* (6 vols., Cambridge, 1974–81), vol. 2, pp. 20–3.

[384] Lord Mahon, *History of England from the Peace of Utrecht to the Peace of Versailles 1713–1783*, vol. 4 (1844; 5th edn., London, 1858), pp. 22, 98, 207, 213–5.
[385] *The Edinburgh Review* 37 (June–November, 1822), pp. 1–46. The authorship is established by Walter E. Houghton, *The Wellesley Index to Victorian Periodicals 1824–1900* (Toronto, 1966), vol. 1, p. 463; 'part' of the article was claimed by Francis Jeffrey: Lord Cockburn, *Life of Lord Jeffrey* (2 vols., Edinburgh, 1852), vol. 2, p. 212.
[386] John Allen (1771–1843); born near Edinburgh, son of a bankrupt lawyer; qualified as a doctor at Edinburgh University, but failed to build up a practice. Associated with the cause of political reform in Scotland; drawn into the Holland House circle via the *Edinburgh Review*.
[387] Francis Bickley (ed.), *The Diaries of Sylvester Douglas (Lord Glenbervie)* (2 vols, London, 1928), vol. 2, pp. 71–2.
[388] T.B. Macaulay to Hannah Macaulay, 25 July 1831: Pinney (ed.), *Letters of Macaulay*, vol. 2, p. 76.
[389] Earl of Ilchester (ed.), *The Journal of the Hon. Henry Edward Fox . . . 1818–1830* (London, 1923), p. 125.
[390] Discussed in P.B.M. Blaas, *Continuity and Anachronism: Parliamentary and Constitutional Development in Whig Historiography and in the Anti-Whig Reaction between 1890 and 1930* (The Hague, 1978), pp. 83–94.

Growth of the Royal Prerogative in England (London, 1830), in its polemic an offshoot of Lord John Russell's less scholarly *An Essay on the History of the English Government and Constitution, from the Reign of Henry VII to the Present Time* (London, 1821). These works emerged from the intellectual milieu of that remarkable group of writers and politicians drawn to the salon of the third Lord Holland and his dominating wife. In literary as well as political society, Holland played the role of a powerful patron; careers depended on his favour. When in 1833 the young T.B. Macaulay wrote his first essay on Horace Walpole for the *Edinburgh Review*, he deliberately disguised his hostile opinion of the first Lord Holland in order to ingratiate himself with Henry Fox's descendant.[391]

The influence of patrician Whig patronage went much deeper than this, however. The Holland House circle was profoundly involved with English history as a sphere of public doctrine.[392] Traditionally this doctrine had concerned itself, first and foremost, with the Tudor and Stuart monarchy. The 1640s had been depicted as a libertarian apotheosis, and the editor of the *Edinburgh Review* duly hailed an antidote to Hume's royalist interpretation which appeared in 1822:

> The true source of practical Toryism, or, in other words, of personal servility to the Government, is no doubt self-interest, or a strong desire for unearned emoluments and undeserved distinctions – but the great support of *speculative* servility and *sincere* Tory opinions – to which we are liberal enough to allow an actual existence, has of late years been found chiefly in Hume's history ... [393]

George Brodie, the subject of that notice, was hardly of sufficient calibre to stand against the orthodox in the long term, however, and the hunt was on for an historian of commanding stature to give expression to the Whig world-view. A possible candidate was James Mackintosh (1765–1832). Earlier notorious as the author of *Vindiciae Gallicae* (London, 1791), he had seemingly recanted his youthful enthusiasms and amassed a modest fortune as Recorder of Bombay in 1804–12. Back in England, he used his new financial independence to sit in the Commons in the years 1813–32 and to reaffirm in a mature form his earlier principles: a celebrity at Holland House, he agitated for Catholic 'emancipation' and finally voted for the Reform Bill. Meanwhile, his main efforts were devoted to historical scholarship, a career cut short in 1832. Lord Holland had originally

---

[391] T.B. Macaulay to Hannah Macaulay, 14 Oct. 1833: Pinney (ed.), *Letters of Macaulay*, vol. 2, pp. 316–7.

[392] Some of its later influences are traced in Olive Anderson, 'The Political Uses of History in Mid-Nineteenth-Century England', *Past & Present* 36 (1967), 87–105. See also T.P. Peardon, *The Transition in English Historical Writing 1760–1830* (New York, 1933).

[393] [Francis Jeffrey], review of George Brodie, *A History of the British Empire, from the Accession of Charles I to the Restoration* (4 vols., Edinburgh, 1822) in *The Edinburgh Review* 40 (March–July 1824), pp. 92–146, at 93.

Introduction

suggested Mackintosh as the most appropriate editor of Walpole's *Memoirs*,[394] but his attention was fixed on his own writings. His *History of the Revolution in England in 1688* was published posthumously in 1834, and attracted a famous essay by Macaulay in *The Edinburgh Review*. Mackintosh had been assiduously collecting materials for a complete history of England, but his text had only reached 1572 by his death. Its introduction nevertheless classically formulated the general purposes of Whig history. The aims of that work must be

> most of all, to strengthen the moral sentiments by the exercise of them on the personages conspicuous in history ... the characteristic quality of English history is, that it stands alone as the history of the progress of a great people towards liberty during six centuries ... the statement offered here ... may much facilitate the right understanding of more recent controversies and changes.[395]

Mackintosh's death prevented him from working out his historical vision for the century following 1688, as he had intended. His surviving writings, however, contributed importantly to two of the three episodes in English history which were to receive special emphasis in the nineteenth century: the Glorious Revolution, with the publication of T.B. Macaulay's *History of England from the Accession of James the Second* (1848–55); the Reformation, with J.A. Froude's *History of England from the Fall of Wolsey to the Defeat of the Spanish Armada* (1856–70); and the theme of E.A. Freeman's *History of the Norman Conquest* (1867–97).[396] The earlier and seminal works of the Holland House school were eclipsed in retrospect by the more meretricious achievements of Macaulay,[397] whose golden prose gave an undue importance to the events of 1688. But in the last decades of the eighteenth century and the first three decades of the nineteenth, present-minded historical polemic was chiefly focussed on two other episodes: the Civil War, and the early years of the reign of George III.

The origin of the Civil War was, of course, an ancient topic of controversy, and its place in the Whig mausoleum was destined to be confirmed by S.R. Gardiner's *History* of the years 1603–42, published in 1863–82. Yet all these works of scholarship came later in the century; by then, the guidelines had been established. None of these episodes played as

---

[394] Holland was evidently referring to Walpole's *Memoirs of George III*: Holland to Waldegrave, 22 March 1820: Waldegrave MSS at Chewton.

[395] Sir James Mackintosh, *The History of England from the Earliest Times to the Final Establishment of the Reformation* (new edn., ed. R.J. Mackintosh, 2 vols, London, 1853), vol. 1, p. viii.

[396] These three themes are discussed, with William Stubbs, in John Burrow, *A Liberal Descent: Victorian Historians and the English Past* (Cambridge, 1981). Professor Burrow does not deal with the debate in the 1820s on the early years of George III's reign, which is here argued to be of seminal importance in the evolution of the nineteenth century's vision of English history.

[397] See Joseph Hamburger, *Macaulay and the Whig Tradition* (Chicago, 1976).

important a part in the crystallization of a certain framework of interpretation as did the early years of the reign of George III, and the constitutional issues then raised. It was this crystallization to which the Waldegrave and Walpole *Memoirs* so importantly contributed, for it was in the 1820s that the reign of George III overtook the Civil War as the main subject for present-minded historical study and the major quarry of historical 'relevance'.

There was an additional reason for the contemporary political significance of the 1750s and 60s beyond Holland House's concern to vindicate its family's political record and in a general sense to carry forward the Foxite torch. The patrician Whig programme for parliamentary reform derived more from a theory of English history than from any body of abstract principle, whether Benthamite claims about utility or Paineite assertions of natural rights. Francis Jeffrey,[398] writing in the *Edinburgh Review* in 1810, employed not untypically extravagant language in tracing the impregnability of the ministry and the seeming permanence of Whig exclusion to the growing power of the monarchy. He had, he believed,

> traced the causes of the disappointment so sorely felt by the whole nation in common with ourselves; – the cause, let us rather call it – the single but fruitful cause, of all our calamities at home and abroad – of the misgovernment which reigns in every department of affairs – the ENORMOUS INFLUENCE OF THE CROWN.

His prescriptions for parliamentary reform were therefore aimed at improving 'the constitution of the House of Commons, by curbing the overgrown influence of the Executive in that assembly', not at subjecting the Commons more closely to the control of the people. Adjustments in the franchise and in the distribution of seats might be valuable, but in promoting liberty, not democracy. Such changes would operate

> not so much in directly improving the House of Commons, as in diffusing a more popular spirit, by increasing the number of great popular elections, and in giving certain classes of the people an interest in the management of public affairs; which is highly beneficial to liberty. These advantages we are very far from undervaluing; but they belong to a class quite different from that which we have ventured to point out as the first and most important, namely, the direct limitation of ministerial influence in the House of Commons. It appears to us, that this should be the first object of reform, as it is indisputably the first evil in the present system; and that a wise and prudent statesman would stop at this point, and be satisfied with having gone thus far, when he had brought forward the measures above suggested with such a view.[399]

---

[398] Francis Jeffrey (1773–1850): called to bar in Scotland 1794. One of the founders of *The Edinburgh Review*, 1802; its editor 1803–29.

[399] [Francis Jeffrey], review of George Rose, *Observations Respecting the Public Expenditure and the Influence of the Crown* (London, 1810) in *The Edinburgh Review* 16 (April-August 1810), pp. 187–213.

Introduction

The same strategy was employed by Henry Brougham, reviewing John Allen's *Inquiry* in the *Edinburgh Review* of 1831. Whigs had quickly learned the advantages of reviewing each others' books,[400] and Brougham predictably lavished anonymous praise on Allen's: 'This is beyond all comparison the most important book upon constitutional antiquities and law that has appeared for many years ... it breathes throughout a warm love of freedom, and a firm spirit of resistance to the slavish maxims, which lawyers unhappily, as well as courtiers, have almost always been prone to inculcate'. Allen's treatise was unashamedly historical; this aligned him with the Whigs against both 'the intolerant and dogmatical utilitarians', and the exponents of natural rights: 'Indeed, the importance which our author attaches to the authority of former ages, and which is avowed by the very undertaking of the enquiry, squares but little with the rash and sweeping nature of the modern zealots for liberty and popular rights'.

The historical approach appeared to offer an effective strategy against the major threat to the Whigs. It showed how 'The pious sycophancy of churchmen carried the title of kings a step higher than even the profane adulation of the Romans, who deified their princes, had ventured to do'. It showed how 'allegiance was held to be conditional' until early Stuart usurpations.

> It shows us that, whatever the slavish propensities of priests or lawyers may have affected to believe, absolute power never was of right, and by law, naturalized in England; that freedom never was an exotic or a stranger, but the birthright and inheritance of Englishmen; that the presumption where no law or usage appears is always in favour of liberty, and against royal prerogative; that it is in no case for the subject to show his title to be free, but for the monarch to prove his right to oppress.[401]

Such a self-interested strategy could only be made plausible by a sustained denunciation of the faults of the monarchy, linked to an academically respectable interpretation of the recent past which at once explained and condemned the Crown's changing role. This interpretation was provided not least by the Holland House circle. John Allen and Lord John Russell, among its other authors, played leading roles in the invention during the early decades of the nineteenth century of that 'Whig interpreta-

---

[400] Lord Holland had planned that Sir James Mackintosh should write on the Waldegrave and Walpole *Memoirs* for *The Edinburgh Review*; when Mackintosh proved too busy, Holland had the task assigned to the equally 'sound' John Allen: Mackintosh to Holland, 18 Dec 1821; Holland to Mackintosh, 20 Dec 1821: Add MSS 51653, n.f.

[401] [Henry Brougham], review of John Allen, *Inquiry into the Rise and Growth of the Royal Prerogative in England* (London, 1830), in *The Edinburgh Review* 52 (October 1830-January 1831), pp. 139-57.

tion' of the English past which has distorted historical understanding until even quite recently.[402]

In fabricating that interpretation, a particular section of English politics played a key role. In his *Edinburgh Review* essay on Waldegrave and Walpole, Allen acknowledged:

> It is indeed very remarkable that no part of our domestic history since the Reformation is so imperfectly known to us, as the interval between the accession of the House of Hanover and the death of George II. Of this period, remarkable for the establishment and consolidation of our present internal system of government, the traditionary accounts are become faint and obscure; while the authentic memorials have not yet appeared. Events of public notoriety are to be found, though often inaccurately told, in our common histories; but the secret springs of action, the private views and motives of individuals, the quarrels and reconciliations of parties, are as little known to us as if the events to which they relate had taken place in China or Japan.

Allen was able to write at a time when this blank was being partly (though inadequately) filled up, and the interpretations then developed were destined to have a lasting influence. The two works together, he recognised, were 'the most valuable addition made to English memoirs, since the publication of Burnet's History of his Own Time; and, with the exception of Lord Clarendon's account of his own life,[403] we know of no works in our language that contain such minute and circumstantial details from an eyewitness, of so many persons remarkable in our history'.

To Waldegrave's and Walpole's *Memoirs* he therefore devoted an interpretive essay of some 20,000 words. But it was the Waldegrave volume to which he turned first and which provided the occasion for the framework of interpretation to be established. In the disputes over the Princes' education, Allen was willing to see merit on both sides; but his sensitivity (drawn partly from Horace Walpole) to the Jacobite danger led him to incline against the dowager Princess while censoring Harcourt and the Bishop of Norwich:

> Which of the parties, the mother, or the governor and preceptor, was most to blame in this rupture, so briefly noticed by Lord Waldegrave, it is not easy, nor perhaps material, to decide. On the one hand, it is clear, by the whole tenor of her conduct, that from the death of her husband, the great object of the Princess Dowager, was to obtain the government of her son; and from the investigation set on foot it appeared, that Cresset, her confidant, 'had dealt out very ungracious epithets, both on the governor and preceptor,' without being dismissed, or even reprimanded for his

---

[402] Its teleological bias was already evident. Commending Horace Walpole, Allen wrote: 'With all his defects of temper and littlenesses of character, he appears, however, on general questions, to have had a soundness of thinking and rectitude of judgement, which led him, on many occasions, to anticipate the decisions of posterity'!

[403] *Bishop Burnet's History of His Own Time* (2 vols., London, 1724–34); *The Life of Edward Earl of Clarendon . . . Written by Himself* (Oxford, 1759).

presumption. On the other hand, it is not denied that Lord Harcourt, the Prince's governor, who owed his appointment to the Pelhams, was a man totally unqualified for so important a trust; and that the Bishop of Norwich, the preceptor, 'though sincerely zealous for the education of the Princes,' was hot in his temper, haughty and violent to the inferior officers of the establishment, and uncourtly enough to 'thwart the Princess herself, whenever, as an indulgent, or perhaps a little as an ambitious mother (and this happened but too frequently), she was willing to relax the application of her sons.' To believe the friends of the governor and preceptor, where the Bishop ventured to have an opinion of his own, it was from his anxiety for the education of his pupils, which had been scandalously neglected, or miserably conducted in the lifetime of their father; and where he and the governor attempted to form an interest independent of the mother, it was to counteract the dangerous influence of Cresset her secretary, of Stone, the subgovernor and confident of the Duke of Newcastle, who had wormed himself into her good opinion, and of Scot, the subpreceptor, who had been recommended to her by Lord Bolingbroke. To take our account from the opposite party, the Bishop was a conceited pedant, devoured with ambition, who had formed a plot to make the governor and preceptor the sole directors of the young Prince, and not allow his mother to have the least influence over him; and had persuaded Lord Harcourt to concur in this notable project; which the Princess was too quicksighted not to discover, and with the help of Stone and Cresset, too dexterous not to defeat. If such was the true origin of the quarrel, the Princess had the prudence to enjoy her victory, without drawing attention to the real grounds of the contest.

Suspicions of Jacobite influence could nevertheless be built up by an innuendo combined with a real truth:

The only part of this squabble in which the public had an interest, was far from being satisfactorily cleared up. It was alleged against the subgovernor and subpreceptor, that they were Jacobites; and imputed to them that they had endeavoured to instil their own arbitrary and unconstitutional doctrines of government into the minds of their pupils. this was the charge of Lord Harcourt and the Bishop, laid before the King. But the Bishop was not admitted to an audience, to explain the grounds of his accusation; and Lord Harcourt expressed himself so vaguely and unintelligibly, that he made no impression on his Majesty. Certain it is, that a book in vindication of the arbitrary and illegal acts of the Stuarts found its way into the hands of the young Prince, without the knowledge of his preceptor. The subgovernor protested his innocence; but, when afterwards accused with Murray, and Johnson, Bishop of Gloucester, of having professed the most violent Jacobitism in his youth, the inquiry was stifled in the House of Lords in a manner that leaves an unfavourable impression against the accused. There were discrepancies, indeed, if not prevarications, in the evidence of Fawsset the informer; but it was proved he had been tampered with, and it was evident he was intimidated. It is very probable that despair of success might have converted these young Jacobites into sincere friends of the House of Hanover; but experience shows that such converts, though they transfer their allegiance from one family to another, commonly retain their old principles of government, and are therefore unfit persons to direct the education, or form the character, of a King of England, who ought to observe the spirit, as well as respect the letter, of the Constitution; and never forget that it was a straining rather than violation of the law, a disregard of the sentiments rather than an actual oppression of the people, that precipitated the Stuarts from the throne.

Such, implied John Allen, had been the point at issue in George III's own use of the prerogative in the previous sixty years.

Arguing by implication against Croker's review in the *Quarterly*, Allen went on to disparage the character of Prince George and the influence of his mother through the evidence of Harcourt's successor. Waldegrave was taken very much at his word, and credited with 'discreet and considerate conduct' which preserved an 'outward calm' until the king's departure for Hanover in 1755. Nevertheless, the Princess was

> inwardly dissatisfied with the King and his Ministers, though she thought it prudent to dissemble her resentment. The grounds of her displeasure appear to have been – that her husband's debts were not paid, which, be it observed, had been contracted by his opposition to his father's government – that his servants had not been brought into office, which most of them had formerly quitted in order to join him in opposition – that she herself was not sufficiently consulted or attended to by Ministers – and that her son, a lad not 16, was still kept under subjection to governors, &c., which, it seems, he felt, though, in his brother Edward's opinion, a boy under 15, he did not resent it with proper spirit.

In 1755, these resentments came to a head as a result of the King's plans for his grandson's marriage, and the Duke of Cumberland's being placed at the head of the Regency in the King's absence abroad. The 2nd Earl himself, insisted Allen, had 'no share' in producing this schism in the royal family; 'Lord Waldegrave, be it remembered, was no follower or partisan of Mr. Fox'. Instead, Allen found for him a more familiar label.

> Though a man of strict honour and exemplary private worth, Lord Waldegrave belonged to that description of persons, known in our practical constitution by the name of the King's friends, – persons unconnected with political parties, and, in general, destitute of parliamentary interest or abilities, who look for honours and preferments to Royal patronage alone. It is perhaps impossible, in a monarchy, that persons of that description should not be found. In arbitrary governments they are often placed at the head of public affairs, with neither virtues nor talents to justify their elevation. In a monarchy like ours, they are commonly confined to inferior and subordinate situations. A step in the Peerage, or a place in the Household, is the utmost height to which their ambition usually aspires. By associating themselves with men of higher views and greater capacities, they sometimes contribute, by their intrigues, to form or subvert an administration. But when the change is once effected, they descend to their natural level, and are content with acting under those to whose rise they have contributed. It must be owned, that Lord Waldegrave appears to have been one of the best and most unexceptionable of this class of persons; and, as the Editor of his Memoirs has justly remarked in his preface, it reflects no small credit on the discernment and liberality of George II, that in

Introduction

chusing a private friend, 'he selected a man of sense, honour, and sincerity, who had few exterior graces to recommend him; and at a period of no unreasonable alarm, placed him, though a near relation to his competitor for the Crown, immediately about his own person'. Lord Waldegrave appears to have returned the confidence and partiality of his Sovereign with affection and sincere attachment; but though grateful for his master's kindness, and warmly devoted to his interests, he appears, from the concluding sentence of his Memoirs, to have felt and appreciated, though he endured, the misery of *his* situation, who, from interest or ambition, seeks for honour and promotion, by depending on the favour and partiality of one so much his superior as his present or his future Sovereign.

Waldegrave's political dependence on George II was a stance, implied Allen, which had done too much harm under George III, whose reign saw a 'silent but steady growth of power in the Crown'. Moreover, the lethargy and aversion to business on which the 2nd Earl had dwelt in his pen-portrait of his royal pupil were soon to be transformed into a much more purposeful and assiduous personal rule. Allen seemingly clinched this argument by quoting a passage from the newly discovered Chewton manuscript:

'Be that as it will hereafter, when the Prince shall succeed to his grandfather, there may possibly be changes of greater consequence. He will soon be made sensible that a Prince who suffers himself to be led, is not to be allowed the choice of his conductor. His pride will then give battle to his indolence; and having made this first effort, a moderate share of obstinacy will make him persevere'. Lord Waldegrave then goes on to add – 'His honesty will incline to do what is right, and the means cannot be wanting, where a good disposition of mind is joined with a tolerable capacity: for a superior genius does not seem to be a *sine qua non* in the composition of a good king'.

Never was prophecy more exactly fulfilled than the first part of the preceding paragraph. If there was one quality more characteristic than another of his late Majesty, in his Royal capacity, it was a determination not be led in the choice of his ministers. If there was any doctrine to which he adhered with pertinacity, it was to the principles of that party in our Constitution who hold that the King ought to have the free and unfettered choice of his servants. At times he was compelled, by the calamities and misfortunes of his reign, to intrust with his affairs an administration formed in repugnance to his wishes. But his pride never forgave the violence to his dignity. Continually on the alert, he watched his opportunity; and no indolence ever interfered to prevent his availing himself of the first occasion that offered to regain what he considered the brightest flower of his prerogative.[404]

Allen's case dovetailed importantly with the line of argument being devised by another rising star of the Holland House circle, Lord John Russell.[405] His book of 1821 on the English constitution was an interpretive

---

[404] [John Allen] in *The Edinburgh Review* 37 (June-November 1822), pp. 1–46.
[405] Lord John Russell, 1st Earl Russell (1792–1878): ed. Westminster and Edinburgh Univ.; MP 1818–61; a succession of high offices in early nineteenth-century ministries; Prime Minister 1865–6; President of the Royal Historical Society, 1872–8.

essay, largely without references and heavily larded with abstract reflections on liberty. Nevertheless, its thesis openly depended on a particular historical argument. 'The accession of George I,' claimed Russell, 'was the era when government by party was fully established in England'.

> We now find, therefore, a party ruling the country through the House of Commons; a species of government which has been assailed with vehemence, with plausibility, eloquence, and wit, by Swift, and Bolingbroke, and the whole party of Tories in the reigns of George I and II; by Lord Bute and the King's friends in the commencement the late reign, and by a party of parliamentary reformers in our own time.

The Whig aristocracy, he argued, had preserved English liberties by steering between democracy and royal absolutism. But in 1760 this delicate balance, preserved by patrician wisdom, had been upset.

> The important feature of the new reign was the experiment of a new project of government. Among other disastrous consequences of the want of public spirit in England, was a total neglect of the political education of the young king; and hence he came to be placed in the hands of men who had but recently shaken from their minds their allegiance to the house of Stuart. It occurred to these persons that, in the general blight of political virtue and public confidence, an opportunity was given for raising the household standard of the sovereign, and rallying around his person the old relics of the Jacobite party, with the addition of all, who, in the calculation of chances, might think the favour of the Sovereign as good an interest as the countenance of any minister whatever. To form and consolidate this party they studiously spread all the doctrines which place the whole virtue of a monarchy in the supreme sanctity of the royal person. They endeavoured to obtain a certain number of seats in the House of Commons, which, with the help of a proportionate quantity of patronage, might make the tenure of any ministry uncertain. They made loud professions of honesty and of conscience, which wholly consisted in an obstinate adherence to certain narrow-minded tenets, and which did not prevent the most shameful violations of sincerity and truth, whenever it suited their purpose to deceive and to betray. They assiduously planted their maxims of government in the mind of their royal pupil, and as he was naturally slow, obedient, good-tempered, and firm, he too easily admitted, and too constantly retained the lessons of his early masters.

This was the system exposed in Burke's *Thoughts on the Cause of the Present Discontents*.[406]

Russell's problem was that he, like others before the 1820s, was hardly able to demonstrate the genesis of the new monarchical absolutism in events of the 1750s at Leicester House. The publication of the Waldegrave and Walpole *Memoirs* offered the prospect of seemingly doing just that.[407]

---

[406] Lord John Russell, *An Essay on the History of the English Government and Constitution, from the Reign of Henry VII to the Present Time* (London, 1821), pp. 160–2, 173–4.

[407] An early contribution to this myth was made by the reformer and Foxite MP John Nicholls (?1745–1832), author of *Recollections and Reflections, Personal and Political, as connected with Public Affairs, during the Reign of George III* (London, 1820), a work reviewed together

Those two documents apparently confirmed the position to which Holland House had already committed itself. Lord Holland, editing the Waldegrave text, was delighted to find that (as he believed) the 2nd Earl had perfectly captured the character of the future George III, 'a character in which his admirers pretend not to recognise him, but every trait of which, I who neither am nor ever was an admirer of him, I think was lamentably confirmed in his subsequent career'.[408] Both memoirs were consequently seized on and used in a similar way by successive Whig-Liberal authors, with varying degrees of subtlety or polemical force. The 'Whig interpretation' henceforth grew by accretion, repetitions of what was essentially the same argument and the same evidence seemingly deriving authority from the accumulation of grave authors and weighty tomes repeating similar conclusions.

Lord Holland thought it sufficient to publish Walpole's *George II*; that author's later manuscripts, as well as being more discreditable to the memory of Holland's ancestor Henry Fox, covered a too recent and too controversial period. Only in 1845 did Sir Denis Le Marchant publish Walpole's *Memoirs of the Reign of King George the Third*. Not until 1845, therefore, was it generally known that Walpole had seen and drawn on the Waldegrave *Memoirs*,[409] and the question of the interdependence of the two sources was hardly raised in the early historiographical debate.

To his famous passage expounding his 'conspiracy theory' of the recent past,[410] Walpole later added a disclaimer. His account, he insisted, owed nothing to borrowing from the *Diary* of George Bubb Dodington, Lord Melcome, published in 1784:

as far as it goes his *Diary* is most uncommonly authentic... Where he and I write on the same passages we shall be found to agree, though we never had any connection, were of very different principles, and received our information from as different sources. My whole account of the reign of George the Second was given about

with the Waldegrave *Memoirs* in the left-of-centre *Monthly Review* 95 (June 1821), pp. 178–95. His father, Dr. Frank Nicholls, had been one of George II's physicians, and the son retailed (without documentary evidence) a number of Court anecdotes of the 1750s. In particular, John Nicholls depicted the Dowager Princess of Wales as the champion of those ideas of princely absolutism which she had allegedly learned in the court of her father, the Duke of Saxe Gotha, and put into print the influential legend: 'it is well known that she ever impressed upon the King from his early years this lesson, "George, be King". And this lesson seems to have influenced the King's conduct through the whole of his life' (pp. 6, 382–3). The author was, perhaps, not wholly impartial. Samuel Johnson observed in 1775: 'Lord Bute showed an undue partiality to Scotchmen. He turned out Dr. Nichols, a very eminent man, from being physician to the King, to make room for one of his countrymen, a man very low in his profession': James Boswell, *Life of Johnson* (Oxford, 1965), p. 620.

[408] Holland to John Murray, 5 May 1821: draft, Add MSS 51832, n.f.
[409] Walpole, *George III*, vol. 1, p. 212: quoted below, p. 140.
[410] Walpole, *George III*, vol. 4, pp. 90–7.

twenty years before I saw Lord Melcombe's *Diary*, or knew it existed; nor did I ever see it till published.[411]

But Walpole never warned his future readers of the extent to which he had relied on the testimony and written memoirs of Earl Waldegrave as a source, and historians finding an agreement between Walpole and Waldegrave have too readily assumed that one account confirmed the other.

In respect of the early years of George III's reign, Lord John Russell carried the story a stage further in 1846. The introduction to the third volume of his edition of the fourth Duke of Bedford's letters covering 1761–70 was a synthesis of sources including Adolphus, Burke, and Brougham.[412] His second volume, covering the years 1749–60, had strangely ignored Waldegrave's account of those years. But in the third volume the Waldegrave and Walpole *Memoirs* occupied an important place, not as a route to a more authentic understanding of the 1750s but as an aid to a polemical misunderstanding of the 1760s. The whole point of Waldegrave and Walpole was to give an unfavourable twist to the cautiously approving scenario outlined by John Adolphus. Russell accepted Adolphus' account of a royal design to win back via 'the dissolution of party connections' a royal initiative lost to Whig oligarchs under the first two Georges, but redescribed this as a sinister plot to bring about 'the supremacy of the King over the Parliament'. Waldegrave and Walpole thus seemingly provided an explanation of the origins in the 1750s of the conspiracy supposedly unmasked in 1770 by Edmund Burke's *Thoughts on the Cause of the Present Discontents*.[413]

By 1852, when the Earl of Albemarle published his hagiographical but well-documented life of Rockingham, the Whig myth was complete: drawing on Walpole's and Waldegrave's *Memoirs*, the work opened with a disparagement of the character of the new king in 1760, and a denunciation of the arbitrary principles he had imbibed at Leicester House: 'To any "education" befitting the constitutional sovereign of Great Britain he had little or no claim'.[414]

Following Albemarle's lead, judgements of this sort henceforth grew more severe as they became more shallow. In 1861, Erskine May[415] gave

[411] Walpole, *George III*, vol. 1, p. 93.
[412] Lord John Russell (ed.), *Correspondence of John, Fourth Duke of Bedford* (3 vols., London, 1842–6), vol. 3, pp. xi–lxxxiv.
[413] The 'Whig interpretation' in its early form consequently made little play with George III's alleged insanity. On the contrary, his conduct was to be presented as the rationally explicable outcome of his early domination by Bute and the dowager Princess of Wales.
[414] George Thomas, Earl of Albemarle, *Memoirs of the Marquis of Rockingham and His Contemporaries* (2 vols., London, 1852), vol. 1, pp. 1–7, 163.
[415] Sir Thomas Erskine May (1815–86): ed. Bedford Grammar School and Middle Temple; called to the bar 1838. Parliamentary lawyer; from 1856 Clerk Assistant, from 1871 to 1886 Clerk of the House of Commons.

classic expression to the Whig scenario in the *genre* of 'constitutional history'. The work's preface announced it as a story of progress – of 'institutions ... improved' and of 'abuses ... corrected'. In typical Whig fashion, the author sought at the same time both to deny and to justify his polemical bias:

Continually touching upon controverted topics, I have endeavoured to avoid, as far as possible, the spirit and tone of controversy. But, impressed with an earnest conviction that the development of popular liberties has been safe and beneficial, I do not affect to disguise the interest with which I have traced it, through all the events of history.

Many of his chapters were devoted to demonstrating the alleged advance of various forms of individual 'liberty', in elections, in opinion and press freedom, in the individual's dealings with the executive, in the colonies and Ireland, in local government, and, at great length, in the sphere of religion. But all these spheres were placed in a particular perspective by the first four chapters of Erskine May's first volume. They established a framework of interpretation for what was to follow.

Those four chapters dealt with the Crown.[416] Erskine May, like others of his party, had a paranoid obsession with what he chose to call 'the vital power of the monarchy'. Somehow the Crown had steadily strengthened its position, they believed, in the teeth of all those modernising and progressive tendencies which ought to have moved English society in the opposite direction. English history since 1760 witnessed the reassertion of royal power, followed by the final 'subjection' of kings to 'the will of Parliament'. Popular liberties were therefore to be pictured as the reciprocal of the power of the crown: the decline of the second and the rise of the first were to be inseparably (and unquestioningly) linked within the analytical framework of Victorian constitutional history.

Under the first two Hanoverians, claimed Erskine May, the theory of ministerial responsibility was fully established: 'The King reigned, but his Ministers governed'. If such a premise was necessary to give Victorian conventions the air of ancient ancestry, some decisive discontinuity was needed to explain the monarchy's lasting threat. Erskine May discovered this, of course, in the policy of the young George III. Its origins were traced in turn to his education at Leicester House. The charges of 1752 about the

[416] Parliamentary parties, which came first in the scale of priorities of most twentieth-century historians, occupied only the last chapter of his first volume; in the second volume no chapter was devoted to that theme. This neglect partly explains the crude dualism of Erskine May's unexamined and undefended assumption: 'The parties in which Englishmen have associated at different times, and under various names, have represented cardinal principles of government, authority on the one side, popular rights and privileges on the other' (vol. 1, p. 397). Modern scholarship has dissolved this false antithesis.

Jacobite bias of his instructors were not proved at the time; 'but the political views of the king, on his accession to the throne, appear to confirm the suspicions entertained concerning his early education'. Dodington's *Diary*, the Walpole *Memoirs* and Albemarle's *Rockingham* were drawn on in evidence; Waldegrave's *Memoirs* contributed the decisive judgement. Prince George was, to his governor, 'full of princely prejudices contracted in the nursery, and improved by the society of bedchamber-women and pages of the back-stairs'. It was an easy inference that Bolingbroke's *Patriot King* was the blueprint for the new reign. 'The young king, brought up at Leicester House, had acquired, by instruction and early association, the principles in favour at that little court ... He at once became the regenerator and leader of the Tory party.'[417]

Erskine May's account of political history, although it made reference to original sources, was highly abridged and strong in unsupported generalisation.[418] Its strength was that it appeared to offer the sanction of a lawyer, of an alternative *genre* of academic enquiry, and almost (through Erskine May's position as Clerk of the House) of the Commons itself. Its weakness was that it achieved these effects by imposing on the eighteenth century the practices or, worse still, the platitudes of the mid-nineteenth century.

By 1882, when Lecky[419] came to publish the third volume of his *History*, he was able to draw on almost all the major sources which were to appear in print for the 1760s, including the Bedford and Chatham papers, Albemarle's *Rockingham*, Harris's *Hardwicke*, Fitzmaurice's *Shelburne*, and Burke. Erskine May's *Constitutional History* prompted Lecky to preface his account of the constitutional significance of George III's accession with a panegyric of limited constitutional monarchy, that unique English invention (as Lecky complacently hailed it), an 'ideal' which had achieved 'substantial realisation' since 1688 largely from the 'steady subsequent growth of the popular element in the Constitution' and the 'silent strengthening of party government, that has virtually deprived the Sovereign of his legally unrestricted power of choosing his ministers'. It was an achievement for which Lecky (following Albemarle) gave his putative ancestors

[417] Sir Thomas Erskine May, *The Constitutional History of England since the Accession of George III* (1861–3; ed. Francis Holland, 3 vols., London, 1912), vol. 1, pp. vii-viii, 1, 5, 7–8, 402–3.
[418] Modern readers expecting to find dryasdust history exemplified in these closely printed Victorian tomes will be surprised at the shallowness and the rhetorical nature of many of their judgements: 'The infatuated assaults of James II upon the religion and liberties of the people ... the Revolution was the triumph and conclusive recognition of Whig principles as the foundation of a limited monarchy' (vol. 1, p. 399), etc. etc.
[419] William Edward Hartpole Lecky (1838–1903). Scots-Irish family; ed. Trinity College, Dublin; private means. Lost his early vocation as a clergyman and became an author, initially on militantly agnostic themes, e.g. *The History of the Rise and Influence of the Spirit of Rationalism in Europe* (2 vols., London, 1865). A Gladstonian Liberal; supporter of Irish Church disestablishment; MP for Dublin University 1895–1902, as a Liberal Unionist. His *History of England in the Eighteenth Century* was published 1878–90.

the whole credit: 'the form which popular government has assumed in England is mainly to be attributed to the Whig party', who 'have combated steadily the Tory doctrine of the divine right of kings, and the conception of monarchy that flows from it, and have restricted within very narrow limits the political functions of the Sovereign'.

George III played a crucial role in this scenario. He was pictured as 'the last instance of an English sovereign endeavouring systematically to impose his individual opinion upon the nation'. It was an attempt destined to fail, of course, in the face of Lecky's assumptions about the broadening stream of liberty and democracy flowing so strongly in the other direction. But what defined George III as a champion of the forces of reaction against the forces of progress were his Leicester House experiences of the 1750s.

Once more, therefore, Waldegrave's *Memoirs* were coupled with Horace Walpole's *Memoirs of George II*. The character defects of the young Prince and his mother ('deeply imbued with the narrow prejudices of a small German Court ... Like most members of German royal families, she exaggerated the prerogative of monarchy to the highest degree'), the illegitimate status of Bute, the lurking influence of Bolingbroke, the Jacobite stigma attaching to Stone and Murray, all were combined by Lecky, allegedly demonstrated from Waldegrave and Walpole, and now used to establish the inevitable apotheosis of late-nineteenth-century constitutionalism.

Conveniently, the story could be personalised, could be given a villain and an excuse for the tardy triumph of 'modernity'. George III was held up as 'a sovereign of whom it may be said, without exaggeration, that he inflicted more profound and enduring injuries upon his country than any other modern English king'.[420] So it was that from Waldegrave's frustrated ambition, personal bitterness and perceptive but moderate criticisms of his royal pupil had flowed the most extravagant misstatements. Thanks to Whig artifice, English historiography was imbued with the perspective embodied in the libel which had amused Lord Holland in December 1821:

> In the first year of Freedom's second dawn[421]
>   Died George the Third; although no tyrant, one
> Who shielded tyrants, till each sense withdrawn
>   Left him nor mental nor external sun:
> A better farmer ne'er brushed dew from lawn,
>   A worse king never left a realm undone!
> He died – but left his subjects still behind,
>   One half as mad – and t'other no less blind.

---

[420] W.E.H. Lecky, *A History of England in the Eighteenth Century*, vol. 3 (London, 1882), ch. ix, *passim*.
[421] An allusion to the revolution in 1820 against the restored Bourbon monarchy in Spain.

> He ever warred with freedom and the free:
> Nations as men, home subjects, foreign foes,
> So that they uttered the word 'Liberty!'
> Found George the Third their first opponent. Whose
> History was ever stained as his will be
> With national and individual woes?
> I grant his household abstinence; I grant
> His neutral virtues, which most monarchs want;
>
> I know he was a constant consort; own
> He was a decent sire, and middling lord.
> All this is much, and most upon a throne;
> As temperance, if at Apicius' board,
> Is more than at an anchorite's supper shown,
> I grant him all the kindest can accord;
> And this was well for him, but not for those
> Millions who found him what Oppression chose.[422]

THE TEXT OF THE MEMOIRS

The *Memoirs* survive in three main versions, referred to as the Chewton manuscript, the Murray manuscript, and the Euston manuscript, with some scattered drafts of other passages; only the Murray ms. is in the handwriting of the 2nd Earl. The Chewton ms. was at Melbury House, Sherborne, Dorset among the Holland House papers, was included in the sale of those papers in 1967, and bought by the American scholar W.S. Lewis, the famous collector of Walpoliana. He presented it to the present Earl Waldegrave. The Murray ms. was in the possession of the publishing firm of that name from 1821; it was sold by the late Sir John Murray in 1970, and bought by the present Earl Waldegrave. The Euston manuscript has a prefaratory note:

Augst. 10th 1797.
A Faithful Copy of an original Manuscript written by my Father in the Year 1758. This Copy was taken by me in the Year 1797.

C. Maria Euston

Lady Euston was Charlotte Maria, the second daughter of the 2nd Earl Waldegrave. She married in 1784 George Henry Fitzroy, Earl of Euston, eldest son of the 3rd Duke of Grafton, in whose family it remained. This manuscript was bought at auction by William Waldegrave in 1980, so that the three versions are now reunited in the family's possession, and can be studied together.

The Euston manuscript is prefaced by a note written by Henry, 5th Duke of Grafton (1790–1863):

[422] Lord Byron, *The Vision of Judgement*, stanzas VIII, XLV, XLVI.

Introduction

This Copy in the handwriting of my dear Mother is preserved for her Sake by her unworthy Son Henry born in 1790 – and now bordering on his Grave with the hope through Jesus Christ of going where that blessed Saint now is. Altho' It is not needful as the Work is now printed and in this Library – But this Manuscript is also of Value for the Comments upon it which My Dear Mother seems to have as My Grandfather Expresses it, Commanded him to make –
Wakefield Lodge July 30. 1862

His grandfather, Augustus Henry, 3rd Duke of Grafton (1735–1811) was himself the author of political memoirs,[423] focussing on the years 1763–85 but opening, like Waldegrave's, with a consideration of the crisis which unfolded following Henry Pelham's death in 1754. The first chapter of that work was dated 9 October 1804, the second chapter 19 February 1805. It was therefore of particular interest to the 3rd Duke that in the latter month Lady Euston showed him her copy of her father's memoirs. Grafton wrote some observations in reply:

Feby. 1805

After expressing my sincere thanks to Lady Euston for her allowing me the full Inspection of those invaluable Observations of my late much respected friend; I shall, in consequence of her Ladyship's Commands put down a few short remarks I had made in the perusal of them.

Lady Euston will forgive me, when I say, that her Father was always prejudiced to some Degree against Mr Pitt: and tho' few People knew Men & Manners better, than his Lordship, yet, he did not know him much personally; if at all: and Lord W[aldegrave] owns in one place, that he was not partial to him.

I am of Opinion, that the Accounts of all that passed between the late King, & others, will not be found any where, to be equally made Clear, as it is in this Relation; where my worthy friend bore himself so great & honorable a Part.

My Grandfather's Fall, early in 1757, soon followed by his Death,[424] happened about the time, that this Confusion of things, & Factions began. Lord W[aldegrave] does not attribute to the late Duke of Grafton more natural & unacquired Talents, & knowledge of Mankind, than he certainly possessed: But it appears to me, that he is not here sufficiently brought forward, particularly in the Transactions with Leicester House, in which Business, I have good Reason, for believing, that he was much consulted by his Majesty; as he indeed was on most confidential Affairs. My G[rand] Father saw a great deal, & lived much with my respected friend: and I know, that no Person was more esteemed by him, than Lord Waldegrave. I do not recollect, that Lady Yarmouth is ever mentioned, which I much wonder at. The Expressions, in spite of "*spotless Innocence*" Page *30*,[425] ironically introduced, speaks plainly the Writer's Opinion, & Conception of the Conduct of the Mother. No one can say, what, under such Circumstances, the Effect might not have been of such an alarming whisper from the Old King.

---

[423] Sir William Anson (ed.), *Autobiography and Political Correspondence of Augustus Henry Third Duke of Grafton K.G.* (London, 1898).
[424] Charles Fitzroy, 2nd Duke of Grafton, died in 1757 as a result of a fall from his horse.
[425] The pagination establishes that it was the Euston ms. which Grafton saw.

The whole Tenor of these Observations from so intelligent and honorable an Adviser, (and himself often a principal Actor) is very edifying, and can not be too highly estimated: and I am particularly flattered, when I find, that many Points advanced by me, in my Memoir, stand on so good Ground, agreeing almost in every thing with this, the most genuine, & best of all Informations.

I ever remain, Lady Euston's obliged & affectionate friend & Servant

Grafton

The immediate family of James, 2nd Earl Waldegrave was obviously well aware of the historical value of the *Memoirs*, and clearly sought to preserve them as a tribute to his memory. Lady Euston transcribed her version of the *Memoirs* at a late date from her father's revised copy, the Murray ms., and the Euston ms. consequently adds nothing to the text. The more interesting problems are raised by the relations between the Murray ms., the Chewton ms., and other papers now in the Holland House collection in the British Library.

The main body of the *Memoirs*, covering 1754–7, is present both in the Murray and Chewton mss. The relevant section of the Chewton ms. is in the hand of Maria Waldegrave; it seems highly probable that the 2nd Earl dictated this first version to his wife, later using it as the basis for his own fair copy, the Murray ms.

Part of the evidence for this thesis is stylistic. The Murray version often softens the expression of the Chewton ms., sometimes omitting a harsh word; the Chewton version often has the sound of a dictated text, which the Murray version amends to more formal prose, and rearranges into longer paragraphs. Stronger evidence is provided by the physical state of the text. The author of the Murray ms. frequently begins by copying a word or phrase from the Chewton ms., then deletes or erases it and inserts a different version. To move from the Murray to the Chewton text is to remove a layer of varnish; the 2nd Earl's freshest and most unrestrained opinions are brought into sharper focus. It is the Chewton ms. which has therefore been used for the main body of the *Memoirs* of 1754–7; material alterations in the Murray version, which affect the sense and not merely the style, are recorded in the footnotes.

The Chewton ms. was probably dictated in the summer of 1758, after Prince George's 20th birthday on 4 June, and, if the opening section is accurate, before George II's 75th birthday on 10 November. In the Murray ms., Waldegrave's failure to note the translation of John Thomas to the bishopric of Salisbury in October 1761 may suggest that the transcription was completed before that event. The Murray version's omission of the early paragraph reflecting on the future accession of Prince George may equally date that manuscript to a period after the demise of George II on 25 October 1760. Sections 3 and 4 below, left as incomplete fragments, were

Introduction

(presumably for that reason) not copied by Waldegrave into the Murray ms.

The situation is complicated by the survival of drafts of other passages in the hand of the 2nd Earl (sections 1, 5, 9–14 below). Sections 5, 6 and 7 have been copied into the Chewton ms. by another hand, now identified as that of Frederick Keppel, Waldegrave's brother-in-law;[426] the survival of Waldegrave's draft of section 5 is evidence for their authenticity and suggests that his drafts for sections 6 and 7 are now lost. Sections 5–7 were obviously written in the period between 25 October 1760 and April 1763, and probably within the two years following George III's accession.[427] It may have been that event which prompted Waldegrave to transcribe his earlier *Memoirs* of 1754–7; if so, his failure to transcribe sections 3–7 suggests either a stylistic desire to preserve the unity and self-sufficiency of the 1754–7 part, or a wish not to compromise the *Memoirs* by juxtaposing them with his bitter attacks on Bute and the dowager Princess of Wales.

Sections 5, 6 and 7 were copied into the Chewton ms., apparently at a later date, and probably after Waldegrave's death. His extant draft of section 5 shows the Chewton copy to be an exact one, without emendations: this may imply that the 2nd Earl was no longer present to make, or authorise, revisions. The copyist also had access to the Murray ms., for as well as transcribing these three sections he also went carefully through both texts of the *Memoirs* of 1754–7: in several places where the syntax of the Chewton ms. is incomplete, Keppel supplied the word from the Murray ms. and wrote it in, first in pencil, then in ink. These emendations are almost never more than minor stylistic ones,[428] which suggests that they were done (and sections 5–7 transcribed) after Waldegrave's death; but that the alterations were made at all confirms the identity of the copyist as a close member of the family circle. Other manuscripts to which Keppel presumably had access were not copied, including section 1; but it was clearly too late to include this in its correct place in the text.

The remainder of the sections have been reprinted from Waldegrave's drafts. The relation of the manuscript versions is summarised in Table 4.

It remains to explain the role of the Chewton manuscript's copyist. The Hon. and Rev. Frederick Keppel (1729–77) was the fourth son of the 2nd Earl of Albemarle.[429] Educated at Westminster and Christ Church,

[426] The identification, which I endorse, was first made by Mrs. Catherine Jestin of the Lewis Walpole Library.
[427] Section 7 seemingly refers to the situation in the autumn of 1762.
[428] There is an important exception: *C*, p. 85 and *M*, p. 53 verso, have a passage heavily deleted by the same hand. In both mss, Keppel has replaced the original: that Prince George was 'full' of princely prejudices 'contracted in the Nursery, and improved by the Society of Bed Chamber Women and Pages of the Back Stairs'.
[429] His mother was Anne, youngest daughter of Charles, 1st Duke of Richmond, natural son of Charles II.

Table 4 *The location of manuscript sources*

The handwriting is indicated thus: [W] for James, 2nd Earl Waldegrave; [MW] for Maria, Lady Waldegrave; [FK] for Frederick Keppel

Section	Chewton Ms	Murray Ms	Other Sources
1. Memoirs of the Leicester House Years, 1752–1756	no	no	51380 ff. 85–6 [W]
2. Memoirs of 1754–1757	pp. 1–172 [MW]	pp. 1–98, i.e. the whole ms. [W]	Grafton ms.
3. Memoirs of the Seven Years' War	pp. 173–4 [MW]	no	no
4. Memoirs of the Accession of George III	pp. 176–89 [MW]	no	no
5. Reflections on the New Reign: 'A Parallel'	pp. 193–206 [FK]	no	51380 ff. 90–105 [W]
6. An Allegory of Leicester House	pp. 209–29 [FK]	no	no
7. A Satire on Bute's Ministerial Power	pp. 231–4, the end of the ms. [FK]	no	no
8. Speeches in the House Lords, 1742–1763	one speech at Chewton House [W]	no	the remainder in 51380ff. 108–89 [W]
9. Notes from Plutarch	no	no	51380 f. 233 [W]
10. Notes from Montaigne	no	no	51380 ff 245 [W]
11. Notes from Montesquieu	no	no	51380 ff 241–4 [W]
12. Notes on Constitutional Law	no	no	51380 ff 234–7 [W]
13. Notes on the Constitution	no	no	51380 ff 238–40 [W]
14. Notes on English History	no	no	51380 ff 231–2 [W]

Oxford, he took his BA in 1752, his MA in 1754, and a DD in 1762. With such antecedents, his career in the church was smooth. Ordained in February 1753, he became in April one of the chaplains-in-ordinary to George II, and retained this office under George III. From 19 April 1754 he held a canonry of Windsor,[430] exchanging it for the bishopric of Exeter in 1762. He obtained a promise of translation to the see of Salisbury at the

---

[430] This he owed to the King's favour. George II, according to Horace Walpole, 'having a mind to make Mr. Keppel Prebendary of Windsor, to which [the] Duke of Newcastle was averse, but said he loved Lord Albemarle and his family, "but Mr. Keppel was very young". [The] King replied, "So do I, and I am very old". Keppel received the post'. W.S. Lewis (ed.), *Memoranda Walpoliana* (Farmington, Conn., 1937), p. 15.

Introduction

next vacancy, but relinquished this in favour of the lucrative Deanery of Windsor, holding it *in commendam* with Exeter until his death.

His family was closely involved in public affairs. William Anne Keppel (1702-54), 2nd Earl of Albemarle, was an army officer, rising to the rank of Major General and fighting at Fontenoy and Culloden. Sent as Ambassador to Paris in 1748, he died there suddenly on 22 December 1754 leaving a family of eight sons and seven daughters. His eldest George, 3rd Earl (1724-72) had followed him into the army, fought similarly at Fontenoy and Culloden, and commanded the land forces at the capture of Havana in 1762 (his share of the prize money amounting to £122,000). The same campaign proved lucrative also for the second son, Augustus (1725-86), a naval officer whose distinguished career included Anson's world voyage, Byng's court-martial (1757), the battle of Quiberon Bay (1759) and the capture of Belle Isle (1761). It was even rumoured (probably wrongly) that the see of Exeter for Frederick was part of the family's reward for the victory at Havana. At all events, Horace Walpole acknowledged that Frederick, 'like his own and wife's family, is tolerably warm' – that is, belligerent.

The family alliance was created when on 12 September 1758 Frederick married Laura, the eldest daughter of Sir Edward Walpole. 'We are very happy with the match', commented Edward's brother Horace. When James, 2nd Earl Waldegrave married Sir Edward's second daughter Maria on 15 May 1759, the Rev. Frederick Keppel officiated. Horace Walpole found it ironic that his own family, via his brother's daughters, had married descendants both of James II (Waldegrave) and Charles II (Keppel)!

The Bishop remained closely in touch with the Waldegrave family. He it was who acquainted Maria with the contents of her late husband's will in April 1763, and he spent much time at Strawberry Hill, with Horace Walpole, to comfort the Countess in her grief. Conversation naturally turned to state affairs; on 1 September, Walpole recorded: 'on Sunday the Bishop of Exeter and I were talking of this new convulsion in politics[431] – she [Maria] burst out in a flood of tears, reflecting on the great rank her Lord, if living, would naturally attain on this occasion'. The connection continued: on Keppel's own death in 1777, Horace Walpole remarked how Maria's daughter Lady Laura Waldegrave 'had lived a great deal with the Bishop and loved him like a father'.[432]

Frederick Keppel was clearly the man to whom Maria Waldegrave

[431] Caused by the sudden death of Lord Egremont, Secretary of State for the Southern Department, on 21 August. After some dramatic negotiations, Lord Sandwich kissed hands to succeed him on 9 September.

[432] Horace Walpole to Mann, 9 Sept 1758, 11 April 1759, 10 April 1763, 1 Sept 1763; to G. Montagu, 14 April 1763; to Lord Hertford, 22 Jan 1764; to Lady Ossory, 27 Dec 1777.

would turn for advice over her husband's papers. With a strong stomach and some knowledge of the political world, he would have taken the 2nd Earl's revelations in his stride. At the same time, however, he did not share Waldegrave's resentments. Keppel owed his position in the Church to Court patronage.[433] His family had similar obligations. His brother Augustus, a protégé of Anson, sat in the Commons from 1755 to 1782 – initially with Treasury backing, then from 1761 as MP for New Windsor on the Duke of Cumberland's interest. The 3rd Earl of Albemarle had been rescued from poverty by a ministerial pension after his father's death in 1754, and was by the 1760s even more closely tied to Cumberland.[434] Frederick Keppel would have taken care not to jeopardise his family's position. He had no quarrel of his own to pursue, either with the Pelhamite ministers or with his new sovereign. He arranged his brother-in-law's papers, carefully compared the manuscript versions, filled in a gap here and there, transcribed the conclusion to the Chewton manuscript – and left the *Memoirs* unpublished.

Horace Walpole, too, was obliged to keep his hatreds largely secret, although he shared some of them with Waldegrave himself. After the 2nd Earl's death, Walpole recorded that Waldegrave

> had been so thoroughly fatigued with the insipidity of his pupil the king [George III], and so harrassed and unworthily treated by the Princess and Lord Bute, that no one of the most inflammable vengeance, or of the coolest resentment, could harbour more bitter hatred and contempt than he did for the King's mother and favourite. This aversion carried him to what I scarce believed my eyes when he first showed me – severe satires against them. He has left behind him, too, some Memoirs of the few years in which he was governor to the Prince, that will corroborate many things I have asserted, and will not tend to make these Anecdotes be reckoned unjust and unmerciful.[435]

Yet Walpole, too, wrote for posterity. No-one in Waldegrave's immediate circle had an interest in the early publication of his *Memoirs*, and it was left to the inducements of present advantage, not historical truth, to bring them into print six decades later.

---

[433] George III agreed, evidently at Bute's suggestion, that Keppel would be 'very fit for the Deanery of Exeter': George III to Bute, [12 Jan 1762]: Romney Sedgwick (ed.), *Letters from George III to Lord Bute 1756–1766* (London, 1939), p. 79. When he refused the Deanery, it was again Bute who told him of the king's offer of the now-vacant bishopric: Keppel ms. memoir, Lewis Walpole Library.

[434] When Cumberland died in 1765, George III entrusted Albemarle with the disposal of his papers. The job was done all too well: the Cumberland Papers at Windsor have been 'weeded' of almost all politically sensitive material. We should be grateful that Albemarle's brother did not similarly censor the Waldegrave *Memoirs*. But almost none of the 2nd Earl's correspondence survives in the family's hands: whether the bulk of it was destroyed after his death is unknown.

[435] Walpole, *George III*, vol. 1, p. 212.

James, 2nd Earl Waldegrave by Sir Joshua Reynolds, at Chewton

Maria, Countess Waldegrave by Sir Joshua Reynolds, at Chewton

1

MEMOIRS OF THE LEICESTER HOUSE YEARS, 1752–1756

The date of composition is not known. The section is not present in the Murray or Chewton manuscripts and survives only in Waldegrave's draft, with his corrections, Add MSS 51380 ff. 85–6. It was printed from this draft, with minor inaccuracies, in the Earl of Ilchester, *Henry Fox, First Lord Holland* (2 vols., London, 1920), vol. 1, pp. 361–2.

Memoires from December 1752 to the latter End of the Year 1756 during which time I was Governor to the Prince of Wales.

The King soon after his Return from Hanover in November 1752 found great Confusion in the Prince of Wales's Family. Earl Harcourt[1] and the Bishop of Norwich,[2] the one Governor the other Preceptor to his R.H. were both much displeased. The Persons they chiefly accused, were Mr Stone[3] the Subgovernor, Mr Cresset[4] Treasurer to the Prince, also Secretary and first Minister to the Princess of Wales, and Scot[5] the Subpreceptor.

---

[1] Simon Harcourt (1714–77), 2nd Viscount Harcourt (succ. 1727), created 1st Earl Harcourt Dec. 1749. Ed. Westminster and Grand Tour. A Lord of the Bedchamber to George II 1735–51; Governor to Prince of Wales April 1751-Dec. 1752. Envoy to Mecklenburg to arrange George III's marriage 1761; Ambassador to France 1768–72; Lord Lieutenant of Ireland 1772–7.

[2] Thomas Hayter (1702–62): ed. Balliol Coll. Oxf., BA 1724, Emmanuel Coll. Camb., MA 1727; chaplain to Abp. Lancelot Blackburn of York, whose protégé he became, receiving various prebends. Bp. of Norwich 1749; Preceptor to Prince of Wales 1751–2; Bp of London Oct. 1761.

[3] Andrew Stone (1703–73). Son of a banker; ed. Westminster and Christ Church Oxford. His brother-in-law William Barnard, chaplain at Claremont, introduced him to the Duke of Newcastle, whose private secretary he became in 1732. Under-Secretary of state 1734–51; various sinecures; MP Hastings 1741–61; a Lord of Trade 1749–61; Sub Governor to Prince of Wales 1751–6; Secretary to Prince of Wales 1756–60; Treasurer to Queen Charlotte 1761–d. His brother George Stone (?1708–64) was Archbishop of Armagh and Primate of Ireland, 1751–64.

[4] James Cresset (d. 1775), Secretary to the Princess of Wales 1746–8, joint Secretary 1748–51, sole Secretary 1751–2; Treasurer to George, Prince of Wales 1752–6.

[5] George Lewis Scott (1708–80), son of a diplomat. Mathematician. Became tutor to Prince George Nov. 1750. Sub-preceptor 1751–6. A Commissioner of Excise 1758–80.

The Crimes objected against them were Jacobite Connections, instilling Tory Principles and Scott was more over pronounced an Atheist on the presumptive Evidence of being a Philosopher and a Mathematician.

The real Fact was this, the Bishop of Norwich who from having been first Chaplin to an Arch Bishop, and afterwards chaplin at Court, thought himself equally quallified to govern both Church and State, persuaded Harcourt, an honest worthy Man, but whose Heart was better than his Head, that they as Governor and Preceptor must be the sole Directors of the young Prince, and that not even the Princess herself ought to have the least Influence over him.

Harcourt having approved the Proposal, they form'd their Plan of Operation and began to carry it into Execution.

But the Plot was soon discover'd, the Princess took the Alarm, Stone and Cresset were consulted, and Harcourt and the Bishop were soon defeated without the least Difficulty.

This pass'd while the King was in Germany, on His Majesty's arrival[6] they made their last Effort that Stone Cresset and Scott might be turn'd out for the Reasons already mention'd. They also endeavor'd to raise Jealousies against the Princess as secretly favoring the Opposition form'd by her late Husband. But again failing in their Attempt, they both resign'd their Employment.

However tho Harcourt and the Bishop succeed[ed] so ill at Court, they had better Success with the Publick, for the Nation in general was on their Side. There is a certain Popularity which usualy attends a voluntary Resignation, especially when it proceeds from a Point of Honor.

Many even of those who were Friends to the Pelham's and the Administration were much dissatisfied. Others exclaim'd loudly that we were govern'd by Jacobites that Stone and Murray the Duke of Newcastles two Cabinet Councelors, were known Jacobites at Oxford,[7] and that if they had changed their old Principles, they still adhered to their old Connections.

That on the other Hand Lord Harcourt was a Nobleman of know[n] Honor, Spirit, and Integrity. A steady Whig, every way qualified for the Education of the Heir Apparent.

In a Word the Names of Lord Harcourt and of the Bishop of Norwich were artfully made use of[8] to raise such a Clamor that it was much doubted whether proper Persons could [be] found who would dare to be their Successors.

[6] George II arrived back at St James's on 18 November 1752.
[7] Both were at Christ Church: Andrew Stone in 1722–6, William Murray in 1723–7.
[8] Waldegrave was evidently unaware that it was his friend Horace Walpole who had artfully made use of Harcourt and the Bishop to forward the rumour.

Under these Circumstances, I was applyed too, as one who was more attached to the King than to his Ministers, for they would not venture to put in a known Creature of their own.

In this Respect I fully answer'd their Purpose, for tho none of their Dependants, I had a very sincere esteem and Friendship for Mr Pelham, and was at least a well wisher to the Duke of Newcastle.

About a fortnight after Lord Harcour[t']s Resignation the Affair was mention'd to me from the King by the Duke of Newcastle, who told me his Majesty did not chuse to speak to me himself, that I might be at full liberty to either accept or refuse as I liked best.

Waldegrave accepted, so laying the best possible foundation (as he must have presumed) for his future political career. Whatever the date of composition of section 1, there is no evidence that Waldegrave felt the need to keep autobiographical notes during his time as Governor to the Prince of Wales. Only after his career had gone disastrously wrong for the second time did he set down an account of events. This forms section 2.

2

MEMOIRS OF 1754–1757

This text is taken from the Chewton manuscript, pp. 1–172. The significant variations in the Murray manuscript are noted.

Written in the year 1758

I shall give a short account of our political Contentions, party quarrels, and of all Events of any Consequence, from the begang[1] of the year 1754 to the middle of June 1757. I will advance no Facts which are not strictly true, & do not mean to misrepresent any man; but must make no professions of Impartiality, because I take it for granted that it is not in my power to be quite unprejudiced. Having given this caution, I shall sketch out the Portraits of some of the principal Actors, endeavoring rather to preserve a Likeness than to catch the Eye with the beauties of couloring or of high finishing.

The King is in his 75th year,[2] but Temperance and an excellent Constitution have hitherto preserved him from many of the Infirmities of old Age.

He has a good understanding tho not of the first Class; and has a clear Insight into Men, & Things[3] within a certain Compass.

He is accus'd by his Ministers, of being exceeding[4] hasty and passionate, when any Measure is propos'd which he does not approve of. Tho, as far as my own Experience, I never knew a Person of high Rank bear contradiction better; provided the Intention was apparently good, and the manner Decent. When any thing disagreeable passes in the Closet when any of his Ministers happen to displease him, it cannot long remain a Secret, for his countenance can never dissemble; but to those Servants who

---

[1] *Sc.* beginning.
[2] George II was born on 10 November 1683. This dates the composition of the *Memoirs* to 1757–58.
[3] *M* adds a comma after 'Things', perhaps softening the sense. [4] *M* omits 'exceeding'.

attend his Person, and do not trouble him with frequent Sollicitations, he is ever gracious and affable.

Even in the early part of Life, he was fond of Business: at present it is become almost his only amusement.

He has more knowledge of foreign Affairs than most of his Ministers; and has good general notions of the Constitution, Strength and Interest of this Country.

But being past thirty when the Hanover Succession took place;[5] and having since experienced the violence of Party, the Injustice of popular Clamor, the Corruption of Parliaments and the selfish Motives of pretended Patriots, it is not surprising that he should have contracted some Prejudices, in favor of those Governments where the Royal authority is under less Restraint.

Yet Prudence has so far prevail'd over these Prejudices, that they have never influenced his Conduct: on the contrary, many Laws have been enacted, in favor of public Liberty; and in the Course of a long Reign, there has not been a single attempt to extend the Prerogative of the Crown beyond its proper Limits.

He has as much personal Bravery as any Man, tho his political Courage seems somewhat Problematical: However it is a Fault on the right Side for had he always been as firm and undaunted in the Closet, as he shew'd himself at Oudenarde, and Dettingen,[6] he might not have proved quite so good a King, in this Limited Monarchy.

At the Drawing room he is gracious and polite to the Ladies; and remarkably cheerful, & familiar with those who are handsome or with the few of his Old Acquaintance, who were Beauties in his younger Days. His Conversation is very proper for a Tete à Tete; he then talks freely on most Subjects and very much to the Purpose: But he cannot discourse with the same Ease, nor has he the Faculty of laying aside the King, in a larger Company: Not even in those Parties of Pleasure which are compos'd of his most intimate Acquaintance.

His Servants are never disturbed with any unnecessary waiting, for he is regular in all his Motions, to the greatest Exactness; except on particular occasions, when he outruns his own Orders, and expects those who are to attend him before the time of his Appointment. This may easily be accounted for; He has a restless Mind which requires constant Exercise; his affairs are not sufficient to fill up the day; his amusements are without Variety & have lost their Relish; he becomes fretful and uneasy merely for

[5] Queen Anne died on 1 August 1714. The future George II's 30th birthday was in November 1713.
[6] The battles of Oudenarde (1708) and Dettingen (1743). George II was vain about his military record. It was the mark of a true courtier to flatter him about it; to cast doubt on it was the surest way to lose his favour.

want of Employment, and presses forward to meet the succeeding Hour, before it arrives.

Too great Attention to Money seems to be his Capital Failing; however he is always just, and sometimes charitable, tho seldom generous: and[7] when we consider how rarely the Liberality of Princes is directed to the proper object, but is usually bestow'd on a rapacious Mistress, or an unworthy Favorite; want of Generosity, tho it still continues a Blot, ceases at least to be a Vice of the first Magnitude.

Upon the whole, he has some Qualities of a great Prince, many of a good one, none which are essentially bad; and I am thoroughly convinc'd that hereafter when Time shall have wore away those Specks & Blemishes which sully the brightest Characters, & from which no Man is totally exempt, He will be number'd amongst those patriot Kings, under whose Government, the People have enjoy'd the greatest Happiness.[8]

The Prince of Wales is entering into his 21st year,[9] and it would be unfair to decide upon his Character, in the early Stages of Life, when there is so much time for Improvement. His Parts, tho not excellent, will be found very tolerable, if ever they are properly exercised. He is strictly honest, but wants that frank and open Behavior, which makes Honesty appear amiable.

When he had a very scanty Allowance, it was one of his favorite Maxims, that Men should be just before they are generous. His income is now very considerably augmented but his generosity has not increased in equal Proportion.[10]

His Religion is free from all Hipocrisy, but not of the most charitable sort; he has rather too much attention to the sins of his Neighbour.

He has Spirit, tho not of the active kind; and does not want Resolution, but it is mixed with too much obstinacy. He has great command of his Passions, and will seldom do wrong, except when he mistakes wrong for right; but as often as this shall happen, it will be difficult to undeceive him, because he is uncommonly indolent, and has strong Prejudices.

His want of Application, and Aversion to Business would be far less

---

[7] *M*: 'but'.
[8] This was written even before the troubles of the 1760s led many to look back on George II's reign as a golden age. The strength of the young Earl's attachment to the aged king is remarkable. Also evident is Waldegrave's care to place George II's shortcomings in the best light. This contrasts with his subtle disparagement of the Prince of Wales which follows.
[9] Prince George was born on 4 June 1738; his 20th birthday in 1758 dates the composition of the *Memoirs*.
[10] As Prince of Wales, George II had received an allowance of £100,000 p.a.; but he gave his own son, Frederick, only £24,000, raised to £50,000 after his marriage. After Frederick's death in 1751, the king continued that sum as an allowance to Princess Augusta. When Prince George came of age in 1756 a separate household was created for him: the warrant dated 10 November 1756 provided for an annual allowance of £40,000. McKelvey, *George III and Lord Bute*, pp. 7, 36; Brooke, *George III*, p. 53.

dangerous, was he eager in the persuit of Pleasure; for the Transition from Pleasure to Business is both shorter and easier, than from a State of total Inaction.

He has a kind of unhappiness in his Temper, which if it be not conquer'd before it has taken too deep a Root, will be a damp to all his Pleasures, and[11] a Source of frequent Anxiety. Whenever he is displeas'd his anger does not break out with Heat, or Violence, but he becomes Sullen, & Silent, and retires to his Closett; not to compose his Mind by Study or Contemplation, but merely to indulge the melancholy Enjoyment of his own ill Humor. Even when the Fit is ended unfavorable Symptoms very frequently return, which indicate that on certain occasions his R:H has too correct a Memory.

Tho I have mentioned his good and bad qualities without Flattery and without Aggravation, Allowances should still be made on account of his Youth, & his bad Education: For tho the Bishop of Peterborough, now Bishop of Salisbury, the Preceptor,[12] Mr. Stone the Sub-governor, & Mr. Scott the Subpreceptor were Men of Sense, Men of Learning, and worthy, good Men, they had but little weight and Influence; the Mother's opinions[13] always prevail'd.

During the Course of the last year, there has indeed been some Alterations; the authority of the Women had gradually declined, and the Earl of Bute, by the assistance of the Mother, has now the intire Confidence. But whether this Change will be greatly to his Royal Highness's Advantage, is a nice question, which cannot hitherto be determined with any Certainty.

Be that as it will: hereafter when the Young Prince shall succeed his Grandfather, there may possibly be Changes of greater Consequence. He will soon be made sensible that a Prince who suffers himself to be led, is not allow'd the choice of his own Conductor. His Pride will then give Battle to his Indolence and, having made the first Effort, a moderate share of Obstinacy will make him persevere. His Honesty will incline him to do that which is Right; & the Means cannot be wanting where a good Disposition of Mind is join'd with a tolerable Capacity: for a superior Genius does not seem to be a *Sine qua non* in the Composition of a good King.[14]

[11] *M* omits 'a damp to all his Pleasures, and'.
[12] *C* has a footnote in Maria Waldegrave's hand: 'now Winchester'. John Thomas (1696–1781), Bishop of Peterborough 1747, was appointed Preceptor to Prince George in December 1752, succeeding Bishop Hayter; he was translated to Salisbury in 1757 and to Winchester in October 1761. James, 2nd Earl evidently copied out the Murray ms. before 1761.
[13] *C* has 'the Mother & the Nursery', deleted and replaced by 'the Mother's opinions'; *M* reverts to 'the Mother and the Nursery'.
[14] The foregoing paragraph is omitted in *M*, possibly dating it after George III's accession on 25 October 1760.

The Duke of Newcastle is in his 35th year of Ministerial Longevity;[15] has been much abused, much flatter'd, and still more ridiculed. From the year 1724 to the year 42 he was Secretary of State, acting under Sir Robert Walpole: he continued in the same station during Lord Granville's short Administration:[16] but Granville, who had the Parts without the judgement of a great Minister,[17] treated him with too much Contempt: especially as he wanted his assistance in the House of Commons where he had no[18] Interest of his own.

After Granville's defeat, the Duke of Newcastle and Mr Pelham became joint Ministers: here he seems to have reach'd the highest Degree of Power where he can reasonably hope to maintain himself.

Ambition, Fear, and Jealousy are his prevailing Passions. In the midst of Prosperity and apparent Happiness, the slightest disappointment, or any imaginary Evil will in a moment make him miserable; his Mind can never be composed, his Spirits are always agitated. Yet this constant Ferment, which would wear out and destroy any other Man, is perfectly agreeable to his Constitution: he is at the very Perfection of Health, when his Fever is at the greatest Height.

His Character is full of Inconsistencies: the Man would be thought very singular who differ'd as much from the rest of the World, as he differs from himself. If we consider how many years he has continued in the highest Employments; that he has acted a very considerable Part, amongst the most considerable Persons of his own time; that when his Friends have been routed, he has still maintain'd his Ground; that he has incurr'd his Majesty's displeasure on various Occasions, but has always carried his Point, and has soon been restored both to Favor and Confidence; it must be allow'd[19] that he possesses many[20] Qualities of an able Minister.

Yet view him in a different light, and our Veneration will be somewhat abated. Talk with him relating to public or private Business of a nice or delicate Nature, he will be found confused, irresolute, continually rambling from the Subject, contradicting himself almost every Instant. Hear him speak in Parliament, his manner is ungraceful, his Language barbarous, his Reasoning inconclusive.

---

[15] Thomas Pelham-Holles, 1st Duke of Newcastle (1693–1768) became Secretary of State for the Southern Department in 1724.

[16] Of February 1745/6. John Carteret (1690–1763), succeeded as Baron Carteret 1695; a Lord of the Bedchamber 1714–21; Secretary of State (S) 1720/1–1724; Lord Lieutenant of Ireland 1724–30; Secretary of State (N) Feb. 1741/2 – Nov. 1744, virtually heading the ministry; succ. as Earl Granville 1744; Secretary of State 10–14 Feb. 1745/6; Lord President 1751-*d*.

[17] *M*: 'who had the parts, and knowledge, yet had not, at all times, the Discretion of an able Minister'.

[18] *M*: 'little'.   [19] *M*: 'it cannot be denied'.

[20] *M*: 'some'. Waldegrave added some minor disparagements in *M*.

Memoirs of 1754–1757

At the same time he labours thro all the confusion of a Debate without the least distrust of his own abilities, fights boldly in the Dark; never gives up the Cause nor is he ever at a loss either for words or argument. His Professions & Promises are not to be depended on, tho at the time they are made he often means to perform them; but is unwilling to displease any man by a plain Negative, and frequently does not recollect that he is under the same Engagements to at least ten Competitors.

If he cannot be esteem'd a Steady Friend, he has never shewn himself a bitter Enemy; and his forgiveness of Injuries proceeds as much from good Nature, as it does from Policy.

Pride is not to be number'd amongst his faults; on the Contrary, he deviates into the opposite Extreme, and courts Popularity with such extravagant eagerness, that he frequently descends to an undistinguishing and illiberal Familiarity.

Neither can he be accused of Avarice or Rapaciousness; for tho he will give Bribes, he is above accepting them, and instead of having enrich'd himself at the Expense of his Master, or of the Public, he has greatly impair'd a very considerable Estate by electioneering and keeping up a good Parliamentary Interest, which is commonly, tho perhaps improperly, call'd the service of the Crown.[21]

His extraordinary care of his Health is a jest even amongst his Flatterers. As to his Jealousy, it could not be carried to a higher Pitch, if every Political Friend, was a favorite Mistress.

He is in his 64th[22] year, yet thirsts for power in a future Reign with the greatest Solicitude; and hereafter should he live to see a Prince of Wales of a year old, he will still look forward not without hopes,[23] that in due course of time he may be his Minister also. Upon the whole he seems tolerably well qualified to act a second Part, but wants both Spirit and Capacity to be first in Command: neither has he the smallest Particle of that Elevation of Mind, or of that dignity of Behavior, which command respect, and characterise the great Statesman.

---

[21] Newcastle succeeded in 1712 to one of the best estates in England, unencumbered by debt and worth about £27,000 p.a. By the last year of his life, 1767–8, he had reduced its gross value by some £320,000 and his annual income to about £9,000. See Ray A. Kelch, *Newcastle: A Duke Without Money: Thomas Pelham-Holles 1693–1768* (London, 1974), pp. 36–7, 182–3, 191–2. Various but quite accurate estimates were public knowledge at the time: cf. 'It moves one to compassion to think of the poor old Duke himself. A man once possessed of £25,000 per annum of landed estate, with £10,000 in emoluments of government, now reduced to an estate of scarcely £6,000 per annum': Mr. Symmer to Sir Andrew Mitchell, 31 Dec. 1762, in Henry Ellis (ed.), *Original Letters Illustrative of British History* 2nd series (4 vols., London, 1827), vol. 4, p. 452.

[22] *M*: '64th or 65th'. Newcastle was born on 21 July 1693; he was 64 in 1757. Waldegrave was evidently uncertain of the date.

[23] *M*: 'Expectation'.

Mr Pitt,[24] has the finest Genius, improv'd by Study, and all the ornamental Part of Classical Learning. He came early into the House of Commons where he soon distinguish'd himself; lost a Cornecy of Horse, which was then his only subsistence; and in about[25] twenty years, has raised himself to be first Minister, and the most powerful Subject in this Country.

His Eloquence is nervous, natural, correct, and elegant.[26] He has an astonishing[27] Clearness, and Facility of Expression, and has an Eye as significant as his Words. He is not always a fair or conclusive Reasoner, but commands the Passions with Sovereign Authority, and to inflame or captivate a popular Assembly, is a consummate Orator.

Tho his Passions are strong, and fiery, they are all obedient to his unbounded Ambition.[28]

He has courage of every sort, cool or impetuous, active or deliberate.

At present he is the Guide and Champion of the People: whether he will long continue their Friend, seems somewhat doubtful. But if we may judge from his natural disposition, as it has hitherto shewn itself, his popularity, and Zeal for public Liberty will have the same Period: for he is imperious, violent, and implacable; impatient even of the slightest contradiction; and under the mask of Patriotism, has the despotick Spirit of a Tyrant.

However, tho his political Sins are black, and dangerous, his private Character is irreproachable; he is incapable of a treacherous or ungenerous action; and, in the common offices of Life, is justly esteem'd a Man of Veracity, & a Man of Honour.

He mixes little in Company, confining his Society to a small Juncto of his own Relations with a few obsequious Friends who consult him as an Oracle, admire his superior Understanding and never presume to have an Opinion of their own.

This Separation from the World is not entirely owing to Pride, or an unsociable Temper, as it proceeds partly from bad Health and a weak Constitution. But he may find it an impassable Barrier in the Road of Ambition: for tho the Mob can sometimes raise a Minister, he must be supported by Persons of higher Rank, who may be mean enough in some particulars, yet will not be the patient Followers of any Man, who despises their Homage, and avoids their Sollicitations.

Besides, it is a common Observation, that Men of plain Sense, and cool Resolution, have more useful Talents, and are better qualified for public

---

[24] William Pitt (1707–78), MP 1735–66, created Earl of Chatham 1766. Cornet of Cobham's Horse 1731–6; dismissed for his opposition activities in the circle of Lord Cobham, George Lyttelton and the Grenvilles. Pitt went over to support the Pelham ministry in May 1745, but George II prevented his promotion to more than minor offices for a decade.
[25] *M*: 'less than'.   [26] Sentence omitted in *M*.   [27] *M*: 'a peculiar'.
[28] This sentence deleted in *M*.

Business, than the Man of the finest Parts, who wants Temper, Judgement, and Knowledge of Mankind. Even Parliamentary abilities may be too highly rated; for between the Man of Eloquence, and the Sagacious Statesman there is a wide Interval.

However if Mr Pitt should maintain his power, a few Years, Observation and Experience may correct many Faults, and supply many Deficiencies: in the mean time, even his Enemies must allow that he has the Firmness, and activity of a great Minister: that he has hitherto conducted the War with Spirit, Vigor, and tolerable Success: and tho some favorite Schemes have been[29] visionary and impracticable, they have at least been more honorable, & less dangerous, than the passive, unperforming Pusillanimity, of the late Administration.[30]

Mr Pelham[31] died in March 1754, and our Tranquillity, both at home and abroad, expired with him.

He had acquired the Reputation of an able, and honest Minister, had a plain, solid Understanding improved by Experience in Business, as well as by a thorough knowledge of the World; and without being an Orator, or having the finest Parts, no Man in the House of Commons argued with more Weight, or was heard with greater attention.

He was a frugal Steward to the Public, averse to continental Extravagance, and useless Subsidies; preferring a tolerable Peace, to the most successful War; jealous to maintain his personal Credit, and authority; but nowise inattentive to the true Interest of his Country.[32]

Fox[33] at that time Secretary at War, was thought the most proper Person to be his Successor, under certain Limitations: but the Duke of Newcastle very prudently consider'd that a Man of Fox's Abilities who held the Purse, regulated our Finances, and govern'd the House of Commons, must in effect be first Minister. He therefore took the Resolution of presiding himself at the Head of the Treasury, and made choice of Legge to be his Chancellor of the Exchequer, thinking him a quiet Man who understood the Business of his Office, and having been accustom'd to act in a Subordinate Station, would do whatever he was directed. Fox was now to

---

[29] *M*: 'may have been'.
[30] Waldegrave is evidently writing before the great series of military and naval victories of 1759.
[31] Hon. Henry Pelham (1695–1754), MP 1717-*d*, Treasurer of the Chamber 1720–2; a Lord of the Treasury 1721–4; Secretary at War 1724–30; Paymaster General 1730–43; First Lord of the Treasury and Chancellor of the Exchequer 1743-*d*.
[32] The large extent to which Waldegrave shared this aversion to continental involvement is clear from his speeches, section 8 below.
[33] Henry Fox (1705–74). Ed. Eton and Christ Church. MP 1735–63; created Baron Holland 1763. Surveyor General 1737–43; a Lord of the Treasury 1743–6; Secretary at War 1746-Oct. 1755; Secretary of State for Southern Department Oct. 1755-Oct. 1756; Paymaster General June 1757-May 1765.

be Secretary of State, and under the Duke of Newcastle, to have the Conduct of the House of Commons; the Articles of Union being settled by the Marquis of Hartington, with all the Appearance of mutual satisfaction.

But before the Treaty could take Place,[34] the Duke of Newcastle changed his Mind: however, not daring to deny his Agreement with Lord Hartington, he endeavor'd to palliate, explain, and excuse himself: that his anxiety of mind, the affliction of his Family, & Grief for the loss of his Brother, had quite disorder'd his Memory: that possibly he might have express'd his Meaning in improper words, but certainly, it could never have been his Intention to give Fox that Share of Power which he now claim'd.

Fox, on the other hand would make no abatement; wrote a Letter of Refusal; was immediately taken at his word; Sir Thomas Robinson[35] was made Secretary of State, and the Duke of Newcastle became nominally the sole Minister.[36]

But without affecting the Name, or Parade of a Minister, Lord Hardwick[37] had also great Weight, and Authority:[38] he seldom chose to interfere in affairs of little Consequence, but was consulted on every occasion; and no important Measure of Government was carried into Execution, without his previous Consent. Before I proceed further in my Narrative, it may be necessary to make some Observations on the several Parties which divided the Court and Parliament.

When the Hanover Succession took Place, the Whigs became the Possessors of all the great Offices, and other lucrative Employments, since which time, instead of quarrelling with the Prerogative, they have been the Champions of every Administration.

However they have seldom[39] been united in one Body, under one

[34] *M*: 'be carried into execution'. Whether terms had been agreed or not was precisely the point at issue; Waldegrave amends his text in a sense unfavourable to Newcastle.

[35] Thomas Robinson (1695–1770). Ed. Westminster and Trinity College, Camb., MP 1727–34, 1748–61, knighted 1742; created Baron Grantham 1761. Diplomatic career 1723–48; a Lord of Trade 1748–9; Master of the Great Wardrobe 1749–54, 1755–61; Secretary of State for the Southern Department March 1754-Nov. 1755.

[36] Waldegrave played no part in the negotiations to establish the succession to Henry Pelham, and repeats here the version of events given him by Henry Fox or Lord Hartington. Yet although Fox began the race as the favourite at White's, his claims automatically to inherit Pelham's position were widely disputed; Waldegrave's account of Newcastle's duplicity in frustrating the obvious candidate needs careful qualification. See Clark, *Dynamics of Change*, pp. 44–97, for an interpretation less favourable to Fox.

[37] Philip Yorke (1690–1764). Ed. Bethnal Green Dissenting Academy and Middle Temple, called to the bar 1715. Protégé of Lord Chancellor Macclesfield. MP 1719–33; Solicitor General 1720–4; knighted 1720; Attorney-General 1724–33; Chief Justice of King's Bench 1733–7; created Baron Hardwicke 1733; Lord Chancellor 1737–56; created Earl of Hardwicke 1754.

[38] *M* deletes the remainder of this sentence and includes instead: 'He was undoubtedly an excellent Chancellor, and might have been thought a great Man, had he been less avaricious, less proud, less unlike a Gentleman, and not so great a Politician.'

[39] *M*: 'not always'.

General, like a regular and well disciplined Army: but may more aptly be compar'd to an Alliance of different Clans, fighting in the same Cause, professing the same Principles, but influenced, and guided by their different Chieftains.

Amongst these, the Party of the Pelhams was undoubtedly the Strongest: for besides the personal Interest of both Brothers, which was very considerable, they had long been the Distributors of all the Favors of the Crown; the last House of Commons had been elected[40] whilst they were joint Ministers; and the Duke of Newcastle was to begin his Administration with the Choice of a new Parliament.

Fox had also many personal Friends and more political Followers; being look'd upon as the rising Minister in the House of Commons, in case either of Mr Pelham's Death, Resignation, or Removal to the House of Peers.

He had moreover the Support of the Duke of Cumberland,[41] & the distribution of military Preferments; which added greatly to his Strength by furnishing the means of gratifying his Dependants.

On the other hand,[42] tho Fox derived these Advantages from his Attachment to the Duke, the Prejudice might upon the whole, be still greater than the Benefit.

His Royal Highness had Strong Parts, great Military Abilities, undoubted Courage, and had gain'd the Victory of Culloden which Saved this Country.

But his popularity ended with the Rebellion, his Services were immediately forgot, and he became the Object of Fear and Jealousy. The Severe Treatment of Scotland after the Defeat of the Rebels was imputed to his cruel and sanguinary disposition;[43] even the Army had been taught to complain of the unnecessary Strictness of his Discipline; that they were treated rather like Germans, than English Men: all his good qualities were overlook'd, all his Faults were agrevated: false Facts were advanced against him, and falser conclusions drawn from them; whilst the late Prince of Wales[44] gave too much countenance to the most malignant and groundless accusations by Shewing Favor to every Man who aspersed his Brothers Character.

Fox had also his share of Calumny, being represented as a Man of Arbitrary Principles, educated in the School of Corruption: a proper

[40] In June-July 1747.
[41] William Augustus, Duke of Cumberland (1721–65), 3rd son (the second having died) of George II. Military career: fought at Dettingen (1743); 1745 Captain General of British army; Fontenoy (1745); Culloden (1746); Laffelt (1747); commanded British army in Germany 1757. Incapacitated by ill-health after 1760.
[42] *M*: 'At the same time'.
[43] See W.A. Speck, *The Butcher: the Duke of Cumberland and the Suppression of the 45* (Oxford, 1981).
[44] Cumberland's brother Prince Frederick (1707–51).

Minister to overturn the Constitution, and introduce a military Government.

As I had Opportunities of knowing them both, I will risk my opinion concerning them, endeavoring as far as I am able, to avoid Partiality.

His R.H.'s Judgement would be equal to his Parts, were it not too much guided by his Passions, which are often violent, and ungovernable. He has Abilities to perform things which are difficult, but sometimes loves an Impossibility.

In his Military Capacity, he appears greatly Superior to any Man in this Country: and I have frequently wish'd that he had confined himself to that department, without entering into party Disputes, or interfering in the affairs of civil Government: the first of which is below his Dignity, and for the latter he is not qualified.

His notions of Honor, and Generosity are worthy of a Prince. That he is ambitious is not to be doubted, and had his Majesty died, during the present Prince of Wales's Minority, he would most reasonably have expected to have been the young King's General; or if he could have form'd a Party in Parliament strong enough to have repeal'd the Act of Regency,[45] the Princess of Wales's Authority might have suffer'd great diminution. But that he had ever[46] the most distant Design of a more criminal Nature, that he meant any thing hurtful to his Nephew, or dangerous to the Public, the Insinuation was base and villainous.

As to Fox, few Men have been more unpopular yet when I have ask'd his bitterest Enemies, which crimes they could alledge against him; they always confined themselves to general accusations; that he was avaritious, encouraged Jobs, had profligate Friends, and dangerous Connections, but never could produce a single[47] Fact of any Weight or Consequence.

His Warmth, or Impetuosity of Temper, led him into two very capital mistakes: he wantonly offended the Chancellor by personal Reflections, or Ridicule, in the Affair of the Marriage Act:[48] he also increased the number

---

[45] The Regency Act of 1751 (24 Geo. II, c. 24) settled the Regency on the dowager Princess of Wales in case of George II's demise before his grandson reached the age of majority; but the Act also established a Council of fourteen members, the Duke of Cumberland being its president, the consent of which was necessary for the exercise of the royal prerogative in many specified areas. The ability of the Princess and of the Duke to act independently was thus circumscribed. For debates on the Bill, see *Parl. Hist.*, vol. 14, cols. 992–1057; Walpole, *George II*, vol. 1, pp. 78–103.

[46] *M*: 'even'.   [47] *M*: 'particular'.

[48] The Clandestine Marriage Act of 1753, 26 Geo. II, c. 33, introduced a requirement for the publication of banns, parental consent, the registration of marriage and prohibited marriage in private houses without special license. The idea was started by Lord Bath, but the Lord Chancellor, Hardwicke, became heavily involved in drafting a revised Bill. Bedford used it as an occasion for opposition in the Lords; when the Bill reached the Commons, Bedford's ally Henry Fox made an impassioned speech against it on 21 May

Memoirs of 1754–1757

of his Enemies by discovering an Eagerness to be the Minister, whilst Mr Pelham was still alive: many of whose Friends might possibly have attach'd themselves to him, if, instead of snatching at the succession, he had cooly waited till it had been deliver'd into his hands.

He has great parliamentary Knowledge, but is rather an able Debater, than a complete Orator; his best Speeches are neither long, nor premeditated; quick and concise Replication, is his peculiar Excellence.

In Business he is clear, and communicative, frank and agreeable in Society:[49] has too much Pride to be a Flatterer, and too much Spirit to be a Hipocrite.

Upon the whole, he has some Faults but more good Qualities: is a Man of sense, and Judgement, notwithstanding some Indiscretion: and in Spite of[50] ambition, Party, and Politics, is a warm Friend, a Man of Veracity, and a Man of Honor.

Mr Pitt's Followers were scarce a sufficient Number to deserve the Name of Party, consisting only of the Greenvilles,[51] and Sir George Lyttelton.[52] The latter was an Enthusiast both in Religion and Politics, absent in Business, not ready in a Debate, and totally ignorant of the World: on the other hand, his Studied Orations were excellent, he was a Man of Parts, a Scholar, no indifferent Writer, and by far the honestest Man of the Whole Society.

The late Duke of Devonshire[53] had great Credit with the Whigs,[54] both on account of his Family and of his personal Merit: many would have follow'd him, had he given the least[55] Encouragement, particularly those who profess'd the purest Whigism, and were neither quite satisfied with the Administration, nor quite ready for Opposition.[56]

1753, for which he later apologised. See *Parl. Hist.*, vol. 15, cols. 1–86; Walpole, *George II*, vol. 1, pp. 225–33.

[49] The sentence in *M* concludes: 'and tho he can pay his court on particular Occasions, he has too much Pride to flatter an Enemy, or even a Friend, where it is not necessary'.

[50] *M*: 'with some allowances for'.

[51] Richard Grenville (1711–79), MP 1734–52, succeeded as Earl Temple Oct. 1752; George Grenville (1712–70), MP 1741-d; James Grenville (1715–83), MP 1742–70.

[52] George Lyttelton (1709–73), succeeded as 5th Bt. 1751, created Baron Lyttelton Nov. 1756. Ed. Eton and Christ Church, Oxford. Secretary to Frederick, Prince of Wales 1737–44; a Lord of the Treasury 1744–54; Cofferer of the Household March 1754-Nov. 1755; Chancellor of the Exchequer Nov. 1755-Nov. 1756.

[53] William Cavendish (1698–1755), 3rd Duke of Devonshire. Succeeded 1729. Ed. New College, Oxford: MA 1717. MP 1721–9. Captain of Gentleman Pensioners 1726–31; Lord Privy Seal 1731–3; Lord Steward 1733–7, 1745–9. A Lord Justice 1741, 1743, 1745, 1748; Lord Lieutenant of Ireland 1737–45. Died 5 Dec. 1755.

[54] *M* continues: 'being a man of strict Honor, true Courage, and unaffected Affability. He was sincere, humane, and generous; plain in his Manners, negligent in his Dress; had Sense, Learning, and Modesty, with solid, rather than showy parts; and was of a Family which had eminently distinguished itself in the Cause of Liberty. Many would . . .'

[55] *M*: 'proper'.   [56] *M*: 'with our Ministers, nor quite determined to oppose them'.

But he did not affect to be a Party Leader; besides, he had a real[57] Esteem and Friendship for Mr Pelham, tho he had not the most favorable Opinion of the Duke of Newcastle.

The Opposition, which under the Protection of the Heir apparent, had been growing strong and formidable; after his Royal Highness's decease, became languid and inanimate.

A few unbeneficed Patriots voted against the Court, but their Principle of Dissatisfaction being thoroughly understood, those who had Parts or Activity to be dangerous, or even troublesome Enemies, were soon quieted.

As to the Jacobites, or Tories, their Numbers in Parliament were not considerable, they had lost their ablest Leaders; and had neither Spirit to make themselves fear'd, nor Abilities to give any disturbance.[58]

This was the State of Parties, at the time of Mr Pelham's Death, from whence it is evident that the Administration, King, and Royal Family might be expos'd to real danger from private Animosity, and Disunion amongst themselves: but had nothing to apprehend from their declared Enemies.[59]

In October 1754 Major General Braddock[60] was sent to North America, to oppose the Hostilities of the French,[61] who had invaded our Frontiers, murder'd the Inhabitants, and built a Chain of Forts to protect, and maintain their usurpations. The Force he commanded was nowise adequate to any great Plan of Operation, and might have gone imperceptibly without giving the least Alarm. But the whole was conducted with all the Pride and Solemnity of a formidable Armament, by which injudicious ostentation, an European as well as an American War became inevitable.[62]

Early in the Spring following, we received certain Intelligence that the French were fitting out a very powerful Fleet, which was to convoy a considerable Body of Land Forces to their Colonies in North America.

On our Part, we were no less diligent in making such necessary

---

[57] *M*: 'an Esteem'.

[58] The unimportance of Jacobitism by 1758 encouraged Waldegrave to omit mention of the extreme difficulties which the issue had posed for his career only a few years earlier.

[59] *M*: 'but had little to apprehend either from declared, or secret enemies'.

[60] Edward Braddock (1695–1755). Army Officer: Ensign 1710, Lieutenant 1716; Lieutenant-Colonel 1745; fought in Flanders; Colonel 1753; Major General 1754; Commander in Chief, North America 1754; led expedition against Fort Duquesne (now Pittsburgh); fatally wounded when his column was ambushed, 9 July 1755. The ministry is sometimes criticised for sending regular troops to fight a guerilla war. For a corrective, which reveals the familiarity of professional soldiers with such methods, see Peter E. Russell, 'Redcoats in the Wilderness: British Officers and Irregular Warfare in Europe and America, 1740 to 1760', *William and Mary Quarterly*, 35 (1978), 629–52.

[61] *M* erases the rest of the sentence.

[62] This was not the case. For the inaccuracy of Waldegrave's account of military and diplomatic planning in 1754–5, see pp. 64–72 above. For the political dimension of the reinforcement sent to America in late 1754, see Clark, *Dynamics of Change*, pp. 98–105.

Preparations as might enable us to set them at defiance: which being accomplished, on a sudden our conduct changes: In [the] Autumn we had been Bullies, with a Force quite contemptible:[63] now we are become formidable we grow circumspect, and fearful of giving the least Offence. *France has only attacked us in North America: what will be the Conduct of our Allies? Will not Spain be dissatisfied, should Boscowen block up Brest, or attack them in the Channel? In the American Seas he may be left at Liberty to fight: it is probable indeed he may not meet them, but for this, we are not responsible.* Such was the Reasoning of the British Ministers; the French sail'd unmolested; two of their Men of War were afterwards taken by Boscowen,[64] when they had almost reached their Port; the rest escaped in a Fog, and got safe to Louisbourg and Quebec.

At the time Boscowen sail'd from England, the King set out for his German Dominions[65] leaving his R:H: the Duke [of Cumberland] one of the Lords Justices, which caused great uneasiness at Leicester House. The Princess of Wales was reputed by those who knew her very imperfectly, a Woman of excellent Sense, and extraordinary Prudence; when in reality she was one of those moderate Geniuses, who without Parts or Knowledge of their own, can act with tolerable Propriety as long as they are conducted by wise and prudent Counsellors.[66] Her Secretary Cresset had been hitherto her principal adviser, a cautious Man, uncommonly skilful in the Politics of the backstairs, trusted by Lady Yarmouth,[67] Munchausen[68] and all the German Faction, giving little[69] Hints & Intelligence both at St James's and at Leicester House; yet it must be acknowledged that he acted no dishonest Part, that the Information he gave[70] was perfectly innocent, and that the good understanding between the King and his Daughter in

---

[63] *M* deletes this, and inserts: 'we had display'd our Intrepidity, whilst our Force was quite contemptible'.
[64] On 8 June 1755. Edward Boscawen (1711–61): entered navy 1726; Captain 1737, Rear-Admiral 1747, Vice-Admiral 1755, Admiral 1758; a Lord of the Admiralty 1751-*d*; MP 1742-*d*; distinguished record of service.
[65] Boscawen sailed on 21 April 1755; George II set out for Hanover on 28 April.
[66] *M* deletes this and inserts: 'The Princess of Wales was reputed a Woman of excellent Sense, by those who knew her very imperfectly but, in fact, was one of those moderate Geniuses, who with much natural Dissimulation, a civil Address, an assenting Conversation, and a few Ideas of their own, can act with tolerable Propriety, as long as they are conducted by wise and prudent Counsellors'. Waldegrave evidently still sought ways of disparaging the character of the dowager Princess of Wales without overstepping the bounds of decency.
[67] Amalie Sophie von Wallmoden (1704–65), George II's mistress from 1735; naturalised 1740 and created Countess of Yarmouth (life peerage). According to Lord Hervey, she obtained a Barony for Stephen Fox in 1741.
[68] Philip Adolf, Baron von Münchhausen. From 1749 to 1762 he headed the chancery in London which administered Hanover on the Elector's instructions. His elder brother Gerlach Adolf (1688–1770) was a leading minister in Hanover: cf. A.W. Ward, *Great Britain & Hanover. Some Aspects of the Personal Union* (Oxford, 1899).
[69] *M* omits 'little'.
[70] *M*: 'that every article of his Information'.

law, had been chiefly owing to his good Offices. The Princess of Wales retain'd all the Jealousy which divided the Royal Family during the Life of the Prince her Husband, dreaded the Power of the Duke, and hated him, as much as she fear'd him. His R.H. was nominally only one of the Regency, but she consider'd him as being, in effect, sole Regent, during the King's Absence. She consider'd also that his great Abilities, with the command of the Army, in a War which seem'd inevitable, must give such additional Strength as might be fatal to her principal Object of governing in the name of her Son, in case of a Minority.

Her Resentment fell chiefly on the Duke of Newcastle, not on this Account only, but for having admitted Fox to the Cabinet Council; which made him also one of the Lords Justices.[71]

It certainly was in the Duke of Newcastle's power to have prevented both; and he was, if possible, more jealous of the Duke and Fox, than the Princess herself: but his fears prevail'd over his Jealousy.

That these Events may be better understood, I shall enter into a more minute Explanation of the causes which produc'd them.

First in relation to Fox, during the preceding Winter, he had join'd Pitt in a kind of Parliamentary opposition.[72] They were both in Place, the one Paymaster, the other Secretary at War, and therefore could not decently obstruct the Public Business, or censure those Measures, which themselves had already approved of: But still they might attack Men, or[73] oppose in questions of an indifferent Nature, where the affairs of Government did not appear to be immediately concern'd.

Pitt undertook the different[74] Task of silencing Murray[75] the Attorney General; the ablest Man, as well as the ablest debater in the House of Commons. Whilst Fox entertain'd himself with the less dangerous Amusement of exposing Sir Thomas Robinson, or rather assisted him, whilst he turn'd himself into Ridicule. For Sir Thomas, tho a good Secretary of State, as far as the Business of his Office, and that which related to foreign affairs, was ignorant even of [the] Language of an House of Commons Controversy, and when he play'd the Orator, which he too frequently attempted it was so exceeding ridiculous, that those who loved and

[71] England in the absence of the sovereign (like Ireland in the absence of the Lord Lieutenant) was administered by a Council of Lords Justices. This Council was by this date virtually synonymous with the Cabinet, and was consequently directed by the smaller group of ministers generally termed the Inner Cabinet. See E.R. Turner, 'The Lords Justices of England', *EHR* 29 (1914), 453–76.
[72] For the covert opposition in the autumn of 1754, see Clark, *Dynamics of Change*, pp. 105–26.
[73] *M* deletes this, inserts: 'attack Persons, tho not Things; or might . . .'.
[74] *M*: 'difficult'. *C* is presumably an error in dictation.
[75] Hon. William Murray (1705–93). Ed. Westminster and Christ Church, Oxford. MP 1742–56; created Baron Mansfield 8 Nov. 1756, Earl Mansfield 1776. Solicitor General 1742–54; Attorney General 1754–6; Lord Chief Justice of the King's Bench 1756–88.

Memoirs of 1754–1757

esteem'd him, could not always preserve a friendly composure of Countenance.

Murray & Sir Thomas Robinson were at that time the only leading Members, in the House of Commons, in whom the Duke of Newcastle had a thorough Confidence but the one wanted Abilities, the other wanted Spirit; and tho the Administration had in every Division, a very great Majority, many of their steadiest Voters were laughers at least, if not Encouragers on the other side of the question.

It therefore became necessary that Pitt and Fox, should be disunited. One of them must be treated with, and Fox was first apply'd to, as being thought more practicable, less disagreeable to the King, and more a Man of Business.

As Fox was apt to be warm, and the Duke of Newcastle as apt to be shuffling, it seem'd necessary that some Neutral Person should negotiate between them; and his Majesty thought proper to employ me on this occasion, because I belonged to neither of them, but was a friend[76] to both.[77]

That the Progress of this amicable Treaty might not be interrupted by a fresh Quarrel I persuaded them to defer their Meeting, till they had settled Preliminaries, and clearly understood each others Meaning.

Fox very readily gave me his Demands in writing, which I reported to the King, and enter'd into a[78] minute Explanation of every particular[79] with the Duke of Newcastle: who made some Objections and propos'd some Alterations, but consented to most of the material articles. There would have been many more difficulties, if I had not begun by terrifying his Grace with a melancholy representation of the fatal Consequences of Fox's uniting with Pitt in open opposition: How he would be expos'd to all the Virulence of abusive Oratory: How his Leaders in the House of Commons would be treated with contempt: and how his numerous Parliamentary Forces, having learnt to despise their Generals, would soon become mutinous and ungovernable.

On the other hand I assured Fox, that the King had, if possible still less inclination to make him a Minister, than the Duke of Newcastle himself. I therefore advised him as a Friend, to rest satisfied with a moderate share of Power, and to wait for a more favorable opportunity; unless he had absolutely determined, to join Pitt, enter into all the Violence of Opposition set the whole[80] Nation in a Flame, and take the Closet by Storm.

All material Difficulties being, at last, remov'd, I propos'd an Interview,

---

[76] *M* erases 'friend', inserts 'Wellwisher'.
[77] On Waldegrave's role as a mediator with Fox in December 1754, see Clark, *Dynamics of Change*, pp. 123–30. Waldegrave was unaware that Newcastle had long-standing plans to reinforce the ministry.
[78] *M*: 'a more'.   [79] *M* omits 'of every particular'.   [80] *M* omits 'whole'.

which produced the following agreement: That Fox should be call'd up to the Cabinet Council, that Employments should be given to some of his Friends, who were not yet provided for, and that others, who had Places already, should be removed to higher Stations. Fox during the whole Proceeding[81] behaved like a Man of Sense, and a Man of Honor; very frank, very explicit and not very unreasonable. But the Duke of Newcastle lost all the Merit of every concession by conferring his Favors with a bad Grace; and it was easy to foresee that this Peace and Amity would be of short Duration.

As to the other affair, the Duke's being one of the Regency: it was as follows.[82]

The King having taken the Resolution of going to Hanover at the Eve of a War, many considerable Persons particularly the late [third] Duke of Devonshire, declared to the Duke of Newcastle that his R:H: being the only General, capable of commanding our Forces, in case of an Invasion it was necessary he should have some share in framing of orders; as well as in executing them. That they would not insist on making him sole Regent, which might give umbrage at Leicester House; but that proper Precautions must be taken, and that it was necessary for the public safety, that during the King's absence his R:H: should be one of the Lords Justices.

The Duke of Newcastle, tho tenacious of Power and full of Jealousy, in quiet times, had not Courage to stand single at the Helm, in the approaching Storm. He therefore agreed to the Measure, & recommended it to the King, who most readily gave his consent, as he would have done to any Proposal whatsoever; provided it made us quiet in England, and prolong'd his stay at Hanover. But tho he was suffer'd to depart, without much murmuring, our domestic Tranquillity was of short Duration. New Factions arose, which possibly might never have existed, could his Majesty have been dissuaded from this unfortunate Journey.[83]

The Princess of Wales, during the life of the Prince her Husband, had distinguished herself by a most decent & prudent Behaviour; and the King, notwithstanding his aversion to his Son, behaved to her not only with great Politeness, but with the appearance of cordiality and Affection.

When the Prince died, his Majesty gave still stronger Proofs of his Favor and Confidence: he patronized the Act[84] by which she was appointed Regent, in case of a Minority: and, what was of greater Importance, he suffer'd the Heir Apparent to remain under her sole Direction.

[81] *M*: 'Negotiation'.
[82] For the creation of the Regency in the spring of 1755, see Clark, *Dynamics of Change*, pp. 154–8.
[83] Nevertheless, at the time Waldegrave was apparently willing to oppose Earl Poulett's attempt to prevent the King from leaving for Hanover: see speech no. 9 below.
[84] The Regency Act of 1751 (speech no. 5 below).

Memoirs of 1754–1757 163

For tho Preceptors and Governors were chose by the King, or rather by his Ministers, they had only the Shadow of Authority; and the two principal, the Earl Harcourt, and the Bishop of Norwich were soon disgraced, because they attempted to form an Interest independent of the Mother, and presumed, on some Occasions, to have an opinion of their own.

In the mean time the Princess's Behaviour to the King was wise and dutiful; she consider'd him as her Protector, Benefactor, and Friend; and took no Step, of any consequence without his Approbation.

In a Word, his Majesty's Tenderness for the Princess and her Family, and the Princess's Duty & Obedience to the King, were equally applauded by the whole Nation; and this Harmony continued without the least Interruption till his Majesty's Departure for his German Dominions.[85]

Here on a sudden the scene changes; the Duke of Newcastle who had hitherto been her R:H: Favorite Minister, and who had shewn himself, on many occasions a very useful Friend, is now to be treated with the coldest civility; whilst Pitt, who had been a Groom of the Bedchamber to the Prince her Husband, and had not quitted his Master in the most decent manner,[86] makes a Tender of his Services, with the assistance of his Relations and Friends, which are joyfully accepted.

This Treaty was negotiated by the Earl of Bute,[87] at that time, a Favorite of little Fame, but who has since merited a very uncommon Reputation; and who is supposed to execute a most honorable Office with great Ability. He had been a Lord of the Bedchamber to the late Prince, has a good Person, fine Legs, and a theatrical air of the greatest Importance.

There is an extraordinary appearance of Wisdom both in his look, and manner of speaking: for whether the Subject be serious or trifling, he is equally pompous, slow, and sententious. Not contented with being wise, he would be thought a polite Scholar, and a Man of great Erudition; but has the Misfortune never to succeed, except with those who are exceeding ignorant; for his historical Knowledge is chiefly taken from Tragedies wherein he is very deeply read; and his Classical Learning extends no farther than a French Translation.[88] The late Prince of Wales, who was not

---

[85] The King embarked for Hanover on 28 April 1755. For the launching of an opposition in the summer of that year, see Clark, *Dynamics of Change*, pp. 158–95.

[86] Pitt had been a Groom of the Bedchamber to Prince Frederick from 1737 until he went over to support the Pelham ministry in 1745.

[87] John Stuart, 3rd Earl of Bute (1713–92), succ. 1723. Ed. Eton. Representative peer for Scotland 1737–41, 1761–80. A Lord of the Bedchamber to Frederick Prince of Wales, 1750–51; Groom of the Stole to George, Prince of Wales 1756–60; and to him as George III 1760–61; Secretary of State for the Northern Department 25 March 1761–29 May 1762. K.G. 1762, First Lord of the Treasury 29 May 1762–15 April 1763.

[88] The injustice of this portrait was pointed out, when Waldegrave's *Memoirs* were published, by those who still remembered Bute. A reviewer in *The British Critic* 16 (August 1821),

over nice in the choice of Ministers, used frequently to say that Bute was a fine Showy Man, who would make an excellent Embassador in a court where there was no Business. Such was his R: Highness Opinion of the Noble Earl's political abilities.[89] But the Sagacity of the Princess Dowager has discover'd other accomplishments, of which the Prince her Husband may not perhaps have been the most competent Judge.

The Substance of the Treaty was that Pitt and his Friends should, to their utmost, support the Princess and her Son; that they should oppose the Duke and raise a Clamor against him; and as to the King himself, they were to submit to his Government, provided he would govern as they directed him.

An Event happen'd about the middle of the Summer, which engaged Leicester House still deeper in Faction than they at first intended. The Prince of Wales was just entering into his 18th year, and having a healthy vigorous Constitution with a modest sober disposition, it might reasonably be supposed that a matrimonial Companion would be no unacceptable amusement. The Dutchess of Brunswick Wolfembuttle,[90] with her two

p. 166, protested: 'That Lord Bute was the handsomest man of his time anyone must be prepared to admit who has seen a portrait of him; that he was vain of his person as Lord Waldegrave more than once insinuates, we may safely deny on yet living authority. That he pretended to polite scholarship which he did not possess, and that his "classical learning extended no farther than a French translation," is, to say the least of it, directly false. Few testimonies to the extent of classical scholarship can be more unexceptionable than that of the late Mr. Bryant, and Mr Bryant, as a brother Etonian, repeatedly spoke in high commendation of Lord Bute's attainments in this path'. Jacob Bryant (1715–1804), classicist; ed. Eton, King's College Cambridge 1736; Fellow of King's; Secretary to the Duke of Marlborough, as Master General of the Ordnance; a placeman in the Ordnance Department. Pensioner of the Marlborough family; prolific author. Latterly resided near Windsor, where George III 'often visited him'; the King 'passed hours alone with him enjoying his conversation' (DNB). It should be noted that Horace Walpole was, in private, by no means as disparaging in his estimate of the character of Waldegrave's rival: 'Lord Bute was my schoolfellow. He was a man of taste and science, and I do believe his intentions were good'. *Walpoliana* (2 vols., London, [1799]), vol. 1, p. 2.

[89] This anecdote occurs also in Walpole, *George III*, vol. 1, p. 237. It seems likely that Horace Walpole copied it, with a literary embellishment, from the manuscript of Waldegrave's *Memoirs*.

[90] 'Philippina Charlotte, Princess of Prussia, sister of Frederick the Second, and wife of Charles, Duke of Brunswick Wolfenbuttel, was born in 1716, and died in 1780. Her two eldest daughters were Sophia Caroline Maria, born in 1737; and Anne Amelia, born 1739. Sophia Caroline Maria was married in 1759 to the Margravine of Bareuth; and died at an advanced age, in 1817 or 1818. And Anne Amelia was married to the Duke of Saxe Weimar, in 1756; and died in 1807'. This was Lord Holland's only annotation to the text of the *Memoirs*. The information was mostly provided by the genealogist John Burke or Bourke (1787–1848), founder of *Burke's Peerage*: see Bourke to Holland, 2 Dec. 1820: Add MSS 51831, nf. Even so, the printer blundered and Holland was obliged to ask the publisher to make a correction in any future edition: for 'Margravine' read 'Margrave'. Holland to J. Murray, 5 May 1821: Add MSS 51832, nf; Holland to Mr. Davison, printer, nd: JMP.

ummarry'd Daughters waited on his Majesty at Hanover: the elder both as to person, and understanding, was a most accomplished Princess. The King was charm'd with her cheerful, modest, and sensible behaviour; and wish'd to make her his Gra[n]ddaughter, being too Old to make her his Wife. I remember his telling me with great Eagerness, that, had he been only twenty years younger, she should never have been refused by a Prince of Wales, but should at once have been Queen of England.

Now whether his Majesty spoke seriously, is very little to the purpose: the young Prince's Happiness was undoubtedly his principal object; and he was desirous the Match might be concluded before his own Death; that the Princess of Wales should have no Temptation to do a Job for her Relations, by marrying her son to one of the Saxe Gotha family who might not have the Amiable Accomplishments of the Princess of Wolfembuttle. The King's intentions could not long be a secret in England, and it may easily be imagined that they were not agreeable to the Princess of Wales. She knew the Temper of the Prince her Son; that he was by nature indolent, hated Business, but loved a domestick Life, and would make an excellent Husband. She knew also that the young Princess having merit and understanding equal to her Beauty, must in a short time have the greatest Influence over him: In which Circumstances, it may naturally be concluded that her R:H: did every thing in her Power to prevent the Match. The Prince of Wales was taught to believe, that he was to be made a Sacrifice merely to gratify the King's private Interest in the Electorate of Hanover. The young Princess was most cruelly misrepresented[;] all her Perfections were aggravated into Faults; and the Prince, without further Examination, was so willing to believe whatever could be invented to her disadvantage, that[91] his Prejudice against her amounted almost[92] to aversion itself.

From this time all Duty and Obedience to the Grandfather entirely ceas'd; for, tho it would have been difficult to have persuaded him to do that which he thought wrong, he was ready to think right, whatever was prompted, either by his Mother or by her Favorite.

Negotiations also of a different Nature were carried on in the course of this Summer.[93] Two Treaties were sign'd, the one with the Landgrave of

---

[91] *M* deletes 'misrepresented ... that', inserts 'misrepresented; many even of her Perfections were aggravated into Faults, his Royal Highness implicitly believing every idle Tale, and improbable Aspersion, till'.

[92] *M* omits 'almost'.

[93] For European diplomacy at this period and the nature of Waldegrave's attitudes, see above, pp. 64–72. Waldegrave omits to record that he was in favour of the Russian and Hesse Cassel Treaties when they were laid before Parliament on 10 December 1755: cf. speech no. 12 below.

Hesse Cassel;[94] the other with the Czarina:[95] the Force we should have acquired by the latter would have been considerable, and the Terms were reasonable but this Treaty was never carried into Execution. However, tho the Court of Russia[96] did not fulfil their Engagements, they behaved with more generosity than is usual on the like Occasions, for as they would not earn our Money they refused to take it. Our Treaties with Saxony[97] and Bavaria[98] expired about the same time, and might both have been renew'd: the former amounted to £32000, the latter to 20000 pounds a year.

The Consequences of such a Renewal cannot now be ascertain'd; but if the mischiefs which have arisen from the Junction of Saxony with France and the Court of Vienna, could have been prevented for £32000 it had undoubtedly been a cheap Purchase.

Be that as it will, it either was extravagant to make these Treaties, or absurd to let them expire. For we paid Troops when they were of no use, in years of Peace and Tranquillity, and afterwards discharged them, or in effect assign'd them over to the Enemy, at the Eve of a War: neither will our Policy be more excusable, tho the original design of the Treaties, might have been to facilitate the Election of a King of the Romans: a Measure which never took Place, which the Austrians themselves, thought of little Consequence, and wherein the interest of Great Britain could be nowise concern'd.[99]

The Court of Vienna was also treated with: they were ready to declare War against France, provided we were ready on our part to furnish all the

---

[94] Signed at Hanover, 18 June 1755; printed in *Commons Journals*, vol. 27, pp. 313–15. The Landgrave contracted for 8,000 men, rising to 12,000 on requisition, under a complex financial formula. These troops were summoned to England in March 1756 to counter the French invasion threat; they arrived in May, and returned in December. Hesse Cassel was overrun by the French army in the ensuing war.

[95] Signed at St Petersburg on 19/30 September 1755; printed in *Commons Journals*, vol. 27, pp. 308–10. Russia engaged to maintain an army of 55,000 men in Livonia and a naval force of 'forty or fifty' galleys, to be called on in the event of an attack on Hanover. The subsidy, initially of £100,000 p.a., would rise to £500,000 p.a. from the moment the Russian forces crossed their frontiers in response to a requisition from George II. The treaty was to run for four years, from the date of its ratification. Ratifications were exchanged in St. Petersburg on 12 February 1756. Following the Prussian invasion of Saxony on 29 August 1756, Russia refused to accept the first payment of this subsidy, and the Anglo-Russian alliance was soon understood to be a dead letter: D.B. Horn, *Sir Charles Hanbury Williams & European Diplomacy (1747–58)* (London, 1930), pp. 268–93.

[96] M: 'the Russians'.

[97] The Treaty of Dresden, 2/13 September 1751; printed in *Commons Journals*, vol. 26, pp. 371–2. It expired on 29 September 1755.

[98] Signed at Hanover 11/22 August 1750; printed in *Commons Journals*, vol. 26, pp. 24–5. It expired on 21 July 1756.

[99] Waldegrave's interpretation is doubtful. Saxony's alignment with Austria and France was a consequence of the Anglo-Prussian alliance, not a cause of the outbreak of war. Waldegrave once more reveals his failure to understand either the purpose or the consequences of Newcastle's Imperial election plan.

Expenses: provided also that we would quarrel with the King of Prussia to give them an opportunity to recover Silesia:[100] in which case it was not difficult to foresee against which of the adverse Powers the Austrian Force would have been chiefly directed. But we had been so often the Dupes of the House of Austria; and their Cause was become so very unpopular that our Ministers durst not engage on these disadvantageous Terms. Our Plan therefore if we had any, was contracted to a narrower Compass; to secure his Majesty's Electoral Dominions by preserving the Tranquillity of Germany; to support our Colonies in North America; to carry on a Sea War against France; and as to Affairs in General, we were to wait for Events, and trust to Chance and Accident.[101] In the mean time the Duke of Newcastle Lord Hardwicke and the most considerable of their Party,[102] foreseeing the confusion which was likely to arise from the State of our affairs at home as well as abroad; obtain'd his Majesty's leave to strengthen themselves, in their Ministerial Capacity by forming new Alliances. Pitt was now the first Person to be treated with;[103] he still continued Paymaster, but was[104] much dissatisfied; had been in a kind of Opposition the preceding Winter, and had just enter'd into Engagements with Leicester House.

Terms being proposed, Pitt was very explicit and fairly let them know that he expected to be a Secretary of State, and would not content himself with any meaner Employment. Neither was it his Intention to be a Secretary merely to write Letters, according to order, or to talk in Parliament like a Lawyer from a Brief; but to be really a Minister. He also declared against Continental Measures and against all Treaties of Subsidy. But as this Declaration was reserved to the last, it seems possible it might have been entirely forgot, if the answer to the preceding articles had been quite Satisfactory. For a short time, it was expected that some agreement would have been made, but Pitt adhered to his first demands; and the Duke

[100] It was certainly an Austrian ambition to recover that province. Waldegrave offers no evidence for his claim, not elsewhere supported, that Austria was really willing to declare war on France in order to forward her designs on Silesia. Kaunitz's final demands were so high that English ministers realised they were meant to be rejected: Horn, *Hanbury Williams*, p. 200. For the Austrian ultimatum, enclosed in Keith's despatch to Holdernesse of 19 June 1755, see W. Coxe, *History of the House of Austria* (3 vols., London, 1807), vol. 3, pp. 379–82.

[101] On the contrary: the ministry's policy was to refuse, at Austria's request, to 'transform the colonial struggle with France into a general European war' or to join in the destruction of Prussia (Horn, *Hanbury Williams*, pp. 200–01), but to conclude an alliance with Frederick the Great. In this they were quickly successful. England's policy was now to avoid continental involvement via the Prussian alliance, and to concentrate on the colonial and naval dimension. Waldegrave should have approved.

[102] *M* omits 'and . . . Party'.

[103] For the ministry's unsuccessful overtures to Pitt in September 1755, see Clark, *Dynamics of Change*, pp. 182–90.

[104] *M*: 'seemed'.

of Newcastle was not sufficiently intimidated to make any Man a Minister who had frankly told him, he would not be directed.[105]

On this Occasion his Grace had recourse to the neverfailing Excuse, that for his own Part, he had the greatest honor and Esteem for Mr Pitt, and wish'd to satisfy him in every particular; but that the King would never give his Consent, and so this Treaty ended.

The Lords Justices, I mean the Leaders only, who in their Private meetings, determined all affairs of Consequence: were the Duke [of Cumberland], the Chancellor, Lord Granville President of the Council[,] the Duke of Newcastle first Lord of the Treasury, Lord Anson first Lord of the Admiralty, Sir Thomas Robinson Secretary of State, and Mr Fox Secretary at War and Cabinet Counceller.

The Preparations for War and all military Operations were chiefly conducted by the Duke [of Cumberland], Fox, and Lord Anson. The Duke of Newcastle, and the Chancellor, follow'd by Sir Thomas Robinson took the lead in our domestic Politicks, and in all affairs of civil Government. As to Lord Granville he sometimes sided with the Duke, sometimes with the Duke of Newcastle and frequently differ'd from both.

An Affair came now under their consideration of the greatest importance.[106] A very powerful Fleet was ready to sail under the Command of Sir Ed: Hawke,[107] and the King trusted to his Regency to prepare proper Instructions. *Was Hawke to have hostile Orders? If hostile Orders were given, must they be unlimited? ought War to be declared when the Fleet sail'd, or were we to commence Hostilities without any Declarations?* These were serious questions, and as they were to be determined by Men of very different Tempers, it is not surprising there should be some difference of Opinion. The Duke, naturally inclined to vigorous Measures, seeing the whole[108] Nation impatient for War, it being also the General Opinion that the Enemy was yet unprepared, thought it advisable to strike the blow whilst our Fury was at its greatest height: at the same time he was very sensible, that notwithstanding our formidable Fleet we were not ourselves in such perfect Readiness as many People imagined. On the other hand, the Duke of Newcastle, who was not fond of danger at a Distance, and seldom grew bolder, on its nearer Approach, was for keeping off the Storm as long as possible, and gave his Opinion that Hawke should take a Turn in the

---

[105] This may be a more just estimate than Waldegrave's earlier claim that he had 'terrified' Newcastle into an accommodation with Fox in December 1754.

[106] For naval dispositions in 1755, see pp. 67–70 above.

[107] Edward Hawke (1710–81). Naval officer; entered as a Volunteer, 1720; Captain 1734; Rear Admiral 1747; 2nd Battle of Finisterre 1747; knighted 1747; Vice-Admiral 1748; MP 1747–76; Admiral 1757; Rochefort expedition 1757; battle of Quiberon Bay 1759; First Lord of the Admiralty 1766–71; created Baron Hawke 1776.

[108] *M* omits 'whole'. Waldegrave's initial instinct is to overstate the desirability of an immediate declaration of war.

Channel, to exercise the Fleet, without having any Instructions whatsoever.

The Chancellor had more courage than the Duke of Newcastle; but, agreeable to the common Practice of the Law, was against bringing the Cause to an immediate Decision. Lord Anson, as usual said little but, as an Admiral, & first Lord of the Admiralty, thought it became him to seem rather inclined to the spirited side of the question.

After mature Deliberation, it was resolved *that Hawke should sail with hostile orders; but War was not to be declared*. Either Extreme had been better than this compromise for it was in our Power to have remain'd quiet till we had been thoroughly prepar'd for Action; or, if we were inclined to more vigorous Measures Hawke's Departure might have been Defer'd a few Days; the King might have been intreated to return to England; and War might have been immediately proclaim'd on his Majesty's arrival. In which case, even our Enemies must have allow'd that we had acted fairly, and like Men of Spirit, who would not bear ill usage.

Whereas, on the contrary, without the least previous Notice, we at once commence Hostilities; Hawke in Pursuance of Orders, seizes every trading Vessel, which has the misfortune to meet him; whereby a Foundation is laid for much dispute and caviling; perhaps also for a considerable Retribution, if the War should prove unprosperous; and in the meantime we are call'd Robbers and Pirates.

Such was the situation of our Affairs when his Majesty return'd in September 1755.[109]

I never heard with any Certainty, whether the King, when he left Hanover, was acquainted with the Intrigues of Leicester House; but I know from the best authority, that before he had been a week in England, he had received thorough information.[110]

The Plan of Opposition in Parliament, was confined within a narrow compass: the Hessian, and Russian Subsidies afforded only a small supply of new matter; and the old Topics of Declamation, like Jests too frequently repeated, had lost their force and Poignancy.

But that which animated the cause, and gave Spirit and Vigor to our worthy Patriots, was the pleasing Prospect of an unfortunate War.[111]

The Prince and Princess of Wales were not openly to declare themselves,

---

[109] After passing the summer in Hanover, George II returned to Kensington Palace on 16 September.

[110] The clear implication of this and subsequent passages is that Waldegrave himself told George II everything that happened at Leicester House.

[111] The ministry was handicapped during parliamentary debates on the Russian treaty, 10–12 December 1755. The opposition's main objection was that the treaty was clearly aimed at Prussia and would only provoke a Prussian attack on Hanover. The ministry was unable to reveal that secret negotiations were already in progress for an alliance with Frederick the Great, which was to be signed on 16 January.

unless the King's obstinacy in the affair of the Marriage, should lay them under the immediate Necessity of pulling off the Mask.

But they were to shew strong Symptoms, by taking that kind of notice of the King's Principal Servants,[112] which at Court is call'd *rumping*; whilst Pitt and his Relations were most graciously received; and whilst the Earl of Bute was distinguish'd by the most particular marks of Favor and Confidence: a Notification to all Men who sought for future Preferment that without his Lordship's Mediation, there was no political Salvation.

The King who had early intelligence of every thing they did, and of most things they intended, treated the Princess[113] with almost[114] the same coldness, with which she and her Son treated his Ministers.

About three months after his return to England,[115] his Majesty sent for the Prince of Wales into his Closet; not to propose the Match knowing it would be to little purpose; but to find out the extent of his political Knowledge, to sift him in relation to Hanover and to caution him against evil Councellors. The Discourse was short, the Substance kind and affectionate, but the manner not quite gracious. The Prince was fluster'd and sulky, bow'd, but scarce made any answer, so the Conference ended very little to the satisfaction of either Party.

Here his Majesty was guilty of a very Capital Mistake: for instead of sending for the Prince, he should have spoke firmly to the Mother: told her that as she govern'd her Son, she should be answerable for his Conduct: that he would overlook what was past, and treat her still like a friend; if she behaved in a proper manner: but, on the other hand, if either herself, her Son, or any Person influenced by them, should give any future Disturbance, she must expect no quarter: He might then have ended his admonition, by whispering a Word in her Ear, which would have made her tremble, in spight of her Spotless Innocence.[116]

The Ill Success of the Duke of Newcastle's Negotiation with Pitt, has been already mention'd. *Fox* in his turn must again be treated with;[117] for the Session of Parliament approached, and it was become almost[118] a general Maxim, that the House of Commons had been so long[119] accustom'd to have a Minister of their own, that they would not any longer be govern'd by Deputy.[120]

[112] Especially, it seems, of Waldegrave himself.   [113] *C* has 'and her son' deleted.
[114] *M* omits 'almost'.
[115] In fact, before 18 October. See Newcastle to Hardwicke, 18 Oct. 1755: Add MSS 35415 f. 108.
[116] For Waldegrave's possible contribution to these developing rumours, see above, pp. 76–9.
[117] For Fox's promotion to a Secretaryship of State in September 1755, see Clark, *Dynamics of Change*, pp. 190–5.
[118] *M* omits 'almost'.   [119] *M*: 'so much'.
[120] For a different interpretation, Clark, *loc. cit.*, pp. 93–8, 151.

Memoirs of 1754–1757

Fox insisted on being made Secretary of State much against the King's inclination, as well as the Duke of Newcastle's: For tho his Majesty prefer'd Fox to Pitt, he liked Sir Thomas Robinson better than either of them: for Sir Thomas was diligent in his office, did as he was directed, understood foreign affairs, and pretended to nothing farther. However Fox carried his Point; Lord Barrington,[121] succeeded him as Secretary at War, and Sir Tho: Robinson went back to his old Place at the Wardrobe, with a considerable Pension on the Irish Establishment. At the opening of the Session, the Court had a great Majority, the ill humor of Leicester house if it had any effects rather doing good than harm. This may at first appear extraordinary, but the Wonder ceases when we examine the conduct of the Princess of Wales, who had not acquired that Freedom, and openness of Behavior which gains the Profligate, whilst the Sober and conscientious part of the World, doubted whether it was strictly right that a Boy of seventeen should be taught to set his Grandfather at defiance: nor were they much edified with other Rumors of a very particular[122] Nature, which were now universally credited.

But the Court did not prevail by Numbers only: in all Debates of consequence, Murray the Attorney General had greatly the Advantage over Pitt, in point of argument; and, abuse only excepted, was not much his Inferior in any Part of Oratory.[123]

During the course of the Winter, a Treaty[124] was sign'd with the King of Prussia, to prevent the introduction of Foreign Troops into the Empire.

The Intention of this Treaty was to stop the Russians, that they might not attack the King of Prussia, under the Name of assistance to the House of Austria; and on the other hand that the French might not overrun his Majesty's Electoral Dominions, under the Pretence of defending their Ally the King of Prussia.

This Measure, tho chiefly calculated for German Purposes was generally approved of, for it seem'd equitable as well as Humane that Hanover should not be exposed to the Resentment of our Enemies in a quarrel entirely English. Yet the consequences were fatal, tho the design was

[121] William Wildman Barrington (1717–93), 2nd Viscount Barrington (Irish peerage). MP 1740–78. A Lord of the Admiralty 1746–54; Master of the Great Wardrobe April 1754-Oct. 1755; Secretary at War Oct. 1755-March 1761; Treasurer of the Navy 1762–5; Secretary at War 1765–78.

[122] M deletes 'very particular', inserts 'less serious'.

[123] For the parliamentary session of 1755–6, see Clark, *Dynamics of Change*, pp. 210–22, 225–30. Waldegrave's estimate of the relative strengths of Murray and Pitt is just.

[124] The Convention of Westminster, signed 16 January 1756; printed in *Commons Journals*, vol. 27, pp. 602–3. It comprised a mutual non-aggression pact, together with a stipulation that if 'any foreign Power should cause Troops to march into the said *Germany*', the contracting powers 'shall unite their Forces, in order to oppose the Entrance or Passage of such Foreign Troops'. No subsidy was involved, though a single payment of £20,000 was made to Prussia in settlement of an old dispute.

honest.[125] For when the Court of Vienna perceived that there was no farther Expectation of English Assistance, to recover Silesia, they immediately treat with the common Enemy; the unnatural conjunction is form'd between France and Austria, the Russians, and Saxons becoming Part of the Confederacy:[126] the King of Prussia foresees the Storm which is gathering over him, and with unparallel'd Activity, Courage, and Sagacity, strikes the first blow whilst the Enemy is yet unprepared.[127] Thus a War is kindled in Germany which has hitherto been carried on with unusual Ferocity, which may prove more bloody and destructive, than any which we meet with in modern History; and which hereafter may reduce England to the cruel alternative of pursuing a continental War, at an immense Expense, which in the End must prove unfortunate; or of abandoning our only ally, the greatest Prince and most fortunate General of the present age, in Contempt of National Faith, and of the most Solemn Engagements.[128]

But to return to our affairs at home. Towards the end of the year 1755 and at the beginning of 56,[129] we were frequently alarm'd with intended Invasions, numbers of Troops swarming on the Coast, flatbottom'd boats Embarcations and the like. We also heard that a considerable Armament was fitting out at Toulon, but this danger being at a greater distance, did not at first give any great uneasiness. However it soon became the general Opinion that the reports from Toulon were too well founded; and that the Island of Minorca could only be preserved by sending immediate and Vigorous assistance.[130]

Our Ministers alone, seem'd still incredulous pretending this to be nothing more than a Feint to facilitate a descent upon England or Ireland; whilst our fleet was employ'd in blocking up ten or twelve old Ships, the rotten part of the French Marine, in the Harbour of Toulon.

[125] Waldegrave was unaware of the effective collapse of the Anglo-Austrian alliance by late 1754. The Prussian alliance arguably retrieved a potentially disastrous situation: see above, p. 71. Waldegrave was not alone in deploring the effect of Frederick's pre-emptive strike, however. This was not England's purpose in signing the Convention of Westminster. It crystallised a Franco-Austro-Russian alliance against Prussia and drew French troops into Germany at a time when Prussia was unable to shield Hanover. For some months after the invasion of Saxony, 'the Anglo-Prussian *entente* hung by a thread': Horn, *Hanbury Williams*, p. 265.
[126] *M* erases 'the Russians . . . confederacy', inserts: 'the Czarina engages to assist them with all her force; and the E[lecto]r of Saxony whose Territories lay most exposed, and who was least able to defend himself, most imprudently confederates with these great Potentates.'
[127] The Prussian invasion of Saxony began on 29 August 1756. See Christopher Duffy, *Frederick the Great: A Military Life* (London, 1985).
[128] This passage was obviously written before Pitt had committed substantial land forces to the war in Germany.
[129] *M*: 'the year 1756'. *C* again sounds like a dictated text.
[130] *M* erases 'only . . . assistance', inserts 'not possibly be saved, without the most immediate, as well as the most vigorous Assistance'.

Undoubtedly our Situation was somewhat delicate; there being a wide difference between our real, and nominal Strength; between our effective Men, and the Numbers voted by Parliament. For, tho Lord Anson had done every thing in his Power, that our Fleet might be in the best Condition, Boscowen had return'd from North America, much later than was[131] expected; had lost a great Number by sickness, and his Ships were not yet refitted. Saylors were wanting even for the Western Squadron, tho this Part of our Marine had always been the most compleatly Man'd, and the best appointed. As to the land Service, we first engaged in a War, and then began to prepare ourselves; consequently our internal Force must be very deficient.

This might have been foreseen, and prevented without any extraordinary Sagacity; for it certainly was in our Power to have defer'd the War, till the Nation had been in a better State of defence: but the Die being unfortunately thrown, before we were sensible of our danger, and the Evil requiring an immediate Remedy, both Houses of Parliament address'd the King that the Hanoverians and Hessians might be brought over to our Assistance.[132] His Majesty granted their Request without the least Hesitation; yet fitting out Transports, and other necessary Preparations, must occasion some delay, and in the meantime Security at home, was our principal object.

Unfortunately our Ministers, blinded by their Fears, confined their attention to this object only. At[133] last they were rous'd from their Lethargy, and Byng sail'd to the Mediterranean: but the French were already landed; St Phillips's was already besieged.[134] Even could our Fleet have arrived a Month sooner common Sense might have inform'd us, that we ought either to have employ'd a more considerable Force, or an Admiral of more experienced Bravery. The Engagement of the 20th of May, with the surrender of Fort St Phillip are but too well known, and will be long remember'd, equally to the disgrace of the Arms and Councils of this Country.

This loss was the principal Cause of that popular discontent and Clamour which overturn'd the Administration; or rather occasion'd the Panick which obliged our Ministers to Abdicate.[135]

The Session had been brought to a conclusion as early as possible, least

---

[131] *M* erases 'was', inserts 'had been'.
[132] This may have been the occasion of Waldegrave's speech no. 14, below.
[133] *M*: 'However, at'.
[134] This was not the case. Byng's fleet sailed on 6 April; a French force landed on the island of Minorca on 18 April; the British garrison surrendered on 28 June.
[135] For the events of April–October 1756 which culminated in Newcastle's resignation, see Clark, *Dynamics of Change*, pp. 231–82.

an[136] account should arrive of the taking of Fort St Phillip, whilst the Parliament was still sitting.[137] In which case there would have been a Motion in the House of Commons for an immediate Inquiry, which could not have been oppos'd with any Decency: and tho a Steady Majority might have protected our Ministers against Impeachments, or any Parliamentary censure, it could have been no security against National Clamor,[138] or against that Torrent of abuse which was reasonably to be expected from our enraged Patriots: for Pitt and his Party were become quite desperate having been all dismiss'd from their Employments[139] at the beginning of the Winter, except Sir George Lyttelton, who did not chuse to[140] resign when his Friends were turn'd out, but on the contrary was made[141] Chancellor of the Exchequer in the room of Legge, which was resented with the greatest acrimony by the whole Cousinhood. Another event happen'd about the time I have been mentioning,[142] which, tho of a private Nature, was a dangerous Blow to the whole Administration particularly to the Duke of Newcastle.

The Chief Justice of the Kings bench, Sir Dudley Rider, died very unexpectedly.[143] He was an honest Man, and a good Lawyer, but not considerable in any other Capacity. Murray the Attorney General, was so greatly superior to the rest of the Profession, that he stood without a Rival and his merit, and abilities must have ensured his Promotion had he been known only in Westminster hall, and at the Bar of the House of Lords. The immediate Loss of the ablest Debater in the House of Commons, at a time when he was so much wanted, was indeed a strong Obstacle. But the Place of Chief Justice with a Peerage having been the Point he had long aimed at; having declined all Preferment, out of[144] his Profession, and having a great independent Fortune, without any Children, it seem'd difficult to find an Equivalent in any other Shape. However, tho no single Weight would turn the ballance, they endeavor'd to overload the Scale with a Profusion of

---

[136] *M*: 'the'. This strengthens the implication that the fall of Minorca was to be expected, an implication derogatory to the ministry. A naval victory on 20 May would have had the opposite result.

[137] The date on which Parliament was prorogued for the summer recess varied considerably; there was no general norm. Dates in surrounding years were: 1754, 6 April; 1755, 25 April; 1756, 27 May; 1757, 4 July; 1758, 20 June.

[138] *M* deletes 'against National Clamor, or'.

[139] On 21 November 1755, Pitt was dismissed from his post of Paymaster General; Henry Bilson Legge from the Chancellorship of the Exchequer; and George Grenville from the Treasurership of the Navy.

[140] *M* deletes 'chuse to'.   [141] *M*: 'chusing rather to be made'.

[142] *M*: 'about the same time'.

[143] Sir Dudley Ryder (1691–1756). Called to bar 1719; Solicitor General 1733-7, Attorney General 1737-54, Chief Justice of the King's Bench 1754-d, MP 1733-d. He died on 25 May 1756.

[144] *M* deletes 'out of', inserts 'foreign to'.

Favors, of less specific Gravity: a very honorable Employment, with an ample Salary for his own Life, a considerable Reversion for his Family, and a Peerage in Futurity: But he wisely refus'd them, knowing that the acceptance of such Bribes, instead of raising him above Envy, would lower his Reputation and create new Enemies.

At last after various Proposals on one Part, & as many Refusals on the other, Murray was obliged to tell them in plain Terms, that if they did not think proper to make him Lord Chief Justice, he would no longer continue Attorney General, and as to the business of the House of Commons he should leave them to fight their own Battles.

This Declaration had an immediate effect; the Affair was settled without any farther delay, &[145] Murray took his Seat in the House of Lords the Winter following: whereby the Duke of Newcastle was depriv'd of his only friend & Advocate in the House of Commons, on whose Integrity as well as[146] Abilities he could thoroughly depend and undoubtedly had great reason to be sorry tho he had no Reason to complain.

The Summer 1756 was the triumph of Faction and of Party Violence: Remonstrances were presented to the King under the Name of Dutiful & Loyal Addresses, not inferior to those of the year 41 in the last century.[147] Whilst the Freedom of Cities and Corporations were presented to Pitt and Legge in gold Boxes accompanied with letters of thanks, not for any Services perform'd, but for those which they were supposed to have intended had they found[148] a proper opportunity.

On the other hand, it must be acknowledg'd that the Nation had sufficient reason to complain tho the manner of expressing their Dissatisfaction was not to be Justifyd: Many Millions having been raised, our Debt considerably increased, Minorca lost, and the War in North America no wise prosperous. But what inflamed the Multitude and shook the very Foundation of Government, were those treasonable Falsehoods pointed even at the Throne itself. His Majesty's very Natural affection for his German Electorate was brought as an undoubted Proof of his Settled Aversion to his British Subjects. All those Calumnies were revived which had been formerly very successfully employ'd by some of the same Persons,

---

[145] *M* omits 'the ... delay, &'.   [146] *M* omits 'Integrity as well as'.

[147] See Paul Langford, 'William Pitt and Public Opinion, 1757', *EHR* 88 (1973), 54–80; Marie Peters, *Pitt and Popularity: The Patriot Minister and London Opinion during the Seven Years' War* (Oxford, 1980). One Whig observer noted: 'In the addresses for enquiries, a Jacobite spirit has mixed itself very strongly with the discontent infused or encouraged by the late opposition': Lord Lyttelton to William Lyttelton, 25 Nov. 1756, in R.J. Phillimore (ed.), *Memoirs and Correspondence of George, Lord Lyttelton, from 1734 to 1773* (2 vols., London, 1845), vol. 2, p. 533. Waldegrave, in the *Memoirs* (below) similarly recognised that although formal Jacobitism was 'at a low Ebb', there was 'a mutinous Spirit, in the lower Class of People'.

[148] *M*: 'been allowed'.

when Lord Granville was Minister[149] and had rais'd that National Discontent which had been the Forerunner of the last Rebellion. Not that Rebellion was the Point they then aim'd at nor did they mean it on the present Occasion. They only desired to create as much confusion as might be necessary to bring themselves into Power; which being once obtain'd they were ready to talk a different Language; to say that the object was changed, and to persue the same political System which had ruined the former Administration.

In the mean time these factious or rather treasonable[150] Proceedings were not in the least discouraged at Leicester house: on the contrary those who by the severest Insinuations, or by ironical Panegyrick, had thrown the most indecent Reflections on Majesty itself, were caress'd in the most public manner; and were honor'd with all the nonsense of gracious Smiles, misterious Nods, and endless Whispers, in every corner of the Drawing Room.

The Princess of Wales's unlimited confidence in the Earl of Bute, has been already mention'd; and, by the good offices of the Mother, he also became the avow'd favorite of the Young Prince: who was just entering into his nineteenth year, the time of his Majority in case the King had been dead; and as very considerable changes must soon be made[151] in his Royal Highness's Family, the great Point they aimed at was to place the Earl of Bute at the head of the New Establishment.

I had been appointed Governor to the Prince of Wales, towards the end of the year 1752, when Lord Harcourt resign'd: and as my Predecessor did not quit on the most amicable Terms, I was very kindly received.

I found his Royal Highness uncommonly full of Princely Prejudices, contracted in the Nursery, and improved by the society of Bed Chamber Women and Pages of the Back Stairs.[152] As an entire change of the whole System of Education was impracticable, I soon perceived that the best which[153] could be hoped for, was to give him right[154] notions of common things, to instruct him by Conversation rather than by Books; and sometimes, under the Disguise of amusement, to entice him into the Persuit of more serious Studies.

The next Point I labor'd, was to preserve Union and Harmony in the Royal Family; and having free access to the Closet, I had frequent Opportunities of doing good Offices: was a very useful Apologist whenever

[149] As Secretary of State for the Northern Department, February 1741/2-November 1744.
[150] M omits 'or rather treasonable'.   [151] M: 'were soon to be made'.
[152] M p. 53 verso, C p. 85 both have this sentence heavily deleted, then written in again, first in pencil, then in ink, in the hand of Frederick Keppel.
[153] M deletes this, inserting: 'As a right System of Education seem'd quite impracticable; the best which'.
[154] M: 'true'.

his Majesty was displeas'd with his grandson's Shyness, or want of attention; and never fail'd to notify even the most minute Circumstance of the young Prince's behavior, which was likely to give Satisfaction.

On the other hand, the Princess and her Son seem'd fully satisfied with my Zeal, diligence, and faithful Services; and I was treated with so much Civility, that sometimes[155] I thought myself almost a Favorite.

This continued near three years, till the time already mention'd, when they changed their Plan, and began by their actions without directly avowing it, to set the King at Defiance. The Governor's Apologies being no longer necessary the best Use they could make of me was to provoke me to some hasty imprudent Action, by which I might be obliged to quit my Station, and make way for Bute's Advancement. However they could not find even the slightest Pretence for shewing any Public mark of their Displeasure; and tho many[156] hard things were said to me in private, I always kept my Temper, giving the severest answers in the most respectful Language, and letting them civilly understand that I fear'd their anger no more than I had deserved it; and tho it might be in their Power to fret me I was determined not to be in the wrong.

During these Transactions[157] the Prince and Princess of Wales forgetting their former Resentment, sent messages to the Duke of Newcastle in the most submissive terms: assuring him that if by his Interest in the Closet, Lord Bute could be made Groom of the Stole, they should ever remember it as the greatest Obligation: that it was the only Point which they had really at heart, and that they were more desirous of obtaining such[158] a Favor by his means, because they had rather be oblig'd to him, than to any other Minister. The Duke of Newcastle either doubted their sincerity, or was not sufficiently frighten'd to give a satisfactory answer. Besides he knew that his Endeavors to please Leicester House would not be quite[159] agreeable at St James's; and did not chuse to incur the displeasure of the King, who, tho in his 73d year was Strong & in perfect Health. Accordingly he went no farther than[160] general Professions of Respect, and of his Inclination to obey their Commands; but avoided an Interview, and made no particular Promises.

However his Majesty was immediately acquainted with their Royal Highnesses Request; and as a new Establishment, in some shape or other,

---

[155] *M* omits 'sometimes'. Waldegrave strengthened, in retrospect, his idea of his entitlement to favour at Leicester House.
[156] *M*: 'some'.
[157] On the negotiations for the creation of the Household of the Prince of Wales in the summer of 1756, see Clark, *Dynamics of Change*, pp. 240–61; McKelvey, *George III and Lord Bute*, pp. 33–47.
[158] *M* deletes 'more'; erases 'such', inserts 'so considerable'.   [159] *M* erases 'quite'.
[160] *M* erases 'went no farther than', inserts 'strictly confined himself to'.

was to be form'd as soon as possible, he order'd a Meeting[161] of his principal Servants, amongst whom, as the Prince of Wales's Governor, I had the honor of being admitted.

It was unusual for the King himself to be present at such Consultations; but he had already declared his opinion, by speaking of the Princess's Favorite, and of her Partiality towards him, with the greatest Contempt.

The Chancellor with his usual Gravity, declared that for his own Part, he had no particular Objection to the Earl of Bute's Promotion; neither would he give Credit to some very extraordinary Reports; But that many sober & respectable Persons might[162] think it indecent; for which reason he could never advise his Majesty to give his Consent.

Lord Granville did not treat the Affair quite so seriously; told three or four very good Stories which were nothing to the Purpose; and concluded, that the King was the only proper Judge in the affairs of his own Family.

The Duke of Newcastle gave his opinion, that the King would never suffer Bute to be Groom of the Stole; but that something might be done for him in some other Shape. That undoubtedly their Royal Highnesses must soon be convinced of the great Impropriety of what they now desired; that it was a very nice Affair, and required the most mature Considerations; and therefore he was against any immediate, or final determination.

When it was my turn to speak, I told them I was fully convinc'd, that Leicester House would never be contented, unless their Request was granted in its full Extent. That I was also persuaded that this Request, however unreasonable, would be complied with, rather than cause an open Rupture by an obstinate Refusal. That it was undoubtedly[163] better to do the thing soon, and with a good Grace, than hereafter, when it would be thought an Act of Necessity, & no Favor whatsoever. But that I had nothing to say as to the Propriety, or Decency of the Measure, whereof I did not think myself a competent Judge.

During the whole Summer there were several Consultations on the same Subject; frequent Letters, and Messages past between Kew and Kensington; but instead of any Agreement, the Breach was daily growing wider: when at last, about the beginning of October, the Ministers not daring to meet the Parliament whilst Leicester House was dissatisfied, obtain'd the King's Consent, that the Prince of Wales should not remove to Kensington, but should still continue with his Mother, and that Bute should be Groom of the Stole at the head of the new Establishment.

By this Means, was I delivered from the most painful Servitude.[164] Even

---

[161] Evidently, the meeting of the full Cabinet on 7 July 1756: Walpole, *George II*, vol. 2, pp. 160–1. There had already been a number of more confidential ministerial meetings on the question since 19 February: cf. McKelvey, *George III and Lord Bute*, p. 36.
[162] *M*: 'would'.   [163] *M* omits 'undoubtedly'.
[164] I.e. of continuing in the Prince's service as his Groom of the Stole.

in the best of times, I had found little Satisfaction in my most honorable Employment; and my Spirits and Patience were at last so totally exhausted that I could have quitted his Royal Highness, & have given up all future Hopes of Court Preferment, without the least Regret or Uneasiness.

But by good Fortune, I did not think myself a free Agent. I was[165] under the greatest personal[166] Obligations to the King, the many Favors I had received having been confer'd by him only without any ministerial assistance: It would therefore have been[167] ungrateful as well as impolitick to have abandon'd[168] my Station without his Majesty's Consent. On the other hand[169] the King thought it absolutely[170] necessary that whoever was at the head[171] of the new Establishment, should be a person, in whom he could repose a thorough Confidence; and was desirous I should continue in the Prince's Service, not only because he was partial in my Favor, but also on account of his Dislike to my intended Successor.

As often therefore as I talked of resigning, his Majesty changed the discourse, & seem'd not to understand me; tho when he thought proper, he could take a hint as quick as any Man.

I next apply'd to the Duke of Newcastle who had not the least conception how my situation could be so very unpleasant as I represented it: Measuring perhaps my feelings by his own, and, thinking that from long attendance at Court, with four years Practice in the School of Politicks, I must have lost all Sensibility. As the clearest Hints had been to no purpose, I was now reduced to the Necessity of speaking plainly and directly to the King himself. His Majesty heard all I had to say with the greatest Condescension and Goodness; own'd I had great Reason to be dissatisfied but press'd me in the strongest Manner to continue with his Grandson, sometime longer. To which I answer'd, that if my situation was still more disagreeable, I never would desert my Post, whilst there remain'd a Possibility of doing any good, in any Shape whatsoever. But, with the loss of his Royal Highness's favor and Confidence, I had lost the only means of doing any real Service, and therefore hoped his Majesty would grant my Dismission whenever it should be his Pleasure to form the new Establishment. At last after much Persuasion, and many unconvincing Arguments, he put the decisive Question, whether I had taken my final Resolution; to which, in the most respectful manner possible, I answer'd in the affirmative. He then reply'd, *I am heartily sorry for it, but cannot say you are in the wrong.*

[165] *M* deletes the para. to here; inserts 'But being'.　　[166] *M* omits 'personal'.
[167] *M* deletes 'It . . . been', inserts 'I thought it would be'.
[168] *M* deletes 'have abandon'd', inserts 'abandon'.
[169] *M* erases 'On the other hand', inserts 'At the same time'.
[170] *M* deletes 'absolutely'.
[171] *M* erases 'whoever . . . head', inserts 'the principal Director'.

The next time I had the Honor of speaking to his Majesty he very graciously told me, that as I had incurr'd the displeasure of Leicester House on Account of my Attachment to him, and because I had acted an honest Part, he was determined to shew his Approbation of my Behavior, by giving me something permanent, which could not be resumed when he should be dead. That he was not resolv'd either as to the thing itself, or the manner of doing it, but that he would consult the Duke of Newcastle and would order him to talk to me more fully on the subject.

Accordingly in a few Days, the Duke of Newcastle after a pompous Preamble of the King's great Goodness, his own good Offices, and my good Fortune, came at last to the Point, and acquainted me with his Majesty's intention of granting me a Pension for my Life of £2000 a Year on the Irish Establishment.

As I was prepared for a Proposal of this Sort, I did not hesitate an Instant to give my Answer, and told him that I was thoroughly sensible of his Majesty's goodness, from long Experience; nor had I ever doubted his Grace's good Offices; and as to my own good Fortune, it was very certain[172] that £2000 a year added to my paternal Estate was as much as I wanted or wish'd for. At the same time, it was my determined Resolution never to accept a Pension in any shape whatsoever. That I asked for nothing, at present, except my Liberty; but if it should be his Majesty's Pleasure to grant me a Reversion, that I might hereafter be one of the Tellers of the Exchequer, it would make me perfectly easy during the Remainder of my Life: and that I imagined, the King himself would prefer this to an Irish Pension, as it would cause no Clamor or Uneasiness,[173] and would be no Diminution of his Majesty's Revenue.

The Duke of Newcastle who wanted this Reversion for one of his Favorites, used many arguments to prove that the present Possession of a Pension for Life, granted by the Crown as a Reward for my Services, ought to be esteem'd honorable as well as profitable. But finding me obstinate he was under the necessity of acquainting the King with what had pass'd, who had not the worse opinion of me for having refused the Pension, and my Request was granted without the least difficulty.

I had not acquainted either the Prince or Princess of Wales with this Transaction, who strongly suspected that notwithstanding the ill usage I had received, I might still have some Inclination to continue in his Royal Highness's Service: and having often perceived that I would not understand the most intelligible Hints, they now resolved to explain themselves in the clearest and most precise Manner.

Accordingly, one day after Dinner, the Prince of Wales began the Conversation by desiring I would take nothing amiss; and then proceeded,

[172] *M* deletes 'it was very certain'.   [173] *M* omits 'or Uneasiness'.

with much Hesitation and Confusion, that he certainly should be exceeding glad to employ me hereafter, but that just at present he had very particular Reasons against my continuing in his Service, that it would be very improper for him to give me a Negative, hoped I would not lay him under such a difficulty, and that he should esteem it a real obligation if my Resignation could have the appearance of being entirely my own Act.

I answer'd, that far from taking any thing amiss I return'd his R:H: my humblest Thanks for the very gracious Manner in which he had express'd himself. That as to my quitting his Service, I had often proposed it to the King, who, tho much averse to it, had at last given his Consent.

That this had long been my Object: for that several months ago, when his Royal Highness had thought proper to tell me that he expected to have the Nomination of the Person who was to be at the head of the new Establishment, it being necessary there should be a Man, in such a Place, whom he could thoroughly confide in: when he had added, that unless he was gratified in this particular, he should consider all those who were placed about him as his Enemies and when it was very apparent that I was not the Person in whom his Confidence was reposed; I should undoubtedly have resign'd my Employment, the next morning, if I had not been apprehensive that it might have produced an immediate Rupture; for that I was determined, that if there must be a Quarrel between him and his Grandfather, which I thought most probable, it should never be placed to my Account.

That I had persisted in doing all good Offices as long as they were practicable; that when it was no longer in my Power to do any[174] Good, I still[175] endeavor'd to do as little Harm as possible; and had made use of every Opportunity to soften, and alleviate whatever was[176] amiss; But at the same time, the King having appointed me his Royal Highness Governor, I was accountable to his Majesty, and it was my Duty to give Informations as to some particulars, when he required it: or supposing it had been my Intention to deceive the King, even in that case it would have been absurd to have denied those things, which might be seen at every Drawing room, and were the subject of conversation at every Coffee House.

Those who had persuaded his R:H: to speak to me in the manner I have mention'd, had forgot to furnish him with a proper Reply: possibly they did not expect that I should have presumed to return so uncourtly an Answer.[177] He was much embarrass'd, said little, and went immediately to his Mother, to give an Account of what had pass'd.

In about two days I was sent for by her R:H:, who began by apologizing

---

[174] *M*: 'any real'   [175] *M*: 'still had'.   [176] *M* erases 'was', inserts 'had been'.
[177] Brooke, *George III*, p. 52 suggests the 'uncourtly answer' was a hint of the Dowager Princess's adultery with Bute.

for her Son's Behavior; telling me that I must certainly have misunderstood him on several occasions, or that he had said more than he really intended: that he had a great Regard for me, did not like new Faces, and was very desirous I should continue in his service. But that he had a very particular Esteem for the Earl of Bute, and had set his heart upon making him Groom of the Stole: that being Master of the Horse was equally honorable and if I would accept that Employment every thing might be made easy, and the King and her Son would both be satisfied. The Prince who was present assented to every thing she said, but enter'd no farther into the conversation.

I return'd their R:R:H:H: my humblest Thanks, assured them that whether I quitted, or whether I remain'd his R:H: Servant, I should always be desirous of doing every thing which they should approve of, as far as was consistent with the superior Duty I ow'd to the King; that nothing could give me more real satisfaction, than to see perfect Harmony and Union Establish'd[178] in the royal Family.

Many other[179] Compliments pass'd between us, without the least Insincerity on either Side; for we did not mean to deceive each other: but, as we were soon to be divided for the rest of our Lives, it seem'd best to part, with the appearance of good Humor, and Civility.

One of my Compliments might, indeed, be somewhat equivocal: I told her R:H: that I had frequently taken the Liberty of speaking to the King concerning Lord Bute's Promotion, but had never obtain'd a serious Answer; and[180] that as often as I touched on the Subject, he immediately laugh'd in my Face.[181]

After this friendly Conference, which was about a Month before the new Establishment took Place, I was treated with the greatest Politeness; and when his Majesty granted their Request, he made Choice of me to be the Messenger of good News.[182] As soon as the happy Event was notified, his R:H: wrote a Letter to the King full of the Strongest Professions of Duty, Respect, and Gratitude, wherewith his Majesty was highly satisfied. It was now the general Opinion that Leicester House would enjoy the Fruits of their[183] Victory, and cause no future disturbance; the Prince of Wales having given the Strongest Assurances that Lord Bute's Promotion was the only part of the Establishment which he had really at Heart, and that if he could be gratified in this particular, he should make no further Demands.

But his Request was most injudiciously complied with, about a week before the new Establishment was entirely settled; during which Interval,

---

[178] *M* omits 'Establish'd'.   [179] *M* omits 'other'.   [180] *M*: 'for'.
[181] Waldegrave's extreme bitterness shows through passages like this. He evidently burned his bridges with the dowager Princess and Lord Bute, whatever were to be his future relations with George III.
[182] On 4 October: McKelvey, *George III and Lord Bute*, p. 45.   [183] *M*: 'the'.

the Language was entirely changed: they acknowledged that the King had been exceeding gracious, and had treated the Prince with the greatest Tenderness; but that neither his R:H: nor the Princess, were under the least obligation to any of the Ministers. That an Establishment had been form'd without consulting them, consisting only of the Duke of Newcastle's Followers and Dependants; that many of their Faces were unknown at Leicester House, and even amongst those who might have been approved of, had they apply'd in a proper Manner, very few had condescended to make the least Inquiry whether their Services would be agreeable.

Now tho this reasoning was neither quite fair, nor quite true, it served at least[184] as a Pretence for their appearing still dissatisfied with the Duke of Newcastle, who alone[185] had prevail'd with the King to grant their[186] Request: a very important Service, which ought to have been longer remember'd.

I received his Majesty's Commands to send letters of Notification to his R:H: new Servants; and when the long expected Day arrived, I introduc'd them first at Kensington, and then return'd to Saville House,[187] where I presented them to the Prince of Wales.[188]

The King could not be persuaded to look kindly on the Groom of the Stole, neither would he admit him into the Closet to receive the Badge of his Office; but gave it to the Duke of Grafton, who Slipt the Gold Key into Bute's pocket, wish'd it could have been given in a more proper manner, but prudently advised him to take no notice.

When the whole Ceremony was ended, I went to take leave of His R:H: who was uncommonly gracious; assuring me that he was thoroughly satisfied with every Part of my Behavior, and that if others had acted in the same Manner, he should have had no Reason to complain.

After these Compliments we had a very chearful Conversation, which being ended, I made my Bow, and parted from him with as much Indifference as was consistent with Respect and Decency.

Whilst these Affairs were in Agitation a very unexpected Event gave a violent Shock to the tottering Administration.

I have already taken Notice of Fox's having been made Secretary of State, at the beginning of the preceding Winter: The Duke of Newcastle by the advice of Murray, Stone, and other Friends, had also admitted him to

---

[184] *M* omits 'at least'.

[185] *M* erases 'alone', inserts 'had gratified them in most of their Recommendations, tho he had not consulted them in every Particular: and moreover'.

[186] *M*: 'their principal'.

[187] Savile House adjoined Leicester House: Prince Frederick had taken a lease of it in 1743, and in 1751 had made it the residence of his two sons, George and Edward. Savile House remained Prince George's actual residence after his father's death.

[188] On 28 October 1756, Waldegrave's last day at the junior court. For the Prince's Household, see Walpole, *George II*, vol. 2, p. 182.

an inferior degree of Ministerial Partnership; and tho there was little Probability that such different Tempers could admit of real Friendship; there would have been no Disagreement of any Consequence, if weak and peevish Counsellors had not interfered.

His Grace had a select Committee of Relations his principal Advisers in affairs of the greatest Importance: these excellent Politicians had a secret Satisfaction in doing ill offices, and lost no Opportunity of giving the worst Interpretation to every doubtful Circumstance of Fox's Behavior:[189] whilst the Duke of Newcastle, to gratify their ill Humor, and his own Jealousy, treated him rather like an Enemy whom he fear'd, than as a Minister whom he had chose for his Assistant.

But the Secretary received greater[190] Mortification from the Treatment he met with in the Closet. His Majesty could not readily forget that Sir Tho: Robinson had been removed to make way for Fox's Promotion: who, with abilities equal to any Employment,[191] had been less conversant in foreign Affairs, than in the Business of Parliament; and his Majesty is supposed to have given some ungracious Hints, how a Man might be a Talker in the House of Commons, tho, at the same time,[192] a very indifferent Secretary. In a word, Fox thought himself ill used both by King and Minister: he also foresaw that the loss of Minorca must add Strength to the Opposition in Parliament,[193] the Nation being now on their Side: moreover, if any personal attack was made against him, that he should be weakly supported. He therefore thought it prudent to avoid the Storm, asked an Audience of the King, enter'd into a short Detail of his Grievances, and obtain'd his Majesty's Permission to resign his Employment.[194]

This Resignation was nowise pleasing to the Duke of Newcastle, who meant that Fox should have continued in a responsible Office, with a double Portion of Danger and Abuse, but without any Share of Power.

The whole System of the House of Commons was at once entirely changed, Fox no longer a Minister, Murray retiring to the House of Peers, Pitt standing without a Rival, no Orator to oppose him who had Courage even to look him in the Face. However the Duke of Newcastle still flattered himself that Art and Negotiation might set every thing right; but Pitt would listen to no Terms of Accomodation, and absolutely refused to treat; declaring that he had infinite Respect for his Grace, in his private

---

[189] Waldegrave's bias in favour of Fox and against Newcastle is here made explicit.
[190] *M*: 'still greater'.
[191] *M* deletes 'with . . . Employment', inserts '(tho his political knowledge was not confined to a particular Branch)'.
[192] *M* erases 'at . . . time', inserts 'in every other Respect'.   [193] *M* omits 'in Parliament'.
[194] For Fox's resignation by letter on 13 October 1756, see Clark, *Dynamics of Change*, pp. 261–70. Fox's audience took place on 18 October.

Capacity; but that a plain Man unpractised in the Policy of a Court, must never presume to be the Associate of so experienc'd a Minister.[195]

Proposals were then made to the Earl of Egmont[196] who was a good Speaker in Parliament, had an excellent Character in private Life, and was thought to have a Spirit which would not be easily intimidated. Business and Politics were his only Amusements. And he had Parts as well as Application. But there is a certain wise saying that every Man should have a Respect for *himself*: which Maxim was[197] understood by his Lordship in the literal sense; and[198] it appear'd both by his Manner and Discourse that he was rather too respectful.[199]

The Duke of Newcastle offer'd to make him Secretary of State; but Egmont, whose Object was an English Peerage, and who had no[200] great Faith in Ministerial Promises, refused to engage unless he was immediately removed to the House of Lords; which was directly contrary to the Duke of Newcastle's Purposes, the House of Commons being the only Place where he wanted Assistance.

His Grace next apply'd to my Lord President, and the Proposal made, was Exchange of Employments; the Duke of Newcastle, to be President of the Council; Lord Granville to be at the head of the Treasury, and first Minister. But Granville soon convinced him that, whatever might have been his object ten years ago, Experience had made him Wiser; and that he was perfectly contented with the Ease and Dignity of his present Situation.

At last when every Proposal had been rejected, when no Man would stand in the Gap, the Duke of Newcastle unwillingly resign'd his Employment[201] which he had not Courage to hold.

He was follow'd by his Friend the Earl of Hardwick, who resign'd the Great Seal much to the Regret of all good[202] Men, and indeed of the Nation in general. He had been Chancellor near twenty years, and was inferior to few who had gone before him, having executed that high office with Integrity, Diligence, and uncommon Abilities. The Statesman might perhaps be nowise equal to[203] the Judge, yet even in that capacity, he had been the chief Support of the Duke of Newcastle's Administration.

Lord Anson was also dismiss'd from the Admiralty, a violent Clamor

---

[195] Pitt actually insisted on Newcastle's resignation in his interview with Hardwicke on 19 October.

[196] John Perceval (1711–70), 2nd Earl of Egmont in the Irish peerage. English MP 1741–62; received English Barony May 1762. A Lord of the Bedchamber to Frederick, Prince of Wales 1748–51; Privy Councillor 9 Jan. 1755; joint Postmaster General 1762–3; First Lord of the Admiralty 1763–6.

[197] *M*: 'may have been'.   [198] *M*: 'for'.

[199] *M* deletes 'that ... respectful', inserts: 'that he respected himself rather more than the World respected him'.

[200] *M*: 'not'.   [201] On 26 October.   [202] *M* deletes 'good', inserts 'dispassionate'.

[203] *M* deletes 'be ... the', inserts 'in some particulars, be the Reverse of the'.

having been raised against him, of which he was no more deserving than of the high Reputation which preceded it. He was in reality a good Sea Officer, and had gain'd a considerable Victory over the French in the last War; but Nature had not endow'd him with those extraordinary Abilities, which had been so liberally granted him by the whole Nation. Now on the contrary he is to be allow'd no Merit whatsoever, the loss of Minorca is to be imputed to his Misconduct, tho many were equally, some infinitely more blamable; his Slowness in Business, is to be call'd Negligence, and his Silence and Reserve, which formerly pass'd for Wisdom, takes the Name of Dullness, and of want of Capacity.

The Duke of Devonshire[204] who had all[205] the good Qualities of his Father, and[206] seem'd less averse to Business,[207] succeeded the Duke of Newcastle as first Commissioner of the Treasury: but did not accept till his Majesty had given his Word that[208] he should be at full Liberty to resign his Employment, at the end of the approaching Session of Parliament.

Legge was appointed Chancellor of the Exchequer in the room of Sir George Lyttelton who was made a Peer. Pitt succeeded Fox as Secretary of State. Lord Temple was placed at the head of the Admiralty. The great Seal was put in Commission, Willes Chief Justice of the Common Pleas being first Commissioner. George Grenville[209] succeeded Doddington[210] as Treasurer of the Navy; and the remaining Friends and Relations[211] of the New Secretary were all provided for, either in the Treasury, Admiralty or other Places of less Consequence, in Proportion to their Interest or their Abilities.

There was indeed one Exception, Charles Townshend[212] being made Treasurer of the Chambers, tho he seem'd better[213] qualified for a more active Employment. But Pitt did not chuse to advance a Young Man to a Ministerial Office, whose Abilities were of the same kind, and so nearly equal to his own. Both had fine Natural Parts: both were capable of great Application: which was the greater Master of Abuse, could not easily be determined: and if there was something more awful and compulsive in

---

[204] William Cavendish (1720–64), 4th Duke of Devonshire. Styled Marquess of Hartington 1729–55. MP 1741–51. Succeeded 5 Dec. 1755. Summoned to House of Lords 13 June 1751 in his father's barony as Lord Cavendish of Hardwick. Master of the Horse 1751–5; Lord Lieutenant of Ireland March 1755-Nov. 1756; a Lord Justice of England 1755. First Lord of the Treasury Nov. 1756-June 1757. Lord Chamberlain 1757–62.
[205] *M* erases 'all', inserts 'many of'.   [206] *M*: 'but'.
[207] *M* inserts: 'and better qualified for a Court'.
[208] *M* inserts: 'in case he disliked his Employment'.   [209] *M*: 'Greenville'.
[210] *M*: 'Dodington'.
[211] *M* omits 'and Relations'.
[212] Charles Townshend (1725–67), MP 1747-d; a Lord of Trade 1749–54; a Lord of the Admiralty 1754–5; Treasurer of the Chamber 1756–61, etc.
[213] *M* deletes 'better', inserts 'fully'.

Pitt's Oratory, there was more Acuteness, and more Wit, in Charles Townshend's.

Tho the settling this New Administration was the work only[214] of a few days, there had been sufficient time for much caballing, and for raising many Difficulties. Pitt's Demands were at first thought so unreasonable, that the King had authorised the Duke of Devonshire to form an Administration in Concert with Fox, the Duke of Bedford, and some of the Duke of Newcastle's Friends; with any other assistance which could be obtain'd, provided Pitt and his adherents might be totally excluded. Fox and some others were ready to engage,[215] a meeting was proposed of those who were call'd the King's Friends, and for two days it seem'd doubtful who were to be our Governors. But during this Interval Pitt became more reasonable, and the Duke of Devonshire advised his Majesty to comply with his Demands; whereupon the Administration was form'd in the manner already mention'd. On which account the Duke of Devonshire was very[216] unjustly censured by many of his[217] Friends; for he join'd Pitt rather than Fox, not because he liked him better, but because he had the Nation on his side, and consequently had the means of doing most Service, to his King & Country.[218]

All previous Articles being now settled, the Session of Parliament open'd with a Speech from the Throne, which by its Stile and Substance appear'd to be the Work of a new Speechmaker. The Militia, which his Majesty had always turn'd into Ridicule, was[219] strongly recommended; the late Administration censured; and the very insolent[220] Addresses of the preceding Summer received[221] the highest Commendations.

But tho his Majesty found it necessary to talk this Language to his Parliament, he had no Inclination that the Nation should be deceived as to his real Sentiments; for being told[222] that an impudent Fellow[223] was to be punish'd for having publish'd a Spurious Speech, his Majesty answer'd, he hoped the Man's Punishment would not be very Severe, for that[224] he had

---

[214] *M* omits 'only'.
[215] The initiative was actually taken by Fox, not Devonshire: on 27 October, the day after Newcastle's resignation, Fox accepted the King's invitation to form an administration of his own: Clark, *Dynamics of Change*, pp. 283–9. This episode calls in question Waldegrave's earlier picture of the innocence of Fox's motives in bringing down Newcastle.
[216] *M* deletes 'very'.   [217] *M* erases 'many of his', inserts 'some unreasonable'.
[218] *M* deletes 'not . . . Country', inserts: 'not from any Change of friendship, or any Partiality in Pitt's Favor; but because it was more safe to be united with him who had the Nation of his Side, than with the Man who was the most unpopular. A Reason which will have its proper Weight with most Ministers.'
[219] *M*: 'being'.   [220] *M*: 'uncourtly'.   [221] *M*: 'receiving'.
[222] *M* deletes 'he had . . . told', inserts 'in common Conversation, he made a frank Declaration of his real Sentiments: particularly, being inform'd'.
[223] *M*: 'Printer'.   [224] *M* deletes 'not . . . that', inserts 'be of the mildest Sort, because'.

read both, and, as far as he understood either of them he liked the Spurious Speech better than his own.

An Event happen'd the first day of the Session, which did not greatly add to the King's Partiality for some of[225] his New Ministers.[226] It had been mention'd in the Speech that the Electoral Troops were immediately to return to their own Country and it was proposed in the Lords Address to thank the King for bringing them[227] to England at a time when we wanted their Assistance; which seem'd a compliment of mere Decency, his Majesty having order'd them over at the Request of both Houses of Parliament. But the new Chief of the Admiralty was of a contrary Opinion: he came, as he told the Lords, out of a Sick Bed, at the Hazard of his Life, (indeed he made a very sorrowful Appearance) to represent to their Lordships the fatal Consequences of the intended Compliment. That the People of England would be offended even at the name of Hanover, or of Foreign Mercenaries; that the Thanks proposed might raise strong[228] suspicions that a total Change of Measures was not intended; which might[229] break that Harmony and Union now so happily establish'd. He added many other Arguments of the same kind,[230] and having finish'd his Oration, went out of the House, fully convinced that such weighty reasons must be quite unanswerable.

If his Majesty was dissatisfied with the Parliamentary Conduct of his Ministers, their Behavior in the Closet, tho hitherto not very offensive, was at least very disagreeable.

The King who had a quick Conception, and did not like to be kept long in Suspense, expected that those who talk'd to him on Business should use no superfluous Arguments, but should come at once to the Point. On the other hand Pitt and Lord Temple who were Orators even in familiar Conversation endeavor'd to guide his Majesty's Passions, and to convince his Judgement by Rules of Rhetorick.

But their Art was Strangely misapply'd, for before they could ever finish their Exordium, his Majesty had both forgot the Subject, and lost his Patience.[231] Their Mutual Dissatisfaction was soon increased by the Affair of Admiral Byng,[232] who had been condemn'd by a Court Martial, but at

---

[225] *M* omits 'greatly' and 'some of'.
[226] For the Lords' debate on the Address in reply to the King's Speech, 2 Dec. 1756, see Waldegrave's speech no. 19 below.
[227] *M* erases 'bringing them', inserts 'having brought them'.   [228] *M* omits 'strong'.
[229] *M*: 'would'.
[230] *M* inserts: 'without mentioning the true Reason of his Disapprobation, namely, the Duke of Devonshire's having added this Compliment, with out consulting him;'.
[231] *M* deletes this sentence.
[232] For Byng's court martial and its political repercussions see Clark, *Dynamics of Change*, pp. 323–35. Waldegrave's account of the ministers' intentions is just.

Memoirs of 1754–1757

the same time[233] strongly recommended to his Majesty's Mercy: The popular Clamor[234] was violent against the Admiral, but Pitt and Lord Temple were very[235] desirous to save him; partly to please Leicester House, and partly because making him less Criminal, would throw greater Blame on the late Administration. At the same time,[236] to avoid the Odium of protecting a Man who had been hanged in Effigy in almost[237] every Town in England, they wanted the King to pardon him without their seeming to interfere; agreeable to the Practice of most Ministers, who take all merit to themselves when Measures are approved of, and load their Master with those Acts of Prerogative which are most unpopular.

His Majesty however not chusing to be their Dupe, obliged them to pull of[f] the Mask; and the Sentance against the Admiral was not carried into Execution,[238] till by their Behavior in Parliament, they had given public Proof of their Partiality.

In the mean time, Mr. Pitt had some Merit in providing for the Security of North America, which during our political Squabbles had been much[239] neglected. After Braddock's defeat near Fort du Quesne, a Reinforcement had been sent from England, a Regiment had also been raised consisting of four Battalions of German Protestants, and Lord Loudon[240] had been appointed Commander in Chief, who had seen some Service in the preceding War, and was, at least, as good[241] an officer as any who would undertake the Command. Yet, our affairs[242] were in a bad Situation:[243] our Colonies were indeed greatly[244] Superior to the Enemy in respect of Numbers,[245] but the French were as much our Superiors in Point of[246] Discipline: almost every Man amongst them was a Soldier, most of the Indians were attach'd to them,[247] and they had a Chain of Forts at the back of our Settlements, where we lay open and defenceless.

All these Evils were now to be remedied: Holbourn[248] was to command a powerful Fleet, with a considerable number[249] of Land Forces who were to join Lord Loudon: Louisbourg was to be attack'd by Sea and Land: from

---

[233] *M* inserts 'had been'.   [234] *M*: 'cry'.   [235] *M* omits 'very'.   [236] *M*: 'But'.
[237] *M* omits 'almost'.   [238] Byng was shot on 14 March 1757.   [239] *M*: 'shamefully'.
[240] John Campbell, 4th Earl of Loudoun (1705–82), succ. 1731. A representative peer of Scotland 1734–82. Entered army 1727; ADC to George II 1743–45. Fought in the '45; Commander in Chief, America, 1756–57. Major General 1755, Lieut. General 1758, General 1770.
[241] *M*: 'was esteem'd as good'.
[242] *C* has 'officers' deleted, 'affairs' inserted by Frederick Keppel: presumably an error of dictation.
[243] *M* inserts 'for tho'.   [244] *M*: omits 'indeed greatly'.
[245] *M*: 'in Wealth and the Number of Inhabitants'.
[246] *M*: 'in military'.   [247] *M*: 'their Interest'.
[248] Francis Holburne (1704–71): entered Navy 1720; Captain 1739; Rear-Admiral Feb. 1755; Vice-Admiral Feb. 1757; Admiral 1767; a Lord of the Admiralty 1770–1.
[249] *C* has 'number' inserted by Frederick Keppel; *M*: 'Body'.

thence, we were to proceed to Quebec, take that also: which being effected, the French must soon be routed[250] out from the whole Continent.

This was indeed a bold Project: desponding Politicians may perhaps call it a wild one: at the same time, such a formidable Armament, must naturally raise our Expectations, and give hopes of a Successful Campaign; wherein we were greatly disappointed the Summer following.

But to return to our Affairs at Court. His Majesty became every day more averse to his new Ministers. Pitt indeed had not frequent occasions of giving offence, having been confined by the gout, the greatest part of the winter; and when he made his appearance, he behaved with proper Respect; so that the King, tho he did not like his long speeches, always treated him like a Gentleman. But to Lord Temple he had the strongest Aversion, his Lordship having a pert Familiarity which is not always agreeable to Majesty. Besides in the Affair of Admiral Byng, he had used some insolent expressions which the King would never forgive.

His Majesty had now determined to dismiss them both as soon [as] possible, which opens a new Scene, wherein I must be guilty of much Egotism, having been a principal agent in most of the Subsequent Transactions.

After I had quitted the Prince of Wales's Service, in October 1756 I remain'd quiet, troubling myself very little about Politics, till the February following, when by the Death of Lord Walpole,[251] I came into Possession of my Place in the Exchequer, about[252] two months after the reversionary Patent had pass'd the great Seal.

On this occasion I thought it right to wait on the King, both to return Thanks and to resign my Employment in the Stannaries; the Place of Teller alone, being as I told his Majesty as much as any Man was entitled to, and full as much as I either wanted or wish'd. He received me very graciously, told me how glad he was that he had granted the Reversion at the right time for that at present it would not have been in his Power. He moreover insisted that I should continue Warden of the Stannaries some time longer, if it were only to exclude some impertinent Relation of his new Minister.

He then express'd his dislike to Pitt and Lord Temple in very Strong Terms; the Substance of which was, that the Secretary made him long Speeches which possibly might be very fine, but were greatly beyond his Comprehension; and that his letters were affected, formal, and pedantic. That as to Temple, he was so disagreeable a Fellow there was no bearing him: that when he attempted to argue he was pert, and sometimes insolent:

[250] *M*: 'driven'.
[251] Horatio Walpole (1678–1757), created on 4 June 1756 Baron Walpole of Wolterton. Younger brother of Sir Robert Walpole. Diplomat; MP 1710–17, 1718–56. Various offices and sinecures, including that of a Teller of the Exchequer 1741-d. Died 5 Feb. 1757.
[252] *M*: 'in less than'.

that when he meant to be civil, he was exceeding[253] troublesom; and that in the Business of his Office he was totally ignorant.

He next question'd me concerning the Duke of Newcastle; to which I answered, that tho he was no longer a Minister, it was very apparent, a great Majority in both Houses of Parliament, still consider'd him as their Chief, and were ready to act under his Direction. That some of these might possibly be attach'd to him by a Principle of Gratitude; but far the greater Number were his Followers, because they had reason to expect[254] that he would soon be in a Condition to reward their Services. That as to his[255] Grace himself, he was quite doubtful what part he should take, being almost equally ballanc'd between Fear on one Side, and Love of Power on the other.

To this the King reply'd, I know he is apt to be afraid, therefore go and encourage him; tell him I do not look on myself as King, whilst I am in the hands of these Scoundrels; that I am determined to get rid of them at any rate; that I expect his assistance, and that he may depend on my Favor and Protection.

In Obedience to these Instructions, I had several conferences with the Duke of Newcastle, the Substance of which I reported to his Majesty.[256] That I found his Grace just as I expected, eager and impatient to come into Power, but dreading the danger with which it must be accompanied. That he had indeed made one Objection, wherein I entirely agreed with him; that it was not yet the proper season for the changes his Majesty propos'd:[257] that when the Supply was granted, the Inquiry at an end, and his late Ministers honorably acquitted, which would probably happen in less then two months, Pitt and his Followers might then be set at Defiance without any considerable Danger. But that an immediate Change of Administration was a desperate Measure, which would create much Confusion, and might involve his Majesty in new and perhaps insuperable Difficulties.

To this the King made answer, neither the Duke of Newcastle nor yourself are Judges of what I feel: I can endure their Insolence no longer. I reply'd, that I certainly did not mean to be an Advocate for Men against whom his Majesty was so justly offended; and that I wish'd to defer the Blow, for this Reason only, that we might strike with more Force, and greater Certainty.

I then proceeded, and told his Majesty that the Duke of Newcastle had also given other Reasons which I thought necessary to be mention'd,

[253] C: 'exceeding' inserted by Frederick Keppel.
[254] C: 'expect' inserted by Frederick Keppel.
[255] C: 'his' inserted by Frederick Keppel.
[256] For these negotiations in March 1757 see Clark, *Dynamics of Change*, pp. 335–53.
[257] M: 'intended'.

because they were of a different nature from the former, and might operate as strongly two months hence, as at the present Instant.

That he seem'd quite[258] terrified with the Dangers to which this Country was exposed, dreading the Consequences of an unsuccessful War, jealous of Fox and of those who were to be his Associates in the new Administration, yet not daring to make himself[259] the only responsible Minister by taking the whole authority into his own Hands. Therefore, tho it might be his present Intention to resume his Seat at the Head of the Treasury, towards the end of the Session of Parliament, he seem'd too irresolute to know his own Mind, and consequently was not to be depended on.

His Majesty now order'd me to talk again to the Duke of Newcastle, giving me leave to say, in his name, whatever I should think necessary, and to endeavor by any means to bring him to some final Determination.

He also directed me to talk with his R:H: the Duke and with Fox,[260] that some Plan of Administration might be form'd in case the Duke of Newcastle should persevere in his present System of Irresolution. His Royal Highness press'd the King very Strongly that Pitt and Lord Temple might be turn'd out without farther deliberation: being desirous that a new Administration should be form'd before he set out for Hanover, where he was to take the Command of his Majesty's Electoral Forces.

Fox was also desirous that a Plan of Administration should be prepared, which being in Readiness might as Circumstances should require, either be delay'd or carry'd into immediate Execution. As to the Duke of Newcastle, in Proportion as the King grew more determined he became more irresolute. He was subject to such frequent changes that I found it necessary to declare, that he must employ a new Commissioner, unless he would assist my Memory, and set down his Proposals in writing: being really[261] vex'd, and ashamed, that I could hardly say a word in his Grace's name, which I was not obliged to contradict the Day following. However, if my Veracity was suspected, it was also soon clear'd, for when he explain'd himself by letter or Memorial there was still the same Inconsistency.

One Morning when his Majesty was complaining how ill he had been used, he ask'd me the following Question. *What must be done if, after all this Delay, the Duke of Newcastle at last fail me?* I answer'd that notwithstanding his present Indecision I hoped that in the end, he would do what his Majesty required; but that at all Events, the Duke of Devonshire, tho somewhat uneasy in his present Employment,[262] might be persuaded to keep it some months longer, during which time, if the Duke of Newcastle should perceive that Business could be carried on without him, his

---

[258] *M* omits 'quite'.   [259] *M*: 'to be'.
[260] Probably on 4 March: Clark, *loc. cit.*, p. 336.
[261] *M* omits 'really'.   [262] First Lord of the Treasury.

Jealousy would get the better of his Fear; and tho the Duke of Devonshire might be very willing to resign the other would be still more eager to succeed him. His Majesty answer'd this will never do: the Duke of Devonshire, has acted by me in the handsomest Manner, and is in a very disagreeable Situation entirely on my Account. I have promised that he shall be at full Liberty, at the end of the Session, and I must keep my Word: He then added, if the Duke of Newcastle should disappoint me, I know but one Person whom I could[263] trust at the Head of the Treasury: can you guess whom I mean? Then after a short Pause, *Why it is Yourself.* Tho I had had long experience of his Majesty's Partiality towards me, I was under some Confusion at this very extraordinary[264] Instance of his Favor, and Confidence. But I soon got the better of my Surprise, and gave, as I thought, very Sufficient Reasons to prove my Unfitness for such an Employment: His Majesty immediately[265] changed the Discourse, and I went out of the Closet, imagining it to have been only[266] a Sudden Thought, which had occur'd whilst he was speaking, and that I should hear nothing farther on the Subject. However, this Alarm made me still more earnest to encourage the Duke of Newcastle, tho I had little Expectation of Success.

He frequently complain'd that I was continually pressing him to be Minister, offering, in the King's Name, almost his own Terms; when at the same time, his Majesty's Confidence in the Duke and Fox, became every day more apparent. I answer'd, that the Fact was true, and might very easily be accounted for; that necessity obliged the King to trust somebody, and that their Influence must[267] naturally increase or diminish, in Proportion, as his Grace shew'd more or less Inclination to give his assistance: and as to the other Part of his Accusation, tho I had encouraged his Return to his former Employment, and had press'd his Reconciliation with the Duke and Fox, I had never deceived him with false Professions of their personal Regard, and Friendship having Strictly confined myself to the Single Assertion that they would support him to their utmost in his Ministerial Capacity, because they had rather the King should be in his Hands, than in the Power of Pitt, Lord Bute, and of Leicester House.[268]

Affairs remain'd, several Weeks, in the same State of Uncertainty. At last, the King growing more impatient, Fox received his Commands[269] to form a new Plan of Administration, in Concert with the Duke: I was also to be consulted, and made acquainted with every Particular, that when the Scheme was fully prepared, and ready for his Majesty's Inspection, I might

---

[263] *M*: 'would'.   [264] *M*: 'particular'.   [265] *M* omits 'immediately'.
[266] *M* omits 'only'.   [267] *M*: 'the Influence of others would'.
[268] Clark, *Dynamics of Change*, p. 340.
[269] Probably on or about 18 March: *ibid.*, pp. 345–6.

lay it before him, and be able to clear up those Points, which required farther Explanation.

The Scheme was soon compleated,[270] the Substance of which was, that Lord Holdernesse should write letters to Pitt and Lord Temple to dismiss them from his Majesty's Service: that the Duke of Newcastle and Lord Hardwick should be immediately acquainted with this Dismission, and with the intended Arrangement: by which it would be evident that their Friends were all[271] to be employ'd, and that whenever they should be dispos'd to appear themselves upon the Stage, his Majesty would be ready to receive them. The Persons who were to have the Refusal of the principal Employments, were Lord Egmont, Lord George Sackville, Lord Hallifax, Charles Townshend, Lord Strange, and Dodington. Fox was to be Paymaster, and an Irish Reversion was to be granted to his Children, as a Compensation for giving up all Hopes of Preferment, in a future Reign.

When I shew'd the Plan to the King,[272] he made many Objections; saying, that it might possibly be a very[273] good Scheme for Fox, his Friends and Relations; but that for his own Part, it did not answer his Purposes.

To which I reply'd, that in Obedience to his Majesty's Commands, I had been informed of every Particular; but at the same time,[274] there had not been a single article of my framing; nor was I anywise prejudiced in its Favor. That Fox's Request in behalf of his Friends and Family might be unreasonable; But that I imagined, whoever were employ'd in forming a Plan of Administration, his Majesty would find none of them forgetful of their own Interest. That as to the Persons named for the principal Employments, most of them were good Speakers in Parliament, and that Oratory was now esteem'd the First Quality of a Minister.

That, indeed, some of these Gentlemen, might be already engaged on the side of the Opposition, and others might not be inclin'd to take any Part whatsoever, in the present State of Confusion. But that they might be talk'd to; and when his Majesty knew their Terms, and how far they were to be depended on,[275] he might then determine whether he would accept their Services; and as to Fox himself, I was persuaded he would be thoroughly satisfied with whatever Mark of Favor his Majesty should think he[276] deserved.

After some Consideration, the King told me that I might authorize Fox to treat with the Several Parties: whereupon the Negotiation was begun, and the Success was just as I had expected. Lord George Sackville tho he had been violent against Pitt at the beginning of the Session, was now

[270] Clark, *Dynamics of Change*, p. 347.   [271] *M* omits 'all'.
[272] On 19 March: Clark, *Dynamics of Change*, p. 348.
[273] *M* omits 'very'.   [274] *M* omits 'at the same time', inserts 'that'.
[275] *M* omits 'and . . . on'.
[276] *C* has 'he' inserted by Frederick Keppel.

connected with him, and had enter'd into engagements with Leicester House.

Lord Egmont's Object was a Peerage: he therefore pleaded bad Health, which could not bear the Fatigue of the House of Commons. Lord Hallifax would not undertake the Direction of the Admiralty unless the Duke of Newcastle would promise to support him, and his Grace did not chuse to give any Encouragement.[277] Charles Townshend[278] hated Pitt, and disliked his Employment which was merely[279] a Sinecure. Yet did not think it advisable to undertake the Defence of an Old King, or to be connected with unpopular Associates. Lord Strange being then in the Country was not apply'd to; so Dodington was the only person ready to engage, and he was to be Treasurer of the Navy his former Post[280] which had never been esteem'd a Ministerial Employment.[281]

These Transactions prove how necessary it is that Princes should on some[282] Occasions, do their own Business.

Instead of negotiating by Deputy, the King should have spoke separately to all the principal Persons, told them that tho he wanted their assistance, he had no service to require of them, which he had not[283] a Right to expect from honest Men and good Englishmen.

But that they must make their Option; for if they refused to engage as his Friends, he would risk even the Crown itself, rather than receive them hereafter, as the dependents and Followers of any insolent Minister. Such an Explanation would have had an immediate Effect, and their Pride as well as their Interest would have determined them to support their Sovereign, when they had found him resolute, and, in his turn, ready to protect them.

It was now the End of March; and it being resolv'd that a decisive Step should be taken before the Duke left England; an Offer was made to the Earl of Winchelsea,[284] of his being appointed first Commissioner of the Admiralty, which was accepted by him with most unfashionable Readiness;[285] and Lord Temple was acquainted that the King had no further occasion for his Lordship's Services.[286] This dismission did not cause the

[277] *M*: 'had not any Inclination to give the least Encouragement'.
[278] *M* has, deleted and erased: 'was not satisfied with Pitt's Behaviour, but did not think these present advantages a sufficient Inducement to give up all future Expectation'.
[279] *M*: 'almost'. [280] *M* omits 'his former post'.
[281] Clark, *Dynamics of Change*, pp. 348–51.
[282] *M*: 'many'. [283] *M*: 'except such as he had'.
[284] Daniel Finch, 8th Earl of Winchelsea (1689–1769), succ. 1730. MP 1710–30; Gentleman of the Bedchamber to the Prince of Wales 1714–16; a Lord of the Treasury 1715–16; Comptroller of the Household 1725–30; First Lord of the Admiralty March 1742-Dec 1744, and April-June 1757; Lord President of the Council July 1765-July 1766.
[285] Lord Winchelsea evidently accepted on 3 April.
[286] *M* deletes 'the King ... Services', inserts 'his Lordship's Services were no longer necessary'.

least Clamor or Uneasiness; for Winchelsea had held the same Office when Lord Granville was Minister, and the Conduct of our Naval Affairs had never given more general Satisfaction than when he directed them. Besides, he was known to be Steady and resolute; not one of those who can only act according to order, and are at all times ready to answer all Purposes.

It was imagined that on this occasion, Pitt would immediately have resign'd; but he did not chuse to save his Enemies any Trouble, and attended his Duty at Court with great[287] assiduity, till he was turn'd out, which happen'd about a week after Lord Temple's dismission.[288] This was follow'd by Legge's resigning the Chancellorship of the Exchequer, and some other Resignations.

I was now charged with a new Commission,[289] being order'd by the King to notify to Sir Thomas Robinson, and Lord Duplin[290] his Majesty's Intention of appointing the former Secretary of State, the other Chancellor of the Exchequer. I was to acquaint both that the King had made Choice of them as men in whom he had a[291] thorough Confidence, that he knew their Abilities, and expected their assistance. I added many[292] Reasons of my own to little Purpose: Lord Duplin excused himself as not being equal to so high an Employment even in times of the greatest Tranquility, more particularly at present, when our Affairs were in the utmost Confusion.[293]

Sir Thomas Robinson pleaded also his Incapacity, having already experienced that a Secretary of State was under the Constant Necessity of defending himself in the House of Commons: that he had never been an Orator, was too Old to learn, neither would his Health suffer him to undergo the fatigue of Business. Both express'd great Concern, hoped his Majesty would not be offended, but ended with an absolute Refusal.

At last[294] when every body had refused, the Enquiry being over, and his Royal Highness gone to Hanover, the Duke of Newcastle became more Couragious and seem'd willing to make a bold Effort, provided he might be at liberty to treat with proper Persons to which Proposal his Majesty consented without much[295] difficulty.

[287] *M*: 'unusual'.
[288] Lord Temple was dismissed on 5 April; Pitt attended at Court on 5th and 6th, and, evidently unwilling to resign, was dismissed on the evening of 6th. Legge resigned the same day. Clark, *Dynamics of Change*, p. 357.
[289] Clark, *Dynamics of Change*, p. 357.
[290] Thomas Hay (1710–87), Viscount Dupplin. Elder son of 8th Earl of Kinnoul. MP 1736, 1741–58. A Lord of Trade 1746–54; a Lord of the Treasury 1754–5; joint Paymaster General 1755–7; succeeded as 9th Earl 1758. A Pelhamite hack.
[291] *M* deletes 'as . . . a', inserts 'because they were Men in whom he could repose a'.
[292] *M*: 'other'.
[293] *M* omits 'more . . . Confusion'.
[294] For Newcastle's overtures on and after 3 May, see Clark, *Dynamics of Change*, pp. 384–6.
[295] *M*: 'the least'.

Memoirs of 1754–1757

To render this Negotiation more effectual, his Powers were greatly enlarged; there was a kind of tacite Permission to treat even with Pitt himself. But this Treaty was of short Duration, for Pitt, conscious of his own Strength would not allow the Duke of Newcastle any real Authority and his Grace could not yet submit to be only a nominal Minister.[296] In Consequence of this Disagreement, another Plan of Administration was immediately form'd,[297] whereby Pitt and his Adherents, were to be totally excluded: the Duke of Newcastle to resume his seat[298] at the head of the Treasury, Sir George Lee to be his Chancellor of the Exchequer.

His Grace was now to make his appearance at Court, that the affair might be finally settled. Accordingly he went to Kensington;[299] was graciously received; the King consented to whatever he propos'd; and all that remain'd was to carry the Scheme into immediate Execution. But the Duke of Newcastle beg'd a Delay of a few days,[300] that he might communicate the[301] Plan to his principal Friends, and make some necessary Preparations; which Request appear'd so very reasonable, that his Majesty could not object tho he was convinc'd that this Procrastination foreboded some Mischief.

Affairs of this Nature are seldom long a Secret; Leicester House was greatly alarm'd, for they never imagined that the Duke of Newcastle could have[302] Courage to be the only responsible Minister, in open Defiance of the Heir Apparent.

Even Pitt himself began to wish that his Demands had been less unreasonable. But there was no time for Deliberation, so Bute was dispatch'd[303] to the Earl of Chesterfield,[304] with a Proposal[305] to the Duke of Newcastle, that the Treaty might again be renew'd.

They certainly could not have chose a more prevailing Negotiator than the Earl of Chesterfield. For besides being a Man of Letters and a Wit, which carries great Weight and Authority amongst the dull and ignorant, he had distinguish'd himself as a Man of Business in many of the highest Offices; and, having given up all Ministerial Views of his own, might now be[306] esteem'd a Man totally [un]prejudiced and disinterested.

---

[296] Clark, *Dynamics of Change*, p. 391. [297] *Ibid.*, pp. 391–9.
[298] *M* omits 'resume his seat', inserts 'be'.
[299] On 27 May: Clark, *Dynamics of Change*, p. 400.
[300] Subsequently extended to 7 June: *ibid.*, p. 407.
[301] *M*: 'his'. [302] *M*: 'had'. [303] On 3 June: Clark, *Dynamics of Change*, p. 407.
[304] Philip Dormer Stanhope, 4th Earl of Chesterfield (1694–1773); succ. 1726. MP 1715–23; a Gentleman of the Bedchamber to the Prince of Wales 1715–27, a Lord of the Bedchamber to George II 1727–30; Ambassador to the Hague 1728–32; Lord Steward 1730–33; Lord Lieutenant of Ireland Jan. 1745-Oct. 1746. Secretary of State for the Northern Department Oct 1746-Feb 1748.
[305] *M* omits 'with a Proposal', inserts 'to engage him to propose'.
[306] *M*: 'very justly be'.

He wrote a very able Letter[307] to the Duke of Newcastle, the Purport of which was, that his Administration would never be Strong and permanent, till he was firmly united with Pitt and Leicester House; without whose assistance he could never be safe, nor would the King be ever at ease: he also mention'd his Conversation with Lord Bute, and seem'd convinc'd that the Princess and her Son were better disposed; and that Pitt would be found more reasonable,[308] than his Majesty expected.

The Duke of Newcastle shew'd me this Letter a few hours after he received it: I told his Grace that it contain'd a great deal of Truth, and a great deal of Wisdom, but I fear'd it would be somewhat difficult to persuade his Majesty to be of the same Mind. That tho I had never been one of Pitt's Admirers, nor had much Partiality for Leicester House, I had always press'd the King to be reconciled to both, even at the time when in Obedience to his Majesty's Commands, I was acting against them.[309] That I had often told his Majesty that Pitt was proud and resolute, but that good Usage would make him Tractable: That Leicester House was weak and obstinate; but by conniving at their Folly, indulging them in Triffles and making them know that he was resolved to be Master in Affairs of Consequence, he might bring them also under proper Subjection: But that all this Advice had been to little Purpose; and I was very apprehensive that Lord Chesterfield's Letter would have no better Effect.

However the Letter was shewn,[310] and his Majesty most unwillingly consented that Pitt and his Friends should once more be treated with: the Duke of Newcastle having first given his Word, that in case they still continued unreasonable, he would perform his Part, and carry the former Scheme into immediate Execution.

The Duke of Newcastle and Lord Hardwick had Several Conferences with Pitt and Lord Bute;[311] Articles of Peace and Amity were at last agreed upon; and a Plan of Administration was prepared, which was carried to Kensington[312] to receive the Royal Assent, without having given the least notice to Sir George Lee, or to any of those Gentlemen who, a few days before, had enter'd into Engagements with the Duke of Newcastle, and were waiting in their best Cloaths, in hourly Expectation of being sent for to Court to kiss his Majesty's Hand.

But when the King examined this new Agreement, he soon perceived that all his favorite Points were entirely given up: Winchelsea was to be displaced with a total Change of the Admiralty: Fox was not to be

---

[307] Chesterfield to Newcastle, 3 June 1757: Add MSS 32871 f. 199.
[308] *M* deletes 'more reasonable', inserts 'less unreasonable'.
[309] In *C*, Frederick Keppel deletes 'both', inserts 'them'.
[310] Newcastle forwarded Chesterfield's letter to the King on 4 June: Clark, *Dynamics of Change*, p. 408.
[311] *Ibid.*, pp. 409–12.   [312] On 7 June: *ibid.*, p. 412.

Paymaster: and Lord Temple to whom he had given a Negative was to have a Cabinet Council Employment.

His Majesty cut the Affair short, and at once rejected their Proposals; whilst on the other hand the Duke of Newcastle, notwithstanding his most solemn Promises, refused to execute the former Plan, or to take Part in any Administration, unless he had the Assistance of Pitt, and his Associates.

The Death of the Duke of Grafton,[313] which happen'd during these Transactions, was very prejudicial to his Majesty's Affairs. He was a few Days older than the King, had been Lord Chamberlain during the whole Reign, and had a particular Manner of talking to his Master upon all Subjects, and of touching upon the most tender Points, which no other Person ever ventured to imitate.

He usually turn'd Politics into Ridicule, had never apply'd himself to Business, and as to Books was totally illiterate; Yet from long Observation and great natural Sagacity, he became the ablest Courtier of his time: had the most perfect knowledge both of King, and Ministers; and had more opportunities than any Man of doing good or bad Offices.

He was a great Teaser; had an establish'd right of saying whatever he pleas'd; was thoroughly acquainted[314] with all the Duke of Newcastle's Evasions; and had obtain'd such an Ascendant over him, and kept him in such perfect awe,[315] that, had he negotiated in my Stead, he probably would have succeeded where I fail'd.

It was to the best of my Memory, on Tuesday ye 7th of June that the Duke of Newcastle made his final Declaration. The morning following I went to Kensington knowing his Majesty must be under great Difficulties, and thinking it right to shew myself, in case it should be his Pleasure to charge me with any new Commission.[316]

After the Levee, the Duke of Devonshire, the Duke of Bedford, and Lord Granville went seperately into the Closet. When they came out, they all talked to me of the King's very disagreeable situation, that this was no time for consulting our own Ease, and that it was our Duty to assist him to the utmost of our Strength and Abilities.

During this Conversation his Majesty sent for me, and began by accusing the Duke of Newcastle, saying that he had now proved himself what he had long thought him equally false and ungrateful. That he believed few Princes had ever been expos'd to such scandalous Treatment; But that it was in my Power to disengage him from all his Difficulties, by

---

[313] Charles Fitzroy, 2nd Duke of Grafton (1683–1757), succ. 1690. A Lord of the Bedchamber 1714–17; Lord Lieutenant of Ireland 1720–4; a Lord Justice during the monarch's absence in Hanover, 1720, 1723, 1725, 1727, 1740, 1743, 1745, 1748, 1750, 1752, 1755. Lord Chamberlain to George I and George II 1724–57. Died 6 May 1757.
[314] *M*: 'by a most intimate Acquaintance'. [315] *M* omits 'and . . . awe'.
[316] Clark, *Dynamics of Change*, p. 414.

accepting the Place of first Lord of the Treasury. That he would hear no Excuses of my want of Experience, or want of Abilities for that he had not trusted to his own Judgement, but had taken the best Advice; and that all who he had consulted were unanimous in this Particular, that in his present Circumstances, he could not make Choice of a more proper Person.

I answer'd, that in return for so much Favor and Goodness, I would lay myself open without the least Reserve; disguising neither my own Strength nor my own Weakness. That as an independent Man who was known to be honor'd with his Majesty's Confidence, I might be useful on many Occasions; and having no private Views, neither the Jealousy of his Ministers, nor the anger of his Successor would in the least intimidate me; but, on the contrary, would raise my Spirits, and make me still more active in his Majesty's service.

On the other hand, whenever I acted on my own Account, my Insufficiency would immediately appear: all my Weight, and Influence would vanish in an Instant.

That I did not mean to magnify the Dangers or Difficulties of a Ministerial Employment; nor did I think there was any mistery in Government[317] which might not be attain'd by proper Application and a tolerable Capacity: But that Prudence and Diligence in the Business of Office were only to be rated amongst the inferior Qualities of a first Lord of the Treasury; that nothing could be done for the publick Service, without a Steady Majority in both Houses of Parliament; and that a Minister must expect few Followers, who had never cultivated political Friendships, and had always abhorr'd Party Violence.

These and many other Reasons had not the least effect, the King continuing to press me in the Strongest and most affecting Terms.

At last, partly moved by his Distress, partly yielding to his Persuasion, or perhaps fired by some latent Spark of Pride or Ambition, I told his Majesty that if he really was convinc'd it was in my Power to serve him, I would no longer be guided by my own Judgement, and whatever might be the Consequence, I was ready to obey his Commands.

I had scarce utter'd my Consent, when his Majesty took me by the hand, saying with great Eagerness, I heartily thank you; you have now given your Word, and cannot go back.

Our Conversation being ended, the King sent for the Duke of Devonshire, told him what had pass'd and order'd him and Fox to talk with me that Evening, that a new Scheme might be form'd, with all possible Expedition.

I went from Kensington to the House of Lords to acquaint the Duke of

---

[317] *M* deletes 'any mistery in Government', inserts 'anything mysterious in the Art of Politics'.

Newcastle with my very unexpected Promotion. His Grace seem'd much embarrass'd, lamented that the King's Affairs were going into great Confusion, said that he had done every thing to assist his Majesty, as far as it was practicable, tho he had been suspected very unjustly, and had been treated very unkindly. That he was under great Concern on my Account; that I might depend on his personal Regard and Friendship, but hoped I did not expect that he should make any farther Promises. I answer'd, that I was much obliged to him for his Professions of personal Friendship, and expected nothing more, for as to his political Assistance, if he did not owe it to the King, I had not the least Reason to hope for it. That I had accepted an Employment, not from Choice, but because I thought it a Duty to obey my Sovereign's lawful commands: that I was sensible I must be exposed to many Difficulties, perhaps to some Danger; but should make myself easy as to that particular, being determined to do nothing which I should be either afraid, or ashamed to answer for.

In the evening,[318] I went with the Duke of Devonshire to meet Fox at Holland House, and was surprised to find him much changed since the Morning, more apprehensive of Danger, more doubtful of Success. He had been talking with some Gentlemen whose assistance in the House of Commons he had much depended on; and had not found them so ready to engage as he might reasonably have expected. He had also been discouraged by the King's Conversation in the Morning, who had received him with Coolness, and seem'd to mistrust him, even whilst he was requiring his Services.

Indeed it was very apparent that his Majesty had neither forgot the Circumstances of his being made Secretary of State, nor the Consequences of his late Resignation; and that he made use of him, on the present Occasion, not from Choice, but because he was the only Man of Abilities who had Spirit to answer Pitt in his own Language.

After various Discourse on the several Topicks of foreign and domestic Politics, we proceeded to our Plan of Administration which was somewhat confused and imperfect, for we were obliged to take many things for granted, which at best were doubtful; and to rely on many Persons who had not yet enter'd into any Engagements.

The principal Points were, indeed, settled, Winchelsea had already form'd his Admiralty, I was to be first Commissioner of the Treasury, Fox Chancellor of the Exchequer, and the Earl of Egremont Secretary of State.

As to the Inferior Places, there were Numbers ready to take them, tho not exactly the Men we would have chose; as to other particulars, we were to wait for Events, and avail ourselves of such future Advantages as Fortune should please to bestow on us.

[318] Of 8 June: Clark, *Dynamics of Change*, pp. 414–5.

The Earl of Holdernesse[319] surprised every body, the next morning, by resigning his Employment, without having given the least previous notice. He had been made Secretary of State merely because he was the King's Favorite,[320] and had been ready on all occasions to act according to Direction. His Majesty not only rais'd him, but had always strongly supported him; particularly in the last Change of Administration, when there was a violent Run against him. I remember his Majesty telling me at that time, how happy he was, that he had just been able to save poor Holdernesse.

The King behaved on this occasion, with great Temper, and proper Dignity. He did not condescend to expostulate, or to take Notice of his Ingratitude; but stopt him short with these words, *You come here to resign, I have no Curiosity to know your Reasons.* When I went into the Closet,[321] soon after,[322] he told me with great Coolness, *Holdernesse has resign'd; you may think I was surprised, but the Loss is not Considerable.*

I then gave him an account of what had pass'd the preceding Evening; and he order'd us, to meet again, that night, with the Addition of Lord Granville and Lord Winchelsea.

We met at the appointed time, Fox still seem'd anxious, and doubtful, having received no new Encouragement since the last Meeting. However he was[323] somewhat animated by Lord Granville, who assur'd us in his lively Manner, that we could not fail of Success. That the whole Force of Government was now firmly united, Army, Navy, Treasury, Church, with all their subordinate Branches. That tho Volunteers did not come in so fast as had been expected, we had the whole summer before us to raise Recruits; and tho of late years, Ministers did not think themselves safe without a Majority in the House of Commons of 150 or 200, he remember'd the time when 20 or 30 were thought more than sufficient.

Winchelsea also seem'd quite easy and determined; and we parted in tolerable good Spirits. The next morning I received a letter from the Duke of Newcastle, desiring I would call on him before I went to Court.[324] I waited on him immediately, and he began by expressing great uneasiness least the King should suspect him of having been the Cause of Holder-

---

[319] Robert Darcy, 4th Earl of Holdernesse (1718–78), succ. 1722, ed. Westminster and Trinity College, Cambridge. A Lord of the Bedchamber 1741–51; with George II at Dettingen, 1743; Ambassador to Venice 1744–6; Minister at the Hague 1749–51; Secretary of State: for the Southern Department 1751–54, and for the Northern 1754–March 1761. A Lord Justice 1752, 1755. Lord Warden of the Cinque Ports 1765–78; Governor to the Prince of Wales 1771–76.

[320] *M*: 'one of the King's Favorites'.

[321] On the morning of 9 June: Clark, *Dynamics of Change*, p. 416.

[322] *M* omits 'soon after'.   [323] *M*: 'we were'.

[324] For Waldegrave's interview with Newcastle on 10 June, see Clark, *Dynamics of Change*, pp. 416–8.

nesse's Resignation; call'd God to witness that so far from having given any sort of Encouragement, it was quite unknown to him, till he received a Letter from Lord Holdernesse, acquainting him with his Resolution, a very few hours before it was executed. He then shew'd me the Letter, and beg'd I would state the case fairly to [his] Majesty that he might know the whole Truth.

We then talk'd on other Subjects: he told me that the King did him great Injustice, thinking him capable of every thing that was bad; and that whoever resign'd, or whoever refused to engage, was supposed to act under his Direction.

I answer'd, it was very certain the King did suspect him, as to some particulars, and I would give one Instance. The Earl of Hallifax having been offer'd a very considerable Employment, had declared to several Persons, that he should have accepted with the greatest Readiness, had he been at Liberty to follow his own Inclination; But was under a necessity of refusing, because he thought himself bound in Honor not to take any Part without the Duke of Newcastle's Consent. I then mention'd other similar cases, and appeal'd to himself whether there might not be some Foundation for his Majesty's Suspicions.

His Grace did not chuse to make any answer to the particular Fact,[325] but said in general, that it was hard he should be condemned because some gentlemen endeavour'd to clear themselves, by loading him: that it was not his Fault if many Persons did apply to him, and that he wish'd with all his Heart, they would judge for themselves. That he had given me Notice, some days ago of a Man near the King's Person, a Favorite, one in whom his Majesty had the greatest Confidence, who would soon resign his Employment: that I might easily guess he meant Holdernesse, tho he had not named him; and that with a single Word, he could cause so many Resignations, as would give the Court a very empty appearance.

I did not think it necessary to add to his Confusion, by comparing his last words with the Solemn Declaration, which I was to make in his Grace's Name, concerning Holdernesse's Resignation: but contented myself with telling him, that if it was in his Power to deprive the King of his Servants, and if he really intended it, the sooner it was done the better, that his Majesty might know with Certainty, what he had to expect, and who he had to depend on. As there had been some Acidity, in the latter Part of our Discourse, we endeavour'd to correct it, by exchanging a few compliments, which, being ended, I took my leave, and went to Kensington.

I found the King much dispirited; complaining that Fox did not succeed in his Negotiations; that there would be many[326] more Resignations; and

---

[325] *M*: 'think it necessary to make Answer to particular Facts'.
[326] *C* has 'many' added by Frederick Keppel.

that almost every body abandon'd him. He assured me that he should always remember how I had Stood by him to the last; but being now in the hands of his Enemies, he would not expose those whom he esteem'd, and who had served him faithfully, to any further Danger: that we were to have another Meeting in the Evening, but was very sensible it would be to no Purpose.

I answer'd, that tho I had never been very Sanguine in my Expectations, I did not think our Case quite Desperate: for, tho we might not have sufficient Strength to form an Administration, we were certainly[327] strong enough to give our Opponents some Uneasiness; and by a firm and steady Behavior, might oblige them to accept reasonable Terms. That it would be bad Policy, first[328] to lay down our arms, and then Negotiate; for that in political, as well as military, Warfare, it was most safe, as well as honorable, to capitulate Sword in Hand. His Majesty was[329] somewhat animated by this Conversation, which gave him momentary Relief; but his Doubts and Apprehensions return'd, after a short Interval, and I was sorry to find so much Despondency, where, I lately wish'd there had been less Confidence.

Our Meeting in the Evening consisted of the Duke of Devonshire, the Duke of Bedford, Lord Granville, Lord Winchelsea, Lord Gower, Fox, and Myself.[330]

If Winchelsea and Granville continued stout and resolute, the Duke of Bedford was still greatly beyond them: he insisted that our Administration would be infinitely the strongest that had ever been known in this Country; and was almost in a Passion with[331] Fox for having started some difficulties, and for seeming even[332] to doubt our Success.

That as to replacing Holdernesse, Lord Gower, at present Lord Privy Seal, and fond of Ease and Pleasure as much as any Man, was ready to change for a more laborious Employment, and would be Secretary of State, in case we thought it necessary; and as to other Resigners, he wish'd their Numbers were more considerable, for that every Vacancy would either serve an old Friend, or gain a new one.

Lord Gower Confirm'd what the Duke of Bedford had said,[333] spoke with great Modesty, but declared he would take the Employment without the least Hesitation, if we thought him capable, and could not find a more proper Person.

As to Myself, I plainly perceiv'd by the King's discourse in the Morning, and by some private Conversation with Fox and the Duke of Devonshire,

---

[327] *M* omits 'certainly'.   [328] *M* omits 'first'.   [329] *M*: 'seem'd'.
[330] For this meeting on 10 June, see Clark, *Dynamics of Change*, pp. 421–2.
[331] *M*: 'against'.   [332] *M* omits 'even'.
[333] *M* deletes 'said', inserts 'promised for him'.

that our Plan would never[334] be carried into Execution, and might possibly be given up, the day following. However it seem'd mean and pitiful to yield tamely, and[335] leave the King in a worse Situation than that in which we had found him. I therefore took the spirited side of the Question and told them that tho I had never been ambitious of being a Minister, and tho our affairs did not appear to me in the most favorable Light, the King having thought proper to require my Assistance, I had consider'd the Consequences, had given my Word, and was ready to perform my Part whenever I was call'd upon.

The Duke of Bedford was pleased with this Declaration; but whisper'd me at parting, that it would be to no Purpose to give ourselves any further Trouble; for we could not possibly go on without a principal Actor in the House of Commons, and that Fox had not Spirit to undertake it.

In spite of all our Difficulties, it was still the Opinion without Doors, that we were too desperate to desist, and that our Plan of Administration would be immediately executed.

Lord Chief Justice Mansfield was order'd to be at Kensington the next Morning;[336] the Reason assign'd was that he should deliver back the Exchequer Seals, which had been in his Possession from the time of Legge's Resignation; but the real Business was of a very[337] different Nature.

The King discoursed him, a considerable time, in the most confidential Manner, enter'd into a particular Detail of all his Grievances; and as bold, and vigorous Measures were no longer necessary, he certainly could not have advised with a more prudent, or more able Counsellor.

The Conversation ended by giving Lord Mansfield full Power to negotiate with Pitt and the Duke of Newcastle, his Majesty only insisting that Lord Temple should have no Employment which required frequent attendance in the Closet, and that Fox should be appointed Paymaster, which last demand did not proceed from any present Partiality, but was the fulfilling of a former Engagement.

Before the final Resolution was taken, his Majesty thought proper to ask my Advice,[338] and encouraged me to speak my Mind with a Freedom which I should have thought indecent, if I had not been commanded to conceal nothing from him.

I told him, I was clear in my Opinion that our Administration would be routed at the opening of the next Session of Parliament; for that the Duke of Newcastle had a considerable Majority in the House of Commons, whilst the popular Cry without doors was violent in Favor of Mr Pitt: and tho the Duke of Newcastle hated Pitt, as much as Pitt despised the Duke of

---

[334] *M*: 'not'.   [335] *M* omits 'yield tamely, and'.
[336] On 11 June: Clark, *Dynamics of Change*, pp. 422–4.
[337] *M* omits 'very'.   [338] At an audience the same day, 11 June.

Newcastle, they were united in one Particular, that nothing should be done for the public Service, till they were Ministers.

That the whole Weight of Opposition rested on a single Point, his Majesty's supposed Partiality to his Electoral subjects, which would at any time set the Nation in a Flame; and that being thought an Enemy to Hanover, was the solid Foundation of Pitt's Popularity.

That as to Jacobitism, it was indeed at a low Ebb; but there was a mutinous Spirit, in the lower Class of People, which might in a Moment, break out in Acts of the greatest Violence; whilst others were sullen and discontented, ignorant of the Blessings they enjoy'd, sensible only that they paid heavy Taxes, and quite indifferent who were their Governors.

That in times of Peace, we might have had Opportunities of undeceiving the People, of restoring them to their Sober Senses; or, if our Administration had been overturn'd, his Ministers would have been the only Sufferers. But in our present State of Confusion, delay was absolute Ruin; for that doing Nothing, was worse than doing wrong.

It was therefore my very humble Advice that his Majesty should give way to the necessity of the times; and if he would graciously overlook some past Offences, and would gratify Pitt's Vanity, tho it were only[339] with a moderate share of that affability and Courteousness, which he so liberally bestow'd on so many of his Servants, I was convinced he would find him no intractable Minister.

That I was not ignorant that Pitt could be guilty of the worst of actions whenever his ambition, his Pride, or his Resentment were to be gratified; but that he could also be sensible of good Treatment; was bold and resolute; above doing things by halves; and, if he once engaged, would go farther than any Man in this Country. Nor would his former Violence against Hanover be any kind of Obstacle, as he had given frequent Proofs that he could change Sides whenever he found it necessary, and could deny his own words with an unembarrass'd Countenance. That as to the Duke of Newcastle, who lately fancied himself independent, and had given so much uneasiness, he would find himself entirely[340] in his Majesty's Power, the Moment he enter'd into Employment: for, as all the Offices of Business would be under the Direction of his new Allies, he could only be considerable by his Interest in the Closet; and that his Fear and Jealousy of Pitt would be better security for his good Behaviour, than a thousand Promises.

His Majesty heard every thing I said with great Patience, and answer'd with some Chearfulness, that according to my Description, his Situation was not much to be envied; but he could assure me it was infinitely more Disagreeable than I represented it. That he believed few Princes had ever

---

[339] *M* omits 'tho it were only'.   [340] *M* omits 'entirely'.

met with worse Treatment: that we were angry because he was partial to his Electorate, tho he desired nothing more to be done for Hanover, than what we were bound in honor and Justice, to do for any Country whatsoever, when it was exposed to Danger entirely on our Account. That we were indeed a very extraordinary People, continually talking of our Constitution, our Laws, and our Liberties. That as to our Constitution, he allow'd it to be a good one, and defied any Man to produce a single Instance wherein he had exceeded his proper Limits: that he never would attempt[341] to screen or protect any Servant who had done amiss, but still he had a right to chuse those who were to serve him; tho at present, so far from having an Option, he was not even allow'd a Negative. That as to our Laws we pass'd near a hundred ev'ry Session, which seem'd made for no other Purpose, but to afford us the Pleasure of breaking them: and as to our Zeal for Liberty, it was in itself highly commendable; but that our Notions must be somewhat singular, when the chief of the Nobility chose rather to be Dependents and Followers of a Duke of Newcastle, than to be the Friends and Councellors of their Sovereign.

The Negotiation with Pitt and the Duke of Newcastle did not remain long in Lord Mansfield's Hands, some thinking him too able, others that he was not enough their Friend.

The Duke of Newcastle, after what had pass'd, was ashamed and afraid to appear in the King's Presence; so the Treaty was undertaken and concluded by the Earl of Hardwicke, a proper Person to negotiate, having great Influence over the Duke of Newcastle, as well as some credit with Pitt, without being disagreeable to the King himself.

For tho his Majesty had not been quite satisfied[342] with his late Behaviour, he could not accuse him either of Breach of Word, or of having given any personal Offence.

The whole Business between the King, and the different Factions, might have been settled in a few Hours; but when they found that his Majesty comply'd with all their Demands, and would not give them even[343] a Pretence to be Dissatisfied, they quarrel'd amongst themselves, and it was at least a Fortnight, before they could be brought to a perfect[344] Agreement.[345] At last the Treaty was concluded, the Substance of which was, that the Duke of Newcastle should be first Commissioner of the Treasury, without one Man at the Board, who really belong'd to him; and Legge was to be once more his Chancellor of the Exchequer.

Pitt was to be again Secretary of State; Lord Temple to be Privy Seal, in

[341] *M*: 'that he never meant'.
[342] *M* erases 'not been quite', inserts 'been somewhat dissatisfied'.
[343] *M* omits 'even'.   [344] *M* deletes 'perfect', inserts 'tolerable'.
[345] For the final negotiations, see Clark, *Dynamics of Change*, pp. 425–41. The ministry kissed hands on 29 June.

the room of Lord Gower, who was to be Master of the Horse, in the room of the Duke of Dorset, who was to have a large Pension, under the name of additional Salary annex'd to his Place of Warden of the Cinque Ports.

Pratt was to be made Attorney General in the room of Sir Robert Henley, who was made Lord Keeper, with a Pension, and a good Reversion for his Son. Fox was to be Paymaster; and Potter who formerly held half that office, was to be made one of the Vice Treasurers of Ireland, in the room of the Earl of Cholmondeley, who was also to have a very considerable Pension on ye Irish Establishment.

But the most surprising Phenomenon was Lord Anson, returning to his old Employment, in spite of his Unpopularity, and of all the Abuse which had been raised against him by the very Men who were now to be his Associates either at the Cabinet Council, or at the Board of Admiralty.

During these Negotiations I received a Letter from the Duke of Devonshire, acquainting me that his Majesty intended to give me the vacant Garter, and that a Chapter was to be held for that Purpose, as soon as possible: Such a Mark of Distinction would at all times have been highly honorable, but was doubly acceptable in my present Situation: it was also the first Instance in his Majesty's Reign, of a Garter being given when there was only one Vacancy: and, as it was very apparent that the King had not consulted his new Ministers on the present Occasion, it shew'd the World, that he had not entirely devested himself of all his Authority.[346]

When I went to return Thanks, he was pleased to express some Concern that I could not still be one of his Ministers; to which I answer'd that my Hopes and Fears being entirely at an end, I might speak of past Transactions, as of things quite indifferent.

That, tho I had obey'd his Majesty's Commands, without any shew of Uneasiness, I had no Conception how a reasonable Man, who was not necessitous, could have any Inducement to undergo the Fatigue, and anxiety of a Ministerial Employment, unless he was animated with a probable Expectation, of rendering his King and Country some important Services, and of being afterwards rewarded with that general Approbation, which such Services merited.

But that knowing the first to be impracticable, and the latter unattainable; being quite easy in my Circumstances; having obtain'd the highest Honors; and being admitted to the nearest approach of his Majesty's Person, which I esteem'd the only[347] valuable Part of a Ministerial

---

[346] In December 1768, George III appointed his brother the Duke of Cumberland to the single vacancy in the Order: 'an evidence of his dislike of the Bedfords, the more marked, as I do not remember an instance of a single Garter given but to Lord Waldegrave': Walpole, *George III*, vol. 3, p. 99.

[347] *M* deletes 'only', inserts 'most'.

Employment; I consider'd the Place of Minister, in every other respect, as the greatest Misfortune, which could hereafter befall me.

At the same time, I was not totally disengaged from Politics, and should always be in readiness to oppose either his Ministers, or his Heir Apparent, if they presumed to act in an improper Manner: but if they behaved well, which did not seem quite impossible, I should think I could do no better service, than to remain quiet, avoiding to give any kind of Offence, or even the slightest Cause of Jealousy.

I had still a more cogent Reason to wish for a private Station, which I had formerly hinted to his Majesty, but had never fully explain'd.

I must irretrievably have lost both his Favor and Confidence the Moment I became an acting Minister. For I had the Misfortune to differ from my Master, in the most tender Point, in relation to German Politicks; and tho I might perhaps[348] have done more for the support of Hanover, than was consistent with the true[349] Interest of my Country: it would have been far short of his Majesty's Expectations: short even of that which has lately[350] been comply'd with, by our Patriot Minister.

On the Day they were all to kiss Hands, I went to Kensington, to entertain myself with the innocent, or perhaps ill natured amusement of examining the different Countenances.

The Behavior of Pitt, and his Party was decent and sensible, they had neither the Insolence of Men who had gain'd a Victory, nor were they awkward and disconcerted, like those who come to a Place where they know they are not welcome.

But as to the Duke of Newcastle and his Friends, the Resigners, there was a Mixture of Fear, and of Shame in their Countenances; they were real Objects of Compassion.

The Man who made infinitely the most respectable appearance was old Winchelsea: As soon as[351] the King had determined to dismiss Lord Temple, he came to his Majesty's Assistance the Moment he was call'd upon, without making any difficulties;[352] tho he knew that the Place had been offer'd to the Earl of Hallifax, who had refused it. Whilst he continued in the Employment, he not only shew'd himself greatly superior to his Predecessor, which indeed did not require any very extraordinary Talents, but his whole Conduct was so unexceptionable, that even Faction itself was obliged to be silent.

On the present occasion, the King was willing to support him, and would have insisted, as far as he was able, that he should either have continued where he was, or that he should have changed for some Cabinet

---

[348] *M* omits 'perhaps'.   [349] *M* omits 'true'.
[350] *C* has 'lately' inserted by Frederick Keppel.
[351] *M* erases 'As soon as', inserts 'when'.   [352] *M* deletes 'without . . . difficulties'.

Council Employment; But he very handsomely declined both; saying, that his Majesty should be under no difficulties, on his Account. That as to being at the Head of the Admiralty, the new Ministers would never suffer it; nor would he[353] act with Men, to whom he had declar'd himself an Enemy: and as to having one of the great Offices, it might answer his Purpose, if he wanted a large Pension or Salary;[354] but could not possibly do the King any sort of Service.

Having frequently mention'd the Duke of Devonshire, I shall add some Particulars concerning him, which might have interrupted my narrative, had they been related in their proper Place.[355]

He had been appointed Lord Lieutenant of Ireland in the Year 1755, whilst his Father was still alive: and had been sent to his Government before the Declaration of War, partly to inspect the military Affairs of that Country; but more particularly to compose their civil Dissensions which had raged with uncommon Violence during the latter period of the Duke of Dorset's Administration.[356]

His Return to England had been subsequent to the Loss of Minorca, consequently he was clear of that Obloquy and Reproach, to which every other Minister was so deservedly exposed.

When the Administration was changed, he seem'd the most proper Person to succeed the Duke of Newcastle, on account of the King's Favor,[357] and the Number of his Friends.

Pitt, and Leicester House, for a time, paid great Court to him:[358] But when they perceived that he had a Will of his own, in some material articles, that he would neither totally abandon his old Master, nor renounce his former Friends:[359] all Cordiality and Confidence was immediately at an End. Mr Pitt's Dismission from his Majesty's Service, his Reconciliation with the Duke of Newcastle, and his Return to his former Employment, have been already related.

As to the Duke of Devonshire, the King appointed him Lord Chamberlain several weeks before he quitted the Treasury; and tho he had been disgusted by Faction and perplex'd with Difficulties, he lost no Reputation; for great things had never been expected from him as a Minister; and in the

---

[353] *M*: 'nor did he desire to'.   [354] *M*: 'if he wanted an Honourable Pension'.
[355] The 5 paragraphs from 'Having frequently . . . ' to 'Want of Capacity' occur in *M* only.
[356] See J.C.D. Clark, 'Whig Tactics and Parliamentary Precedent: The English Management of Irish Politics, 1754–1756', *HJ* 21 (1978), 275–301.
[357] *M* has, deleted, 'Honest Reputation'.
[358] *M* has, deleted: 'whilst in Return on his Part, he took every opportunity of assisting them in the Closet, and of [breaks off] endeavor'd to doing all good Offices, endeavouring to reconcile them to the king, and to assisting them, with, Zeal and Capacity in whatever related to the Public'.
[359] *M* deletes 'betray his Master, nor sacrifice'.

ordinary Business of his Office he had shown great Punctuality and Diligence, and no Want of Capacity.[360]

I have now finish'd my Narrative of all the Material Transactions wherein I was immediately Concern'd; and tho I can never forget my Obligations to the kindest of Masters, I have been too long behind the Scenes, I have had too near a View of the Machinery of a Court, to envy any[361] Man either the Power of a Minister, or the Favor of Princes.

The constant anxiety, and frequent Mortifications which accompany Ministerial Employments, are, indeed, tolerably well understood; but the World is totally unacquainted with the situation of those whom Fortune has selected to be the constant[362] Attendants, and Companions of Royalty; who partake of its Domestic Amusements and Social Happiness.

But I must not lift up the Veil, and shall only add, that no Man can have a Clear Conception how great Personages pass their Liesure Hours, who has not been a Prince's Governor, or King's Favorite.

---

[360] *M* has, deleted, possibly relating to Devonshire: 'yet had preserved the good Opinion of his Country. His Behaviour to his Colleagues had at first been friendly; at the last, was honourable; and he had conducted the Affairs of his own Department with Diligence, Judgement and Integrity'.

[361] *C* has 'any' inserted by Frederick Keppel.

[362] *C* has 'constant' inserted by Frederick Keppel.

3

MEMOIRS OF THE SEVEN YEARS' WAR

This section is present in the Chewton manuscript only, pp. 173–4, and is in Maria Waldegrave's hand. Presumably the 2nd Earl's exclusion from the inner circles of politics after the summer of 1757 deprived him of the information which alone would make political memoirs worthwhile.

Some particular Friends[1] to whom I communicated the foregoing Narrative, have advised me to continue my Observations to the end of the War. I shall give an Account of the most remarkable Occurrences, but not having at all times the most certain Information, I shall relate rather what I have heard than what I have seen, therefore must not decide with my former Confidence.

Tho the King was most passively Obedient to his New Ministers, he wanted sufficient Dissimulation to submit with a good Grace. He behaved to Pitt, as to a Prince who had conquer'd him, and to the Duke of Newcastle, as to a faithless Servant who had deliver'd him into the hand of an Enemy.

The Administration being settled, his Majesty prorogued the Parliament on Monday ye 4th of July 1757. I shall leave the Detail of the Military Operations in Germany to those who can relate them with greater Accuracy. Yet without taking some Notice of the most decisive Battles, as well as of other continental Transactions, it might be difficult to form a true Judgement of our Situation at Home.

On the 6th of May the King of Prussia with an inferior Force had gain'd a compleat Victory over the Austrians, commanded by Prince Charles of Lorraine and Marshal Brown. The routed Army retreated to Prague which was immediately blockaded by the Prussians.

[1] We may guess that Horace Walpole was among these friends.

4

MEMOIRS OF THE ACCESSION OF GEORGE III

This section is present in the Chewton manuscript only, pp. 176–89, in Maria Waldegrave's hand. It follows immediately after the foregoing: no space was left for a continuation of the *Memoirs* from mid–1757, which suggests that the project was soon abandoned.[1]

Anecdotes

The King died suddenly on Saturday the 25th of October 1760 at Seven in the Morning. His Majesty had been out of Bed almost an hour, had drank his Chocolate with a good Appetite, and was preparing to walk in the Garden, passing thro a little Anti-chamber joining to the Back Stairs he fell on the Floor.[2] One of the Pages heard the Fall, ran into the Room and found him at the last Gasp. The King was carried to his Bed, a Surgeon who happen'd to be in the Palace, open'd a Vein, but no Blood follow'd, nor was there the least Sign of Life. His Death was occasioned by the bursting of one of the Ventricles of the Heart, an accident which could neither have been foreseen nor prevented.

He seems to have been particularly fortunate both in the time and Manner of his Death. He was older by some years than the oldest of our Kings since the Conquest had few bodily Infirmities died without Sickness or Pain, and Maintain'd the Quickness as well as the Solidity of his Judgement to the last Hour of his Life. The Success of his Arms had exceeded even the most Sanguine Expectations particularly in those great

---

[1] Waldegrave's account may be compared with Henry Fox's memoir of the events of 1760–3, printed in the Countess of Ilchester and Lord Stavordale (eds.), *The Life and Letters of Lady Sarah Lennox 1745–1826* (2 vols., London, 1901), vol. 1, pp. 3–79. The close similarity between Waldegrave's account and Walpole's (*George II*, vol. 3, p. 118) suggests that Walpole had access to Waldegrave's manuscript after the Earl's death. The section of Walpole's *Memoirs* for 1760 is dated, in the rough draft, 29 October 1763.
[2] Waldegrave tactfully disguises the place of his sovereign's death: the privy.

Objects of the War, the destruction of the French Marine, and the Conquest of Canada.

Having heard the News of his Majesty's death, between nine and ten o'clock, I immediately went to Kensington; where I found some Lords and Grooms of the Bedchamber, with other Attendants of his Majesty's Person, all looking decently grave, tho I did not observe one sorrowful Countenance.

I also observed many Inhabitants of the Palace of Inferior Rank, earnestly soliciting Admittance into the Bedchamber, that they might gratify their Curiosity with the Sight of a Dead King.

I went from Kensington to Saville House, where the Privy Council was order'd to attend. The Duke of Cumberland arrived from Windsor at twelve o'Clock, his Behavior was steady and composed, he spoke of his Father's Death with decent Concern, yet as of an Event which might naturally be expected, tho not so suddenly.

After having waited almost an Hour, he desired me to ask for a private Room, where he remain'd till near four o'Clock, when he received a Message from the King to attend him at Carlton House.

The two Secretaries of State were sent for at the same time, soon after there came a Second Message for the other Privy Counsellors.

The first Act of the Privy Council was to notify to the young King the Death of his Grandfather, which being perform'd with proper Gravity by the Arch Bishop of Canterbury, we return'd to the Council Chamber, to sign the Orders for the King's Proclamation. After which his Majesty came into Council and read his Declaration. We then proceeded to those Matters of Form which are necessary on the like Occasions, but being quite unprepared for such Business, our Proceedings were somewhat irregular. Particularly, tho we were summon'd by Virtue of an Act of Parliament, as the Council of the late King, and were entitled to act in that Capacity, we were immediately sworn Privy Counsellors to King George the third, an Honor which unless by Mistake some of us perhaps might never have obtained.

His Majesty appear'd grave and thoughtful, tho it might be perceived by his Countenance that he was not sorry to be a King.

He spoke little, except to the Duke of Cumberland, but his Looks and Manner were gracious to every one. The Duke of Cumberland, the Duke of Newcastle and Mr Pitt had had private Audiences, but his Majesty had not consulted them concerning his Declaration.

It was immediately known that this Declaration had been prepared by the Earl of Bute, whether the Production was really his, or whether it was his by Adoption only, was somewhat doubtful.

Be that as it will, when the Council was over Mr Pitt expostulated very warmly with the Earl of Bute and insisted that the Declaration should not be made public till the King had consented to two very material Alterations. Mr Pitt's first Objection, was to an Expression relative to the *War*, which was call'd *bloody and expensive*. A Strong Implication that the Blood as well as the treasure of the Nation had been lavishly employ'd. Mr Pitt's Amendment was to leave out the Epithet bloody, and to substitute two others, *just and necessary*. Mr Pitt's second Objection was to his Majesty's Silence concerning his Allies. The difference will be better understood by transcribing both Paragraphs the first as it was read in Council, the Second as it was publish'd by Authority after it had received Mr Pitt's Emendations.

1st. As I mount the Throne in the midst of a *bloody and expensive War*, I shall endeavor to prosecute it in the manner most likely to bring on an honorable and lasting Peace.

Second. As I mount the Throne in the midst of an *expensive but just and necessary War*, I shall endeavor to prosecute it in the Manner most likely to bring on an honorable and lasting Peace, *in Concert with my Allies*.

The King Consented to these Alterations with great Unwillingness. It was indeed a rough Measure to overrule the first Act of a young King, who only exerted a Power which must have been allow'd to the meanest of his Subjects, the Declaration of his own Sentiments, in Words of his own Choice. On the other hand, it was rather Indiscreet in the Earl of Bute, to take so decisive a Step before he had consulted the Principal Ministers of the late King, whereby he expos'd his Master to a public affront almost in the first Hour of his Reign.[3]

An Order being issued for proclaiming the King the next Morning, the Privy Council was summoned to attend the Proclamation at Saville House.[4]

The King did not appear in public but the Duke of Newcastle, the two Secretaries of State, and such Cabinet Counsellors who had not been at Council the preceding day had private Audiences. It was observed that the Earl of Bute was some minutes with his Majesty before each Audience. Amongst others the Speaker of the House of Commons desired leave to kiss his Majesty's Hand; but was told that none were to be admitted that day except Cabinet Counsellors. Whereupon the Speaker immediately quitted the Council Chamber, saying that if he was not thought worthy of having an Audience, he must think himself unworthy of remaining in that Place, therefore would retire amongst his Majesty's inferior Servants in the

---

[3] 'I believe Lord Bute did not wish to make the King avow the war, or engage to carry it on, nor, indeed intend to carry it on a moment longer than he should be forced to it. And yet surely these alterations were very proper, tho' not agreed to till Sunday afternoon': Fox, *Memoir*, p. 6.

[4] On Sunday 26 October.

outward Room. This being told to the King, the Speaker was desired to return to the Council Chamber, and from thence was conducted to his Majesty's Closet where he was most graciously received.

The Duke of York and the Earl of Bute were sworn Privy Counsellors the Day following,[5] and were both named by the King in the Commission for proroguing the Parliament. But when the Council was over it was recollected that it would be improper for the Earl of Bute to act as a Commissioner because not being one of the Sixteen he was not a Peer of Parliament; his Lordship's name was therefore omitted.[6]

His Majesty was civil and gracious to the Duke, the Ministers, and other Servants of his Grandfather, but seem'd to have little Confidence in any of them. He told the Duke of Cumberland in his first Audience, that he was determined to break an Old Custom of their Family by living in a friendly manner with all his Relations. However tho he discoursed with his Uncle as a Friend he gave him no trouble as a Counsellor.

When the Duke of Newcastle had his first Audience, his Majesty said to him, You have been a good and faithful servant to the King my Grandfather, and I am fully convinced that you will serve me also with the same Fidelity. But when the Duke of Newcastle encouraged by these gracious Words, was beginning to enter upon Business, His Majesty changed the Discourse.

Mr Pitt, was received with the highest Civility, but without much Cordiality or Openness.

By these and Indications of the like Nature the new political System was discovered to the World, before it was thoroughly understood even by the King himself. Whilst the Earl of Bute was Groom of the Stole to the Prince of Wales, his Uncle the Duke of Argyle[7] a Shrew'd and experienced Politician, had frequently advised him to prepare a Plan of Administration in case of the old King's Death, that tho his Majesty might possibly disappoint them by living longer than they expected, which would oblige them to form new Plans according to times & Circumstances, it would still be necessary that some regular system should be always in Readiness.

[5] On 27 October. The clear implication of Waldegrave's account of the Privy Council meeting on 25 October is that Bute, not yet a member, did not attend: cf. Brooke, *George III*, p. 76.

[6] After the Union of 1707, sixteen Scots peers were allowed to take their seats at Westminster. They were newly chosen, for each Parliament, by vote among themselves. Bute sat in the Lords in that capacity between 1737 and 1741, and again from 1761 to 1780; but since the election after George III's accession did not take place until 5 May 1761, his inclusion was considered inappropriate. See, in general, Sir James Fergusson of Kilkerran, Bt., *The Sixteen Peers of Scotland: An Account of the Elections of the Representative Peers of Scotland 1707–1959* (Oxford, 1960).

[7] Archibald Campbell, 3rd Duke of Argyll (1682–1761); succ. 1743. A Lord of the Treasury 1705–6; cr. Earl of Ilay 1706; a representative peer of Scotland 1707–13, 1715–61.

Bute, had too much Knowledge of his own to follow any Mans Advice, particularly when he did not like the Adviser: no Plan was form'd, and the Sudden Death of the King allowed no time to recollect himself.

In such a Situation, to have displaced the old Ministers, would have been a dangerous Experiment. It was therefore determined that Pitt should remain Secretary of State, the Duke of Newcastle first Commissioner of the Treasury, but that the Authority of both should be diminished, that Pitt should no longer be the Sole Conductor of the War, nor should the Duke of Newcastle have the Distribution of all the Favors of the Crown, Civil, Military and Eclesiastical. These were Powers too great to be trusted in any Hands but the King's. A Maxim which in itself seem'd wise and Constitutional, yet can never be reduced to Practice, unless there be on the Throne a Prince of Abilities and Experience, who is guided by no Favorite, and is known to act for himself.

Mr Pitt and the Duke of Newcastle were nowise connected by personal Friendship and differ'd widely in their Politics. But perceiving that the Earl of Bute would soon be a Rival to both, it became their mutual Interest to give a Check to his Power, before it had arisen to Maturity. Whereupon the Duke of Newcastle agreed to Pitt's Amendments of his Majesty's Declaration: and in return Mr Pitt publickly declared that had it been the King's Intention to have appointed him the first Minister, he would most humbly have declined so high an Honor. That whilst he was Secretary of State in the late Reign, as often as it had been necessary to make a Request to his Master either in his own behalf, or in behalf of his Friends instead of addressing himself directly to the King, he had made his Application to the Duke of Newcastle: and that he should be thoroughly satisfied in receiving the Favors of his present Majesty thro the same Channel. This was directly pointed against the Earl of Bute. Nevertheless Mr Pitt and the Duke of Newcastle, whilst they attacked him as a Minister, paid great Court to him as a Favorite: and each of them would have connived at Bute's Encroachments in the Province of his Ally, tho neither of them would suffer it in his own.

These were the Principal Occurrences of the first three days of the New Reign.

5

REFLECTIONS ON THE NEW REIGN

This section is present in the Chewton manuscript, pp. 193–206, in the hand Frederick Keppel, and in draft in Add MSS 51380 ff. 90–105 in Waldegrave's hand. It is here printed from the Chewton ms. The title and date are Keppel's.

A Parallel

1760

To compare the present times with the past, or present Ministers with those who preceded them, is the Right of every Englishman.

But Kings are not to be examined with the same familiarity: it would be a Work of too delicate a nature to make a fair Comparison between a Prince on the Throne, & his immediate Predecessor.

However there are certain happy Resemblances between our most gracious Sovereign and his Royal Grandfather, which may be mentioned without disrespect or flattery either to the living or the dead.

Strict honour and integrity, great temperance and fortitude, a sincere affection to their People, and a Reverence to our excellent Constitution, are virtues, that have been common to both.

Our young Monarch has moreover the singular advantage of being born and educated a Briton, and is free from the imputation, as well as, from the influence of any foreign partiality.

I shall now proceed to characters of inferior rank, and shall begin with our old Statesman the first Commissioner of the Treasury, who began to be a minister under King George the first, has taken a new lease under his great Grandson, and probably will continue a Minister to the last hour of his Life.

For though he will always struggle for as much power as he can get, he will think a little, better than none; and tho' the dreadful word Resignation

Reflections on the New Reign: 'A Parallel'

has formerly carried terror, and amazement, it may hereafter be understood in a milder sense: for in a Glossary which has lately been discovered in his Grace's library, Resignation is defined to be the art of Saving the employment, as well as, the act of quitting it.

As his Grace continues in the same high office, which he held under his late Majesty; there is no successor who can be weighed against him, and to compare him with himself would be a work of too much difficulty.

The sudden, tho' not unexpected, promotion of the Earl of Bute, was the first considerable change after the accession of his present Majesty.

No man can have a right to complain, because one noble Lord is removed, and another succeeds him, it being the undoubted Prerogative of the Crown to make choice of its own Ministers, as well as, of its own Favorites.

Yet in all free governments where ministers are accountable to the Public, every man thinks himself at liberty to speak freely of his superiors, particularly of those who have received the largest portions of favour, profit, or authority.

The noble Peer who was Secretary of State, and the noble Peer his successor,[1] are of the same degree of Nobility, the former amongst the English Earls, the latter amongst those of North Britain. So far there seems to be little superiority on either side.

The late Secretary when he removed from Westminster to Cambridge, had as much school learning as most of his Cotemporaries. Since which time having been constantly employed either as a man of pleasure, or as a man of business, it cannot be supposed that he has made any considerable improvement in Classical Knowledge.

But our present secretary having laid in his stock of Erudition since he arrived at years of discretion, whatever he has known at any time, must still be fresh in his memory: and tho' he be less correct in his mother tongue, than in the learned languages, it must proceed from inattention, not from ignorance: For if Vouchers should be required to attest his excellence in every branch of polite literature; there are discreet, grave, perhaps even Right Reverend Personages, who free from all worldly considerations, for the sake of truth only, will be ready to give proper Certificates.

Soon after the Earl of Holderness was of age, he was chose by the late King to be one of the Lords of his Bedchamber, he had the honour to attend his Royal Master at the Battle of Dettingen, and was afterwards employed in different Embassies: during which time he acquired a competent knowledge of foreign affairs, and shewed so much capacity for business, that after his return from Holland, he was appointed Secretary of State.

[1] The Earl of Bute succeeded the Earl of Holdernesse as Secretary of State for the Northern Department on 25 March 1761.

The Earl of Bute was also a Lord of the Bedchamber to the late Prince of Wales, he distinguished himself on the Stage, very early in life, & was allowed to be an excellent Tragedian.

It seems probable that if the Prince had lived, his Lordship might have travelled abroad in a public character, his R H having frequently declared that he was the only nobleman of his Court, who could look the part of an Embassador with becoming solemnity.

Amongst the inferior duties of a Secretary of State, it is expected that he should contribute to the magnificence of his Court by giving entertainments to foreign ministers, and to other Strangers of distinction.

On these occasions, few men can excel the Earl of Holderness, there is no sullen Pride, no false dignity, no smile of condescension, no nod of importance, no studied attitudes, no theatrical gesticulation: it is the cheerful easy conversation, it is the unaffected elegant behaviour of the Minister and of the man of Quality. In this particular, a comparison between the two Earls would be quite unnecessary, because the foregoing description, *mutatis mutandis*, may be equally applicable to both.

Both have been distinguished by the Ladies, with this difference, that Girls, and young married Women have been partial to the late Secretary, whilst the knowing ones have maintained the superiority of his more able successor.

After the administration was settled in the year 1757, there were no political disputes, of any consequence, as long as the late King lived.

During the first months of the present Reign, Mr Pitt maintained his ground without any considerable loss, or any considerable advantage. He was as much feared, and as little loved, was as much flattered by his colleagues, and as much abused by their Emissaries, had as great a part in the conduct of the war, and as small a share in the distribution of Preferment, as when he was the servant of the late King.

Notwithstanding much jealousy on one part, and some passion on the other, few men have been less obstructive to each others pretensions, than Mr Pitt and the Duke of Newcastle.

It seems probable that the Union would have continued till the end of the War, if it had not been interrupted by a more favoured minister, who with abilities far inferior to either, became equally formidable to both.

The increasing difficulties which have accompanied Mr Pitt's administration, many that he surmounted, and some which he found insuperable, may hereafter be explained by those who can speak with certainty.

Whatever, or whoever may have driven him from the service of the Public, we have lost the Minister, who found us on the verge of Destruction, desponding, sullen, and mutinous: who rouzed the Great from their Lethargy: who directed the spirit of the People to its proper object: and who raised the glory of his country to a tremendous Height, from whence not even himself could look down quite free from Dizziness.

A Minister whose Genius is not confined to a particular department, who would have executed in a military station with the same spirit he has plan[n]ed. Like Hawke he would have attacked Conflans: like Amherst he would have conquered Canada: like Wolfe he would have fought at Quebec:[2] if like him he had fallen, the Character had then been Complete.

As to our new Secretary, who was not the cause of Mr Pitt's Resignation, it must be allowed that he is a man of sense, that he knows the World, that he possesses the Theory of Business, tho' he may want the Practice, and that amongst men of his Lordships Rank, it would have been difficult to have made a better choice.

It had almost escaped my memory that Mr Legge is no longer Chancellor of the Exchequer: He was turned out[3] without any ceremony, no crime was alleged against him, no Compensation was given him in any other shape.

When his dismission was notified to the Public, it was received with the most perfect indifference, if there was no mark of approbation, there was not even a single Complaint.

Yet this is the gentleman who has been honoured with the thanks and congratulations, of almost every corporation in England, and who is the Possessor of as many gold Boxes as the great Commoner himself.

No objection can be made to the present Chancellor of the Exchequer,[4] who is a man of parts, as well as a man of business.

Yet an easy accomodating temper, with an ambition that will never give umbrage to a superior Minister, may have been more instrumental to his Lordships promotion, than any of his other accomplishments.

It would be unnecessary to make any Comparisons between Masters of the Horse, Grooms of the Stole, Stewards of the Household, Lords of the Bedchamber and the like. Provided they be men of Rank and property, whose characters in private life do no discredit to their offices, it is of little consequence to the Public, whether they formerly have been placemen or

---

[2] Jeffrey Amherst (1717–97). Ensign in Guards 1731; served on staff of Ligonier and Cumberland; Lieut.-Col. 1756; Major-General 1758; Wolfe's commanding officer in the conquest of Canada. Governor-General of North America 1760. Peerage 1776; General 1778; Field Marshal 1796. James Wolfe (1727–59): professional soldier, on active service in Flanders in 1740s; fought at Dettingen, Culloden, Laffeldt; Lieut-Colonel 1750; Rochefort expedition 1757; Major-General in conquest of Canada; died in siege of Quebec.

[3] Viscount Barrington succeeded H.B. Legge as Chancellor of the Exchequer on 12 March 1761.

[4] William Wildman Barrington, 2nd Viscount Barrington (I), (1717–93), succ. 1734. M.P. 1740–78. A Lord of the Admiralty 1746–54; Master of the Wardrobe 1754–55; Secretary at War 1755–61; Chancellor of the Exchequer March 1761–1762; Treasurer of the Navy 1762–65; Secretary at War 1765–78; Joint Postmaster General Jan.-Apr. 1782.

Patriots, whether they be seasoned Courtiers, or have lately been broke into harness. As to the reformation of abuses in his Majesties Stables or Household, it would be useless to inquire which is most commendable, the frugality of the present Reign, or the extravagance of the last.

Tho' a Coachman, grown corpulent and unweildly, should drive by deputy, or tho' a superannuated helper or Postillion should make his place a sine cure, the Public would receive no detriment: nor does it seem to be of greater importance, whether the principal Turnspit of the Court be a two or a four legged animal, or whether the administration of the Kitchen be Scotch or English.

It was a complaint against the late King, that on many occasions, when he might have had ye ocular proof, he formed his opinion of Men and of things from the report of his Ministers.

However, his Confidence in his servants was not unlimited, he sometimes judged for himself, and the characters of Minister and of Favorite were never united in the same person.

Some of his Ministers were men of real abilities: not one of them aspired to be first or second in command, till he had proved his Capacity for business in a preparatory station.

A Man, who had little knowledge of the World, and less of public affairs: who was flighty, without parts: pedantic without learning: and heavy without solidity: might have been Chamberlain to a Queen, or to a Princess Dowager, but had never been the leading Minister.

I shall now compare the measures of the late Reign with those of the present administration, and shall begin with the affairs of Germany.

The late King was supposed to have been strongly prejudiced in favor of his Electoral Dominions, and most of his Ministers have been accused of having paid an unconstitutional deference to their Masters partiality.

That he had a particular affection for his Electoral subjects, and that the assistance of Hanover has been purchased at too dear a Rate, are Truths which cannot denied.

Yet happy had it been for the Electorate, had she never been connected with this country. For in spite of Subsidies, and of other pecuniary advantages, she has lost more in an English quarrel, than England can ever repay.[5]

Those who have asserted that England ought rarely to interfere in the

---

[5] Add MSS 51380 f. 100 has a superseded alternative to this passage: 'But that he ever attempted to sacrifice the English Interest in affairs of the greatest Importance, that Hanover has been more favor'd than England in Treaties with Foreign Powers, except sometimes in a Treaty of Subsidy, is a false and scandalous Aspersion. If at the Demise of the late King, our Account with Hanover had been fully balanced, it would have appear'd that we both had been Sufferers, for tho Hanover has been a weighty Load upon this Country, she has lost more in an English Quarrel than England can every repay'.

Reflections on the New Reign: 'A Parallel'

broils of the Continent, who have never been the friends of Hanover, and who retain their former jealousies, may censure former measures with the greatest consistency.

But to all approvers of our present political Conduct, the authority of the present Reign must be the clearest justification of the last.

Has there been any change in the Continental System?

Has any subsidy been withdrawn?

Have we starved the war in Germany?

Have Prince Ferdinand's services been forgot?

Has it ever been suggested that an army which is paid by Great Britain, should be commanded by an English General?

Have we agreed to a separate Peace?

Most of these questions may be answered in the negative. But[6] instead of having been misled by our national prejudices, we have erred in the opposite extreme.

If all our continental connexions have not only been fulfilled, but renewed.

If every ally receives his former stipend, tho' his Troops want half their Complement, and cannot be recruited till the ensuing Peace.

If Success and Economy are to go hand in hand in Germany, till we have neither money to make payments, Armies to fight for us, nor ground to fight upon. We may talk of British measures and of a British administration, but the interest of Great Britain could receive no greater detriment, tho' every English General was recalled from Germany, and Baron Munichausen was appointed Secretary of State for the Northern Department.

At the same time, it is not my opinion that our Ministers have much Fondness for this German War, nor would they have embarked in so perilous an adventure, had they foreseen its probable consequences. But finding themselves at the brink of a Precipice, and having forgot to secure a retreat, their Courage has been stronger than their Judgement, and most daringly they have leaped into the Gulf.

As to the War at Sea, the War in North America, and other military operations in those parts of the Globe, where the interest of Great Britain is immediately concerned: the extraordinary successes of the last Reign have left us only a narrow field for future acquisitions. Bellisle and Dominica were conquered by the arms of his present Majesty, but the demise of the late King was unknown in the East Indies when Pondicherry surrender'd,[7] and the French Empire in India received its fatal overthrow.

It has been the language of former Reigns, that Placemen and Pension-

---

[6] Add MSS 51380 f. 101: 'But if'.   [7] On 16 January 1761.

ers in Parliament, were the mercenary tools of the Minister, the underminers of our excellent Constitution. A place was the yoke of dependence, a Pension was the wages of Iniquity.

But such is our Confidence in our present Governors, and in all those who shall govern us hereafter, that tho Pensions be increased both on the English and Irish Establishments: tho' dormant places have been revived: and tho' old Places have been multiplied: the man would be thought mad or disaffected who insinuated that this was Corruption, or expressed even the slightest disapprobation.[8]

The Spirit of Party or Faction which in former Reigns has caused so much disorder, and so much Malevolence, seems now to be at its last gasp. Every Barrier is removed, the Road of Preferment lies open to every political adventurer.

This widening of the Bottom must undoubtedly be agreeable to the tories, whose attachment to their rightfull sovereign has seldom been equivocal, and who may find more solid satisfaction in the service of the Crown, than they have felt for some years past in the service of their Country.

On the other hand, the Whigs have no great cause to complain, since most of those, who have been discarded, are succeeded by men who profess the same political principles, therefore in the language of Party are called Friends.

However notwithstanding that perfect harmony and Union which has hitherto subsisted, tho' Whig, Tory, Hanoverian, Jacobite, Courtier, Patriot, Privy Counsellor, Common Council Man, Prince, and Grocer, be all blended together in one mass. These Halcyon days may soon be at an end.

When many mouths are to be filled, when stomachs which have been impaired by long fasting, shall have recovered their digesting faculties, the pasture will not be sufficient.

To preserve us from a calamity which would affect the whole Community, I will recommend a very powerful antidote, and can offer it without Vanity, it being no discovery of my own.

The addition of many Lords and Grooms to the Royal Bedchamber[9] was a masterly stroke of State Policy, and had a surprizing effect.

A short Act of Parliament might be of extraordinary benefit to the Subject, by extending this salutary measure to some more lucrative employments. We might have nine Commissioners of the Treasury,

---

[8] Irony.
[9] 'The King's Bedchamber received six or eight additional Grooms and seven Gentlemen. Most of the late King's were continued; the King's own were joined with them; the rest were taken from the Tories': Walpole, *George III*, vol. 1, pp. 18–19.

Reflections on the New Reign: 'A Parallel'

thirteen of the Admiralty, as many of the Board of Trade:[10] or if it should be necessary, any of the great offices might be put into Commission, the present great Officer retaining his Rank and Salary, under the title of a first Commissioner.

This will be a comfortable maintenance for many worthy Senators who are not yet provided for, every party will have its Share, and we shall continue till Time, or money shall be no more, a Rich, a virtuous, and an United People.[11]

---

[10] The normal establishment was five at the Treasury, seven at the Admiralty, and eight at the Board of Trade.
[11] Waldegrave's suggestion was, of course, ironic.

6

AN ALLEGORY OF LEICESTER HOUSE

This composition distils the interpretation of events at Leicester House set out at greater length in the *Memoirs*, and reveals more fully the depth of Waldegrave's personal animosity towards Princess Amelia and Lord Bute. It may have been intended for publication as a satirical pamphlet, but no such work has yet been located. The text survives only in the Chewton manuscript, pp. 209–29, in the hand of Frederick Keppel.

The following History is translated from the French translation of an ancient Manuscript. The Reader must not be surprized, if in many parts of this work, he should meet with some obscurity. Old Chronicles giving an account of customs which are fallen into disuse, and of manners which are totally changed, must in these times appear fabulous, and will not be understood without great difficulty.

If therefore this History should be tolerably clear, its perspicuity is singly owing to the French translator, who has most judiciously explained many doubtful passages, has made alterations and amendments, where the original meaning could not be properly ascertained, and has even attempted to soften and modernise the enormous vices of antiquity, that they might appear less shocking to the virtuous simplicity of the present age.

Several hundred years ago, there was an Emperor called *Augustus*, but the country where he reigned, and the time when, are both doubtful.[1]

Our history represents him as having been a wise and good Prince, religious without bigotry, of great personal Bravery, yet not delighting in war, an indulgent master to his servants, tho' not governed by Favorites, a kind Father to his People, though not blind to their faults.

Tho' he could feel an injury, he was still more sensible of good and faithful Services, he had a certain warmth of temper which proceeds from a

---

[1] Georg August, otherwise George Augustus (1683–1760), King George II from 1727.

An Allegory of Leicester House

good heart; and could he have been guilty even of the least duplicity, his looks must have betrayed him, for his countenance could never dissemble.

Besides these Kingly Virtues he was temperate, just, humane, strict to his word, firm to what he thought right, and had a plain, solid understanding which went directly to the point.

However it must not be concealed that these and many other admirable Qualities were all counterbalanced by one unpardonable fault; a fault which had been gradually increasing for a very considerable time, and which in the end entirely alienated the affections of his most devoted servants. It is with grief I mention his infirmity, but this in every other respect most excellent Emperor, was far advanced in the evening of his days, between seventy and eighty years of age.

It is true indeed that his health, his spirit, his understanding were still unimpaired. But Patriot Politicians, and Ministers, the faithful followers of a court, in all changes, and under all governments; confine not their care for the public safety to the present instant only, they look farther into futurity, they consider that the greatest Princes are mortal like other men, they know that if the favor of a successor be not properly cultivated, the succession of Employments may fall into bad hands. Which being an evil of the first magnitude, must be prevented by any means; and none so reasonable or so effectual as to secure the successor by a small anticipation, of that power which must shortly be his own: and tho' to forsake a good old master, whose beneficent hand has raised them from the dust, may by certain rigid Moralists be called ingratitude. Yet the nicest casuist must allow that those men deserve best of the common wealth, who shew the most active zeal to serve their Country, that taking possession of all considerable employments is the previous step, without which, such services can never be performed, and consequently they ought to be esteemed the best of Citizens who for this desirable end, make a ready sacrifice of honour, of conscience, and of every moral Virtue.

But to proceed, *Augustus* had two sons, the elder[2] was humane, affable, easy of access, a friend to liberty, and loved his country. There was indeed some slight suspicion that he could not be entirely depended on, that he wanted Steadiness, and was too easily led. But tho' he might be deficient as to some Qualities which form a great prince, he possessed many of those which constitute a good one.

The younger[3] had the full possession of every great and princely qualification, superior understanding, quick Judgment, undaunted Courage, so far excelling others in all military knowledge, that his abilities

---

[2] Frederick Louis, Prince of Wales (1707–51).
[3] William Augustus, Duke of Cumberland (1721–65).

alone must have raised him to the supreme command, had he been born in a less exalted Station.

He was for a time the Idol of the people. A Rebellion breaks out, the rebels advance, armies are put to flight, whole provinces fly before them, a panick seizes upon all men. He comes to the Relief of his distressed Country, guided by his prudence, animated by his Example even Cowards forget their fears. The Rebels are vanquished, the Rebellion quelled, Religion and liberty are no longer in danger, and from that instant he becomes unpopular.

About the time I have been mentioning, the Elder Brother died, leaving a disconsolate Widow, with an only Son, between six and seven years old.[4]

This Lady who acts a principal part in the present history, was called *Penelope*. During the life of her husband, she was all goodness, condescension, affability, moderation, had no passions, no will of her own, was fearful of giving the least offence, a dutifull daughter, an obedient wife. From the moment she became a widow, she looked upon *Augustus* not only as a father, and sovereign, to whom all duty and obedience were now become due; but also as her sole protector, Benefactor and Friend.

The Emperor on his part, treated her with the greatest tenderness, and as the strongest proof of a thorough Confidence, he suffered her son to remain with her. *Augustus* was indeed too wise not to know that in the education of a young prince, there is but one science, where women are qualified to give proper instruction, but he knew also what a mother must feel in being separated from an only child almost at the very instant she loses her husband; and here it must be confessed that his humanity prevailed over his judgement.

Penelope on her part, seemed in every respect worthy of the favours she received. Her behaviour to the Emperor was decent and respectful, and she shewed a satisfaction in receiving his commands by her most chearful obedience.

At the same time it was observed, that the behaviour of the Prince her son was somewhat different.

Tho' *Augustus* did every thing in his power, not only to gain his affection, but to make him easy, and familiar, he could never succeed. When he advanced towards him, the youth drew back; when he asked him any chearful, good humoured Question, he was answered by a respectful bow, and a monosyllable. What ever was done to please him, he seemed quite indifferent: and tho' this was generally imputed to his natural modesty, or

[4] Frederick, Prince of Wales died on 20 March 1751; his son, Prince George, was then aged 12. Waldegrave deliberately exaggerates Prince George's dependence on his mother and on Bute.

An Allegory of Leicester House

to a timidity arising from filial awe and reverence: there were some who did apprehend that such behaviour might proceed from a worse principle.

Moreover *Penelope* not from jealousy, but apprehending the danger of vicious companions, had taken particular care to prevent his mixing with any of the young Nobility: and as to the different setts of Governors, preceptors and others who had the care of his education, such men might possibly instill bad principles: they were therefore in their turns, so properly played off one against the other, that long before his coming of age, none who approached him preserved the least influence, except the mother and those who she confided in.

These were quickly reduced to a sole Favorite, the great *Bombastus Vigorosus*,[5] whom I now must have the honour of introducing to my Readers acquaintance.

Soon after the death of her husband, some think before, a Platonic friendship was formed between the chaste *Penelope*, and the graceful *Vigorosus*.

He was above the middle size, had broad shoulders, great muscular strength, and remarkable fine legs; yet those bodily perfections, (which sometimes may have attracted vulgar widows), would have remained entirely unnoted. His lively wit, his solid judgement, his profound Erudition, his most extensive Knowledge, his instructive Conversation, and above all his unaffected modesty, these were the charms which alone could captivate the incomparable *Penelope*.

But least envious tongues should call this Flattery, I will produce some examples of his most extraordinary genius.

Vigorosus had scarce attained his 20th year, when having finished his Studies at a celebrated College,[6] he could just sign his name, and with a little difficulty could read a newspaper. But hearing of the Fame of Learned men, how much they were esteemed, how much respected, he at once determined to become a man of Letters: and as Lord Clarendon reports of Lord Falkland that he shut himself up in the country, resolving not to see London which he loved above all places, 'till he had learnt the Greek tongue. So our Hero took the resolution neither to use a looking glass, indulge himself with one fine attitude, nor contemplate the beauties of his admirable legs, 'till he had made himself a perfect master of all Classical learning: which by the help of French translations, he fully accomplished in less than six months.

But 'tis observable that superior Geniuses, applying themselves only to that which is great and sublime, are apt to despise common things as

---

[5] John Stuart, 3rd Earl of Bute (1713–92).
[6] Eton. Waldegrave's aspersions on Bute's literacy are otherwise unsubstantiated.

unworthy their attention, and *Vigorosus* thought it Pedantick to be quite correct in the mother tongue, either as to grammar, or orthography.

In the same manner he became a great Algebraist without the least knowledge of vulgar Arithmetick, and was not without hopes of squaring the circle, discovering the Longitude, and finding the Philosophers Stone.

He was also superior to all men in the knowledge of those instructive Histories which give a perfect account of mighty Empires which never existed, of astonishing actions which never were performed, and of extensive countries totally unknown to modern Geographers: and having with infinite Labor compleatly formed himself by examples drawn from the ideal Heroes of these wise Historians, he undertook the education of our young *Telemachus*,[7] equally qualified to lay the foundation, raise the Superstructure, or give the last polish.

But about the time I have already mentioned, when *Telemachus* was entering into his nineteenth year, the Emperor thinking him of a proper age for matrimony, fixed upon a Princess of high birth, great beauty, and excellent understanding, no ways doubting but such a choice must render him compleatly happy. She was indeed so thoroughly accomplish'd, that some were of opinion, had it not been for the great disproportion of years, *Augustus* himself would rather have chose her for a wife, than for a grandaughter.

This greatly alarmed *Penelope* and *Vigorosus*, they knew the amiable character of the young Princess, and they moreover knew that so much merit, with so much beauty could not fail of gaining the entire affection of the Prince her husband: that this must be destructive to their influence over him, was so very obvious, it could not possibly escape them. The obstruction therefore of such a match was nothing more than self defence, or rather self preservation.

In this extraordinary situation, where Truth and plain dealing could do no sort of good, the sincere, the artless, the scrupulous *Penelope*, with the approbation of her conscientious, and Right honorable Friend, found it expedient to make use of a little cunning, or, what in such cases is quite allowable, of a little falsehood.

For this purpose, they extolled the young Princess in publick, if possible, even more than she deserved, whilst in their private lectures all her perfections were aggravated into faults. At length by painting her in the most odious colours, with proper insinuations, concerning the Emperors reasons for promoting this detestable match, they so wrought on the mind of *Telemachus*, that he not only made a solemn resolution never to marry her, but from that moment considered the Emperor himself as his greatest enemy.

[7] George, Prince of Wales (1738–1820).

Here *Vigorosus* and *Penelope* gained a considerable Victory; for a right understanding between the young Prince and his Grandfather, was not only dangerous on account of the match, but might also have produced a friendship between *Telemachus* and the Emperors younger son, whom I have already mentioned.

This Prince who was called *Cambrianus*, had most imprudently neglected the great *Bombastus Vigorosus* who formerly would have condescended to have taken him under his puissant protection: and tho' this neglect alone would have been sufficient cause of enmity; there were still stronger reasons. *Vigorosus* tho' conscious of his own superior abilities, could not help perceiving that they were not held in proper estimation, either by the Emperor or by his country.

So difficult is it for truth to reach the ear of Princes, that for many years *Augustus* was totally ignorant that this great personage had any merit whatsoever. Indeed the world in general was long under the same mistake, except three old Ladys, one Gentleman Usher, and two Pages of the Back Stairs, who were better informed.

These sage and venerable Matrons, these sober and sagacious Gentlemen, who walk steady and secure through all the mazes of a Court, were the only persons, except *Penelope* herself, who enjoyed the benefit of his entire confidence: to them he poured out that torrent of erudition and eloquence, which at once delighted and surprized, tho' far beyond their Comprehension. To them he repeated Speeches out of Plays, for he was an excellent tragedian, and just as he stir'd up, or lull'd their passions, they would either cry, laugh, yawn, or fall fast asleep: to them did he first rehearse those admirable political lectures wherewith he afterwards instructed the young *Telemachus*, and to them only was it known, that he not only excelled the ablest and most experienced Statesmen, but was moreover a greater General than *Cambrianus* himself.

But this amazing superiority being still a secret to the Publick; our Hero looked upon this Prince as a most powerful Rival, who if not immediately subdued, might be a check to his greatness even in a future reign. He therefore represented him to *Telemachus* as violent, enterprising, full of dangerous ambition, not without some insinuations, that even the succession to the crown would be very precarious, as long as *Cambrianus* had the Command of the Army, or indeed whilst he retained any power whatsoever. By these salutary falsehoods, the fears and jealousy of *Telemachus* were raised to such a pitch, that had there been Pretenders in those days, they would have been less hateful to him, than his nearest Relations.

In consequence of these family divisions, new factions arose in the Court, factions in the Senate, and factions amongst the People.

No subordination, no Government: War is proclaimed against a most powerful Neighbour, which in such a situation must prove unfortunate; The Nation is on the brink of destruction.

Here *Vigorosus* and *Penelope* began to have some doubts, whether they had not gone rather farther than they first intended.

They only meant to create a little confusion, humble their opponents, break the old Emperor's Heart, and take all the power into their own Hands. But besides the improbability that persons of such exalted Virtue, could have any bad purposes; they never once imagined that any particular advantage could accrue to them, either from the total subversion of Government, or from the entire ruin of their Country.

Here the ancient Manuscript begins to be very defective; several Chapters are entirely lost, others are so very obscure, that neither the lively imagination of French translators, nor the laborious diligence of Dutch or German Comentators, have yet been able to decypher them. Some fragments however are still preserved, with some titles, or Heads of Chapters lately recovered by a learned Antiquary of the University of Glasgow, and here for the first time presented to the Publick.

Chap: ye 15th

How *Vigorosus* and *Penelope* established a court of Conscience to discuss and determine several important Questions. How three Reverend Foreigners the Fathers Sanchez, Molina, and Escobar, were the leading casuists in this court.[8] Some few Questions are still extant, with their respective answers: but our History gives no information either as to the particular tendency of these Questions, nor concerning the persons by whom they were proposed.

Query ye 1st – Whether the duty of a son to a father descends to the sons children, or whether any duty whatsoever be owing to a Grandfather.

Answer – No duty whatsoever

Query ye 2nd – Whether by the death of a father, all duty does not devolve and become due to the Mother only, and at what age this duty ceases.

---

[8] Three Spanish Jesuits and moral theologians. Thomas Sanchez (1550–1610): famous for his *Disputationes de sancti matrimonii sacramento* (1602), a standard work on the theological and moral significance of marriage. 'As it deals with every possible point in the subject, it has often, quite unjustifiably, drawn upon Sanchez the charge of immorality' (A. Lehmkuhl). Luis de Molina (1535–1600): his writings occasioned one of the greatest theological conflicts of the seventeenth century. Antonio Escobar y Mendoza (1589–1669): prolific author, including *Summula casuum conscientiae* (1627); 'perhaps the most reviled of all Jesuits ... became a symbol of unprincipled sophistry ... His *Handbook of Moral Theology* went through many editions in every Catholic country and for ten years was praised as a useful and unexceptionable compendium, with the usual quota of sexual transgressions. Then, quite suddenly, it was given a wider fame by anti-Jesuit writers as a turgid classic of pornography and equivocation': David Mitchell, *The Jesuits: A History* (London, 1980), pp. 127–8. Waldegrave perhaps displays a greater knowledge of Jesuit theologians than would have been considered proper in a Protestant Englishman.

Answer – The Son must continue an infant during his mother's life, all duty becoming due to her, or to the Person who she shall confide in: which Person ought to be considered as a second father.

Query ye 3d – Whether after the 70th year, a man may not be supposed to dote, tho' in appearance he retains all his faculties.

Answer – This frequently happens. But the precise time when dotage begins cannot be exactly ascertained, and therefore must be fixed at the discretion of the Heir apparent, or of his sufficient Deputy.

Query ye 4th – Whether a married Man who punctually performs the *debitum conjugale*, may not sometimes be indulged with a new object.

Answer – It may be allowed. But the indulgence must be confined to one woman only, and she ought neither to be younger, nor more tempting than his own wife.

Query ye 5th – Whether a widow can be guilty of Adultery.

Answer – A widow can be guilty of simple fornication only. Which proceeding from Constitution, not from any depravity of the mind, is not *malum in se*, and consequently there is no criminality, unless it proceeds from collateral circumstances.

Chap: ye 19th

How *Vigorosus* had a Levée. How he practised fine attitudes before his Glass. How he could nod with great condescention, smile with protection, hear with inattention, decide or give the most judicious answers without knowing what had been said: and how none approached him, who did not feel his great superiority and their own unworthiness.

Chap: ye 21st

How a distant colony was invaded by a powerful Enemy, and how *Vigorosus* discovered a new method of defence, by sending to their succour a whole ship load of sermons against infidelity.

Chap: ye 30th

How *Penelope*, *Vigorosus*, a maid of Honor, & a young Duke went on a Party of Pleasure into the Country. How they play'd at cards, how *Penelope* chose the young Duke for her Partner, how *Vigorosus* discovered that this young Duke had abominable long legs, and that *Penelope* had dropp'd one of her Slippers.

Chap: ye 34th

How during a whole summer, an impudent Fellow of a neighbouring Island, walked every evening under *Penelope's* window. How a Lady of the Bedchamber was sent to reprimand him, and how she returned full of astonishment. How *Penelope* herself condescended to expostulate with him. How *Vigorosus* did not entirely approve of this condescension, & was seized with a nervous Fever.

Chap: ye 41st

How *Vigorosus* condescended to amuse the Court in the capacity of an actor; the different Tragedies wherein he excelled. How he performed the part of Alexander the Great, but entering too deeply into the madness of the last act, became disordered in his senses. How he fancied himself Jupiter Ammon, and how the Lord Treasurer and many of the nobles, his faithful followers, fell down and worshiped him.

Chap: ye 45th

How a certain Gentleman turned away one of his servants who had given abusive language. How all the Family owned he was a very insolent fellow, and quite ignorant of his business; nevertheless insisted he should still be employed, because he had a cousin, a great Talker, who was stout & testy, and might break some of their heads, if his Kinsman was not restored. How the Master refusing to take him again, the whole Family mutinied. One could not in honor take care of his horses; another tho't himself bound in conscience not to dress his dinner; a third out of pure love & affection, could not allow him a clean shirt. Some even talked of a statute of Lunacy, and of putting the heir apparent into immediate possession.

The chapter concludes with an account how the saucy Servant was at last admitted into a profitable sine-cure, on condition that he was never to open his mouth, 'till his Master should think fit to speak to him.

Chap: 50

How the Emperor, much against his inclination, was obliged to have a new body Guard, called Noblemen Pensioners, where those only could be admitted who were most remarkable for publick spirit, and had expressed the greatest contempt for all lucrative Employments. With the Names, and titles of those great Lords, Knights, & Gentlemen, who had the honour of riding in this illustrious Troop. How greatly they were esteemed & respected by their Country, and how the Lord Treasurer was appointed Paymaster, a famous Cornet of Horse carried the Standard, and the Warlike *Bombastus Vigorosus* condescended to be their Captain General.

Chap: 52

How *Telemachus* became lethargick, and how the ablest Physicians were consulted, but could give no relief. How one *Bubo* an irregular Practitioner who had formerly laboured under the same misfortune, undertook to cure him. With *Bubo*'s manner of reasoning as to the cause of the Distemper and the method of treating it. Giving an account how his own disorder first proceeded from living too much with nurses, children, and old women, and was afterwards increased by passing his time with a dull, sententious Gentleman, who taught him Politicks in blank verse.

That tho' the case of *Telemachus* was totally different, who conversed only with persons of the most refined wit, and most consummate wisdom; yet change of company might produce very surprizing effects. How *Penelope* took the Hint, sent her family into the country, kept *Vigorosus* in constant employment about her own Person, and gave her son leave to go abroad and amuse himself. How during this interval, *Telemachus* got acquainted with a beautiful and most engaging Countess, who had an infallible nostrum, against all lethargick Disorders, and how he soon recovered his former chearfulness.

Chap: ye 57th

Gives an account of the Emperors last illness. How he sent for his Grandson and talk'd to him in the tenderest, and most confidential manner. How greatly *Telemachus* was affected by this conversation, and most earnestly desired to make a second visit. How his Mother would have dissuaded him from it, telling him that talking might do the good Emperor harm, that it was a very fine evening, and that he had better take a ride into the Country. How *Telemachus* Contrary to his mothers inclination, went directly to the dying Emperor, who expressed great comfort in seeing him, and concluded a very moving and affectionate discourse in the following manner.

Tho' I am arrived to such an age that it would be Weakness indeed to wish for longer life; I find it impossible to meet death without some anxiety, when I consider the difficulties in which you must soon be engaged; with the danger, or perhaps the misery to which my People are exposed.

From want of Experience it is impossible you can act alone; yet the choice of proper assistants is a work of great uncertainty. Some want abilities, some want Honesty, far the greater Number are equally void of both.

Endeavour as much as possible, to employ men of plain, solid Understanding, capable of application, who have some experience in Business, & have sufficient property to maintain their dignity without an Employment: such men have less temptation to do wrong.

Tho' you meet with ingratitude in a thousand different Shapes, be not discouraged from doing good, nor think all men alike ungrateful. Yet be cautious to whom that power is granted, which cannot be resumed. For I have known Ministers dispute with their Sovereign the command of his own servants, and even bribe against him out of his own Treasury.

Your Disposition will naturally lead you to encourage virtue, and publick spirit. Yet rigid virtue has ever been an object of Contempt and Ridicule. She must suit her behaviour to the temper of the times; She must appear good humoured, and amiable, or she will have few followers.

Be not inattentive to the voice of your people; consider even their inclinations, and particular prejudices. Yet suffer them not to dictate in affairs of state, which are above their Comprehension. For I have experienced that giving way to unjust clamour, encourages Faction, and is subversive of all good government.

Notwithstanding your present most dangerous situation, you must not despair. Your Country may still be saved, as our greatest misfortunes proceed rather from Misconduct, and bad Policy, than from any natural Defect.

Try therefore the bold experiment of doing that which is right. Think not grievances are without a Remedy, because they have been long established. The diminution of the publick Debt, and the abolishing those Taxes which are a load upon industry, would revive the spirit and good humour of the People. Even Corruption itself may be conquer'd by proper resolution.

Put an end to the calamities of the present War, whenever you can obtain a tolerable Peace. At the same time consider what may be your situation some years hence, as well as the dangers of the present moment.

As to what has been said concerning your Mother; I may have been misinformed. If the intelligence you have received, should not be confirmed by your own observation: you ought to think her innocent.

As to myself, tho' I have committed some Errors, I am conscious of having performed my Duty to the best of my capacity: and will not complain of those evils which are inseparable from human nature. Neither will I give you any further trouble, the Ceremony of parting would be painful to us both. May you be happy yourself, and make your subjects happy; May you live to my age, and may your close of life be more fortunate.

Soon after the good Emperor died; and here the ancient manuscript is again very deficient. We only know that *Penelope* was confined in a castle, during the remainder of her life, and that *Vigorosus* was condemned to perpetual banishment in his own Country.

The History also informs us that the contending nations after several Battles, the sinking or destroying a great number of ships, the loss of at least two hundred thousand men and contracting new debts, to the amount of several millions; having sufficiently damaged each other by Sea and Land; at length wisely agreed to make a reasonable Peace: and the People

An Allegory of Leicester House

almost ruined by Faction, and harassed by Squabbling amongst themselves, had almost taken the resolution of hanging up the party Leaders of every denomination. However all escaped as to their Lives, tho' not without some Corporal Punishment. The Orators in particular being distinguished with a seat in the ducking stool, the old Constitutional Rostrum of vituperative Eloquence.

The Citizens also perceiving how egregiously they had been the dupes of these Gentlemen, and that the most considerable Traders in Politics were all of them Bankrupts; took the sober resolution, of retiring behind their long neglected Counters, to administer to their Shops, and as far as their wives would suffer them, to practise the arts of Government in their own families.

All Foreign wars being now ended, and domestic Tranquillity being at last restored; *Telemachus* reign'd happily for many years, was beloved by his subjects and lived to a good old age. But would not be persuaded to marry, till he was near sixty, that he might not live to see his children old enough to become disobedient.

7

A SATIRE ON BUTE'S MINISTERIAL POWER, LATE 1762

This allegory is present only in the Chewton manuscript, pp. 231–4, in the hand of Frederick Keppel.

Bute had been conducting private negotiations for peace, without the knowledge of his cabinet colleagues, since the summer of 1762. The terms of the Treaty were concluded by the Duke of Bedford, heading the British delegation, in October, and were approved by Parliament in December, this success greatly strengthening Bute's position. The Peace of Paris became operative in March 1763.

We can assure the public that as soon as the definitive Treaty is signed, and peace is proclaimed, The Right Honble the Earl of Bute will be escorted from Carleton House to Westminster, with great pomp and solemnity, where he will receive the thanks and congratulations of both houses of Parliament, and will be appointed Minister for life.

On Thursday last there was a private Rehearsal of the whole Ceremony. The Procession began in the Park, at her Royal Highnesses Garden gate, in order as follows.

1. The Briton, The Auditor,[1] the Modest and Judicious Doctor Hill,[2] the Reverend Author of Douglas,[3] and the ingenious Mr Lockman[4]

---

[1] *The Briton* (launched 29 May 1762, written by Tobias Smollett) and *The Auditor* (launched 10 June 1762, written by the St Omers-educated Arthur Murphy) were the leading pro-ministerial journals in the press war of 1762–3 against *The Monitor* and *The North Briton*.

[2] John Hill (?1716–75) apothecary, botanist, scientist, entrepreneur and quack; MD of St Andrews University; a protégé of Bute. In December 1760 the *Gentleman's Magazine* announced his appointment as 'master gardener of the Royal gardens at Kensington', which Horace Walpole described as 'a place worth £2000 a year': Walpole, *Letters*, vol. 16, p. 42; cf. G.S. Rousseau (ed.), *The Letters and Papers of Sir John Hill* (New York, 1982).

[3] John Home (1722–1808). Scot; Presbyterian minister. Author of the tragedy *Douglas*, performed on the London stage February 1757. Tutor to George, Prince of Wales, 1757–60; Private Secretary to Lord Bute 1757-April 1763. Received a pension of £300 p.a. from the accession of his pupil as George III.

[4] John Lockman (1698–1771): minor poet, translator, prolific author, Court sycophant; Secretary to the British Herring Fishery.

Secretary to the British Fishery, dressed like Herb Women at the Coronation, carrying incense in one hand, and strewing flowers with the other.

2. The forlorn Hope, in French, les Enfans perdues, commanded by Lord George Sackville.[5] It was intended that this troop should have led the Van; but it being rumoured that the Schools of Wandsworth and Marybone were in arms, and might attempt to interrupt them in their march, the Commander sent an Aid de Camp to the Minister, and the flower women were posted in the front. They were followed by the noble Lord at a convenient distance, his Lordship halted frequently, and sent for fresh instructions on every new emergency.

3. Colonel Barré[6] at the head of a scalping party. He was ordered to follow Sackville's Corps, that he might not advance too fast, as well as to prevent any unnecessary effusion of Christian blood.

4. The Earl of Litchfield[7] mounted on a white horse from the stud at Hanover, at the head of the Noblemen and Gentlemen Pensioners. The appearance of this troop was very respectable, they marched with great Regularity, and observed the strictest Discipline.

5. The sacred band of Steady Friends, their uniforms turned wrong side out,[8] commanded by the Earl of Sandwich.[9]

6. A Light Troop of Trimmers commanded by the Earl of Hardwick,

---

[5] Lord George Sackville (1716–85), 3rd son of 1st Duke of Dorset; Chief Secretary in Ireland 1751–5 during Dorset's second Lieutenancy. On his return to London in late 1754, Sackville attached himself to Leicester House and slowly forged links with Pitt and Bute. Thanks to Pitt, Sackville was given a senior position in the British army in Germany; but, commanding the British cavalry at the battle of Minden, 1 August 1759, his tactical hesitancy was ascribed to cowardice, and he was disgraced at a court-martial, 29 February – 3 April 1760. Immediately on George II's death, Sackville wrote to Bute for permission to pay his duty to the new monarch; 'He came to Court and kissed hands, but it caused such an uproar that he was asked not to appear again': Piers Mackesy, *The Coward of Minden: The Affair of Lord George Sackville* (London, 1979), p. 245 and *passim*.

[6] Isaac Barré (1726–1802), MP 1761–90. Army officer: Ensign 1746; Captain 1758; served with Wolfe in Rochefort expedition and at Quebec. Brought into Parliament by Lord Shelburne; attached to Bute in early 1760s. Made a sensational debut in the Commons on 10 Dec. 1761 with an attack on Pitt, for which he was honoured at Court and appointed Lieutenant Colonel. The 'scalping party' refers to Barré's savagery in debate.

[7] George Henry Lee, 3rd Earl of Lichfield (1718–72), succ. 1743. MP 1740–3; High Steward, Oxford Univ., 1760–62, and Chancellor 1762-d. A Lord of the Bedchamber 1760–62; Captain of the Gentlemen Pensioners 1762-d. Lady Louisa Stuart wrote that he had been 'the most promising in point of parts amongst all the young men of the Tory party'; he destroyed his constitution with drink.

[8] Sandwich abandoned his patron Cumberland in the autumn of 1762 and attached himself to Fox, then rallying support for Bute's ministry. Sandwich's reward was the Admiralty in April 1763.

[9] John Montagu, 4th Earl of Sandwich (1718–92), succ. 1729. Entered army: Colonel 1745, Major General 1755, Lieut.-General 1759, General 1772. A Lord of the Admiralty 1744–46; Minister Plenipotentiary 1746–9; First Lord of the Admiralty 1749–51 and April-August 1763; Secretary of State for the Northern Department 1763–5, 1770–1; First Lord of the Admiralty 1771–82.

240   *A Satire on Bute's Ministerial Power, late 1762*

and Chief Justice Mansfield. They marched with great dexterity in a kind of zig zag, but could never go the Strait Road. The Motto on their Banner was that excellent Maxim of Law, *Audi Alteram Partem.*

7. The most formidable Troop of duellists, their Standard a Deaths Head. To have been commanded by Major General Townshend, but he arrived too late.[10]

8. A Lady of the Bedchamber, a Maid of Honor, and a Bedchamber Woman, not any of the Queen's,[11] bearing the Champions lance.

9. Earl Talbot[12] in his coat of mail, representing the champion, challenging the whole opposition to single Combat.

10. The Minister in the Dowager Lady Whale's Body-Coach.

11. At the coach doors, George Stevenson dressed like a Bishop, and the Naylor like a Judge, least the mob should suspect their being Bruisers.[13]

12. Buckhorse and the Irish Boy,[14] standing like Pages on the fore braces of the coach, with bags, solitaires, and coats of pompadour velvet.

[10] Hon. George Townshend (1724–1807). Army officer: Major General 1761, Lieutenant-General 1770, General 1782, Field Marshal 1796. He attached himself to George III and Bute at the start of the new reign, and was an assiduous courtier. He enjoyed a reputation as a duellist; after the accession, 'the first gust of faction that threatened the new era was an intended duel between the Earl of Albemarle and General George Townshend': Walpole, *George III*, vol. 1, p. 17. Townshend was serving with the army, in Portugal, during the latter half of 1762.

[11] Implication: the Dowager Princess of Wales'.

[12] William Talbot, 2nd Baron Talbot of Hensol (1710–82), succ. 1737; MP Glamorgan 1734–7; supporter of Frederick, Prince of Wales; created 19 March 1761 Earl Talbot; Lord Steward 1761-*d*. Talbot's Lord Stewardship, and earldom, 'for some time occasioned more speculation than even the credit of the Favourite', Bute; Talbot, according to Horace Walpole, lacked 'gravity, rank, interest, abilities ... morals', and 'was better known as a boxer and man of pleasure, than in the light of a statesman'. Walpole, *George III*, vol. 1, pp. 35–6.

[13] On Lord Mayor's day, 9 November 1761, the new holder of that office held the traditional banquet at the Guildhall, attended by the royal family and the ministers. Pitt and Temple, in one carriage, were given a triumphant reception during the procession. The reaction to another carriage was very different: 'It now comes out, that a party of bruisers, with George Stephenson, the one-eyed fighting coachman, at their head, had been hired to attend the chariot which contained the blazing comet [Bute] and the new chancellor of the exchequer [Barrington] ... and to procure shouts and acclamations from the mob'; instead of which the mob turned on Bute, and 'Before they arrived at Guildhall, the bruisers were almost bruised to death themselves'. Thomas Nuthall to Lady Chatham, 12 Nov. 1761: W.S. Taylor and J.H. Pringle (eds.), *Correspondence of William Pitt, Earl of Chatham* (4 vols., London, 1838–40), vol. 2, p. 166. Bute's reception at the Lord Mayor's Banquet the following year was similar: 'As soon as it was known who he was, he was entertain'd with a general hiss; and if some accounts are true, his chariot was pelted, on each side of which the two famous bruisers, Broughton and Stevenson, are affirmed to have walked as a guard to him, tho' I can scarce credit it'. Thomas Birch to Lord Royston, 13 Nov. 1762: Yorke, *Hardwicke*, vol. 3, p. 431. 'The Naylor' was Bill Stevens, another noted fighter: cf Henry Downes Miles, *Pugilistica: The History of British Boxing* (3 vols., Edinburgh, 1906), vol. 1, pp. 36–7.

[14] 'Buckhorse' was the nickname of John Smith (d. 1772), a famous boxer: Miles, *Pugilistica*, vol. 1, pp. 40–2. The 'Irish Boy' was presumably another pugilist.

Their periwigs, better for having been worn, were given ready curled, and powdered by Welbore Ellis Esquire.[15]

On his Arrival at Westminster Hall, the Minister alighted from his Coach of State, and walked to St Stephens Chapel, preceded by the Champion. He was supported by the Naylor on the left, on the right by Mr Stevenson, and his train was most gracefully lifted up by the two Pages, Mr Buckhorse and the Irish Boy, to the great satisfaction and astonishment of several thousand Spectators, his Lordship being in his Highland dress.

As soon as he entered the Lobby, the Speaker retired to the Treasury Bench: and his Lordship being seated in the chair, the Serjeant at Arms was sent to the other house to require their Lordships attendance. The Peers immediately obeyed, and were admitted within the Bar.[16]

The signal being given, the whole Assembly in Chorus, began their Congratulatory address. Which being ended, his Lordship was anointed perpetual Minister by a Presbyter of the Kirk of Scotland, assisted by his Grace the Lord Arch-Bishop of Canterbury.

The Lords and Gentlemen saluted and did Homage one by one, as vassals to their superior Lord; but kissed rather lower than the face. His Lordship tho' under the necessity of turning his back to the company, behaved with great humility, and thanked them in a most emphatic speech, it is doubtful in what language, whether Greek, Latin, Hebrew, or Erse; it can only be said with Certainty that it was not English.[17]

The Procession then returned in the order it came. The whole was conducted with great decency. The Lord Steward gave a whole kilderkin of mild ale to the populace,[18] to drink the Ministers Health, and the evening concluded with ringing of Bells, illuminations, squibs, crackers, Bonfires, and other rational demonstrations of Joy and Loyalty.

V i v a t   R e x

[15] Welbore Ellis (1713–1802), MP 1741–94. A Lord of the Admiralty 1747–55; Joint Vice-Treasurer, Ireland 1755–62, 1770–77; Secretary at War Dec. 1762–5; Treasurer of the Navy 1777–82; Secretary of State for America Feb.-March 1782. A close associate of Henry Fox in 1750s, he attached himself to Bute in the early 1760s.

[16] This reverses normal procedure: the Lords are here being summoned to attend in the Commons.

[17] Bute was, in fact, thoroughly Anglicised. His daughter pointed out: 'My father, who went to Eton school at seven years old, returned no more to Scotland till almost a man; but passed his holidays at the home of one of his uncles'. 'Memoir by Lady Louisa Stuart' in J.A. Home (ed.), *The Letters and Journals of Lady Mary Coke* (4 vols., Edinburgh, 1889–96), vol. 1, p. xv.

[18] An allusion to Lord Talbot's parsimony in his new office; 'nothing was heard of but cooks cashiered, and kitchens shut up': Walpole, *George III*, vol. 1, p. 36.

8

SPEECHES IN THE HOUSE OF LORDS, 1742–1763

The manuscript drafts of Waldegrave's speeches cover a period during which Lords' proceedings were almost unreported. Ebenezer Timberland's *The History and Proceedings of the House of Lords* (8 vols., London, 1742–4) continue to the end of the session of 1742–3. The Secker Papers in British Library (Add MSS 6043) contain the manuscript notes of debates complied by Bishop Thomas Secker for 15 April 1735 to 25 February 1743, and printed in Cobbett's *Parliamentary History of England*, volumes 9 to 12. The hiatus is all too evident from John Debrett's *The History, Debates and Proceedings of both Houses of Parliament ... 1743 to ... 1774* (7 vols., London, 1792). Volume 1 of that work contains a few Lords' debates on the scale of Timberland up to April 1745; thereafter Lords' reports are confined almost wholly to King's Speeches, Addresses in reply, and signed protests entered in the Journals. Reporting of Lords' debates really only revives in the 1770s with John Almon's *The Parliamentary Register ... 1774–1780* (17 vols., London, 1775–80); the drafts printed below are important in throwing light on a dark age in the history of the upper House.

Timberland, Debrett, and Cobbett all fail to record any speeches by the 2nd Earl Waldegrave; his own drafts are almost our only evidence that he spoke at all in that House. It was clearly not his practice to send copies of his speeches to the press, as other peers were said to do.[1] Nevertheless, Waldegrave's consistency in accurately drafting his speeches over twenty years is evidence for the importance he attached to that exercise, whether as an aid to memory or as a record of what he had said. The endorsement on the back of his speech of 1762, no. 34 below, strongly suggests that he had the draft in his hand while delivering it, and this may have been the case on other occasions.

Waldegrave's careful preparation and *verbatim* texts doubtless contri-

---

[1] See the examinations at the Bar of the House of Edward Cave, editor of *The Gentleman's Magazine*, and Thomas Astley, editor of *The London Magazine*, on 30 April 1747: *Lords Journals*, vol. 27, pp. 107–8.

buted to the gravity and caution for which he was known. At the same time, they suggest a lack of that spontaneity and extempore mastery of his subject which characterised the man of business and the regular parliamentary debater. These are not the speeches of an administrator; neither are they the speeches of a party loyalist. Waldegrave is more than formally apologetic in troubling their lordships; his constant themes are the unity of the House, the defence of its privileges and functions and the need scrupulously to establish the honourable nature of his motives and actions. 'I think myself obliged to trouble Your Lordships with a few Words, tho I never desire to take any thing to myself, or to enter into any debate, wherein I am not immediately concern'd' (51380 f. 124): such is a normal form of Waldegrave's reticence.

These speeches, though carefully drafted, are all undated. This edition supplies an attribution of date and subject, collates the available drafts of the same speech, and sets each document in its political context.

[1] The threatened impeachement of Sir Robert Walpole, 1742. Waldegrave MSS at Chewton House.

Sir Robert resigned on 2 February 1741/2. On 9 February Horace Walpole claimed that the Prince of Wales had first promised Thomas Secker, Bishop of Oxford, that the newly created Earl of Orford would not be persecuted, but that Prince Frederick would now insist on an impeachment. Horace Walpole commented:

As to an impeachment, I think they will not be so mad as to proceed to it; it is too solemn and too public to be attempted without any proof of crimes, of which he certainly is not guilty. For a bill of pains and penalties, they may if they will, I believe, pass it through the Commons, but will scarce get the assent of the King and Lords.[2]

Nevertheless, the preparations went ahead. On 18th Walpole wrote again:

During the recess they have employed Fazackerley[3] to draw up four impeachments; against Sir Robert, my uncle [Horatio Walpole], Mr Keene and Colonel Bladen, who was only commissioner for the tariff at Antwerp. One of the articles against Sir R, is, his having at this conjuncture trusted Lord Waldegrave as ambassador, who is so near a relation of the Pretender – but these impeachments are likely to grow obsolete MSS.[4]

This speech was presumably drafted when it seemed that a trial would take place. Only one page survives: it is not known whether Waldegrave

---

[2] Horace Walpole to Mann, 9 Feb. 1741/2: Walpole, *Letters*, vol. 17, p. 328.
[3] Nicholas Fazackerley (?1685–1767), MP 1732-*d*; Tory and lawyer.
[4] Horace Walpole to Mann, 18 Feb 1741/2: Walpole, *Letters* vol. 17, p. 335. No copy of the articles of impeachment has yet been located.

wrote more, or abandoned the draft when the prospect of an impeachment evaporated. This was not quite a foregone conclusion. On 23 March the opposition in the Commons narrowly passed a motion for a Committee of Inquiry into the ministry's conduct for the last ten years. Horace Walpole spoke in Parliament for the first time on the losing side in defence of his father; this may have induced Horace's friend, the young 2nd Earl Waldegrave, to a similar effort.

In the Commons, however, the Committee's investigations were soon thwarted by refusals to testify. To make its work feasible, an Indemnity Bill was passed by the lower House. On 20 May 1742 the Lords gave a first reading to 'An Act for indemnifying such Persons as shall, upon Examination, make Discoveries touching the Disposition of Public Money, or concerning the Disposition of Offices, or any Payments or Agreements in respect thereof, or concerning other Matters relating to the Conduct of *Robert* Earl of *Orford*'. The Bill was read a second time, and rejected by 109 votes to 57, on 25 May. Waldegrave was present on both days,[5] but no speech by him is recorded;[6] it is possible, though less likely, that this draft is of a speech delivered by him on one of those occasions.

The rejection of the Indemnity Bill rendered the work of the Committee of Inquiry virtually impossible; it produced no hard evidence against Orford. More significant still, the impregnable Court majority in the Lords meant that no trial would stand a chance in that House: the proposed impeachment was silently abandoned. For the young Waldegrave, however, it was an ominous warning: the age of ideology, persecution[7] and rebellion was not yet over. The issues which lay behind this speech were to haunt him as a latent threat for another decade.

My Lords

It is with some concern that I find my self obliged to trouble Your Lordships in the present Debate, but as several things have been said which carry with them the most severe sensure and the strongest reflections upon the Character of a Person for whom I may be allowed to have had the greatest Regard I think it incumbent on me not to leave those Reflections entirely unanswered.

What I have to say relates chiefly to the 14th Article of the Impeachment wherein my Lord O[rford] is imputed guilty of a high Crime and misdemeanour in having employ'd the E[arl] W[aldegrave] for several Years as his Majesty's Ambassador at the Court of France, the said E[arl] W[aldegrave] having formerly been a Roman Catholick, being nearly

---

[5] *Lords Journals*, vol. 26, pp. 125, 129–30.
[6] The debate is reported in *Parl. Hist.*, vol. 12, cols. 643–711.
[7] In 1756, the fall of Newcastle's ministry produced threats of an impeachment of Lord Anson: Walpole, *George II*, vol. 2, p. 189.

related to the Pretender,[8] and therefore reasonably to be supposed to be in the Pretender's Interest.

My Lord O[rford] would certainly have been guilty of a very grievous Offence in employing a person who deserved such a Character, Yet how much more grievous would be the Offence, how much more black would be the guilt of the Person so employed, If these Crimes were as clearly prooved as they are strongly asserted[?] Neither all the Tyes of Blood, nor the stronger Tyes of gratitude and Affection, nor the desire of supporting the reputation of one who can no longer speak for himself, Should ever induce me to say one word in his deffence, but so far are they from being clearly prooved that they have not even probability to support them.

I hope that what I have to say on this subject will not be thought entirely Foreign to the principal Question, since if I can clear my Father's Character from the asspertions that are here thrown upon him, of consequence I must at the same time clear the noble Lord under whose directions my Father was supposed to have acted.

[2] The King's visit to Hanover: spring of 1744 or 1745. Add MSS 51380 f. 115.

During the period when James, 2nd Earl Waldegrave held his title, George II spent the summer abroad six times: in 1743 (being present at the battle of Dettingen), 1745, 1748, 1750, 1752 and 1755. Earl Poulett's motion against the last journey was the occasion of Waldegrave's speech no. 8, below. The King's absences in Hanover in 1748, 1750 and 1752 were in times of international tranquillity: they are unlikely to have aroused alarm. This speech probably relates either to the actual visit of 1745, or to a planned visit in 1744 from which George II was dissuaded by his ministers.

In 1744 Parliament rose on 12 May and in 1745 on 2 May; in neither year was a motion against the King's departure actually made. Nor is it known which Duke contemplated a motion. It may however be significant that the active Jacobite Lord Charles Noel Somerset, MP 1731–45, had emerged as the effective leader of the Tories in 1744; he succeeded his elder brother as 4th Duke of Beaufort on 24 February 1745 and took his seat on 12 March.

Despite the disastrous defeat at Fontenoy on 30 April 1745, and the loss of Flanders which followed, George II left for Hanover immediately after Parliament rose; he remained there until Prince Charles Edward's initially successful rising compelled his return to London at the end of August.

Diplomatic circumstances suggest 1744 as the more likely date, however.

---

[8] James II's natural daughter by Arabella Churchill was Henrietta Fitzjames (c. 1667–1730); she married in 1683 Sir Henry Waldegrave, 4th Bt., created 1st Baron Waldegrave. Their son, James 1st Earl Waldegrave, was thus a nephew of the Stuart King James III, known to Hanoverians as the 'Old Pretender'.

The King's plans for a summer visit to his Electorate were causing concern by late January;[9] this concern soon greatly intensified. On 14 February 1744 the ministry learned through its intelligence sources of the impending French invasion attempt, aimed at a Stuart restoration; it reacted swiftly with military precautions. On 15th a message from the King was read to both Houses announcing the imminent danger, and a joint Address passed in reply the next day. Waldegrave was present both on 16 and 24 February when the Lords debated documents laid before them concerning the invasion. Although the French fleet was blown off station and the transports at Dunkirk badly damaged by the storms which began on that day, a French declaration of war against England followed on 20 March. It was not until 24 June that continual pressure from his ministers finally forced the King to abandon his plans to spend that summer in Hanover.[10]

My Lords

I feel a very particular Uneasiness in opposing the present Motion made by a noble Duke from whom I never can differ but with the greatest Concern.

I entirely agree that his Majesty's leaving this Country in the present Situation of Affairs would be highly dangerous.

At the same time I could wish that his Majesty's Stay amongst us should proceed from himself only.

Besides there is great Probability that the End proposed by the noble Duke, is already answered.

His Majesty must be inform'd of the Question that has been moved. He will also know that he who made the Motion is one who speaks the Sense of almost every wise and honest Man thro out the Kingdom.

We all know his Majesty's great Wisdom and Prudence, as well his constant Endeavours for the Honor, Happiness, and lasting Prosperity of this Country.

Therefore there is the greatest Reason to hope that unaddressed, unadvised, he will defer his Journey to a safer Opportunity.

Even allowing the Motion to be necessary, I do not think there is any necessity for the Address. And therefore am against addressing his Majesty on the present Occasion.

[3] The Heritable Jurisdictions Bill, February-March 1746/7: Add MSS 51380 f. 108.

Following the rebellion of 1745, the Whig regime in London moved swiftly to devise a programme of social engineering aimed at eliminating the

[9] Horace Walpole to Mann, 24 Jan 1744: Walpole, *Letters*, vol. 18, p. 381.
[10] Hardwicke to Newcastle, 24 June 1744: Yorke, *Hardwicke*, vol. 1, p. 347.

Highlands' ability to revolt.[11] An important component of this plan was the abolition of the hereditary legal jurisdictions still enjoyed by the clan chiefs. This authority would henceforth be exercised by the Sheriff Depute, who became the chief local judge in each Scottish county. Waldegrave was present on 17 February 1746/7 when Hardwicke introduced 'An Act for taking away and abolishing the Heretable Jurisdictions in that part of Great Britain called Scotland; and for restoring such jurisdictions to the Crown; and for making more effectual provision for the administration of justice throughout that part of the United Kingdom by the King's courts and judges there; and for rendering the Union more complete'.[12]

When a provision for financial compensation was added it became a Money Bill, and so had to originate in the Commons: a recast Bill was introduced there on 7 April, read a second time on 14 April, passed on 14 May[13] and returned to the Lords. There it was read for the first and second times on 15 and 20 May. Waldegrave was present when the Bill was committed after a long debate on 21 May by 79 votes to 16, and this speech probably relates to that day.[14] He attended again in committee on 26 and 27 May, but not subsequently during its passage.

The Bill became law as 20 George II, c. 43. Waldegrave had attended particularly in his speech to the Bill's provision, in clause 29, that the Sheriffs-Depute were to hold office during pleasure for the first seven years after the Act came into force, and only thereafter for life; he was concerned to defend the measure against objections drawn from the obvious analogy with Stuart claims against the judiciary. This seven-year term expired on 25 March 1755, but in the spring of that year the ministry brought in a Bill to repeal clause 29 in the 1747 Act,[15] later modified into a proposal for postponing life tenure for a final period of 15 years.[16] The Bill went to the Lords on 7 March 1755; Waldegrave was present for its second reading on 13th. There was no division and no record of what was said: it is possible that this speech relates to 13 March 1755; but 21 May 1747 seems the more likely date.

By his support for this measure, Waldegrave identified himself unequivocally with the Lord Chancellor, Hardwicke, who had drafted the Bill and piloted it through Parliament in the face of continuing opposition from

[11] For the consequences of this programme, see A.J. Youngson, *After the Forty-Five: The Economic Impact on the Scottish Highlands* (Edinburgh, 1973).
[12] For Hardwicke's speech, see *Parl. Hist.*, vol. 14, cols. 9–25.
[13] Horace Walpole wrote that the ministry had been alarmed at the prospect of losing this and a related Bill, and had 'whittled them down almost to nothing, in complaisance to the Duke of Argyle': Walpole to Mann, 10 April 1747: *Letters*, vol. 19, p. 386. For the Commons debates, see *Parl. Hist.*, vol. 14, cols. 27–51.
[14] Hardwicke's notes of the debate are printed in *Parl. Hist.*, vol. 14, cols. 51–6. Waldegrave is not mentioned as a speaker.
[15] Walpole, *George II*, vol. 2, pp. 37–40.   [16] *Ibid.*, pp. 44–6.

Tories, Jacobites, and Scots.[17] Waldegrave's talk of Revolution Principles echoes standard ministerial rhetoric.

My Lords

A Government like ours and indeed all limited Monarchies can only be founded on what we call Whig, or Revolution Principles. Every other Rule of Government is Absurdity and Nonsense. And as to the Bill now under Your Lordships Consideration. I am thoroughly convinced we all reason upon the same Principles, tho in some Respects our Conclusions are different.

I shall now trouble Your Lordships with some of my Reasons, and am most heartily for the Bill, as every Objection, every Difficulty which could possibly arise, seem to me to be entirely obviated by the Shape under which it now appears before us.

It is undoubtedly a right political Maxim in all free Governments, not to grant Powers to a great and good Prince, which tho safe in his hands, may in a future Reign, be prostituted to unjust or arbitrary Purposes.

According to which Principle, this Law is not made perpetual, and should it hereafter only be found unnecessary, which I hope will be the Case. It naturaly will expire in the Course of a few Years.

On the other hand, there are other Considerations, founded also on Revolution Principals, which deserve some Attention.

It is not the Power of the Crown only, but Power where ever it is lodged, may be abused. And that Government is certainly the best constituted, wherein not only the different Parts which compose the legislative Power, are mutual Checks on each other. But wherein every delegated Branch of the executive Power is under a proper Restraint.

I make no doubt but these Sherifs Depute are in general well qualified for the Execution of the Trust reposed in them. That they are Men of Probity. That they have a competent Knowledge of the Laws, and Customs of their Country. That they are firmly attach'd to his Majesty's Person and Government, and the Protestant Succession. Friends to Liberty and our excellent Constitution.

Yet at so great a Distance from the Center of Government, Mens private Characters, or political Principles cannot be so thoroughly known.[18]

[17] Yorke, *Hardwicke*, vol. 1, pp. 588–624. By contrast Frederick, Prince of Wales observed a studied neutrality; 'most of his servants have absented themselves whenever it came on': *ibid.*, p. 614.

[18] Waldegrave cannot have been unaware of the long-standing acute difficulty of governing Scotland through a local gentry elite whose loyalty could not be relied on. For a recent study which emphasises the extent of disaffection among JPs, see Elizabeth K. Carmichael, 'Jacobitism in the Scottish Commission of the Peace, 1707–1760', *Scottish Historical Review* 58 (1979), 58–69: 'Jacobitism was a pervasive force in the Scottish commissions of the peace and was to remain so, to a greater or lesser extent, until 1756'.

brought into Employments. Without any ill Design in those who recommend them. And we all know there may be very strong Reasons, which may render a Man very unfit to be trusted. And yet these Reasons may not admit of legal or Parliamentary Proof.

In which case it is certainly less dangerous that a discretionary Power should be lodged in the Crown, which if abused may be soon taken away. Than that any Person should continue in Employment, to the Danger of Government, the Delay of Justice, or the Oppression of his Fellow Subjects.

As to comparing these Sherifs Depute to our Judges here in England. There is certainly a very wide difference, both as to the Extent and Nature of their Jurisdiction. None are admitted into the High Offices[19] but Men whose characters and Principles are thoroughly known. And as to the illegal Practices on Judges in the Reigns of Charles ye 1st and James ye 2d when they held their Places during Pleasure. These are Considerations so totaly different, that they cannot admit even of the least Comparison.

Upon the whole it is my sincere Opinion, that the Power as it is now limited by this Bill, may be safely lodged in the Crown. And on the other hand, that fixing these Sherifs in their Places for Life, would be merely catching at the Shadow of Whig or Revolution Principles, but losing the Substance.

As to the Military Force in Scotland, it appears to me a Consideration of a quite different Nature. At present it can only act under the direction and in Support of the civil Power. And there is the greatest Reason to expect that it will dayly become less necessary.

[4]   The Buckingham Assizes Bill, March–April 1748: Add MSS 51380 f. 110.

In Buckinghamshire it had been the practice since 1720 to hold the winter assizes at Aylesbury, the summer assizes at Buckingham. 'After the 1747 election, when two of the Prince of Wales's supporters were returned unopposed [at Aylesbury] it was alleged by Richard Grenville that the Lord Chief Justice, Sir John Willes, had deliberately removed the summer assizes from Buckingham to Aylesbury, holding them there himself about the time of the election, in order to procure the support of a grateful electorate for his son, Edward Willes', who was duly elected. The borough of Aylesbury was under no consistent domination; Buckingham by contrast was a pocket borough, hitherto the centre of the Grenvilles'

---

[19] I.e. in England. Waldegrave argues that metropolitan ignorance of the allegiance of men at county level in Scotland justifies tenure there for a limited term only.

sphere of influence but now also coveted by the Prince of Wales and his election managers.[20]

The ambitious and disreputable Sir John Willes, though a protégé of Walpole, had attached himself to Prince Frederick after Sir Robert's fall and now aspired to be the Prince's future Lord Chancellor.[21] His electoral initiative was a challenge both to the local stronghold of a family connection, and to the Pelhamite ascendancy. The Grenvilles counter-attacked in force, securing the support of the ministry[22] for 'An Act for holding the Summer Assizes for the County of *Buckingham* at the County Town of *Buckingham*', introduced into the House of Commons on 12 February 1748 by 184 votes to 124, given a second reading on 19 February by 182 to 112, committed on 7 March by 150 to 103, and passed at its third reading on 15 March by 155 to 108.[23]

Horace Walpole observed that although the ministry would carry the Bill the both in the Commons and the Lords, 'it is by a far smaller majority than any they have had in this Parliament'.[24] The Bill was fought, as far as the ministry was concerned, as an issue of confidence and a decisive clash with the Leicester House opposition.[25] Henry Pelham was particularly bitter at Sir John Willes' desertion of the Pelhamite cause.[26] Yet exactly the same prize, local electoral influence, was at stake on both sides. It was not without reason that Sir William Stanhope, MP for Buckinghamshire and supporter of Prince Frederick, allegedly declared on 19 February: 'This Bill is the arrantest job that ever was brought to parliament . . . [the Grenvilles] have solicited the attendance of their friends, and of their friends' friends, with as much importunity, as if their power itself was tottering . . . ', and was called to order after his abuse of the Grenville family became extreme.[27]

Horace Walpole voted throughout against the Bill, from, as he recorded, his personal regard for Sir John Willes.[28] That he should attempt to speak

[20] Sedgwick, vol. 1, p. 197.
[21] Sedgwick, vol. 2, p. 540. Both Edward Willes and Sir John's other son, John Willes (MP for neighbouring Banbury 1746–54) voted with the Prince of Wales' party.
[22] See Lewis M. Wiggin, *The Faction of Cousins. A Political Account of the Grenvilles, 1733–1763* (New Haven, Conn., 1958), pp. 124–9.
[23] *Commons Journals*, vol. 25, pp. 512, 530, 534, 538, 561–3, 570.
[24] Walpole to Mann, 11 March 1748: Walpole, *Letters*, vol. 19, p. 467.
[25] For the vitriolic Commons' debates see *Parl. Hist.* vol. 14, cols. 202–246.
[26] Walpole to Mann, 11 March 1748, *loc. cit.*.
[27] *Parl. Hist.*, vol. 14, cols. 204–5. This version of his speech was written by Horace Walpole, and published on 3 March as *The Original Speech of Sir W--m St--pe*; how far it reflects Stanhope's actual words is not known. Cf. Walpole, *Letters*, vol. 13, p. 21.
[28] Willes was 'one of the principal friends of my father . . . stamped with his approbation in the last solemn act of his life, by having committed to his charge the care of a favourite child': Walpole's undelivered speech on the Bill, 6 April 1748, in *Letters*, vol. 26, pp. 25–8. Sir Robert at his death had entrusted to Willes the care of his illegitimate daughter, Lady Maria Walpole (c. 1725–1801; she married in 1746 Col. Charles Churchill).

in addition is a measure of his personal involvement. Although Horace Walpole sat in the Commons from 1741 to 1768, only six speeches by him are known, five of them in his first decade.[29] One was on 23 March 1742, the Commons' motion for a Committee of Inquiry into Sir Robert Walpole's conduct, which episode occasioned Waldegrave's first drafted speech, printed above. Another was on the Buckingham Assizes Bill. This Bill, too, called forth a speech from his friend. Waldegrave was present in the Lords for the key stages of the Buckingham Assizes Bill's passage: the first reading on 18 March 1748; the second reading on 23 March (passed by the uncomfortably narrow margin of 56 votes to 40); the reception of the report from Committee on 1 April; and the third reading on 4 April (passed by 54 votes to 29).[30] When the Bill was returned to the Commons, Horace Walpole made a last-ditch attempt on 6 April to put it off, but was prevented from delivering his prepared speech.[31]

Waldegrave's opposition to a ministerial measure was remarkable. He was not, so far as can be ascertained, seeking to ingratiate himself with Prince Frederick's Leicester House opposition; it seems likely that he allowed his friendship with Horace Walpole to override his allegiance to the ministry. It was not a wise move.

My Lords

I am against the Bill now under our Consideration, and find myself obliged to trouble Your Lordships with my Reasons, least my Opposition should be imputed to Motives very different from my way of thinking.

And I will begin by admitting every thing that can be said in defence of the Bill to be litteraly true.

First then as to the situation of Buckingham and Aylesbury with regard to the Convenience of the County, I will suppose the Difference not to be so great as what has been represented, yet still it must be allow'd there is some Difference and that Difference must be to the advantage of Aylesbury.

As to the Place where Assises have oftenest been held it is of little Consequence, suppose they had constantly been held at Buckingham and no where else, this must be done at the discretion and by the Appointment of the Judges and not by virtue of any Right inherent in the town of Buckingham, and the tranferring or taking away of that to which I have no right can be no injustice. That a Judge may make a partial use of this Power is what I readily agree too, but if this is thought sufficient reason for passing the Bill it must have equal weight in regard to every County in England,

[29] Walpole, *George II*, vol. 3, p. 177, Appendix 11.
[30] He was not present in Committee on 29 March, when in four divisions the ministry had majorities of 23, 14, 17 and 19. Sainty and Dewar, *Divisions*; *Lords Journals*, vol. 27, pp. 189, 192, 199, 203, 205.
[31] Printed in Walpole, *Letters*, vol. 26, pp. 25–8.

and should this bill once become a law I make no doubt but we shall have frequent applications of the same nature with at least as weighty reasons to support them.

I have also heard it insinuated, why should not this bill pass, it is a very harmless bill it is of very little consequence one way or the other. So far I will readily own that where the consequences are bad the less those consequences are, certainly the better, but that an extraordinary bill should pass meerly because it is of little consequence, is it consistent with Your Lordships' justice is it consistent with Your Lordships' Dignity.

These are reasons that to me appear unanswerable, these are reasons that make me now differ from some Lords for whose judgement I have the highest regard, and from whom I never can differ but with the greatest Concern.

[5]   The Regency Bill, May 1751: Add MSS 51380 f. 184

When Frederick, Prince of Wales died on 20 March 1751, his eldest son George was aged 12; the King was 65. Horace Walpole was at once moved to 'reflections on minorities, regencies, Jacobitism, opposition, factions':[32] the failure of the House of Hanover was, for Whigs, a terrifying thought. The alarming prospect of a minority spurred the ministry to swift action. On 27 April Waldegrave was present in the Lords to hear a message from George II requesting Parliament to make provision for a regency. Waldegrave, newly appointed Warden of the Stannaries, attended the House to see the resulting Bill through most of its stages: the 1st reading on 7 May; the Committee stage on 10th (the ministry winning the only two divisions of the session by 98 to 12 and 106 to 12); the 3rd reading on 13th; and again on 21 May when the Bill was returned from the Commons with certain amendments. It duly passed as 24 Geo. II, c. 24.

The Bill encountered difficulties. On 1 May, Horace Walpole added a postscript to a letter:

the bill was to have been brought into the House of Lords today, but Sherlock the Bishop of London, has raised difficulties against the limitation of the future regent's authority, which he asserts to be repugnant to the spirit of our constitution.[33] Lord Talbot had already determined to oppose it; and the Pitts and Lytteltons who are grown very mutinous on the Newcastle's not choosing Pitt for his colleague, have talked loudly against it without doors ... The Pelhams, taking advantage of this new partiality [of George II for the Dowager Princess of Wales], of the universal dread of the Duke [of Cumberland], and of the necessity of his being administrator of Hanover, prevailed to have the Princess regent, but with a council of nine of the chief great officers, to be continued in their posts till the majority, which is fixed for

[32] Walpole to Mann, 21 March 1751: Walpole, *Letters*, vol. 20, p. 231.
[33] Sherlock had some knowledge of the law relating to regencies, and had discussed it in defending Sir Robert Walpole in the debate of 13 February 1741: *Parl. Hist.*, vol. 11, col. 1212.

eighteen [i.e. on 4 June 1756]; nothing to be transacted without the assent of the greater number; and the Parliament that shall find itself existing at the king's death, to subsist till the minority ceases – such restrictions must be almost as unwelcome to the Princess, as the whole regulation is to the Duke. Judge of his resentment: he does not conceal it.[34]

Waldegrave's position evidently won the gratitude of the King without forfeiting the friendship of Cumberland; as a reward, George II included Waldegrave as one of the four members of the Regency Board within the personal gift of the King.[35]

My Lords

We certainly have not been quite regular in committing this Bill before his Majesty had given his Consent, and some Lords are of Opinion that the Bishop of London's Consent was also necessary. But be that as it will, his Majesty has been pleas'd to overlook the Omission, and most graciously has given his Consent. But the reverend Prelate has thought proper to give a Negative.

Now had his Majesty given his Negative also, I should have been heartily sorry for it, not as a well wisher to the Bill, about which I am very indifferent, but as wishing that the Royal Prerogative had not been exerted on such an Occasion.

I therefore am clear in my Opinion that the reverend Prelate a Man no less respe[c]table for his superior Sence and Judgment, than for his high dignity in the Church, could only mean to express his dislike to the Bill and had he been here in Person that he would have voted against it.

I therefore hope that this seeming Negative will now be overul'd, shoud some particular Parts of the Bill appear justly lyable to exception, Your Lordships will undoubtedly make proper Amendments should Your Lordships agree with the Reverend Prelate, should the whole appear fundamentaly wrong it will then be entirely rejected, for I most heartily wish that abstracted from every other Consideration that the Bill might stand or fall by its own merits.

[6] The Education of the Prince of Wales, 22 March 1753: Add MSS 51380 f. 129

Earl Harcourt resigned as Governor to the Prince of Wales on 5 December 1752. Waldegrave was the King's own choice as a successor, and it took George II's persuasion to induce him to accept. His caution was understandable. It was, on one hand, an offer almost impossible to refuse: it opened the possibility, later seized by Bute, of ingratiating himself with the

---

[34] Walpole to Mann, 22 April 1751, postscript of 1 May: Walpole, *Letters*, vol. 20, p. 244. For proceedings in the Committee on 10 May, see Dodington, *Diary*, 10 May 1751.
[35] See above, p. 50.

next sovereign. On the other hand, Harcourt had resigned on that most sensitive and potentially explosive of issues, Jacobitism. Ironically, the man chosen to succeed had himself an ideologically dubious family background. At any time, this might be drawn into the political arena; Waldegrave's marvellous opportunity might explode in his face. There were early signs that this might happen: his choice, recorded Walpole, was 'severely criticized: Lord Waldegrave's grandmother was daughter of King James; his family were all Papists, and his father had been but the the first convert'.[36] Waldegrave's speech confirms this criticism.

He must therefore have watched with growing alarm as the rumours current at the end of 1752 not only failed to subside, but snowballed. Horace Walpole, careless of Waldegrave's delicate position, wrote and distributed his anonymous memorial on the education of the Prince of Wales which placed the issue at the centre of political attention. From there it was taken up and exploited by the Duke of Bedford, then in opposition to the Pelhams.[37] After the Cabinet's investigation of the charges against Stone and Murray, Bedford brought the issue before the House of Lords on 22 March 1753. Waldegrave evidently prepared a long speech of self-exculpation (no. 6), and a short speech (no. 7) merely affirming his confidence in Andrew Stone.

Possibly Waldegrave waited to see how the debate would develop before deciding which speech to deliver. Would the spotlight fall on him? In the event, it did not.[38] To exculpate the King and blame his ministers, Bedford's tactic was to say that Harcourt 'has been as well replaced as possible; the choice was the more acceptable as it was His Majesty's own – *he* can do no wrong; he always acts right; when he acts himself'.[39] Waldegrave's long speech, no. 6, was therefore unnecessary, and it seems that it was never delivered. He wisely said as little as possible, and made his short speech instead.

My Lords

I do not rise up with an Intention of answering any thing that has been said by the Noble Duke for whom I have the greatest Honor, and whose approbation will ever give me the Highest Satisfaction. But as I have had my Share of that Calumny which has been so liberaly bestow'd on a late Occasion, I rise up to beg Your Lordships Indulgence if I deviate a little

---

[36] Walpole, *George II*, vol. 1, p. 200.   [37] *Ibid.*, pp. 204–11.
[38] For the debate, see Walpole, *George II*, vol. 1, pp. 212–23. Dodington thought it 'the worst judg'd, the worst executed, and the worst supported point that I ever saw, of so much expectation ... the whole was so ill conducted and supported, that I should be almost tempted to believe that the grounds which carried our conjectures almost into certainties, had no foundation at all': *Diary*, pp. 212–4.
[39] Walpole, *George II*, vol. 1, p. 216.

from the present Debate and trouble Your Lordships with a few Words on so tender and so disagreeable a Subject.

Soon after it had been his Majesty's Pleasure to appoint me Governor to his R H the Prince of Wales several of my Friends told me with some Concern[40] that the World talk'd very freely on my Subject. I thank'd them for their Information and ansered I knew very well that prating silly People must have Subject to talk upon, that I was very well persuaded none of them would venture to say any thing improper to my Face, and as for what was said in Whispers or in my Absence it should not give me the least uneasyness. They told me the Affair was more serious than I imagined, and that it was no Wonder half the Town should think me a Jacobite when they knew for certain I was a Papist. And as a Specimen of what was publickly said one of my Friends offer'd to give me an Account of a Conversation which pass'd in a Company where he was present. I promised my Friend I would not insist on being told the Names, and the Account he gave was as follows. Being in a Company where the Discourse turn'd on some late Events one of the Gentlemen express'd a very just Surprise that a Man educated a Papist by the Jesuites at St. Omers should be entrusted with the education of the Prince of Wales. To which my Friend answer'd, Sir I realy believe You must be under some Mistake for I have allways heard Lord Waldegrave was brought up either at Eton Westminster or some of our Schools here in England. Dont say so Sir replys a third Person he was brought up a Papist at St Omers and this I affirm on my own knowledge. My Friend who had only known me since I left School was at once struck Dumb and so their Conversation ended.

This being told me I thought it right to give some account of myself, accordingly I reply'd, that it was very true my Father had been brought up a Papist, but that it was no less certain that he renounced the Errors of Popery[41] when I was too Young to have received any Prejudices, or even to have the least Notion of the Principles of any Religion whatsoever. That soon after I was eight Years Old I was sent to Westminster School where my health did not permitt me to stay two Years, that on leaving Westminster I had a Tutor at home who was then in Orders, and is now Dean of Raphoe in Ireland.[42] From home I was sent to Eaton where I continued till I was seventeen. My Father who was then Ambassador in France thinking me of an Age to leave School I went directly to him at

---

[40] Deleted: 'that realy they never expected to have heard me abused, but that now they thought it necessary I should know'.
[41] Before 12 February 1721/2, when as James, 2nd Baron Waldegrave, he took the oaths and his seat in the House of Lords (his Earldom followed on 13 September 1729). His elder son, later the 2nd Earl, had been born on 4 March 1714/15.
[42] Rev. Antony Thompson (d. 9 October 1756), chaplain to 1st Earl Waldegrave; English *chargé d'affaires* in Paris 1740–44; Dean of Raphoe 1744–56.

Paris, and least I should forgett what little Learning I was then Master of I had a Minister of the Church of Geneva by way of Preceptor.

Having given this account of my Education I added that in case he mett with any honest well meaning Men who had been misinformed I should take it as a Favour if he would sett them Right, but as for his St Omers Friend and those who spoke like him from their own knowledge, I did not think proper to give them any other Answer than that they were Lyars and Scoundrels.

By these plain Facts Your Lordships will see I was not brought up a Papist I shall now beg leave to trespas a little longer on Your Lordships Patience that I may give a short Account of my Political Principles.

In the first Place I look upon the Nature of Jacobitism to have been entirely alter'd for a long time past. Several Years after the Revolution many Persons were still living who had been engaged in publick Affairs before ye year 88, several of these might think themselves bound by personal Obligations, some by private Friendship, some by Party Connections, and others by solemn Engagements, so that tho they had a bad Cause they might still act on Principles of Honour and Consience; But this Generation is now pass'd away, all those Tyes are now disolved, and I look upon a Jacobite of the present Age as the most despicable Being that crawls on the Face of the Earth.

At that glorious Period when Resistance was call'd in to the defence of Liberty our Constitution was settled on the most solid and sure Foundation. The Prerogative of the Crown that discretionary Power so often misused yet so necessary on some Occasions was then confined within its proper Lymits, every thing was then ascertain'd, what ever was formerly doubtful is now made clear, and the Rights of a free People are no longer Problematical.

Yet to this Constitution and to these Principles have I been call'd an Enemy, an Enemy also have I been call'd to the established Religion of my Country, the only clear System of true Piety, good Sence, and Sound Morality. I have even been represented as a Traytor to the best of Masters and the best of Kings, whose repeated Favours never gave me an Opportunity of asking. What return am I to make to such a Master, for such Obligations, for such Confidence reposed in me[?]

I am to poison the Mind of [a] Young Prince, the Heir to his Crown and Dignity, with those mon[s]trous Notions of Popery: Bigotry and Superstition, Persecution and Cruelty. I am to represent in the most odious Colours those very Principles which saved this Country from Destruction, brought about the happy Revolution, and fixed the Succession of the Crown on the House of Hanover. I am to impose on his Understanding by representing a seperate or even opposite Interest between a King and his

Subjects, and that there are Methods by which a Prince may make himself both great and Happy without either the Confidence or Love of his People. In a Word I am to add Folly to Wickedness and Ingratitude to Treason.

If all this Calumny has not been directly let loose against me it has at least been imply'd in what has been Whisper'd about on my Subject.

Whet[h]er any of these Slanderers will ever venture too speak out, I am entirely ignorant, In the mean Time I here bid defiance to Envy and Malice with even Falsehood to assist them.

But should they prevail, and that a Spirit should at last be rais'd against me, I am so concious of my own Integrity, that as far as it relates to myself only, I would give up every thing without the least Concern. I never had that callous Temper which is insensible of publick Reproach. My Ambition shall never interfere with the publick Tranqu[i]llity.

Yet my Lords I ever had Ambition and still I feel it, the Object of which has ever been to gain the good Will and Confidence of those who know me, and the general Character in the World of a Man of Honour. I hope it will not be thought Vanity if in both these Points I flatter myself I have mett with some Success. And as for those who may hereafter attempt to rob me of them, they shall find the undertaking neither free from Difficulty nor free from Danger.[43]

[7] Waldegrave's speech as delivered on 22 March 1753: Add MSS 51380 f. 111.

Horace Walpole's account of what Waldegrave said in the debate[44] tallies closely with the Earl's own draft. It may be significant that in a debate in which both Andrew Stone's and William Murray's principles were called in question, Waldegrave commended Stone and said nothing of Murray.

The extent of Waldegrave's knowledge of Murray's political predilections is not elsewhere made clear. It may, however, have begun at an early date: William Murray had been educated at Westminster from 1718 to 1723, which school Waldegrave, on his own evidence, had also attended in c. 1722–4. Murray's father and elder brother had been arrested on suspicion of treason after the Fifteen; another brother, James Murray, was in the service of the Stuart King James III. The Waldegrave family's contacts in Jacobite circles must have impressed these facts on the 2nd Earl; he may even have heard some rumour of the written profession of alle-

---

[43] Waldegrave implies that he would challenge to a duel anyone who questioned his loyalty to the House of Hanover.
[44] Walpole, *George II*, vol. 1, pp. 220–1. Hardwicke's account of the debate (Add MSS 35877 ff. 104–9) fails to mention Waldegrave; but he is listed as a speaker in Newcastle's fuller notes, Add MSS 32995 ff. 6–13.

giance to James III which William Murray had made, while an Oxford undergraduate, in August 1725.[45] Waldegrave's silence was prudent.

My Lords

I do not rise up to answer any thing that has been said in the present Debate, but as I find it is expected I should speak my Mind on this important Occasion.

I declare to Your Lordships in the most solemn Manner that I look upon Mr Stone as an Able Zealous and Faithfull Servant to the best of Masters and the best of Kings.

I am also thoroughly convinced of his firm Attachment to those Principles which saved this Country from Destruction at that glorious Period, when Resistance was call'd in to the Defence of Liberty, when the Prerogative of the Crown that Discretionary Power which had been so often misused, was confin'd within its proper Lymits; and when our Princes were taught the only safe Road to Prosperity and Greatness by gaining the Affection and Confidence of their People.

These I am persuaded are the Principles of the Gentleman who has been the chief Subject of the present Debate, and it is by such Principles only he can acquire the Esteem and Confidence of a Young Prince of whom I can say with great Satisfaction and without the least Flattery, that he has an uncommon Goodness of Heart, an Understanding far above his Years, with the most steady Adhere[nce] to Sincerity Honour and Justice.[46]

I shall only add that I never will act in Conjunction with any Man of whom I have not as good Oppinion. And that I have hitherto acted in Conjunction with Mr Stone because I think him a Man of Sense a Man of Integrity and a Man of Honour.

[8] The Lords' Address in reply to the King's Speech, 14 November 1754: Add MSS 51380 f. 112.

After the general election in the spring and a token session from 31 May to 5 June, Parliament met again on 14 November.[47] Newcastle was always anxious to secure a show of strength and unanimity at the outset, and that Waldegrave was invited to move the Address in reply to the King's Speech[48] was a mark both of Newcastle's confidence and desire to involve

[45] Sedgwick, vol. 2, pp. 285–6.
[46] These remarks may be contrasted with Waldegrave's disparaging portrait, after he had ceased to be the Prince of Wales' Governor.
[47] For the Commons' debate see Walpole, *George II*, vol. 2, pp. 21–2; *Parl. Hist.*, vol. 15, cols. 333–73.
[48] For the King's Speech and the Lords' Address, see *Parl. Hist.*, vol. 15, cols. 330–2; *Lords Journals*, vol. 28, pp. 282–4.

him in public affairs. This and the three succeeding parliamentary sessions indeed showed a steadily improving record of attendance on Waldegrave's part.

My Lords

Your Lordships have heard his Majesty's Speech from the Throne, relating to the present situation of our Affairs, which are of a very nice and of a very delicate Nature, and which undoubtedly deserve our most serious Attention.

I will not take up Your Lordships time by entering into every particular. But the present amicable Disposition of the Court of Spain is certainly an Event of very great Consequence. It is our mutual Interest that we should continue in Friendship, and there is very great Reason to hope that by his Majesty's wisdom and Prudence we shall be still more firmly united. I shall now proceed to a less pleasing Subject, the present State of our Affairs in North America.

But in the first Place I will observe, that considering our Situation in Europe, America, and the East Indies, every where Neighbors to the French; considering we are Rivals in Trade, and the great superiority of our Maritime Force. It is almost impossible but Disputes and Jealousies must frequently arise, which may sometimes extend themselves even to Acts of open Hostility.

At the same time, I will consider them as Rivals, not as Enemys. I esteem them as a brave, a respectable Nation. And I heartily wish they knew the real Sentiments of almost every reasonable Man in this Country.

Far be it from us to insult them, we desire to continue in Friendship, our affairs require Peace, we know it to be our own Interest, and we think it is theirs.

But be that as it will, Englishmen can never want Spirit to defend their just their undoubted Rights, and whatever may be the event we will maintain them.

The great Consequence of our Possessions in America, how much they contribute to the Strength, as well as to the Riches of this Country; is a Truth which speaks itself and reqires no Argument to support it.

Neither is it less evident, that were we tamely to suffer every Injury which might be offer'd us, we should be hunted from Settlement to Settlement, from Province to Province. Even those who could defend themselves would shake of[f] their Mother Country, when she was no longer in a Condition to give them Protection, and in the Course, of a few Years, all might possibly be lost.

But this can never be our Case, his Majesty is wise, magnanimous, and loves his People. He will avoid all unnecessary Difficulties, he will lead us into no unnecessary Danger. But whatever is just and reasonable, he will not fear to execute.

In the mean time it would be venturing beyond my Depth, should I presume to carry my Conjectures further on this important Occasion. Besides the Conduct of great and National Affairs can never depend on general Rules only. And they alone shew themselves wise, steady, and consistent; whose Sagacity can discover the various Changes as they arise, and without varying their Object, can accomodate their Measures to the flux Condition of human Affairs.

If any particular Occasion, can render every Circumstance of our Conduct of still greater Importance. It must be the Opening of a new Parliament, and in some Measure of a new Administration. And here I cannot but lament a real national Loss. The Death of a Man who by his Abilities, Integrity, and long Experience in great and important Affairs, had acquired the Esteem and Confidence, both of his King and Country. A faithful Servant to his Prince; a frugal Servant to the Public. Amiable in his private as well as in his public Capacity, a wise, an able, an honest Minister.[49]

This may be said of the Dead, even without the Suspicion of Flattery. As for living Ministers, their Actions only ought to speak for them.

However that which I really think I will not fear to express, and it is my sincere Opinion, that his Majesty's Measures which are ever directed to the Security, Honor, and lasting Prosperity of this Country, will be honestly and ably executed.

As I have nothing to propose but general Expressions of Duty and Confidence, and of Zeal for his Majesty's Service, I will not trouble Your Lordships with any further Apology for the Motion I am going to make, which is as follows.

[It may not be coincidence that Waldegrave found it appropriate to include in the Address the following ardently Hanoverian passage:]

Permit us, Sir, to take this Opportunity to renew the most solemn Assurances of our inviolable Fidelity and Affection to Your Sacred Person and Government. In this, our Duty and our Interest unite, and are inseparable. Our Resolution is fixed and unalterable, to strengthen Your Majesty's Hands, for preserving the Peace, supporting the Honour of your Crown, and maintaining the Rights and Possessions of Your Kingdoms against any Encroachments. The Maxim graciously laid down by Your Majesty, 'that a mutual Confidence between You and Your Parliament is the surest Pledge of the Happiness both of King and People', is highly worthy a *British* monarch: And it shall be our zealous Endeavour, to demonstrate to the World the Stability of that Confidence; and, under the Protection of the Divine Providence, to transmit to our Posterity the Blessings of Your Majesty's Reign in the Perpetuity of the Protestant Succession in Your Royal House.

[49] Henry Pelham, First Lord of the Treasury since 1743, died unexpectedly on 6 March 1754.

[9] Earl Poulett's protest against George II's visit to Hanover, 24 April 1755: Add MSS 51380 f. 114.

Waldegrave's defence of the King's intention to visit Hanover in the spring of 1744 or 1745 was the subject of [2] above. George II's practice was to visit his electorate every second year. In 1755,

> It was the year in turn for the King to go to Hanover. The French armaments, the defenceless state of the kingdom, the doubtful faith of the King of Prussia, and above all, the age of the King, and the youth of his heir at so critical a conjuncture, everything pleaded against so rash a journey. But as His Majesty was never despotic but in the single point of leaving his kingdom, no arguments or representations had any weight with him. When all had failed, so ridiculous a step was taken to dissuade him, that it almost grew a serious measure to advise his going. Earl Poulett notified an intention of moving the House of Lords to address against the Hanoverian journey. However, as the motion would not be merely ridiculous, but offensive too, Mr Fox dissuaded him from it. He was convinced; and though he had been disgraced as much as he could be, he took a panic, and entreated Mr Fox and Lady Yarmouth to make apologies for him to the King. Before they were well delivered, he relapsed, and assembled the Lords, and then had not resolution enough to utter his motion. This scene was repeated two or three times: at last on the 24th [April] he vented his speech, extremely modified, though he had repeated it so often in private companies, that half the House could have told him how short it fell of what he had intended.[50] Lord Chesterfield, not famous heretofore for tenderness to Hanover, nor called on now by any obligations to undertake the office of the ministers, represented the impropriety of the motion, and moved to adjourn. Lord Poulett cried, 'My lords, and what is to become of my motion?' The House burst into a laughter, and adjourned, after he had divided it singly.[51]

My Lords

I shall trouble Your Lordships only with a very few Words, and will not consider the Address proposed by the Noble Earl as the highest Indecency offer'd to a great and good King. Which I am persuaded his Lordship cannot mean.

Neither will I presume to guess what are, or are not, his Lordship's Reasons. Because the same Things may appear to different Persons in a very different Light, and it seems to me almost impossible that any national Benefit can any ways be expected from a Motion of this Nature.

Should his Majesty think proper to defer his Journey till our Affairs are in a more settled State. It is undoubtedly our Interest, it is for our Honor as well as the King's, that his Stay amongst us should proceed from himself only.

[50] He also published it, as *Sibylline Leaves, or Anonymous Papers: containing A Letter to the Lord Mayor of London: With a View of inducing that great Metropolis to take the lead in addressing his Majesty for his most gracious and auspicious Residence in these Kingdoms ... together with An Introductory Speech to the Motion* (London: T. Cooper, 1755).
[51] Walpole, *George II*, vol. 2, p. 48.

If on the other hand, his Majesty for Reasons with which we are not acquainted, and of which he only must be the proper Judge, should find it necessary to visit his German Dominions. His Journey being undertaken contrary to an Address of the great Council of the Nation, must render his absence still more dangerous.

Upon the whole tho I am not always for taking things merely upon Trust. Yet in the present Case, where tho we may advise; we certainly have no Right to Dictate. I would submit every thing to that Wisdom, Justice, and paternal Care, and Affection, which we have so long and so often experienced.

[10]   The Education of the Prince of Wales, n.d. [but before June 1756]: Add MSS 51380 f. 126.

After the crisis of late 1752-early 1753 over the alleged Jacobite influences in the household of the Prince of Wales (see speech no. 6 above), Waldegrave's position never settled down to one of trust and confidence. Within the small circle of Leicester House, his own standing with Prince George and Princess Augusta went from uneasy to difficult; the stock of the Earl of Bute steadily rose, and forced Waldegrave's resignation in October 1756. In the wider political world, it seems that Waldegrave could never rest easy that the crisis of 1752-3 would not erupt once more, this time bringing his own political principles and background under critical scrutiny. It seems that Waldegrave kept a speech of self-justification in draft form, ready for just such an emergency. It seems, too, that he updated it on at least one occasion. The version printed here, beginning in Add MSS 51380 f. 126, is dated by the phrase in the second paragraph – 'the experience of more than two years'. The later version, *ibid.* f. 124, reads 'more than three years'. Waldegrave's appointment in December 1752 relates f. 126 to the parliamentary session of 1754–5, f. 124 to that of 1755–6.

Evidence has not yet emerged to suggest that such a speech was delivered in either session. Waldegrave's anxiety, however justified formerly, was now overtaken by events. It was not because of his rival's ideological antecedents that Bute supplanted Waldegrave at Leicester House.

The draft speech is printed here from the earlier version, f. 126; it is copied almost exactly in the later version, f. 124. Significant variations are noted.

My Lords

I think myself obliged to trouble Your Lordships with a few Words, tho I never desire to take any thing to myself, or to enter into any Debate wherein I am not immediately concern'd.

When I first enter'd into my present Employment, I certainly had a very good Opinion of those Gentlemen who were engaged with me in the Education of the Prince of Wales, and I can now affirm without the least Partiality or Prejudice in favor of any Man, that after the Experience of more than two[52] Years, I have not once perceived even the slightest Reason to change my Mind, their Conduct having ever appeared to me clear and uniform.

I must now mention some things which relate chiefly to myself, tho it realy is a Subject I should always choose to avoid.

And in the first Place[53] I believe it is known by many of Your Lordships that my being appointed Governor to the Prince of Wales, was entirely his Majesty's own Act.

If I may presume to guess at his Majesty's Reasons for placing me in so high and so honorable a Situation, it was probably owing to the good Opinion he was pleased to have of me, as One who he could depend upon. And being convinced I should do my Duty like an honest Man, was perhaps inclined to think much better of my Abilities, than what they realy deserve.

But be that as it will, it certainly never was intended to make use of me merely as a Cypher, that I should have nothing to do but to follow the Princes to Court, or some times to the riding house, to receive my Sallary, and quietly to lend my Name whenever it should be thought necessary by wiser Men, who were to have all the Influence and all the Authority.

This I say never could be intended, and I flatter myself nobody can think me mean enough to have accepted of any Employment on such Terms.

But perhaps it may be thought that tho it might be his Majesty's Intention that under him I should have the chief Authority. I either may have been deceived, or that being naturaly indolent, meeting with Difficulties, and being desirous to keep things as quiet as possible, I may have thought it best to shut my Eyes, leaving others at full liberty to act just as they should think proper.

But realy, my Lords, were I capable of acting in so pityful a Manner, were I to excuse myself by saying, I mean no kind of Harm, I am very much concerned any thing should be wrong, But here are a Set of artful cunning Men, connected with others far too able for me to contend with. Whatever Faults are committed it is they who are answerable.

Were I, my Lords reduced so low that this should be the only means by which I could defend myself, what a despicable Figure should I make.

But that which must be the highest aggravation of so great a Breach of Trust, is the natural Disposition of the Prince of Wales, who added to every

---

[52] f. 124: 'three'. [53] The remainder of the sentence omitted in f. 124.

good Quality of the Heart, has an understanding capable of great Improvement, wanting neither Quickness nor Solidity.[54]

To mislead such a Prince by Flattery, or[55] by making him an early Dupe, to the factious and self interested Views, of those who are trusted with his Education, would be so highly criminal as to amount even to Treason itself.[56]

On the contrary, Truth express'd in the strongest Terms, should be set before him in the clearest Light.

He should be informed that tho he is naturaly posses'd of those Qualities, which are the Foundation of every thing which is good. Yet these Qualities alone are not sufficient. That he must know those things which are right before he can practice them, and that Knowlege does not come by Inspiration, but can only be acquired by Application, Observation, and Experience.

A Prince who is one Day to govern this Country should have this Principle strongly fixed in his Mind, That the good of the People is the great End of all Government. And that he is to govern by Laws, by which he is equaly bound with the meanest of his Subjects.

He should have a clear and extensive Knowlege of our happy Constitution.

What is the Duty of a Prince, what is the extent of his Power in his Legislative Capacity, may be known without much Difficulty.

As to flattering Princes with Arbitrary or unconstitutional Notions of Government. Thank God, we live in a Time when men must be Idiots as well as Traytors who can preach such Doctrine.

At the glorious Revolution we were not only preserved from the immediate Dangers of Popery and Arbitrary Power, but the Bounds of Prerogative and Liberty were then fully ascertain'd. Points formerly doubtful and which force alone could decide, are now made clear, and the Rights of a free People are no longer Problematical.

A Government like ours and indeed all limited Monarchies can only be founded on what we call Whig or Revolution Principles, every other Rule of Government is absurdity and Nonsense.

For as to those Gentlemen who distinguish themselves by the Name of Tories I will speak my Mind very freely. I am persuaded there are some still remaining who mean Jacobitisme, there are others who mean nothing more than merely Opposition to the Administration. And there are others who are contented to follow the Cry, with hardly any Meaning at all.[57]

But to have done with this Subject. [f. 124 concludes:] I am fully

[54] Waldegrave's good opinion of his royal pupil in 1753 (speech no. 7) is still repeated as late as the parliamentary session of 1755–6.
[55] f. 124 omits 'by Flattery, or'.   [56] f. 124 omits from here until 'As to flattering Princes'.
[57] f. 124 omits this paragraph. Possibly Waldegrave recognised, by the session of 1755–6, that Jacobitism was fast fading as a preoccupation of politicians.

convinced that it is the most hearty Wish of every honest Man in this Country, that his Majesty's Life may be prolong'd many Years, and that the Prince of Wales, may never be a very Young King.

I hope that long before that Day shall come when he is to reign over us, that he will be capable of judgeing, and of acting for himself, and that I shall have been long discharged from my present Employment.

But be that as it will as long as I am employ'd, I will speak both concerning Measures, and Men, with that Impartiality and Freedom which becomes my Situation.

Whatever he shall hear from me, I neither will be affraid, nor ashamed to avow.

[11] The Education of the Prince of Wales, n.d. [but before June 1756]: Add MSS 51380 f. 120.
Waldegrave is obliged to argue both for the perfection of Anglicanism on the one hand, and on the other for toleration of Protestant Dissenters and Roman Catholics. The occasion of this speech is unknown; it presumably relates to [10] above.

Religion is another Article concerning which it is highly necessary that Princes should have right and proper Notions.

Besides the Respect which is due from every Man to the Religion of his Country. I am clearly of Opinion that the Church of England as by Law established is the most perfect System of Religion that ever existed.

At the same time it is a Subject concerning which Men always have differ'd, and ever will. Nor have I the least Right to think ill of any Man, merely because his Opinion does not in every Respect agree with mine.

As for the Protestant Dissenters they differ from us only in some of the Forms, not in the Substance of Religion. I look on them as Men who have very right Notions of civil and religious Liberty, as firmly attached to his Majesty's Person and Government, and as excellent Members of the Community.

I think them entitled to every Advantage of Society in the fullest Extent, except Power. And I except Power on a political not a religious Principle. For religious Disputes are of all others the most violent, the most destructive of public Tranquillity.

Therefore it is a Maxim wisely adhered to in most considerable States, that whatever is the prevailing Religion, there the sole Power ought to reside.[58]

This Nation also abounds with a Multitude of different sects, many of

---

[58] Waldegrave here echoes standard Whig doctrine, as expressed, for example, in William Warburton, *The Alliance Between Church and State: or, The Necessity and Equity of an Established Religion and a Test Law Demonstrated* (London, 1736).

whom are excellent Subjects and very justly deserve that Toleration which the Law alows them. For in a Country of Liberty every Man has a Right to judge for himself, and to make a free Use of that Reason which God has given him.

But without examining any other Religion I shall only trouble Your Lordships with a few Words concerning Popery.

When I consider the Roman Catholicks in a religious Light only, I am enclined to abandon them to that Contempt which their Bigotry and Superstition so highly deserve, which realy appear to me to be a disgrace to human Understanding.

But their political Principles may possibly deserve our very serious Attention. For how can those Men have any Notion of civil Liberty who dare not so much as think, but as their Priests direct them. I will add that as long as the most powerful Princes of the Continent profess this Religion, and as long as there is a popish Pretender to his Majesty's Crown and Dignity, we cannot be too much on our Guard.

Should they at any time presume to act on factious and seditious Principles, I am for treating them with the utmost Severity.

But as long as they continue quiet and give no Disturbance I am an Enemy to all Persecution, I would not drive the[m] to Despair.

On the contrary, to get the better of Prejudice must be the Work of Time, and I am persuaded that a proper Use of Mildness, Lenity, Resolution, and good Sence, will at length prevail over them.

Another Consideration of very great Importance, is the state of our National Debt. The heavy Taxes which are the Consequences of this Debt, and those prudent Measures of Goverment, with that strict national Oeconomy which must be our only Remedy.

A Country and a Government like ours has so many and so great Resourses, that we may bear a great deal and still be in a florishing Condition. Yet as long as this Evil does subsist we can never expect fully to exert our proper Strength.

Therefore till the Burden is removed it will remain a Chek to our Trade, will lye still heavyer on the Landed Interest. Must lessen our credit and Influence abroad. And will be a Cause of Discontent if not of Disafection at home.

I shall just say one Word concerning Coruption. And it is is undoubtedly true that when this Evil has once raised itself to a very great height, if it be not soon destroy'd, it must end in the Destruction of all free Government.

His Majesty is just, wise, and loves his People, I am convinced that his Measures will never require it. And I heartily wish that the Depravity of the Times may never make it necessary.

The last Article I shall mention as worthy the Attention of a Prince, is the Knowlege of Men. A Knowlege not so difficult to be attain'd as some perhaps may imagine.

The general Opinion of Mankind seldom errs, and those who have never had an Opportunity of shewing their Abilities in a public Station, may have deserved the Esteem of the World, and may have shewn their Capacity for Business, by their Conduct in private Life.

As for those who have long been employ'd in great Offices, of the highest Trust and Confidence. Their Talents, their Characters must be thoroughly understood and their Actions only ought to speak for them.

My Lords, I am fully convinced that it is the most hearty Wish of every honest Man in this Country, that his Majesty's Life may be prolong'd many Years, and that the Prince of Wales may never be a very Young King.

I hope that long before that day shall come when he is to reign over us, that he will be capable of judging and of acting for himself, and that I shall have been long discharged from my present Employment.

But, be that as it will, as long as I am employ'd I will speak my Mind both concerning Measures and Men, with that Impartiality and Freedom which becomes my Situation. Whatever he shall hear from me, I will neither be affraid nor ashamed to avow.

For which Reasons their political Conduct must deserve our most serious Attention; at the same time I can no more be angry with a Man for believing in Purgatory, Transubstantiation or such like Absurdities, than for believing in Gosts Witches or any Miracles whatsoever, except such as are recorded in the Old or New Testament.

[12] The Russian and Hesse Cassel Treaties, 10 December 1755: Add MSS 51380 f. 139. Drafts: ff. 132, 135.

For the terms and significance of the treaties, see pp. 64–72 and 166 above. The Russian and Hesse Cassel treaties were laid before both Houses on 10 December 1755: Waldegrave attended and witnessed a motion of censure moved by Earl Temple but rejected by 85 votes to 12. Horace Walpole, who noted the presence of the Prince of Wales 'taking notes', did not include Waldegrave in his list of speakers.[59] If he did not speak on this occasion, it is understandable that he should have used some of the text again for a speech (no. 19 below) in December 1756; but the three extant drafts show the care of Waldegrave's preparation for a major set-piece debate, and suggest that his participation is likely.

---

[59] Sainty and Dewar, *Divisions*; *Lords Journals*, vol. 28, p. 443; Walpole, *George II*, vol. 2, pp. 94–5. For the Lords debate, see *Parl. Hist.*, vol. 15, cols. 616–60, printing Hardwicke's list of speakers; again, Waldegrave is not mentioned.

My Lords

As the Treatys under your Lordships Consideratiion have my very sincere Approbation I shall beg leave to trouble Your Lordships with a few Words. Both to declare the Reasons why I approve, and how far my Approbation extends.

That the Strength and Security of this Country is owing to our Situation to our being divided from the Continent is a self evident truth which admits of no contradiction.

There is also another political truth which very few will deny, if not universaly assented too. That tho from our Situation as an Island we have the greatest Advantages we are still so far connected with the Continent, that in all material Transactions we must at least be careful Observers and on some Occasions must be under the necessity of taking a Part.

If this be allow'd other Questions must naturaly arise far more difficult to determine, when and how far Alliances on the Continent or what are commonly [called] Continent Measures are repugnant to, or consistent with the true English Interest, what ought to be the principal Object of all our Alliances, and what are the advantages we can reasonably expect to derive from them.

As a Maritime Power, or a trading Nation we must have treaties of Commerce which will be productive of other treaties. We must have Allies who will frequently avail themselves of our Protection and other good Offices, the only tenure on which we can expect to hold them. In which complicated System of Alliances, Negotiations, Guarantees, and the like; how difficult it must be to discover that almost imperceptible Point, where our true Interest centers.

It may be said let us assist our friends in such manner only as to enable them to act for themselves, still taking Part as Allies not as Principals. Still remembering that tho in some Measure we share the Danger, yet, that Danger which is immediate to them is remote to us. Still considering what we are in a condition to undertake, as well as what we could wish to undertake, never giving hopes of doing more than that which we are able to perform. But these Rules are only general, and even the best general Rules will not always suit particular Cases.

As to the other Question what services what Assistance we are to expect in return, tho it be undoubtedly true that political Friendship can only be founded on mutual Interest. Yet mutual Interest does not always imply equal Advantages. From many of our allies we can only expect certain Advantages in Trade. From others perhaps the best we can hope is that they should do us no harm. Some may be useful on particular occasions, and may be inclin'd to do still greater Services, but want the Means, whilst there are very few indeed on whose active immediate and effectual Assistance we can at all times depend.

However far be it from me to draw any Conclusion, because Allies may have a separate Interest, because they may have been ungrateful, or are not always to be depended on, that therefore Alliances give no additional Strength, or that we are on no occasion to avail ourselves of any foreign Assistance. I only mean that even the wisest Measures may be extended to[o] far, and if Alliances on the continent have ever engaged us in a more extensive Plan of Operation than is consistent with the true Interest of this Country, that it may be better on some Occasions to depend chiefly on our own Strength, than to be tyed down to all the Consequences, and bear the unequal Burden of reciprocal Engagements.[60]

Having troubled Your Lordships so far concerning our own Affairs relative to the Continent in general, another consideration will arise of a very particular and of a very delicate nature in relation to his Majesty's German Dominions. That those Dominions may in a short time be exposed to very great Danger is a truth which cannot be deny'd, and were we to leave them without any Assistance, should they now be attack'd on account of a Quarrel entirely English, would it be consistent with Honor or Justice, with that which we owe to a great and good King, or indeed with what we owe to ourselves.

At the same time no country can effectually provide for others, that does not first take Care of itself. And there is a wide Difference between entering *totis Viribus* into all the destructive extravagance of a continent War, or giving such assistance as may enable them to defend themselves, which comparatively speaking, may be done at a small Expense.

Espetialy if we consider the treaties now before us what I really think they are meant, a general Measure of Peace, not of War, and that it is highly probable that by far the heavier Part of the Expense may never be incurr'd.

This Consideration will have still greater Weight, as the same force which gives Security to his Majesty's electoral Dominions, must greatly contribute to the general Tranquillity of all Europe. Nor have I the least Apprehension of such Defensive Measures giving Umbrage or Provocation to any power whatsoever. An army of 60,000 Russians seeming much more likely to appease than to provoke. For I have ever observ'd that nothing

---

[60] This weakens the sense of some of the drafts, e.g. f. 135: 'Is it not better to depend singly on our own strength, and when we find it necessary to support our Allies, to assist them *Gratis*, to assist them generously without any Obligation whatsoever, Than to be tyed down to all the Consequences, and to bear the unequal Load of reciprocal Engagements ... God forbid, that the Preservation or Safety of this Country should depend on any Alliances, or on the Friendship of any foreign Power whatsoever.'

gives greater Provocation to an ambitious Prince than a weak Neighbor who cannot defend himself.

As to the exact Proportion in which we ought to take Part I own myself at a loss. I do not find myself a competent Judge, and consequently must rely upon those of whom in general I have the best Opinion, and who from their Station, Experience, and Knowledge of Affairs seem most capable of forming a right Judgement. Hitherto it is my sincere Opinion we have not exceeded our proper Limits. But should I hereafter be convinced that we change our System, that we engage beyond our Ability, beyond that to which we are bound both in Honor and Justice, I would oppose such measures without the least Regard either from whom I differ or who I offend. My Lords those who are the most apt to be elated by grownless hopes, are commonly most lyable to sink under unreasonable fears, and was our present Condition infinitely more dangerous than what it really is, I never would be one of those who despair of the commonwealth. And tho I cannot but lament the near Prospect of a War with the most powerful Nation in Europe labouring under an immense national Debt. Peace and War being hardly more opposite to each other than war and Oeconomy. Yet we have this Comfort that whatever we spend in strengthening ourselves at home, whatever we spend in naval Preparations, circulates amongst ourselves. What ever we spend in North America must in the End return back to the Mother Country with double Interest. And whatever we spend in Foreign Subsidies will bear but a very small Proportion to our other Expenses. We have also this additional Comfort that the present Hostilities were neither lightly nor inconsiderately undertaken. Even the Name of peace was only to be obtain'd by tamely suffering the most unprovok'd Insults. By departing from our just our undoubted Rights, and Possessions such Terms as Englishmen could never submit to. And there is still Reason to hope that the force of this Country being vigorously directed to its proper Object, every man being ready to perform his Part, neither rashly despising Danger, nor fearing to look it in the Face. We may make that Haughty Nation know that as we have a Prince on the Throne who never exceeds the bounds of Moderation and Justice, there is a Strength as well as Spirit in this country which will not suffer any Power on Earth to insult us with Impunity.

[13] The Russian and Hesse Cassel Treaties, 10 December 1755: Add MSS 51380 f. 162.

That this is a fragment of Waldegrave's draft on this occasion is suggested by its incorporation in another, larger, draft, f.135.

As to N[orth] A[merica] it cannot be denied that our Success hitherto has no ways answerd our Expectations.

But whilst our Collonies are disunited amongst themselves, whilst each particular Province, as in an Army composed of different Nations, considers only its own separate Interest. The common Cause must suffer, one must still be beat in detail, by an inferior Force.

On the other Hand could Harmony and Union be once established, not only between Collony and Colony but also between the regulars, and the Provincial troops. We should undoubtedly have a Force so greatly Superior to the Enemy, that in the End we must prevail over them.

Tho even then we are not to flatter ourselves that there will be no delay, that we are to meet with no Disappointments, when we consider the various Difficulties which naturaly attend such distant Expeditions, and the unforseen Accidents by which even the best concerted Measures may sometimes be defeated.

[14] Possibly the Lords' Address on summoning Hessian troops, 23 March 1756: Add MSS 51380 f. 116.

On 23 March 1756 the Earl of Holdernesse presented in the Lords, and Henry Fox presented in the Commons, a Messsage from the King[61] warning of the imminence of a French invasion 'upon *Great Britain* or *Ireland*', announcing the augmentation of sea and land forces, and notifying Parliament of a requisition of troops from Hesse Cassel under the terms of the recent treaty. Both Houses passed loyal Addresses in reply, approving the summoning of the Hessians, and, in the words of the Lords' Address,

To assure his Majesty, that we will, with unshaken Zeal, Vigour and Unanimity, at the Hazard of our Lives and Fortunes, stand by His Majesty against all His Enemies, and support Him in all such Measures as He shall find requisite in this critical Conjuncture; this House not in the least doubting, that even the Menace of so injurious and presumptuous an Enterprize will create the highest Detestation in all who call themselves *Britons* and Protestants, and raise a becoming Spirit in all his Majesty's Subjects, for the Defence of His Sacred Person and Government, the Protestant Succession in His Royal Family, and the Religion, Laws and Liberties, of these Kingdoms.[62]

Transports sailed on 28 March to bring over the Hessians. The ministry had already, on 13 February, formally requested the 6000 troops which Holland was committed to provide under the treaty of 1678; this request was abandoned at the Cabinet meeting of 15 March when it was learned that Holland would require freedom of trade with France under the terms of the Anglo-Dutch treaty of 1674.[63] On 29 March Fox, in the Commons, moved additionally for the requisition of twelve battalions of Hanoverian troops. William Pitt, and the Tories, opposed.

[61] Printed in *Lords Journals*, vol. 28, p. 537; *Parl. Hist.*, vol. 15, cols. 700–01.
[62] Printed in, *Lords Journals*, vol. 28, pp. 537–8; *Parl. Hist.*, vol. 15, cols. 701–2.
[63] Walpole, *George II*, vol. 2, pp. 124 nn. 1–2, 139 n. 10.

There was a considerable party in the House, to whom such a motion was odious and detestable: but, considering the critical situation of affairs, they were afraid that a direct opposition might expose them to a more odious suspicion: they therefore moved for the order of the day, and insisted on the question being put upon that motion, but it was carried in the negative by 259 against 92.[64]

Waldegrave was present on 30 March when a conference of both Houses drew up an Address to the King endorsing the summons of Hanoverian troops;[65] both Hessians and Hanoverians were soon encamped in southern England. Waldegrave thereby once more squarely aligned himself with the ministry; his position at Leicester House was now beyond recovery.

My Lords, I most heartily wish that this our natural Strength was of itself sufficient, without any other Assistance. But I am sorry to say that with this alone our Security is not compleat.

I am not ignorant of the many Dangers which may arise from too great a Number of Land Forces in a free Country. I know what have often been the Consequences, and that which has happen'd to other Governments, may one Day be the Fate of this.[66]

I will not go so far back as those turbulent days when Kings, Clergy, and Nobility were all Tyrants in their Turns, when Reputation and Power were acquired by Military Virtues only, and the Commons groan'd beneath the Burden of Service, and Vassalage. Every thing was at that Time so different from our present Constitution that it is impossible to draw any Paralel. It is sufficient for my present Purpose that not our Government only, but the Government in France and most other Parts of the Continent, have suffer'd very great alterations. The Art of War has been greatly improved. Armies are more easily governed, being subject to a more exact and more regular Discipline.

But within this last Century, a kind of epidemical Madness has spread itself over all Europe.[67] Even in the midst of Peace we live in a constant State of War. Whilst great and powerful Princes not content with Armies and Garisons of two or three hundred Thousand of their own Subjects, are on every Occasion contracting for fresh Troops, paying Subsidies to poorer Princes, who sell the Blood of their Subjects to the best Bidder. Without inquiring in whose Quarel, or in what Cause they are engaged.

[64] *Parl. Hist.*, vol. 15, col. 702.   [65] *Lords Journals*, vol. 28, pp. 547–8.
[66] The danger of a standing army to English liberties was a Tory platitude after 1714, just as it had been a Whig platitude before 1688. Despite his Tory legacy, Waldegrave was being compelled by circumstances to support not merely a standing army, but mercenaries. For the background to the controversy, see Lois G. Schwoerer, *"No Standing Armies!" The Antiarmy Ideology in Seventeenth-Century England* (Baltimore, 1974). Waldegrave's concern, and other evidence, suggests that Professor Schwoerer exaggerated the importance of 1685 as a 'watershed' in this respect (p. 189); the issue continued to be important.
[67] Waldegrave here echoed his reading of Montesquieu: see section 11 below.

This being the present State of the Continent and when we consider from how many different Ports we may at any time be envaded, how little absolute Princes value the Risque of twenty or thirty Thousand Men. And at least the uncertainty whether in a Case of necessity it might be possible for our Fleets to act.

The Temptation would realy be too great were we to leave ourselves entirely unprovided and to Trust the Winds for our Security.

There is also another Consideration which should have some Weight. For we must not judge of things merely according to what we wish, or according to what the[y] formerly have been. But according to what they now are.

And I am sorry to say that on too many Occasions, even the most necessary Laws would not be carried into Execution without very great Difficulty and Opposition. If it was not known that there is a military Force ever in readyness to act under the civil Powers, and to give them proper Support.[68]

I shall conclude this Subject with this Reflection, that as a certain military Force is undoubtedly necessary. We cannot be too jealous, we cannot be too much on our Guard, we cannot keep too strong a Check over them.

I shall next proceed to foreign Affairs, a Consideration of a very nice and delicate Nature.

As an Island we have great Advantages, and I am far from being of their Opinion, who think we ought to concern ourselves in all the Transaction of the Continent.

At the same Time, our Trade, our Collonies, nay even our domestic Security require that at least we should be careful Observers of what is going forwards, and may some times oblige us even to take a Part.

As a trading Nation we must have Treatys of Commerce, which will be productive of other Treatys. We must have Allies to whom in some cases it will be necessary to give Assistance. In regard to these Alies many Difficulties will naturaly arise, as in some Points our Interests will be mutual in others different.

And as with our best Friends there will always be some cases wherein our Interests differ. So with our most powerful Rivals, even with Enemys themselves in some Respects our Interests may be the same.

---

[68] Waldegrave may have been thinking of riots in Carmarthen, December 1755-January 1756. The early part of 1756 was relatively quiet, but the outbreak of war was soon followed, from August, by 'a widespread breakdown in public order, due to the high price of provisions, and eventually 1756 became almost as bad a year for riots as any in the century'. The Jacobite overtones to some of these disturbances in the Midlands led Newcastle to wonder whether they were a concerted attempt to tie down troops at a time when every man was needed to counter the threat of a French invasion: Tony Hayter, *The Army and the Crowd in Mid-Georgian England* (London, 1978), pp. 75, 81.

But between these Extremes, who can discover that almost imperceptible Point, where our true Interest centers.

[15]   Lord Irwin's Bill, 29 March 1756: Add MSS 51380 f. 154.

This was a private Bill to undo the entail on Lord Irwin's estate. Entitled 'An Act to enable *Henry* Viscount *Irwin*, together with *George Ingram* his Brother and *Charles Ingram* his Nephew, to make such Settlements and Dispositions of their several Estates as are therein mentioned', it was given a 1st reading in the Lords on 8 March, a 2nd reading on 9 March, and was reported from Committee on 24th; Waldegrave was present when it was rejected on its 3rd reading on 29 March.

Waldegrave may have known the Ingram family through Anne, wife of the 7th Viscount; she was a Lady of the Bedchamber to Princess Augusta as Princess of Wales.[69] The object of the Bill was to help Charles Ingram, Whig MP for Horsham 1747–63, who became Groom of the Bedchamber to George, Prince of Wales 1756–60. He was to marry on 28 June 1758 Frances Gibson, illegitimate daughter of Samuel Shepheard (d. 1748), MP and rich London merchant, who had left her a fortune provided she married a peer or one likely to succeed to a peerage.[70]

My Lords.

I entirely agree that Private Settlements or Entails are of a very delicate Nature, and should never be touch'd but on very extraordinary Occasions.

At the same time it must be allow'd there may be Circumstances where the Legislature ought to interpose and the only Question is whether those Circumstances do now exist in the Affair which is now before us.

Were we acting in our Judicial Capacity, and were we to decree conterary to Law, because the Law appear'd a hardship in this particular Case. It would undoubtedly be an Act of the greatest Injustice, it would be assuming a Power which does not belong to us.

But as Part of the Legislature we have greater Latitude. We are to consider the Affair singly on its own Merits, and judge accor[d]ingly.

The State of the Case [is] this. Lord Irwins[71] Estate is settled on himself and his Issue next on his Brother Dr Ingram,[72] and his Issue, after them to Mr Ingram[73] who is here principally concern'd. Lord Irwin is himself advanced in Years, and his Lady also so far advanced that they cannot

[69] Dodington, *Diary*, pp. 69–70.
[70] G.E.C., *The Complete Peerage*, vol. 7 (London, 1929), pp. 74–5; for a different account, Sedgwick, vol. 2, p. 421.
[71] Henry Ingram (1691–1761), 7th Viscount Irwin or Irvine [Scottish title]. He married Anne, daughter of Charles Scarborough; she died in 1766. They had no children.
[72] The Rev. George Ingram (1694–1763); succeeded in 1761 as 8th Viscount Irwin. He was brother of the 7th Viscount; was Prebend of Westminster 1724–63; and died unmarried.
[73] Charles Ingram (1727–78), 9th Viscount Irwin. Nephew of 7th and 8th Viscounts. Whig MP for Horsham 1747–63.

expect Children without a Miracle. Dr Ingram also who is no young Man, has never been married nor has any thoughts of marrying. And both most earnestly desire that this Bill may pass into a Law. Now tho both of them give a very strong Proof of their Affection for their Neveu, it certainly would not extend so far as to disinherite their own Children. If it were not for their Certainty they shall never have any.

It may be objected indeed that they may not know their own Mind. But considering the Age and Charcters of the Persons concerned, this Objection can have but little Weight.

The Settlement now proposed facilitates a Marriage by which great additional Property will acrue to the Ingram Family. And an Evil which is barely possible ought never to be set in Competition with great and certain Advantages.

I hope therefore that the Bill will appear to Your Lordships both just and reasonable, that all objections are founded on the Supposition of Events hardly possible, and that it will pass into a law.

Nor have I the least Apprehention of any ill Use being hereafter made of this Precedent, as I am clear in my Opinion that any future Parliament who would make use of such a Precedent to do an Act of Injustice would not have any great Scruple of doing the same Injustice without any Precedent whatsoever.

[16]   The Paddington Road Bill, April 1756: Add MSS 51380 f. 187.

A number of Road Bills seem possible candidates;[74] but the most famous and keenly contested of such Bills passed in April 1756. A new road to the east, avoiding the City of London,[75] seemed likely to benefit the property interests of the Duke of Grafton and to injure those of the Duke of Bedford. Horace Walpole wrote that Bedford

consequently took this up with great heat. The Duke of Grafton, old and indolent, was indifferent about it. The Duke of Argyll, who did not love the Duke of Bedford, and others who *now* wished to thwart him and his faction, privately spurred up the Duke of Grafton to make a point of this. Fox embraced the occasion as a trial for power with Newcastle: Rigby, who had endeavoured to soften the Duke of Bedford, now to humour Fox, adopted his master's warmth, and added all his own violence, treating the name of the Duke of Grafton (who was much respected) with the greatest licentiousness in the House of Commons. The Duke of Newcastle was frightened, and wished to avoid the decision; but the Duke of Bedford, who had received all manner of encouragement from the Chancellor and his friends, pushed on the determination, was betrayed, was beaten, was enraged[76]

---

[74] See *Lords Journals* under 21–6 Jan 1742/3; 24 Feb. 1742/3; 25–30 April 1744; 10 April 1745; 13–19 Feb. 1746/7; 7–24 June 1751.
[75] See *Commons Journals*, vol. 27, pp. 344, 428–9, 472–7, 546–7, 552.
[76] Walpole, *George II*, vol. 2, p. 141; cf. Walpole to Conway, 25 March, 16 April 1756: Walpole, *Letters*, vol. 37, pp. 451, 457.

as the Bill passed the Lords despite his opposition. Waldegrave was present for the Bill's second reading on 6 April; for the Committee on 12th, 13th and 28th (on 28th, three divisions were won by 58 to 40 and 51 to 35) and for the third reading on 30th (won by 56 to 38).[77] Waldegrave evidently demonstrated that his friendship for Fox did not override his allegiance to the ministry.

My Lords

I am for the bill now under Your Lordships consideration because I cannot conceive but the Mony collected at different Turnpikes in these different Roads, if honestly and prudently apply'd must be sufficient to mentain both, and even supposing the Old Road should in some degree be hurt by it, I think it would be shewing too great a partiality if a new Road was to be refus'd meerly for fear it should do the old one a prejudice.

At the same time to avoid Partiality on the other side I think it reasonable that the Old Road should be rendered as good as possible, and therefore I am for the Amendament propos'd by the noble Lord.

But from what has been said relating to the Effect this alteration may produce in another place, a Consideration arises which appears to me of far greater Consequence.

Now with regard to Mony Bills whither in general we have or have not a Right to make any Alteration, whither a Bill for a Turnpike is or is not a mony Bill, whither our allowing them as such may not bring others that have still less pretence, under the same Denomination, are Questions that I only throw out without presuming to give any determination, but so much at least I will venture to affirm that it is better that neither this nor any other bill of this nature should ever pass again in Parliament than that the House of Peers should want Spirit to make any Amendament when the Ends propos'd appear to be just and necessary.

[17] Townshend's Militia Bill, 24 May 1756: Add MSS 51380 f. 118.

George Townshend, MP 1747–64, had left the army in 1750 out of antipathy to the Duke of Cumberland; the promotion of the Duke's ally Henry Fox within the ministry drove Townshend into the arms of Pitt and the Grenvilles in November 1755. On 8 December Townshend moved, and Pitt seconded, a motion for a Committee of the Whole House to review the militia laws, a measure unwelcome to the army establishment, to Cumberland, and to the King.[78] Nevertheless, the ministry took care to keep the

---

[77] Sainty and Dewar, *Divisions*; *Lords Journals*, vol. 28, pp. 558, 569, 573, 585, 588. The Bill passed the Lords without amendment.
[78] For the 1756 Bill, see J.R. Western, *The English Militia in the Eighteenth Century: The Story of a Political Issue 1660–1802* (London, 1965), pp. 127–34; Walpole, *George II*, vol. 2, pp. 91–4, 122, 144, 149.

resulting militia Bill uncontroversial as it passed its stages in the Commons, being sent to the Lords on 10 May.

Parliamentary approval of the requisition of Hessian and Hanoverian regular troops meanwhile made a militia a military and political irrelevance. Waldegrave was present for all the stages of the Bill's passage through the Lords: for the 1st reading on 11 May; for the 2nd reading on 18th; for the Committee on 21st; and for the 3rd reading on 24 May, when the ministry intervened to secure its rejection, after a division, by 59 votes to 23.[79]

Waldegrave is not listed as a speaker in the account of the Lords' Debate on 24 May printed in the *London Magazine*;[80] but the brevity of his speech, if delivered, was presumably sufficient to escape the notice of the reporter. His position on the issue is exactly that of the ministers: to profess support for the idea of a militia in general, but to object to the terms of Townshend's Bill.[81]

My Lords. When this Affair of the Militia was under Your Lordships Consideration in the Committee, I came here a Friend a wellwisher to the Bill, tho not blind to its Faults.

I was prejudiced in its favor as being founded on a right Principle, I was also prejudiced on account of a Gentleman who had a considerable Share in framing the Bill, as knowing it to be the Work of able, of honest Hands.

However as I said before, not being blind to the Faults of the Bill, and no Amendments having been made in the Committee, I think it lyable to so many Objections, that tho I am for a Militia, tho I most sincerely wish for a good Bill of this sort, I am not for passing it in the Shape it now stands.

And I make this declaration not by way of Excuse or Apology for the part I now take. but freely to speak my Mind without the least Regard either from whom I differ, or who I offend.

[18] The Establishment of the Prince of Wales, June 1756: Add MSS 51380 f. 163.

George, Prince of Wales celebrated his eighteenth birthday on 4 June 1756; although three years short of the full age of majority, he would now succeed at once if George II were to die. A separate Household had therefore to be created for the junior Court; but this was an issue of extreme sensitivity. Not only was the King notoriously parsimonious; in addition, all such expenditure from the Civil List would henceforth go to fund the activities of the main opposition to George II's ministers.

---

[79] Sainty and Dewar, *Divisions*; *Lords Journals*, vol. 28, pp. 594, 604, 610–12.
[80] Reprinted in *Parl. Hist.*, vol. 15, cols. 706–69; cf. Newcastle to George II, [24 May 1756]: Add MSS 32865 f. 102 where, again, Waldegrave was not listed.
[81] It is possible that Add MSS 51380 f. 116, printed as no. 14 above, relates to the Militia Bill; but Waldegrave's opposition to that measure makes it unlikely.

The problems to which this could give rise were fresh in everyone's memory. On 22–3 February 1737, motions were made in the Commons by Pulteney and in the Lords by Carteret for an Address to the King to settle an allowance of £100,000 p.a. on Frederick, Prince of Wales, and after set-piece battles were only narrowly defeated.[82]

Newcastle must have feared a similar crisis when in May 1756 he learned of 'a Resolution to propose an Address for settling a provision on the P. of W. in case Parliamt. sits a day after the Birthday'.[83] Newcastle acted swiftly to head off the threat of open conflict by arranging matters to the temporary satisfaction of Leicester House,[84] but it seems he took the precaution of having Prince George's Governor draft a speech warning Parliament against interfering in a matter belonging to the royal prerogative alone. George II had offered £40,000, an inadequate sum and one which left scope for future demands. In the event, no such motion was made in the Lords, and Waldegrave's speech was evidently never delivered; Parliament rose on 27 May. But the Earl's pro-ministerial line on this issue can only have lowered his stock still further at Leicester House. His departure from the junior Court was only a matter of months away.

My Lords

I never heard a Question moved in Parliament whereby I found myself less embarassed, because I never was more clear in my Opinion, and consequently cannot be under the least Difficulty in taking a Part.

That we are the hereditary great Council of the Nation is undoubtedly true, neither is it less certain that we have a Right, that it is our Duty to advise the Crown on proper Occasions. But when does this Duty exist, when is this Right to be exerted. Why, either in those difficult, and arduous acts of Government wherein the Crown thinks proper to require our Advice. Sometimes unask'd to warn the Crown in cases of imminent Danger. More particularly on those unpleasing Occasions where the Crown, or more properly speaking, those who serve the Crown do wrong.

But this cannot now be the Case, the Prince of Wales, in respect of his Age, is in the strictest Sense still a Minor, therefore as yet there can be no wrong. And as to ancient Precedents quoted by the noble [Lord] in the times of Edward ye 3d Henry ye 4th and others, his Lordship has shewn that which I believe nobody doubted his great Knowlege in English History. But no reasonable Conclusion can possibly be drawn from such distant Examples. For as to Princes who had Dutchies, as it were in their Cradles, and Principalities at 3 or 7 Years old, this would prove too much

---

[82] See *Parl. Hist.*, vol. 9, cols. 1352–1454.
[83] J. West to Newcastle, 8 May 1756: Add MSS 32864 f. 498.
[84] Clark, *Dynamics of Change*, pp. 240–51.

they might be given as a Maintainance but certainly could never be given by way of making them independent.⁸⁵ Unless we suppose those Princes form'd quite different from mankind in general and endowed with a kind of supernatural Understanding which rises up at once Maturity.

As to a precedent of later Date, the Duke of York in the Reign of Charles ye 2d, tho he may be brought as an Example of an Heir Presumptive having more than 100000l a Year, he certainly cannot be quoted as one whose Mind was open'd, whose Understanding was enlarged, by the Advantages of an independent Settlement.⁸⁶

Indeed nothing is more certain than that Independency proceeds from the Mind, and not from Circumstances.

The Prince of Wales besides the Duty of a Subject to a great and good King, has the stro[n]gest additional Tyes of Gratitude, and filial Duty and Affection.

This is the only Influence over a generous Mind, for in every other Respect, he has both Sence and Spirit to feel himself thoroughly independent.

At the same Time, My Lords, I most sincerely wish that His R.H.'s Establishment may soon be very considerably encreased. But let us not by officious and premature Advice, endeavor as it were to rob the King of the Merit, of exerting his paternal Affection by providing for his Heir Apparent. He has already given the strongest Proof of his Inclination towards it. His Majesty is undoubtedly the only proper Judge both as to the time and Manner of forming this Establishment. Therefore whatever is done, let it be *ex mero motu*, unadress'd, unadvised, proceeding from himself only.

As to the Prince of Wales being now entirely independent because he would be of Age in case of his Majesty's Death, neither does this Argument prove any thing. His being of Age in that case is only the *Minus Malum*. A King of 18 is undoubtedly a national Misfortune, but a Minority, a Regency is still worse. But to apply this reasoning to ourselves. Should it be said that as we are the hereditary great Council of the Nation. The Heir apparent of every Peer ought to have such a Proportion of his Fathers Estate from the day he is 18, to give him an early taste of that Independence to which he is born. I really think this would be a Doctrine which very few of Your Lordships who are Fathers would think proper to admitt.

At the same time, My Lords, I make no Doubt but his R.H.'s Establishment will hereafter be considerably encreased. Even at present, I

---

⁸⁵ If this is a speech written in advance, Waldegrave must be speculating that some peer would raise these objections. The precedents had been fully explored in the debates of 22–3 February 1737.
⁸⁶ The Duke of York later became king James II.

give no Opinion whether it be too little, or whether it be sufficient. I only affirm that we are not the proper Judges. We might as justly determine every minute Article, of his Majesty's private Oeconomy, or of his private Amusement. For it appears to me a direct Absurdity that the King who by Law, by our Constitution is intrusted with the whole executive Power, should not be thought a proper Judge in the private Concerns of his own Family. And I shall conclude with this most solemn Declaration that whatever Reasons other Lords may have for voting for this Question, I could have but one and I had rather walk si[n]gly out of this House and never set my Foot again in Parliament, than basely desert a great and good King because he is 74 Years of age, and because the Heir Apparent is no more than 20.[87] Therefore let us not by officious and premature Advice, endeavour, as it were, to rob the King of the Merit of exerting his paternal Affection, by providing for his Heir apparent. His Majesty is undoubtedly the only proper Judge both as to the time and Manner of encreasing this Establishment. Therefore whatever is done let it be *ex mero motu*. Unadressed, unadvised, proceeding from himself only.

[19] The debate on the Address in reply to the King's Speech, 2 December 1756: Add MSS 51380 f. 148; drafts, ff. 141, 144, 146.

Newcastle's ministry had fallen; Waldegrave had resigned his position at Leicester House; Pitt was about to take office as Secretary of State. The Hanoverian and Hessian troops were to be sent back to Germany, to form part of an army to defend Hanover itself; their place was to be taken at home by a militia, the opposition's favourite scheme, which Waldegrave had joined in defeating on 24 May.

What would be his position in these wholly new circumstances? Waldegrave prepared his speech with extreme care, writing draft after draft. Against the threatened isolationism of Leicester House, the Earl produces a measured defence of continental involvement. His own instinct not to be tied to specific engagements, still expressed in an early draft, f. 141, is omitted from the final version. The employment of mercenary troops is defended in the light of England's manpower shortage; and the early consequences of the late ministry's alliance with Prussia are welcomed. Defeats in Minorca and North America are passed over as the normal

[87] It seems likely that Waldegrave is not trying to be precise over the ages. If these ages are precisely meant, however, another date is entailed for the speech. George II's 74th birthday was on 30 October 1759; but by that date the Prince of Wales was no longer a minor, celebrating his 21st birthday on 4 June of that year. If Waldegrave means that the king is in his 74th year, the speech is dated to the period 30 October 1758–4 June 1759. But Waldegrave attended the House only twice in that session: on 5 April 1758, on an issue concerning the Ferrers trial, and on 23 November 1758, the first day, for the King's Speech. Perhaps there was an attempt to add to the Address a request to increase the Prince of Wales' allowance; but no evidence for such an attempt has yet been found.

fortune of war. The prospects are not gloomy; the new ministry does not inherit an impossible position. He therefore ends with a warning to 'those Men . . . rather artful to cajole the People, than skillful to conduct the State' (f. 144) about their conduct of affairs.

Waldegrave's temperate declaration of loyalty to the old ministers was overshadowed by Temple's outburst (see below). In fact, the new ministry steered a deliberately uncontroversial course during the winter of 1756–7.[88]

My Lords

When ever we speak of present times and present Transactions. We naturaly represent them of the most delicate and most important Nature, as being attended with the greatest Difficulties, and requiring the greatest Sagacity, Prudence, and Resolution to carry them into Execution. Which Expressions, tho often made use of on the slightest Occasions, may undoubtedly be apply'd, to those Transactions which are immediately before us, without the least Impropriety.

The particular Circumstances of the present War seem to differ entirely from the Circumstances attending all other Wars in which this Country has ever been engaged. For notwithstanding the frequent Examples of England singly and successfully war[r]ing against France. The Ballance of Power on the Continent, the Power of France itself, and their Alliances with most of the considerable Powers of Europe, are so totaly different from former times, as not to admit of any Parallel.

From these Circumstances, Questions naturally arrise of the utmost Importance, tho not easy to determine. When, and how far, Alliances on the Continent, or what are sometimes call'd continent Measures, are repugnant to, or consistent with the true English Interest. Also whether in the present Situation of Affairs, this Country can carry on a War against France, with any Prospect of Success, by itself, without any Forreign Assistance.

That the Strength and Security of this Country is owing to our Situation, to our being divided from the Continent, is a self evident Truth which admits of no Contradiction. But there is also another political Truth which very few will deny, if not universaly assented to. That tho from our Situation as an Island, we have the greatest Advantages, we are still so far connected with the Continent, that in all material Transactions we must at least be careful Observers, and on some Occasions must be under the Necessity of taking a Part.

As a Maritime Power, as a trading Nation we must have Treatys of Commerce, which will be productive of other Treatys. We must have Allies who will frequently avail themselves of our Protection, and other good

[88] For the texts of the King's Speech and Lords' Address, see *Parl. Hist.*, vol. 15, cols. 771–7.

Offices, the only Tenure by which we can expect to hold them. In which complicated System of Alliances, Negotiations, Guarantees, and the like, how difficult must it be to discover that almost imperceptible Point where our true Interest centers.

It may be said, let us assist our Friends in such manner only as to enable them to act for themselves, still remembering that tho in some measure we share the Danger, yet that Danger which is immediate to them is remote to us. Still considering what we are in a Condition to undertake, as well as what we could wish to undertake. Never giving Hopes of doing more than that which we are able to perform.

But these Rules are only general, and even the best general Rules will not always suit particular Cases.

As to the next Question, what Services, what Assistance we are to expect in Return. Tho it be undoubtedly true that political Friendship can only be founded on mutual Interest, yet mutual Interest does not always imply equal Advantages.

From many of our Allies we can only expect certain Advantages in Trade. From others perhaps the best we can hope, is that they should do us no Harm. Some may be useful on particular Occasions, and may be inclined to do still greater Services, but want the Means; Whilst there are few or perhaps none, on whose active, immediate and effectual Assistance we can at all times depend.

However far be it from me to draw any Conclusion because Allies may have a separate Interest, or are not always to be depended on, that therefore Alliances do not give great additional Strength. I only mean that we should never lose our Principal Object. That we should not so far depend on others, as to neglect ourselves.

Having troubled Your Lordships so far, I shall now proceed to the other Consideration. Whether in the present Situation of Affairs, this Country can carry on a War against France, with any prospect of Success, by itself, without any Forre[i]gn Assistance. And my Lords, when We consider our Situation as an Island, as Great Brittan, to which I will add Ireland. And the great Superiority of our Naval Force. It certainly may be answer'd in the affirmative, we can defend ourselves.

But on the other hand, when we consider that merely to defend these Islands against France is not sufficient. When we consider the Numbers which are necessary for this Defence only. How many are required for the Navy, how many for the Land Service, whether Regulars, Militia, or jointly both.

When we go farther, and consider what is necessary for the Defence of Gibraltar, our Settlements and Possessions in the East and West Indies, and North America. Add to these the Numbers employ'd at home, in

Trade, Agriculture, Manufactures, and civil Services. It is my sincere Opinion that this Country, populous as it undoubtedly is, cannot produce a sufficient Supply of Hands, to answer all these Purposes.

Besides our Enemy, the French, powerful as they are in themselves, nor less vain than powerful. Are yet so far from being Dupes to their Vanity, in depending entirely on their own Strength, that there is not a Power in Europe, from the Republick of Genoa, to the Emperesses of Russia and Germany, whose Friendship, and Assistance they are not ready to purchass, nor think the means disgraceful, when the End is answer'd.

However, My Lords, I am far from recommending this Example in its full Extent. There are many Reasons against it, but one which alone would be sufficient, our Finances do not admit of such Extravagance. But at the same time, should we run too far into the other Extreme, it would be folly, indeed.

The March of the King of Prussia into Bohemia, and the great Success which has hitherto attended him undoubtedly opens a new Scene in Europe.[89] What may be the Consequences of such an Expedition. How far the Protestant Interest in general, how far even this Country may in the end be effected by it. Are Questions which I believe the wisest Politician would find difficult to determine.

But so far at least is certain, that such an Undertaking must have Consequences, either good, or bad, it cannot be of an Indifferent Nature. And that hitherto it appears the vigorous Act of a brave and wise King. Who saw Danger at its Birth, and thought it a safer Choice to face it still an Infant, than to wait its full Maturity.

As to ourselves, considering how far we are already engaged, I do not apprehend that general Confusion, amongst the other Powers of Europe, can possibly do us any Sort of Harm.

Tho I have already given Your Lordships too much Trouble, I cannot conclude without touching on a very unpleasing Subject, without taking some Notice of our great National Misfortune I wish I could not add a great National Disgrace. The Loss of the Island of Minorca and the Manner of losing it.[90]

But amidst the various Events of War, every Man has Sagacity to discover the Evil, whilst few are capable of pointing out the Remedy. The Misfortunes that happen every Man feels, those which have been prevented make so little Impression, that few remember that even the Danger of them ever existed.

[89] The Prussian invasion of Saxony began on 29 August 1756. Bohemia, described by a Turkish diplomat in 1762 as 'the real pride and core of the Austrian power' was invaded on 13 September: Christopher Duffy, *Frederick the Great: A Military Life* (London, 1985), pp. 94, 102.
[90] The garrison surrendered on 28 June 1756.

As to North America, it cannot be deny'd that our Success hitherto has no ways answer'd our Expectations.

But tho from our Superiority over the French, in those Parts, there is great Reason to expect we shall in the End prevail over them. At the same time we are not to flatter ourselves that there will be no Delays, that we are to meet with no Disappointments. When we consider the various Difficulties which naturaly attend such distant Expeditions. and the unforseen Accidents by which even the best concerted Measures may sometimes be defeated.

Those who are the most apt to be elated by groundless Hopes, are commonly the most lyable to sink under unreasonable Fears, and was our present Condition infinitely more dangerous than what it really is, I never would be one of those who despair of the Commonwealth. And tho I cannot but lament our being engaged in a War with the most powerful Nation in Europe, laboring under an immense National Debt. Peace and War being hardly more opposite to each other than War and Oeconomy. Yet we have this Comfort that whatever we spend in naval Preparations, whatever we spend in stre[n]gthening ourselves at home, circulates amongst ourselves. Whatever we spend in North America must in the End return back to the Mother Country with double Interest. And whatever we spend in Forreign Subsidies will bear but a very small Proportion to our other Expences.

We have also this additional Comfort, that Hostilities on our side were neither lightly nor inconsiderately undertaken. Even the name of Peace was only to be obtained by tamely suffering the most unprovok'd Insults, by departing from our just, our undoubted Rights and Possessions. Such Terms as English men can never submit to. And we have still reason to hope, that the Force of this Country being vigorously directed to its proper Object, every Man being ready to perform his Part, neither rashly despising Danger nor fearing to look it in the Face, we may make that haughty Nation know, that as we have a Prince on the Throne who never exceeds the Bounds of true Magnanimity, Wisdom, Moderation, and Justice, there still remains a Strength as well as Spirit in this Country, which will not suffer any Power on Earth to insult us, with Impunity. As to the Hanoverians, last year we thank'd his Majesty for bringing them over. Now we return thanks for sending them away.

However as both their coming and going has been merely to gratify the Inclinations of the People.

The more contradictory our Thanks. The stronger will be the Testimony of his Majesty's Condesension and Goodness.[91]

[91] 'Our first day of Parliament passed off harmoniously; but in the House of Lords there was an event. A clause of thanks for having sent for the Hanoverians had crept into the address of the peers – by Mr Fox's means, as the world thinks: Lord Temple came out of a sick bed

I shall conclude with this Observation, which I mean in no unfriendly Sense, merely as a warning.

As those Men will be justly esteemed the ablest Statesmen, and best of Patriots who can so exert the Strength of this Country, as to render us a Match for France without any Foreign Assistance.

So on the other hand, as there is not a braver, neither is there an honester People than ours, if they are not misled.

But should the free and generous Spirit of Emulation, the old Characteristic of this Country, be ever debased into the sulky, discontented Spirit of Jealousy, should we become too presuming to receive Assistance from others, too indolent to perform the Work alone.

Those Men, who obstinate in the Pursuit of any favourite System, shall wantonly raise this unfortunate Spirit, will have much to answer for.

[The following passages, present in the draft f. 141, are omitted in f. 148:]

The Danger or Advantage of Forreign Assistance must depend upon two Points, the Numbers that are employ'd, and the Services in which we employ them. Should we ever become so degenerate so unfitt for War as to admit Foreign Mercenaries to an equal Share of the Defence of this Country, from that Moment we are devoted to Destruction. On the other Hand Foreign Assistance to make a Diversion on the Continent or on extraordinary Occasions in a moderate Proportion here at home, might enable us to send out our Fleets and Armys to defend our own, and to attack the Possessions of the Enemy, and as long and [sc. 'as'] any martial Spirit any Spirit of Liberty remains amongst us, can never be dangerous . . .

Having troubled your Lordships so far concerning our Connections with the Continent in general, I shall now proceed to another Consideration of a very particular, and of a very delicate Nature, in relation to His Majesty's German Dominions. How greatly those Dominions have already suffer'd, how greatly they are still exposed on account of a Quarrel entirely English are facts which cannot be denied, unfortunately they are too apparent. However I do not mean, because they suffer on our Account, that therefore we must attempt Impossibilities, in order to relieve them. To ruin ourselves would certainly be no very probable Means of serving our Friends. But this I do affirm, that whatever can be done to save them, tho attended with some Expence, with some Difficulties and even with some Danger, to this we are bound by every Tye of Honor and Justice, by that

to oppose it. Next day there was an alarm of an intention of instating the same clause in our [Commons'] address. Mr Pitt went angry to Court, protesting that he would not take the seals, if any such motion passed: it was sunk'. Walpole to Mann, 8 December 1756: Walpole, *Letters*, vol. 21, p. 30.

which we owe to a great and good King, and indeed by that which we owe to ourselves.

As the Preservation of Publick Credit is real Riches, so the maintaining National Honor, is real Military Strength. And this National Honor is so much engaged in the Defence of His Majesty's Electoral Dominions. That to abandon them would be Infamy itself, unless we confess a total Inability to give any Assistance to any Ally whatsoever.

In which unfortunate Situation when many would treat us, as a common Enemy, when none would consider us a Friend, we might then find that it is with Nations as it is with Individuals where some may have Advantages whereby they can support themselves better than others. But none can entirely subsist alone.

However far be it from me to draw any Conclusion that because our Allies may have a separate Interest, or are not always to be depended on, that therefore Alliances on the Continent are of little Consequence. My Meaning is that they ought to be cultivated as giving great Additional Strength. At the same time that we should not lose our principal Object. That we should not so far depend on others as to neglect ourselves.

[20–24] The Militia Bill, March-June 1757

The loss of Minorca in June 1756 transformed the militia into a major issue of Patriot propaganda. Leicester House was thereby committed to introducing another Bill at an early date; Pitt made it a condition of accepting office.[92] A Commons committee, voted on 4 December 1756, eventually produced a Bill similar to that of the previous year; it was fought over in the Commons from 26 January to 25 March 1757, when it passed its 3rd reading without substantial amendment.

The militia was thus, from January 1757, an issue of confidence and a test case for the new ministry. During its passage the Bill acquired an even greater significance. Pitt was dismissed on 6 April, and his associates during the next few days; then began an epic series of manoeuvres which lasted until the formation of the Newcastle – Pitt coalition on 18 June. Would Waldegrave have a political future after the fall of Bute and Pitt? Would a compromise over the militia allow a coalition ministry to emerge? Which plan would triumph – an extensive or a limited force?

The Lords were therefore contesting the future composition of the ministry as much as the composition of the militia: were they willing to insist on their objections to the measure, and to modify it substantially? They were. The Bill was brought from the Commons by George Townshend on 26 March; Waldegrave was present for its 1st reading on 29 March and its 2nd on 20 April. He attended in Committee on 27, 28 and 29 April,

[92] Walpole, *George II*, vol. 2, p. 181.

the first day seeing a Lords' amendment carried by 45 votes to 40, and thereafter a large number of amendments without division: in particular, the size of the proposed force was halved, as Newcastle and Hardwicke had determined to do as early February, and the Leicester House plan for a permanent milita was converted into a plan for five years only. Waldegrave was present again on 9 May when the much-altered Bill passed its 3rd reading by 64 votes to 28.

This did not end the matter. On 25 May Waldegrave attended for the Lords' conference with the Commons on the amendment to the Bill, and again on 26th when the Lords voted by 27 to 25 not to insist on an amendment not accepted by the Commons, but without a division adhered to almost everything else. The division on 26 May was the first and last occasion in his career when the 2nd Earl Waldegrave acted as a Teller – on the side of the Lords not insisting on one amendment.[93] Waldegrave was in the House again on 27 May for the report of the Lords' reasons for adhering to their other amendments, and again on 8 June for the final conference with the Commons, when the lower House accepted most of the points in dispute, and the Lords gave way on the insignificant remainder. The argument Waldegrave employs is the same as that to which he committed himself in the previous session: approval of a militia in principle, but resistance to the specific terms of Townshend's proposal, and principled insistence on the constitutional right of the House of Lords to intervene. 'The final result was thus that the Bill became law, but the new force was to be smaller and a little less under popular control than its advocates had wished and it seemed unlikely to have a long life, even supposing that the difficulties of organising it were overcome'.[94]

[20] The Militia Bill: possibly a draft of a speech on the 1st or 2nd reading, 29 March or 20 April 1757: Add MSS 51380 f. 161.

My Lords

When this Affair of the Militia was before Your Lordships last Winter, I voted for the Bill as thinking it founded on a right Principle, tho at the same time it seem'd lyable to some very material Objections.

However notwithstanding those and other Difficulties which have arisen in the Course of the last Summer, I still like the Principle of this Bill also. I am for explaining, I am for amending, I am for enforcing.

---

[93] Sainty and Dewar, *Divisions*; *Lords Journals*, vol. 29, p. 173. I am grateful to Mr. D.J. Johnson for elucidation of Lords' procedure at this point. The 1st Earl Waldegrave acted as Teller on seven occasions. Divisions in the Lords were rare, averaging 3.5 per session during the 22 full sessions 1741–63; not counting the unusually contentious sessions of 1741–2, 1742–3, and 1747–8, the average falls to 2.32 per session.
[94] Western, *Militia*, pp. 134–40.

But I should hope that proper Amendments, with proper Explanation might be sufficient.

For as to enforcing, it may become necessary but is of a very nice, and of a very delicate Nature. To gett the better of Popular Prejudices requires great Temper and great Moderation. For the Mob must not be holoo'd one day and manacled the next.

Upon the whole, Tho I am not one of the most sanguine Friends to a Militia. Tho I have Doubts as to the Expediency of the Measure, as well as to the Practicability. I still have Hopes that in some Shape or other, some Good may be derived from it. And therefore am still for trying the Experiment.

But on the contrary, if I had changed my Opinion since last Winter, and were now against the Bill. I would not endeavour to spoil it by improper Amendments. But would oppose it openly like a fair and avow'd Enemy.

For either as to Measures or as to Men, I scorn to pretend a Friendship which I do not feel.

[21] The Militia Bill, possibly notes for a speech in Committee, 27–29 April 1757: Add MSS 51380 f. 155

'The Lords had proposed to exempt the Tower Hamlets from the bill, but the Commons refused to strike out their quota and the Lords acquiesced after a division. The Hamlets were left with an organisation under the old acts and a quota under the new'.[95]

My Lords

I shall not trouble Your Lordships at present either as to what Bills are, or are not Money Bills, or as to our Power of Altering them. But in this Affair of the Tower Hamlets, it is the Commons who are making alterations, not Your Lordships. They seem to be of Opinion, that some Points not very material in themselves may be alter'd for the better. Your Lordships say let things remain in their ancient State.

Now My Lords this is not merely saying, this is a Money Bill, you cannot alter it, a Doctrine which Your Lordships can never admit. It is saying in effect Your Lordships shall not even have a Negative, for what is a negative, if it be not a Power of continuing things in their present situation, which is all that Your Lordships now propose. As to the Militia itself, I was very sincerely for trying the Experiment, tho at the same time I thought it a very doubtful one. But be that as it will I had rather neither this Bill nor any Bill of this Nature should ever Pass again in Parliament than that this House should have the least Doubt of making any Amendment, when the end proposed appeard to be just and reasonable.

[95] Western, *Militia*, p. 140 n. 1.

[22] The Militia Bill: variant drafts of passages, n.d.: Add MSS 51380 f. 159.

Of late Years the collective Body of the People have been flatter'd like Princes in a despotic Government, they have been appeal'd too almost on every Occasion, and their Pride has been elated with the wildest notions of their own unerring Judgment, and unbounded Authority. Whilst at the same time their Minds have been sower'd by heavy Taxes, an unsuccessful War, with a Series of national Disgrace. To restore such a People to their sober Senses.

Of late Years Appeals have been made to the collective Body of the People even on the slightest Occasions. And their Pride has been elated with the wildest and most absurd Notions of their supreme Power, and unbounded Authority, almost to the Subversion of our Constitution and of all good Government.

To restore such a deluded People to their sober Senses, to make them feel their Danger[.] But at the same time know their own Strength. To make them know that in a Country of the greatest Liberty, even under the mildest Government, the Laws are absolute and must be obey'd must be a Work of Difficulty as well as of the greatest Importance. Which will require great Temper and great Moderation and which can never be effected by Force and Violence. To make them sensible that the Blessing[s] they enjoy are almost peculiar to themselves, and that the Hardships they suffer are still infinitely greater under every other Government and without damping the Spirit of the People, to direct that Spirit to its proper Object.

[23] The Militia Bill: variant drafts of passages, n.d.: Add MSS 51380 f. 158

For to restore our People to their sober Senses, to make them unlearn those Lessons of Faction which have been taught them with too much success, almost to the subversion of the best Constitution ever existed. To make them sensible that in a Country of the greatest Liberty under the mildest Administration of Government. The Laws are absolute and must be obey'd. And without damping the Spirit of the People, to direct that Spirit to its proper Object. Must be a Work of difficulty as well as of the greatest Importance which will require great Temper, and great Moderation, and which can never be effected by Force, and Violence.

[24] The Militia Bill: possibly a speech on the 3rd reading, 9 May 1757: Add MSS 51380 f. 156.

My Lords. When this Affair of the Militia was before Your Lordships last Winter, tho in some Measure I liked the Bill, as being founded on a right

Principle, yet I voted against it as thinking Experiments of this Nature more proper for times of Peace, that even the Attempt would be burdensom to the People and that in the End it would be found impracticable.

But during the Course of the last Summer, most of the considerable Counties having declared themselves strongly in its favor, the case seems greatly alter'd. For the Gentlemen and others of the Country are certainly the best Judges as to the Burden, and ought to be so far Judges of the Practicability, as the Execution must chiefly Depend on their Activity. Besides in times of national Danger it seems bad Policy to damp the Spirit of the People, when the Object of that Spirit, is their own Defence.

Therefore many proper Amendments having been made, in the Committy most of the material Objections being now removed. I shall be for giving the Bill a fair Tryal.

As to the present popularity of a Militia, I believe nobody doubts it. At the same time popular favor may be too much trusted, as well as it may be too much despised. For tho I know some Gentlemen who convinced of the Utility, will undoubtedly perform their Parts with true publick Spirit, yet this Conduct must be general before it can answer any Good Purpose, and Undertakings of so extensive a Nature, where a whole nation must cooperate, are seldom executed with the same Spirit they are plan'd.

Besides Acts of Parliament far more correct than this which is now before us have not always been explain'd according to their primitive Sense and Meaning. And whether the Power of the Crown over this Militia should hereafter appear to be merely nominal. Or whether this Militia entirely in the hands of the Crown, should too nearly resemble a Standing Army of regular forces. Either Extreme must be dangerous to the Constitution, must be equally repugnant to a limited Monarchy.

But without supposing Cases which may or may not exist. The greatest Friends to the Bill must own that it is merely an Experiment. Many think it a very doubtful one.

Therefore till Experience shews us what additional Strength we really do acquire, how far this Militia may reasonably be depended on, it will deserve the very serious Attention both of Parliament and of the Administration that other legal and necessary means of defence, be not negle[c]ted, least the best Constitution in the World should be the wo[r]st defended. And whilst we are grasping at the Shadow of Security, we should lose the Substance.

[25]   The Seamen's Wages Act, March-April 1758: Add MSS 51380 f. 160
This was the second such Bill to attempt a reform of naval pay and recruitment. The first was a Leicester House measure, brought forward during the Pitt-Devonshire ministry. Sponsored by George Grenville,

Henry Bilson Legge and William Pitt, it passed its 3rd reading in the Commons on 11 May 1757 but was defeated by Newcastle's latent majority in the Lords on 24 May;[96] Waldegrave was not present on that occasion, but attended on the militia issue on the three subsequent days, and was presumably aware that this naval reform and the militia were supported from the same quarter.

After the formation of the Newcastle-Pitt coalition, George Grenville brought the navy Bill forward once more; its former ministerial opponents were now obliged to support it; and it passed the Commons in January 1758, without serious opposition, as 'An Act for the Encouragement of Seamen employed in the Royal Navy; and for establishing a regular Method for the punctual, frequent and certain Payment of their Wages; and for enabling them more easily and readily to recruit the same, for the Support of their Wives and Families; and for preventing Frauds and Abuses attending such Payments'.

The Lords gave it closer scrutiny, however. Waldegrave was present on 2 March when the House addressed for papers relating to the question; on 16 and 17 March when voluminous papers were received; on 21 March when the Bill passed its 2nd reading after a division by 74 votes to 14; on 12 April in Committee, when a crucial division was won by 61 votes to 12; and for the 3rd reading on 13 April, when the Bill finally passed by 65 votes to 9.[97] The tenacity with which this small opposition in the Lords fought every stage of the Bill in an unwinnable battle is remarkable. But Waldegrave now had no personal motive for standing by Newcastle, and every motive for indulging his resentment against Pitt and Bute. Ironically, this measure had much to commend it as an administrative reform; it 'represented a victory for a small group of naval administrators and politicians to overcome the inertia of their colleagues who were content to rely on tradition and the press to man the fleet'.[98]

My Lords. I am against the Bill now under Your Lordships consideration, because I think it fundamentally wrong, and that it will not answer those good Purposes for which it was intended. Our Saylors are not ignorant that in the Merchants Service they receive the best Pay, and enjoy the greatest Liberty. Many of them have been forced into the Kings Ships,

[96] Walpole, *George II*, vol. 2, p. 259.
[97] Sainty and Dewar, *Divisions*; Walpole, *George II*, vol. 3, pp. 13–14.
[98] For a full study, see Stephen F. Gradish, 'Wages and Manning: the Navy Act of 1758', *EHR* 93 (1978), 46–67. Associated with this measure was a more far-reaching proposal to rationalise naval conscription by creating a register of seamen. Originating similarly with the Grenvilles, it was first aired in the Commons on 25 January 1758, and finally rejected there on 27 March 1759 after a long campaign by interested parties. See Stephen F. Gradish, *The Manning of the British Navy during the Seven Years' War* (London, 1980), pp. 107–8.

like Slaves who are drag'd to the Gallies in the most despotic Governments. Such men are Objects of the Greatest Compassion, but certainly are not to be trusted. And as some Restraint is absolutely necessary, it seems the lesser Evil to subsist them well, keeping back such arrears of Pay as may be some Security against their desertion. Than that they should never be suffer'd to go on Shore, and be condemned to constant confinement. I shall not trouble Your Lordships as to the particular Faults of the Bill, for if the most material objections were intirely removed, I should still be of Opinion that Experiments of this Nature, are proper only for times of Peace.

But in our present Situation, as the Bill now Stands, it appears to be greatly prejudicial to the public Service, hurtful even to the Seamen themselves, beneficial to their Families only in a few Instances, and that it will seriously prove what it was ironically call'd in a former Debate, a Bill for the more effectual Encouragement of Mutiny and Desertion.

As to the present popularity of the Bill, I believe nobody doubts it. At the same time popular favor may be too much trusted as well as it may be too much despised. And I remember an Observation of Lord Bacon's, that the true Composition of a Counsellor is rather to be skillful in his Master's Business than in his Nature, for then he is like to advise him, not feed his Humor.[99] Now whether this be applyed to the Counsellors of Princes, or the Counsellors of the People, the Proposition is equally true. For the favor which is acquired by feeding the Humor the Passions of the People, at the Expence of their Safety their true Interest, is dearly purchass'd, and will never be long lived.

[26] The Address in reply to the King's Speech, 13 November 1759: Add MSS 51380 f. 165.

The setbacks and discouragements of the early part of the war were wiped out by an astonishing run of military victories. 'Thus we wind up this wonderful year!' wrote Horace Walpole after the drama of Quiberon Bay; 'Who that died three years ago and could revive, would believe it?' 'Indeed one is forced to ask every morning, what victory there is? for fear of missing one.'[100]

Parliament was opened by commission on 13 November, George II being too infirm to attend in person. His Speech from the Throne was read for him by the Lord Keeper, Henley, and catalogued a long series of victories. The Address in reply was moved by the Earl of Buckingham;[101] Waldegrave, though present on that day, was not a member of the

---

[99] Waldegrave here misremembered his notes; he derived the idea from Montaigne, not Bacon. See section 10 below.
[100] Walpole to Mann, 30 Nov., 13 December 1759: Walpole, *Letters*, vol. 21, pp. 350, 352.
[101] The King's Speech, and the Lords' Address, are printed in *Parl. Hist.*, vol. 15, cols. 947–52.

Committee which drew up the Address. Whether he seconded the motion or spoke for it is not known.

My Lords

Tho Thanks and Congratulation to Princes are frequently, and perhaps very properly ascribed to Flattery, the Successes of the last Summer will fully justify our highest Praise and our warmest Acknowledgements.

Successes which have not proceeded either from Chance or Accident, but from the Wisdom of his Majesty's Measures; the Bravery of his Fleets and Armies; and from the good Conduct, Activity and Example of those who have commanded them.

So many have deserved well of their King and Country, that to do Justice to the Merit of every individual would be a Work of the greatest Extent. I must therefore confine myself to things as they now are, without entering into a particular Examination of the Causes which may have produced them.

In the first Place as to our Marine, there certainly never was a Period wherein it made a more respectable Appearance: whilst on the other hand, our Enemies either remain peaceable in their Harbours, patiently enduring the most humiliating Insults, or sculk from Port to Port, less fearful of Tempests, and of all the Fury of the Elements, than of meeting almost inevitable Destruction from his Majesty's Fleets.

As to the Bravery of our Land Forces, and the good Conduct of those who commanded them, I need only mention the taking of Crown Point, Niagara, and Quebec: the Conquest of the Island of Gardaloupe: the raising the Siege of Madras: and the Victory of Minden.[102]

It is to be lamented that the like Prosperity, and Success has not accompanied our great and powerful Ally the King of Prussia in his late Engagement with the Russians.[103] Yet such is the Superiority of his Genius, and such are his Resources, that tho he has received a Cheque, he still is in a condition to defend himself, and will again be the Terror of his Enemies.

As to Spain, Portugal, Sardinia, and other Princes who have not hitherto taken any part in the War, it seems to be their Inclination, as it undoubtedly is their Interest, that the Power of France should suffer some Diminution.

---

[102] Niagara was taken on 25 July 1759, Crown Point on 4 August; both victories were reported in the *London Chronicle*, 6–8 September. Quebec surrendered on 17 September; it was reported in the *London Gazette Extraordinary*, 17 October. The surrender of Guadeloupe on 1–2 May was reported, *ibid.*, 14 June. General Lally was forced to raise the French siege of Madras in April 1759; the events are reported in the *Gentlemen's Magazine* for October. The battle of Minden was fought on 1 August.

[103] The battle of Kunersdorf, 12 August; Frederick II commanding the Prussian army was defeated by a joint Russian and Austrian force.

I will not even except the Republic of Holand, for it would be unfair to suspect our ancient and natural Ally of those acts of Hostility, or of that unf[r]i[e]ndly Clamor, to which Avarice and French Influence may have prompted some Individuals.

As to our Dispute with the Dutch,[104] I will not trouble Your Lordships with nice distinctions between the Letter and Spirit of a Treaty: nor enter into subtile Arguments whether breach of Treaty in one Particular, makes void all other Contracts. I shall only affirm that it must be equally fatal to this Country whether the French trade for themselves without any Molestation, or whether neutral Powers are suffer'd to trade for them; and that Necessity and self Preservation are superior to every other Engagement.

As to the French invading us, one of their Enterprises has lately fail'd;[105] however it seems probable that they will make other Attempts of the same Nature, perhaps with a more considerable Force. But their greatest Efforts must be languid and inanimate; the Troops destined for these Services, already considering themselves as Men devoted to Destruction. At the same time, too much Presumption on our Part, might be as dangerous as Fear, and Despondency. It therefore becomes us to expect them with cool yet active Resolution; determined to maintain our Liberties, Religion, and all the Blessings we enjoy: God will then deliver them into our Hands.[106]

I come now to my last Consideration and it is of some Importance; what Advantages are we to derive from this expensive, bloody, but successful War. The Question may be answer'd in a few Words, a safe and honorable Peace. Yet my Lords let us not deceive ourselves: Safety and Honor, we have a right to expect; but if we require a solid Compensation for all the Treasure which has been exhausted, and for all the Blood which has been

---

[104] The Franco-Austrian alliance of May 1756 transformed Holland's strategic position. By removing Austria as the guardian of the southern Netherlands, the Dutch republic was left vulnerable to France and compelled to adopt a position of neutrality. Holland thereby violated her defensive treaties with England, especially that of 1678. England in return held Anglo-Dutch trade treaties to be abrogated, particularly that of 1674 which guaranteed to the Dutch a favourable interpretation of the principle 'Free Ships, Free Goods'. Anglo-Dutch relations were then strained almost to breaking point in the summer of 1758 when England intervened to halt Dutch participation in French colonial trade in place of the French merchant marine. See Richard Pares, *Colonial Blockade and Neutral Rights 1739–1763* (Oxford, 1938), pp. 180–204, 242–79; Alice Clare Carter, *The Dutch Republic in Europe in the Seven Years' War* (London, 1971); idem, *Neutrality or Commitment: The Evolution of Dutch Foreign Policy, 1667–1795* (London, 1975), pp. 72–89.

[105] Admiral Boscawen, in pursuit of the French Toulon squadron, had caught up with it and destroyed it in Portuguese waters at the battle of Lagos, 18–19 August. it was reported in the *London Gazette Extraordinary*, 10 September.

[106] News of Admiral Hawke's decisive victory over the French fleet in Quiberon Bay, 20 November, was known in London early on the morning of 30th. The action put an end to the last serious invasion attempt: 'I think our sixteen years of fears of invasion are over', noted Horace Walpole. Walpole to Mann, 30 Nov. 1759: *Letters*, vol. 21, p. 350.

spilt we shall be greatly disappointed. Neither the present system of Europe, nor the Nature of War itself can possibly admit of such Indemnification.

When the Day of Peace is to arrive, or what are then to be the Conditions, far be it from me to presume to give any Opinion. But from his Majesty's Equity, Moderation, and true Magnanimity, we have the greatest Reason to hope that all our Engagements will be fulfill'd, and that the Reputation, as well as the Security of this Country, will be fully provided for.

[27] Bedford's Motion against Continuing the War in Germany, 5 February 1762: Add MSS 51380 f. 170

As early as 1759, William Pitt predicted: 'Perhaps it is not too much to say that sustaining this war, arduous as it has been and still is, may not be more difficult than properly and happily closing it'.[107] This was all too true. Britain's overseas objectives were reached at an earlier stage than her allies' continental objectives: the naval and colonial victories of 1759–60 contrasted sharply with the reverses experienced by Frederick the Great and his allies in Germany. Continental involvements became steadily more unpopular in Britain, a trend accentuated by arguments deployed in pamphlets like Israel Mauduit's *Considerations on the Present German War* of 1760. After the death of George II, ministerial reshuffles eventually called in question this strategy of continental commitment. Bute replaced Holdernesse as Secretary of State for the Northern Department in March 1761; Pitt's resignation from the other Secretaryship in October left Waldegrave's old rival as the dominant figure in the ministry. By early 1762, Bute was exploring the possibility of a negotiated peace and leading the Cabinet in that direction.

The 'Blue Water' school of strategy, which Pitt had deserted by his military engagement in Germany, now reasserted itself. Newcastle (still First Lord of the Treasury until Bute replaced him on 29 May 1762) was inclined to peace by the escalating cost of the war; Bute occupied a similar position; the Duke of Bedford, who became Lord Privy Seal on 25 November 1761, went even further in his advocacy of 'peace at any price'. Britain's declaration of war against Spain on 4 January 1762 and the death of the Czarina Elizabeth on the following day, which took Russia out of the war against Prussia, spurred Bedford to action. On 5 February in the Lords, he moved

To resolve, That it is the Opinion of this House, that the War at present carried on in *Germany* is necessarily attended with a great and enormous Expense; and that, notwithstanding all the Efforts that can possibly be made, there seems no

[107] Pitt to Hardwicke, 20 Oct.1759: Add MSS 35423 f. 193.

Probability the Army there in the Pay of *Great Britain*, so much inferior to that of *France*, can be put into such a Situation as to effectuate any good Purpose whatsoever; and that the bringing the *British* Troops Home from *Germany* would enable His Majesty more effectually to carry on with Vigour the War against the United Forces of *France* and *Spain*, give Strength and Security to *Great Britain* and *Ireland*, support Publick Credit, and, by easing the Nation of a Load of Expense, be the likeliest Means, under the Blessing of God, to procure a safe and honourable Peace.[108]

Bute was persuaded that Russia's *volte-face*, and the possibility of Dutch participation in the war, required Britain to maintain her continental commitments in the short term in order to compel an early peace; yet Bute and Cumberland failed to dissuade Bedford from pressing ahead with his motion. Horace Walpole wrote that Bedford, out of hostility to Pitt,

resisting the most earnest entreaties of the Duke of Cumberland, and even without the approbation of the Court, determined to make his motion, which, however, he softened from a proposal of recalling the troops from Germany, into a resolution of the ruinous impracticability of carrying on the war. He might as decently have termed it an exhortation to Spain not to dread our arms. Lord Bute, to show the Court did not countenance so gross a measure, moved the previous question, and was supported by Newcastle, Melcomb, and Denbigh. Lord Temple of course opposed the Duke of Bedford. The Lords Shelburne, Pomfret, and Talbot spoke for the motion; but the previous question was carried by 105 to 16, which latter were the friends of Bedford and Fox. Six or seven even protested.[109]

Devonshire's list of the minority includes Waldegrave, voting with Earls Talbot and Gower, and the Duke of Bedford himself. Bute was reported as saying he was 'most angry with Lord Waldegrave and Lord Weymouth', two of the deserters; 'Lord Bute told the Duke of Newcastle that the Duke of Bedford sheltered them or else the King would make some example'.[110] Waldegrave's position, as expressed in these drafts, was ambiguous.[111] He avoided praising or condemning the war in Germany: to praise it would be to offend the new King, to condemn it would be to renounce his own alignment with Newcastle. At the same time, he refused to endorse Pitt's claim of 13 November 1761 that America had been conquered in Germany. In one draft, f. 170, Waldegrave argued that war on the continent was unavoidable until peace was made, and that a sound peace would hold out the prospect of a future avoidance of continental entanglements. In other,

---

[108] *Lords Journals*, vol. 30, p. 155.   [109] Walpole, *George III*, vol. 1, p. 107.
[110] P.D. Brown and K.W. Schweitzer (eds.), *The Devonshire Diary* (Camden 4th series, vol. 27, London, 1982), pp. 156–7.
[111] Hardwicke's notes of the debate are printed in *Parl. Hist.*, vol. 15, cols. 1217–19. Waldegrave is not mentioned as a speaker there, or in the much fuller version of the debate drawn up by Sir James Caldwell and printed by K.W. Schweitzer, 'The Bedford Motion and House of Lords Debate 5 February 1762', *Parliamentary History* 5 (1986), 107–23. It seems likely that Waldegrave did not speak in this debate, despite the care he took to draft a speech.

presumably later, drafts this position was reversed. By speech no. 29, the prospect of a further year's warfare in Germany becomes decisive; by speech no. 30, the war in Spain is held to compel a step already recognised to be desirable in itself. Which speech was delivered is unknown; it seems possible that Waldegrave remained silent and merely voted against Bute.

My Lords

That the War in Germany has been a weighty Load upon this Country, is a Truth which is known to every Man. But without enquiring whether our former Conduct has been wise or desperate; without enquiring who were the persons who first engaged us in this German War, or who are those who have adopted it since the Accession of his present Majesty. Let us confine ourselves to a Question of much greater Consequence. What are we to do in our present Situation, are we still to pursue the War, to the utmost of our Ability, or is it to be totally given up.

My Lords, I will very freely declare my Opinion, that if we look back to almost every Speech from the Throne, to almost every Address from Parliament, or to almost every Treaty which has been laid before us, it will appear that we have no Option. Till we can procure a reasonable Security to our Allies either by a separate or by a general Peace, it will be shameful even to think of a Retreat.

When the Day of Peace is to arrive, or what are to be the particular Conditions must depend upon Circumstances of which I am totally ignorant. But from his Majesty's Magnanimity Moderation and Justice, we have great reason to expect that we shall not discover such an Eagerness for Peace, as may render our Enemies overbearing and obstinate: and on the other hand, that we shall not dispute upon Trifles, if ever Terms shall be proposed which are fair and reasonable. That all our Engagements will be fulfill'd, as far as they are practicable. And that the Reputation as well as the Security of our Country will be properly attended to. And if hereafter in the sober Hours of Peace, it should be perceived that we have proceeded on too extensive a Plan. That great and powerful as we are, our Courage has exceeded our Strength. Let us grow wise from dear bought Experience, and for the Sake of our Allies as well as of ourselves let us never more involve ourselves in the like insuperable difficulties, which in the End may prove fatal to both.

My Lords I have deliver'd these my real Sentiments free from all personal considerations, without the least Inclination either to flatter or to offend any Man. On many Occasions I can accquiesce to the Opinion of Others, but in an affair of so great Importance, it is right that I should have an Opinion of my own.

But whether this German War, by exhausting the Strength of the

Enemy, has contributed to our Success in other Parts of the World where the Interest of Great Britain is more immediately concern'd. Is a Question of a more doubtful Nature which does not admit of the clearest demonstration.

[28]   A draft in reply to Bedford's motion, 5 February 1762: Add MSS 51380 f. 174. Further drafts: ff. 168, 180.

My Lord

I shall trouble Your Lordships with a few Words, but without presuming to dive into the Secrets of Government, I shall confine myself to such general Propositions as are within the Compass of every Man.

The several Powers engaged in this bloody and expensive War, have declared their desire of Peace upon just and reasonable Terms.

Yet supposing all these Professions should be equally sincere, and allowing, that the Disputes between France and England may be easily adjusted, a great Difficulty will remain of doing that which is right for our Allies, without doing wrong to ourselves.

That the American War was productive of the War in Germany, that our Allies have distinguish'd themselves by their Courage and Fidelity, and have suffer'd in a Quarrel entirely English, are truth[s] which cannot be denied: and in return we are bound to support them, to the utmost of our Power, by the strongest Tyes of Honor and Justice.

At the same time Honor and Justice like all other virtues have certain Lymits. Therefore because it is a duty to do as much as we can, it does not follow that we are to attempt Impossibilities, nor things which if possible, would be a Prejudice instead of a Benefit.

If, for example, there was a probable Expectation that by carrying on the War another Year we might deliver Hesse, save Hanover, and secure to the King of Prussia a reasonable and honorable Peace: we are bound to try the Experiment, notwithstanding all the Danger notwithstanding all the Difficulties.

But on the other hand, should it be more probable, that after the Expense and Devastation of another Campagne, our Condition may become more desparate possibly that we may neither have Armies to fight for us, nor Grown[d] to fight upon, it were better to compound immediately whilst we are able to assist them in some other Shape. Than to endanger our Credit at home and expose our Allies to a dangerous and dishonourable Dependance on French or Aust[r]ian Moderation.

There is also another Question which deserves the most serious Attention. What Advantages are we to derive from a War wherein as far as England has been immediately concernd, our Success has exceeded even the most sanguine Expectations. The general Question may be answerd in a few Words, a safe and honorable Peace. Yet my Lords let us not deceive ourselves. Safety and Honor we have a Right to expect: but if we require a solid Compensation for all the Treasure that has been exhausted, for all the Blood that has been spilt, we shall be greatly disappointed neither the present System of Europe, nor the Nature of War itself can possibly admit of such Indemnification.

When the Day of Peace is to arrive, or what are to be the particular Conditions, must depend on Circumstances of which I am totally ignorant.

But from his Majesty's Magnanimity, Moderation and Justice we have great Reason to hope that we shall neither discover such an Eagerness for Peace as may render our Enemies overbearing and obstinate. Nor on the other hand we shall not dispute upon Trifles, whenever Terms are proposed which are fair and reasonable: that all our Engagements will be fulfil'd, as far as they are practicable: and that the Reputation as well as the Security of this Country will be fully provided for. I shall only add that I have deliverd my real Sentiments without the least Inclination either to flatter or offend. For tho I shall never be an Enemy to any Man who shall deserve well of my King and Country. I scorn to profess a Friendship which I do not feel.

[29]   A draft in reply to Bedford's motion, 5 February 1762: Add MSS 51380 f. 169.

That our Allies in Germany have distinguish'd themselves by their Courage and Fidelity, and have suffer'd in a Quarrel entirely English is a Truth which cannot be denied; and in return, we are bound to support them to the utmost of our Power, by the strongest Tyes of honor and Justice. Yet Honor and Justice like all other Virtues have certain Lymits, therefore because it is a Duty to do as much as we can, it does not follow that we are to attempt Impossibilities, nor things which, if possible, would be a Prejudice rather than a Benefit.

As to the King of Prussia, I do not insinuate because the annual Treaties are expired, that therefore all Tyes are dissolved, that we are under no Engagement whatsoever. I only say that great and respectable as he is, he is not to dictate to this Country, either in what manner, or in what Degree we are to give him our Assistance. And as to our other Allies, it is time we should discover some new Means of supporting them, since no Condition can be more deplorable, than that unavailing Protection which we have hitherto afforded them.

In a Word, tho there are some weighty Reasons against our withdrawing the Troops, there is one Reason on the other Side which must outweigh all others. The Moment this Negotiation is broken off, a new Scene of War lies open before us, we are not barely to consider whether we can raise Supplies for one Year longer, but in what manner we are to counteract an Enemy, who in Places where she is vulnerable has little left to lose, and who will endeavour to effect by Delay, that which by Arms she can never accomplish.

It is of little Consequence to enquire who were the Persons, who first engaged us in this continental war, who were those who extended it in the last reign, or who were those who adopted it since the Accession of his Present Majesty. I beli[e]ve all of them acted for the best. But if hereafter in the sober hours of Peace, it shall be perceived that we have proceeded on too extensive a Plan. That great and powerful as we are our Generosity has exceeded our Ability, our Courage has exceeded our Strength, let us grow wise from dear bought Experience, and for the Sake of our Allies as well as of ourselves, let us never more involve ourselves in the like insuperable Difficulties which in the End may prove fatal to us all.

[30]   A draft in reply to Bedford's motion, 5 February 1762: Add MSS 51380 f. 168.

That our Allies in Germany have distinguish'd themselves by their Courage and Fidelity, and have suffer'd in a Quarrel entirely English, is a Truth which cannot be denied. And in return we are bound to support them, to the utmost of our Power, by the strongest Tyes of Honor and Justice.

Yet Honor and Justice like all other virtues have certain Lymits. Therefore because it is a Duty to do as much as we can, it does not follow that we are to attempt Impossibilities, nor things which if possible, would be a Prejudice rather than a Benefit.

If for example there was a probable Expectation that by carrying on this continental War another Year we might deliver Hesse, save Hanover, or secure to the King of Prussia a reasonable and an honorable Peace, we are bound to try the Experiment notwithstanding all the danger notwithstanding all the difficulties. But on the other hand should it be more probable that after the Expence and Devastation of another Campaign, our Condition should become more desparate, it were better to compound immediately, whilst it is in our Power to give some Assistance to our Friends in some other Shape.

As far as the King of Prussia is concern'd it does not appear to me that the British Troops in Germany can be of any Use whatsoever. And as to our other Allies, no condition can be more Deplorable than that unavailing Protection which we have hitherto afforded them.

In a Word, tho there are some weighty Reasons against our withdrawing the Troops, there is one Reason on the other Side which must outweigh all others. Since Spain has declared against us, a new Scene of War lies open before us. The withdrawing our Troops from Germany is no longer an Act of Choice, it is an Act of mere Necessity, if that Necessity did not really exist, it would be shameful even to think of a Retreat. Having deliver'd these my real Sentiments free from all personal Considerations, without the least Incilination either to flatter or offend any Man, whatever may be the Consequence of the Motion, so properly made, and so ably supported by the N[oble] D[uke], I shall rest satisfied in having spoke my Mind in having perform'd my Duty to my King and Country.

And if hereafter in the sober Hour of Peace, it shall be perceived that we have proceeded on too extensive a Plan, that great and powerful as we are, our Courage has exceeded our Strength; let us grow wise from dear bought Experience and for the Sake of our allies, as well as of ourselves, let us never more involve ourselves in the like insuperable Difficulties which in the end may prove fatal to us all.

[31] Notes of the Motion, 5 February 1762: Add MSS 51380 f. 167.

This incomplete passage corresponds in substance to the text of the motion moved by Bedford and printed in *Parl. Hist.*, vol. 15, cols. 1218–19, and *Lords Journals*, vol. 30, p. 155. Waldegrave probably took down the text while the debate was in progress, or wrote it out shortly afterwards.

That an humble Address be presented to his Majesty, most humbly to lay before his Majesty the great and extraordinary Expence of the British Troops serving in Germany. The little Probability that an Army so much waisted by Sickness, desertion, and the common Accidents of War, can be recruited in so effectual a Manner as may answer those good Purposes for which it was intended, also that a greater Number of National Troops at home would give Strength and Security to Great Britain and Ireland, would support public Credit, and frustrate the united Efforts of his Majesty's Enemies.

Also to submit to his Royal Consideration the Opinion of this House [breaks off]

[32] The Militia Act, March–April 1762: Add MSS 51380 f. 172.

The Militia Act of 1757 was due to expire in May 1762. George II, still a committed supporter of regular troops, had threatened Newcastle in 1760 that he would veto any Bill to make the militia perpetual, and Newcastle was initially resistant to such a proposal.[112] But the King's death put off the issue for a year, until the session of 1761–2. The end of the war was still not in sight; on the contrary, war had been declared on Spain. With the new King thought to be in favour of a militia, the friends of that scheme took the opportunity to press for its continuance in perpetuity. This

[112] Western, *Militia*, p. 171, 176.

provision was duly embodied in a Bill during its passage through the Commons but deleted in the Commons' Committee on 19 March 1762, being replaced with a clause limiting the Bill to seven years. Newcastle then used his influence to see the Bill through the Lords; it received its 1st reading on 29 March 1762 as 'An Act to explain, amend, and reduce into One Act of Parliament, the several Laws now in being, relating to the raising and training the Militia within that part of *Great Britain* called *England*'. Waldegrave was present for the 2nd reading on 5 April, but not for the remaining stages: the Committee on 6th (an attempt to amend the Bill being defeated by 55 votes to 10), the 3rd reading on 7 April.

Waldegrave's reference in this draft to perpetuity suggests that he wrote it before this provision was deleted in Commons Committee; it seems possible that this speech of protest was never delivered. The militia regulations were eventually made perpetual in 1769, after the expiry of the 1762 Act.[113]

When the settlement of a Militia for a time limited was formerly under Your Lordships' Consideration, I was for giving the Experiment a fair Tryal, and voted for the Bill because it was founded on a right Principle, tho it seem'd lyable to some very reasonable Objections.

As to the present Militia Bill whereby the temporary Law is to be render'd perpetual, I am strongly against it for this plain Reason, because it appears to me to be still an Experiment which has happily succeeded in some Particulars, but has not hitherto been fully tryed.

The Utility of a Militia in the present War we have already experienced: that its Operation may be totally different in time of Peace, seems more than possible. What can be more dangerous than the present military Spirit difused over the whole Nation, when such military Spirit shall be totally unrestrain'd by military Discipline. For tho it may be said that the Militia is not like the Army composed of the Idle, and Profligate, who can only be restrain'd by the Fear of Punishment, but is composed in general of Men of a better Sort Men who have Families and Property to defend: yet how can we flatter ourselves that this better sort of Men will undergo the various Hardships of personal Service, when at the Expence of a few Guineas they can serve by Deputy. For admitting that the Farmer or substantial Tradesman would readily take arms in Defence of his Property, in cases of Rebellion, Invasion or any sudden Emergency: Can it be expected that such Men should leave their Families, neglect their Business, and subject themselves to military Law, merely to enable Government to send more Troops to Germany or to North America.

Besides, Experiments of so extensive a Nature where a whole Nation

[113] Western, *Militia*, pp. 184–93, 199. The Bill became law as 2 Geo. III, c. 20.

must cooperate, will frequently deviate from those good Purposes, for which they were plan'd.

Now whether this Militia hereafter in the Hands of the Crown shall too nearly resemble an Army of regular Forces: or whether in the Hands of Lords Lieutenants, or of any popular Leader, they shall be used as an Instrument to overawe the Crown, in times of Violence, and Civil Disention: either Alternative will be dangerous to the Constitution, may be equally fatal to a limited Monarchy.

At the same time that I have these Doubts concerning a Militia, I admit its Utility, as long as it shall be properly administer'd, and I wish its Continuance by a temporary Law, tho I can never give my Consent to its Immortality.

For notwithstanding the Distinction between a perpetual regular Army, and a perpetual Militia, I must oppose both on the same Principle, the Dangers of both are of the same Nature tho their Degrees of danger be somewhat different.

I shall only add, that we enjoy an excellent Constitution, yet the best Constitution in the World may be endanger'd by too much Refinement: Names may hereafter mislead us, when Things are totally changed; and whilst we are grasping at the Shaddow of Liberty we may lose the Substance.

[33–34] The Lords' Address in reply to the King's Speech, 25 November 1762.

The summer of 1762 witnessed the takeover of the ministry by Bute. On 29 May he succeeded Newcastle as First Lord of the Treasury, and Sir Francis Dashwood deposed Lord Barrington as Chancellor of the Exchequer. George Grenville succeeded to Bute's Secretaryship of State, and the Earl of Halifax replaced the Pelhamite Lord Anson at the Admiralty (Grenville and Halifax were later exchanged in order to reduce Grenville's influence in the Commons). When the Duke of Devonshire was dismissed from his office of Lord Chamberlain in October for refusing to support the peace treaty, the rout of the Pelhamites was complete. Pitt and Newcastle now found themselves heading separate groups in opposition to the ministry; when the peace preliminaries were presented to both Houses on 9 December, Pitt was to speak against.

Meanwhile, even greater importance attached to the impression the new ministry would make at the opening of the parliamentary session on 25 November. The extreme political sensitivity of the peace terms[114] made the ministry's position hazardous, and the possibility of carrying through both Houses a treaty which ceded any of Britain's spectacular conquests was

[114] For the diplomatic negotiations see Z.E. Rashed, *The Peace of Paris 1763* (Liverpool, 1951).

open to question. Bute was obliged to turn to a political figure of surpassing skill and experience as a political manager. In early October, Henry Fox was acknowledged as the leader of the ministerial group in the Commons. The Duke of Cumberland remained opposed to the peace, but Fox detached himself from his patron and seized the chance of power. With him, Fox brought a number of his associates including the Earl of Sandwich and, with qualifications, Waldegrave.

After Devonshire's dismissal, Newcastle openly declared his opposition and called on his followers to resign their offices and join his campaign against the ministry and its treaty; some followed him, but many declined to do so for reasons both of principle and self-interest. Among those who placed loyalty to the King and the desirability of an advantageous peace above loyalty to Newcastle and a continued war on the continent was Earl Waldegrave. He did, indeed, refuse to hold office under Fox, and Waldegrave himself was presumably Horace Walpole's source for the manner of the refusal.[115] Nevertheless, it seems from these two drafts that Waldegrave spoke for the Address in reply to the King's Speech. That Speech itself signalled the ascendancy of the peace party in the Cabinet. In October 1760, Pitt had compelled the alteration for the published version of the new monarch's first Address to his Privy Council: 'a bloody and expensive war' had become 'an expensive but just and necessary war'.[116] On 25 November 1762, the King's Speech at the opening of the parliamentary session began: 'My Lords and Gentlemen: I found, on my accession to the throne, these my kingdoms engaged in a bloody and expensive war'.[117] It went on to look forward to the consideration by Parliament of the peace preliminaries signed at Fontainbleau on 3 November and published in the English press shortly afterwards. The Lords' Address of Thanks was moved by Lord Egmont and seconded by Lord Weymouth;[118] Waldegrave evidently supported it. There was no division. Newcastle complained to Hardwicke: 'I suppose your Lordship, was as little pleased, as I was, with the appearance of the House of Lords, yesterday. Such Shameful Adulation to the Minister & such a Hum of Applause, I never expected to see, in this House of Lords'.[119]

[33]   A draft of Waldegrave's speech on 25 November 1762: Add MSS 51380 f. 176.

The endorsements on f. 178 below suggest that f. 176 is the preliminary draft; but this is not certain.

---

[115] Walpole, *George III*, vol. 1, pp. 155–6: see above, pp. 90–6.
[116] Brooke, George III, p. 75. Waldegrave's account of the Council meeting, in his *Memoirs* of the Accession of George III: section 4 above.
[117] *Parl. Hist.*, vol. 15, cols. 1230–6.   [118] Walpole, *George III*, vol. 1, p. 174.
[119] Newcastle to Hardwicke, 26 Nov. 1762: Add MSS 32945 f. 153.

My Lords

Your Lordships have heard his Majesty's Speech from the Throne and as I have a Motion to make relative to which it is necessary I should trouble Your Lordships with a few words, I will come directly to the Point and not take up Your Lordships time in making any Appology. And in the first place tho Political Reasoning is not allways productive of the clearest demonstration yet if we look round us and consider the present situation of Affairs I believe no proposition can be more self evident than that a reasonable Peace must greatly contribute to the common benefit of all Europe.

The House of Austria for several Years past has been in a constant State of War, ever since the death of the late King of Poland they have scairse had any interval, and tho by the Assistance of their Friends they certainly might have prolong'd the war for some time, yet Peace is the only sure remedy for the recovery of their shatter'd Strength.

The King of Sardinia has certainly made a brave stand against the united force of the House of Bourbon he has both attack'd with vigour and defended himself with resolution, yet when we consider that the common chance of War, that the loss of one Battle, from being master of a considerable part of Italy might soon have reduced him to his own Capital, surely as he is wise as well as valliant he must have dislik'd so precarious a situation.

As for the Du[t]ch I shall only say that a general Peace seems as necessary in their present condition, as their entering vigorously into the war would have been some time ago when the State of their Affairs was very Different.

As for the French tho they have succeeded in many of their undertakings they also have felt the reverse of fortune they have had their share of Publick Calamity, before the war with England the[y] were in effect the second Maritime Power in Europe, and their naval force and Trade dayly increasing would soon have render'd them at least our Equals, this is totaly changed, their Merchants ruin'd, their Stoutest Ships taken or destroy'd reduces them to so low an ebb that nothing but Peace can give them the least chance of a recovery. Even their Victorys by land have been dearly purchass'd, what an infinite loss of Men, what Burdens have been laid on the Subject towards carrying on this destructive war, such a load as we never felt I hope never shall feel. The Spaniards had still stronger reasons to be tir'd of the war for while the[y] labour'd under the same disadvantages as the French the[y] had not the same probability of making themselves amends in any other Shape. With regard to ourselves tho his Majesty's Fleets had obtain'd victorys equal to the greatest examples History can produce, tho they were justly the terror of the World as far as trade and Navigation extend. Tho his land forces ever gave the most undoubted proofs of that true spirit and Resolution which numbers cannot depress nor danger terrify, tho these troops were commanded by a General who must often meet with success because he will allways deserve it, tho in every respect we did our Duty. Yet when we consider, the great expence that naturaly attended the War which tho chearfuly paid must be severely felt, and other reasons which must occur to Your Lordships tho perhaps improper for me to mention, it certainly became our interest to put an end to the War.

But tho the expediency of such a measure was obvious to everyone yet the bringing it into execution must be an affair of great difficulty. We were engaged with a Brave a Politick and dangerous enemy, equal to all the force that had been brought against it far superior to our Allyes, unsupported by our powerful Assistance, when terms of peace were offerd, had we slighted their Proposals and shewn to[o] great an indifference it must have created new confusion, and have t[h]rown our affairs back allmost beyond a Possibillity of reconsiliation, As on the other side too egar a desire of Peace might have obstructed the means of obtiaining it for had our enemys once perceiv'd that we were resolv'd at all events to put an end to the war that we wanted either men mony or Spirit to resist them, weary as the[y] were they would have given us no terms but such as English men could never submit too. Even under the most favourable circumstance the restoring Peace must be attended with great difficulty, for it never can be effected where many different Partys are engaged till many opposite interests are reconsil'd, and not only enemys satisfied but likewise friends often times more unreasonable than Enemyes themselves.

Whither this has been entirely our case I will not pretend to assert so far at least is certain whatever the difficultys were the[y] now no longer subsist, and a Peace is happily concluded which I hope will prove both safe and honourable, and it is a consideration which must give the highest satisfaction when we reflect that it is singly owing to his Majesty's Prudence Magnanimity and Support, duely seconded by a Brave a grateful and a free People that this great end is accomplished. And as Your Lordships example must have very great weight nothing can contribute more to the settling our affairs on a lasting and sure foundation than our giving the most publick testimony of the confidence we so justly repose in his Majesty and our shewing the World that his glorious endeavours for the safety honour and wellfare of his People shall ever meet with our most effectual Assistance.

I therefore humbly move &ra

[34] Waldegrave's speech seconding the Address, 25 November 1762: Add MSS 51380 f. 178

The endorsements on the reverse of the manuscript suggest that Waldegrave had the speech in his hand as he delivered it, using his notes as a prompt.

My Lords.

Your Lordships have heard his Majesty's Speech from the Throne, and as I have a Motion to make, relative to which it is necessary I should trouble Your Lordships with a few words, I will come directly to the Point and not take up Your Lordships time in making any Appology, and In the first Place tho political Reasoning is not allways productive of the clearest demonstration yet if we look round us and consider the present situation of Affairs, I believe no proposition can be more evident, than that the Peace and Tranquillity we now enjoy is not only necessary for our own prosperity and happyness but must greatly contribute to the common benefit of all Europe.

In what proportion every partickular Country is benefited by it I will not pretend to ascertain so far at least is certain that even those who during the war had the greatest appearance of Success whatever they gain'd in one Shape the[y] lost in another and whilst they only plum'd themselves with imaginary advantages were expos'd to all the severity of real distress.

I should not so much as have touch'd on the state of Affairs in other Countrys had they not been so far connected with those of our own that whatever affects them must in some measur affect us also. It is from the continuance of Peace alone that we may expect to see our trade flourish, our taxes lowerd, and the weighty Burden of national debt gradualy deminish, but were these and all other advantages to our selves only the Peace from whence they are deriv'd would stand on a very loose foundation, mutual amity must be founded on mutual Interest. For tho the individuals of which different nations are compos'd may esteem and honour each other, yet between nation and nation no friendship can subsist but that which is meerly political.

The most solemn treatys have sometimes been made use of only as temporary expedients, different Inter[e]sts will easily find different constructions for the same words and when powerfull Princes have a mind to quarel a pretence at least a plausible one will never be wanting, and tho I am thoroughly persuaded that all our friends mean to do every thing that is right, yet to be a little on our guard not to trust ourselves entirely to the faith of others is surely the safest Policy.

My Lords when we consider that our Island is still guarded by those Fleets that have obtain'd victorys equal to the greatest examples History can produce, that have been justly the terrour of the wor[l]d as far as trade and Navigation extend. When we have land forces that have ever given the most undoubted proof of that true Spirit and resolution that numbers cannot depress nor danger terrify. When these troops are commanded by a general who must often meet with success because he will allways deserve it. When we have a Prince on the Throne ever attentive to the true Interest of his People, too wise too prudent to lead them into unnecessary danger and whose magnanimity is equal to his prudence, when we reflect on these advantages it is then our safety seems no longer precarious these are our Guarantees this is our Security.

And as Your Lordships example must have very great weight nothing can contribute more to consolidate every thing and settle our affairs on a lasting and sure foundation, than our giving the most publick testimony of the confidence we so justly repose in his Majesty and shewing the world that his glorious endeavours for the safety, the honour and the wellfare of his People shall ever meet with our most effectuall assistance.

[Endorsed on the back:]
and in the 1st Place the Political Reasoning
in what Proportion every partickular Country
I should not so much have touchd
It is from the continuance of Peace alone
The most solemn Treaty are sometimes
My Lords when we consider that our Island
and as your Lordships example must have very great

[35] The Debate on the Peace Preliminaries, 9 December 1762: Add MSS 51380 f. 181. Draft: f. 180

Horace Walpole wrote:

The memorable day, December 9th, being arrived, both Houses sat on the preliminaries. Lord Shelburne and Lord Grosvenor moved to approve them. The Duke of Grafton, with great weight and greater warmth, attacked them severely, and, looking full on Lord Bute, imputed to him corruption and worse arts. The Duke was answered by the Earl of Suffolk; and then Lord Temple spoke with less than usual warmth. The Favourite rose next, and defended himself with applause, having laid aside much of his former pomp. He treated the Duke of Grafton as a juvenile member, whose imputations he despised; and, for the Peace, he desired to have written on his tomb, 'Here lies the Earl of Bute, who, in concert with the King's ministers, made the Peace'. A sentence often re-echoed with the ridicule it deserved, and more likely to be engraven on his monument with ignominy than approbation. The Duke of Newcastle and Lord Hardwicke censured the preliminaries, which the latter said were worse than could have been obtained the last year; and he reflected on the assiduity with which prerogative was cried up, more than it had been by the most ductile Parliaments. Henley the Chancellor abused them both; but the fine defence of the treaty was made by Lord Mansfield, which, he said, though he had concurred to make, he should still retain his old connections and attachments; a promise he soon violated, with as little decency as his late friends had censured prerogative. At ten at night the preliminaries were approved by the

Lords without a divison.[120]

The Lords then passed an Address of Thanks to the king, moved by Lord Shelburne and seconded by the Earl of Halifax.[121] This relatively quiet debate contrasted sharply with the conflict in the Commons, where a $3\frac{1}{2}$ hour speech by Pitt was insufficient to halt the preliminaries; and the Court triumphed by 319 votes to 65.

Were we to form our Judgment of the Peace by comparing the success of the War with the Articles under Your Lordships Consideration, those who have been the Makers of such a Peace would have much to answer for.

On the other hand, if we consider how much we keep, as well as how much we restore. If we consider the State of our Finances, and above all, the difficuty I will not say the Impossibility of completing our Fleets and Armies. We may perhaps be of Opinion that those who have disengaged us from these Difficulties, have perform'd a necessary Service for their King and Country, and have merited our Approbation, rather than our Reproach.

If at the end of a six Years War, we require a solid compensation for all the Treasure which has been exhausted, for all the Blood which has been spilt, we can never be satisfied. Neither the present System of Europe, nor the nature of War itself, can anywise admit of such Indemnification.

It is easy to point out what might have been better, in some Particulars, but whether that better could have been obtain'd, is exceeding doubtful. Be that as it will, I only pretend to judge for myself, and upon the whole, I am satisfied. I shall only add that I have deliver'd these my real Sentiments, free from all personal Considerations, without the least Inclination to either flatter or to offend any Man.

I shall only add, that if hereafter in the sober Hours of Peace, it shall be perceived that we have proceeded on too extensive a Plan. That powerful and successful as we have been, our Generosity has exceeded our ability, our Courage has exceeded our Strength. Let us grow wise from dear bought Experience. And for the Sake of our Allies, as well as of ourselves, let us avoid the like Extremes, and let us never more engage ourselves in the like insuperable Difficulties, which in the End, might prove fatal to us all.

As to the King of Prussia, tho it would have been wrong to have continued the War till he was satisfied. I most sincerely wish that in the affair of Wesel, and some other Particulars, we had been more attentive to his Interest.

After having assisted him with so much Spirit and generosity whilst he was at the very Brink of the Precepice, it seems bad Policy to cancel all Obligations, when his greatest Difficulties are removed, when he may soon be at Leisure to indulge either his Gratitude or his Resentment.

[120] Walpole, *George III*, vol. 1, pp. 175–6.   [121] *Parl. Hist.*, vol. 15, cols. 1251–7.

However I do not affirm that by the Letter of any Treaty we were bound to do more. I only express my Wishes that more had been done: that we might have finished this glorious War without either Speck or Blemish: as free even from the slightest Suspicion, as from any real Reproach.

And if hereafter in the sober Hours of Peace, we should perceive that we had proceeded on too extensive a Plan, that powerful and successful as we have been, our Generosity had been too great for our Finances, our Spirit has exceeded our Strength: let us grow wise from dear bought Experience, and for the Sake of our Allies as well as of ourselves, let us avoid the like Engagements, which if they should not be accompanied with the like good Fortune and the like Success, might be productive of the most fatal Consequences.

[36–38] The Cider Tax, 28 March 1763.

Bute's nominee Sir Francis Dashwood had become Chancellor of the Exchequer in May 1762; he undertook the duty of drawing up the first postwar budget, an endeavour to close the gap between income and expenditure by finding new sources of revenue. One such was an increase in customs duties on wine and cider, and an additional excise duty on English cider.[122] This made an easier target for the ministry's enemies than the reasonable and advantageous peace terms, and the opposition seized the chance to incite an outcry 'copied from the noise on the Excise in my father's time', as Horace Walpole observed.[123] Pitt and many country gentlemen, especially those for the cider-making counties, fought the Bill in six successive divisions as it passed the Commons with certain amendments.

In the Lords the main clash came on the 2nd reading on 28 March. Waldegrave was present and evidently delivered what proved to be his last speech in the House: two days later we fell ill with smallpox, and died on 8 April. It was also Hardwicke's last speech in the Lords (he died on 6 March 1764). The opponents divided the House both at the 2nd reading on 28 March (the Bill passing by 83 votes to 41) and the 3rd reading on 30th (again a Court victory by 73 to 39). It was, observes Cobbett's *Parliamentary History*, 'the first time the Lords were ever known to divide upon a Money Bill.'[124] Hardwicke's biographer too notes that his subject's 'last recorded

---

[122] Betty Kemp, *Sir Francis Dashwood: An Eighteenth-Century Independent* (London, 1967), pp. 54–62.
[123] Walpole to Mann, 10 April 1763: Walpole, *Letters*, vol. 22, p. 126.
[124] *Parl. Hist.*, vol. 15, col. 1316, listing the minority on 30 March: Waldegrave is not among them. The *Lords Journals* record his attendance on the 2nd reading only. But Hardwicke's list of speakers on 28 March does not include Waldegrave: *ibid.*, cols. 1311–3; cf. Walpole, *George III*, vol. 1, pp. 199–201.

vote was given against a money-bill, a right of the Lords which had been rarely exercised, but which had never become obsolete.'[125]

Whether the Lords could initiate a money bill, or amend one originating in the Commons, were dormant but unresolved questions. Although the Commons had a strong practical case, it could produce 'little or no historical proof of its validity'.[126] Conflict had arisen in 1661, 1665 and 1667 when the upper House had initiated such measures, and in 1671, 1677 and 1679 when Lords' amendments to Commons' money bills were reversed in the lower House. The issue recurred in William III's reign with the Commons sometimes accepting but usually resisting the Lords' alterations, and finally devising the procedure of 'tacking' other measures to money bills to force them through the upper House. This innovation was fiercely contested, however, and proposals for a tack were rejected in the Commons in 1704, 1712 and 1713. Thereafter there was an uneasy truce, though the issue was not as uncontentious a one as is sometimes suggested.[127] In February 1739/40, Lord Carteret reminded the peers that

we have never yet yielded to them [the Commons] the sole and exclusive right of granting supplies, or that we have not a right to alter and amend those money-bills they send up to us. It was but in the year 1696, that they came to a resolution, which they afterwards made a standing order, not to confer with this House about any amendment made by us to a money-bill, and this is the only determination this affair has yet met with, which is a determination we are not in the least obliged to stand to.[128]

A similar claim was made by Lord Shelburne in 1778 and 1782.[129]

In parliamentary terms, these protests were unavailing. The Cider Bill passed, and remained on the statute book until repealed by the Rockingham ministry in 1766. With the peace and the cider duty successfully carried by large majorities, Bute's position seemed secure: 'Now, bating the slight distemperature occasioned by the cider-tax, England seemed to be willingly, and submissively, prostrate at the Favourite's feet'.[130] But the political turmoil of the opening years of the reign, and the outcry fomented over these two issues in particular, had weakened Bute's determination to hold power; on 7 April he gave notice of his intention to resign his office. Whether as a failure of nerve, or as an example of political disinterestedness, it was a remarkable transformation of the political scene. The major

[125] Yorke, *Hardwicke*, vol. 3, p. 383.
[126] Sir William Holdsworth, *A History of English Law*, vol. 10 (London, 1938), p. 586.
[127] E.g. Mark A. Thomson, *A Constitutional History of England 1642 to 1801* (London, 1938).
[128] *Parl. Hist.*, vol. 11, col. 486.
[129] Holdsworth, *loc. cit.*, p. 587. It might be argued that the Commons' claims were not securely established until 1861: cf. Luke Owen Pike, *A Constitutional History of the House of Lords* (London, 1894), pp. 342–5.
[130] Walpole, *George III*, vol. 1, p. 201.

obstacle to Waldegrave's advancement was now removed. It was, tragically, too late: he died the next day.

[36]   A Speech on the Cider Tax, 28 March 1763: Add MSS 51380 f. 183.

I have no particular Objection to the Tax upon Cyder, and so far from having any Dislike to Excise, I think it the best method of collecting, provided it be subject to such Regulations as are agreeable to the Spirit of a free Government.

But if we are to form no Opinion of our own either as to the manner in which money is to be collected, or as to the Purposes to which it is to be apply'd: few Constitutional Questions will come under our Consideration and in our Legislative Capacity we shall be very useless indeed.

Therefore I had rather Risk the confusion of throwing out the whole Bill, than that this House should have the least doubt of making an amendment of real Consequence, if the end proposed by such Amendment appear'd just and reasonable.

[37]   Possibly a speech on the Cider Tax, March 1763: Add MSS 51380 f. 185

My Lords.

If in consequence of any Difference with the Commons, or on any Occasion whatsoever, a Motion should be made in this House, which carried with it the least diminution of their just Rights, and Privileges, it would be acting directly conterary to our own Interest, if we did not immediately discourage such unconstitutional Encroachments.

For whenever the Commons lose any share of that Power which justly belongs to them. We shall never be the Gainers, on the conterary, our own Rights and Priveleges will be very precarious.

But my Lords, as it would be neither just nor prudent to encroach on others, so on the other hand, it would be mean as well as imprudent, were we to suffer Encroachment.

But to come directly to the Point. The great Sourse of Difference between this and the other House of Parliament, has been either when our Judicature has interfered with what they call their Priveleges. Or when we have thought proper to make Alterations or Amendments in what they call Money Bills. I shall not trouble Your Lordships as to the first Article, which no way relates to the present Consideration.

But as to the other Article of Money Bills, it undoubtedly deserves our most serious Attension.

[38] Possibly a speech on the Cider Tax, March 1763: Add MSS 51380 f. 186

My Lords, I neither mean to recur to original Right, or to avail myself of ancient Precedents. Since those times great changes have been made, I think much for the better. For tho the Peerage has lost, the Constitution has been Improved and consequently the Nation has been the Gainer.

For a great Number of Years all Aids to the Crown, have had their Rise in the House of Commons. As the Representatives of the People may naturally be supposed the best Judges, both as to the Burden their Constituents can bare, and as to the easiest Manner of raising it. At the same time no Bill can pass into a Law without our Concurrence. And to say that we have no power over the most Minute Article, and yet have Power over the whole, seems to me a direct Absurdity. Indeed adding to a Tax, may not improperly be call'd laying a new Tax, which by Custom ought to begin in the other House. But this Argument certainly cannot hold good either against lowering a Tax, or against other Alterations of an indifferent Nature.

Another Consideration of a very serious Nature, is what Bills are, what are not Money Bills.

In former times when the Demene of the Crown was sufficient to answer the common expences of Government Aids or Subsidies, then the only Money Bills, were only granted on extraordinary Occasions.

But of late Years not only real Money Bills, but others which improperly go under the same Denomination, are greatly multiplied.

Now my Lords, if every Bill wherein Money is any ways concerned, be admitted a Money Bill, and by a kind of tacit Renunciation, we are to make no Amendments. I can think of no Act either private or publick, which may not be changed into a Money Bill, with very little Difficulty. So that in the Course of a few Years, we may be no more considerable, in our Legislative Capacity, than the Crown itself.

The Crown indeed will always be strong, as it is at present, by its executive Power. But we should be nothing more than a Court of Judicature, and the real Force of the Legislature would be in the Commons only.

But allowing, as I said before that the Representatives of the People are the best Judges what Burden the Nation is able to bare. We are undoubtedly equal Judges of the Measures, of the Exigencies which make that Burden Necessary. and if we disaprove of those Measures or of any Part of them or if it appear to us that the Commons have committed any Mistake to which all Bodys of Men as well as individuals are sometimes lyable, it becomes our Duty to sett it Right.

I know, My Lords it may be said, that tho the Right is undoubtedly on our Side, yet there may be prudential Reasons, why that Right should not now be exerted, and that a Dispute with the Commons in our present Situation, may be attended with very bad Consequences. Nothing indeed can be more certain than that any Part of the Legislature may either claim Powers which do not belong to them or may overturn the Constitution by a desparate Use of those Powers which they really have.

The former will probably sometimes happen. But God forbid, that the latter should ever be the case. The Commons may so far mistake their own Interest, as to wish to acquire Power at our Expence. But they certainly can never mean to stop the wheels of Government. Much less would they ever destroy that Constitution of which themselves are now become so considerable a Part.

Therefore, as Reason and Justice are apparent on our Side, our adhering to our just Rights and P[r]iveleges is a Debt which we owe not to ourselves only, but to our King, and to our Country.

I shall conclude with this Observation that Bodies of Men seldom chuse to set the Bounds to their own Authority. Whatever Concessions are made, tho they may not instanly lay in new Claims, they still look forward and wait the first Opportunity.

Perhaps no House of Parlimaent has ever yet declared, so far our P[r]iveleges do extend and no farther.

[39] Occasion unknown: Add MSS 51380 f. 189

My Lords

I rise up to second the Motion that has been made by my Noble Friend and I do it with less Diffidence and Apprehention, because it has allready been so ably supported and sett before Your Lordships in so clear a light that the thing speaks itself and requires no farther Argument to inforce it.

And I am so well convinced of Your Lordships earnest Desire of expressing in the strongest terms our Duty and Gratitude to the best of Kings, that I need give Your Lordships no farther Trouble but conclude as I began by most heartily seconding the Motion.

[40] Occasion unknown: Add MSS 51380 f. 188

This note of a witty reply suggests that Waldegrave sometimes made notes *after* a debate of what he remembered he had said.

The noble Lord has been pleased to call the Opposition to this Bill, an Opposition of Faction. The Expression may perhaps seem somewhat hard. Yet I am persuaded the noble Lord did not make use of the Word Faction as a Term of Reproach, but rather meant it as a Compliment. For his Lordship must be sensible that whenever he quarels with Faction, he will lose one of the best Friends he ever had in his Life.

9

NOTES FROM PLUTARCH

This section and the following are evidence of Waldegrave's thinking on constitutional questions, and on his sources. Printed from Add MSS 51380 f. 233.

From Plutarch

There were Societies at Lacedaemon, where the Members were chose by Ballot, each of the Electors had a small Ball of soft Bread, a Waiter carried a Pitcher upon his Head, those who approved of the candidate threw in their Ball without altering its Figure: those who disapproved press'd the Ball flat between their Fingers. One Negative excluded.

Lycurgus would never reduce his Laws into writing.

Lycurgus being advised by some pretended Patriot to establish a popular Government. Desired the Adviser to try the experiment in his own Family.

One of Licurgus's Laws was that the Lacedaemonians should not make War often, or long, with the same Enemy, least they should instruct the Enemy in the Art of War.

Solon being ask'd whether he had left the Athenians the best Laws that could be given: answerd that he had establish'd the best Laws they could receive.

It was a saying of Cato's, that wise Men learn more from Fools, than Fools from wise Men.

Some young Men being brought before Pyrrus for having rail'd at him, in their Cups, he ask'd them if they had said such things of him. One of them answer'd, we did Sir, and should have said much more if we had had more Wine. Pyrrus smiled and discharged them.

10

NOTES FROM MONTAIGNE

Printed from Add MSS 51380 f 245.

Montagne's Definition of a Lyer is that he is brave towards God, and a Coward towards Men.

Tacitus says of Tiberius when he was dying, Iam Tiberium vives et corpus, non Dissimulatio, deserebant.

Of all Kind of Men, God is least beholden to Kings, for he doth most for them, and they do ordinarily least for him.

It is a strange desire to seek power and to lose liberty. Or to seek Power over others, and to lose power over a Man's self.

Certainly great Persons had need to borrow other Mens Opinion to think themselves happy, for if they judge by their own feeling they cannot find it.

Preserve the Rights of inferior Places, and think it more Honor to direct in chief, than to be busy in all.

Judges ought to remember that their Office is *Jus dicere* not *Jus dare* to interpret the law not to give law.

It is the Solecism of Power to think to command the End, and yet not to endure the Mean.

Kings have to deal with their Neighbours, their Wives, their Children, their Prelates or Clergy, their Nobles, their second Nobles or Gentlemen, their Merchants, their Commons, and their Military Men, and from all these arise Dangers.

It is not always true that War cannot justly be made but upon a precedent injury or Provocation. For there is no question, but a just fear of an imminent Danger, tho there be no Blow given, is a lawful Cause of War.

It is bad Policy for a King to depress his Nobles, it may indeed make him more absolute, But he will be less safe, and less able to perform any thing he desires.

There is little Danger from the Common People, except where they have great and Potent Heads or where you meddle with Religion, or their Customs, or their Means of Life.

The true Composition of a Counsellor is rather to be skilfull in his Masters Business, than in his Nature, for then he is like to advise him and not to feed his humour.

It is one thing to understand Persons, and another thing to understand Matters, for many are perfect in Mens humours, that are not greatly capable in the real Part of Business.

Cunning is a sinister or crooked Wisdom.

Solon said to Croesus, who in Ostentation shew'd him his Gold, Sir, if any other come who hath better Iron than You, he will be master of all this Gold.

No People over charged with taxes, if they long continue, will be fit for Empire.

The Ambitious Man who seeks to be eminent amongst able Men, hath a great Task, but that is ever good for the publick. But he that plots to be the only figure amongst Cyphers, is the Decay of a whole Age.

Where foreign materials are but Superfluities, foreign Manufactures should be prohibited, for that will either banish the Superfluity, or gain the Manufacture.

11

NOTES FROM MONTESQUIEU

Printed from Add MSS 51380 ff 241–4. Waldegrave's marginal titles are here denoted by italics; the passages referred to are identified in the editor's footnotes.

Charles de Secondat, Baron de Montesquieu (1689–1755) was a friend of the French-educated 1st Earl Waldegrave (1684–1741) and may have met the 2nd Earl also. Significantly, this friendship derived from Montesquieu's acquaintance with the Jacobite Duke of Berwick, which dated from 1716. The Baron thereby gained an introduction to Berwick's nephew, the 1st Earl, and Waldegrave and Montesquieu travelled together in 1728 – the Englishman to take up his post as Ambassador at Vienna, the Frenchman on the Grand Tour into Italy. It was from Waldegrave that Montesquieu received a letter of introduction to Chesterfield, then envoy at the Hague, and thanks to Berwick's and Waldegrave's contacts, the philosopher's stay in England in 1729–31 was passed to a large degree in the company of Tories and opposition Whigs. Back in Paris in 1734, we catch a glimpse of Montesquieu and the 1st Earl as members of the same masonic lodge; and the young Lord Chewton, soon to succeed to the earldom, may have met his father's distinguished friend during these years at the Paris embassy.[1]

Montesquieu's great work had been in preparation for twenty years. When published as *De l'Esprit des Loix* (Geneva, 1748), it enjoyed immediate currency. The 2nd Earl's friend Horace Walpole commended it as 'the best book that ever was written',[2] and Waldegrave himself obviously shared this favourable opinion. The *Monthly Review* was quick to publish translated extracts of passages most relevant to an English audience.[3]

---

[1] Robert Shackleton, *Montesquieu: A Critical Biography* (Oxford, 1961), pp. 90, 93–4, 119–20, 123, 126, 173.
[2] Walpole to Mann, 10 Jan. 1750: Walpole, *Letters*, vol. 20, p. 106.
[3] *The Monthly Review* 1 (1749), pp. 233–7 (July), 241–50 (Aug.), 381–92 (Sept), 401–7 (Oct).

Thomas Nugent's English edition of the whole work was published in London in 1750, and was reprinted in 1751, 1752, 1756 and 1758 during the 2nd Earl's lifetime; but Waldegrave's text differs from both the *Monthly Review* and the Nugent translations, and shows that the 2nd Earl worked from the original.

TRANSLATIONS FROM L'ESPRIT DES LOIX

Of Honour being the Principle of Monarchy.[4] It is true, to speak philosophicaly, it is a false Honour that guides every part of the State, but this false Honour is of the same use to the Publick in general, as the true Honour would be to the particular persons who are possess'd of it.

Of the Formalitys of Justice.[5] If you examine the Formalitys of Justice, relative to the Difficulty a Citizen labours under either to gett back, what has been taken from him, or to obtain redress for an injury he has receiv'd, you will certainly find their number too considerable yet if you consider the relation they have with the liberty and security of the People in general instead of too many forms you will often find them too few. And you will see that the trouble the expence, the Delays and even the Danger of Justice, are only the necessary Price that every Citizen pays for his Liberty.

Of the Dishonour of Punishment.[6] If there is a Country where Dishonour is not a necessary consequence of Punishment, it must proceed from Tyranny which has inflicted the same Punishment on Vilains and Honest Men.

Of setting bounds to a State.[7] The true power of a Prince does not so much consist in the facility he has to conquer, as in the difficulty there is to attack him, and if I may use the expression in the Immutability of his condition, for the agrandising of a State only lays open new sides whereby it may be taken.

Of the Augmentation of Troops.[8] A new disease has spread itself all over Europe, it has seiz'd upon our Princes and has made them keep up an extravagant number of Troops, its malignity is so violent, that it consequently becomes contagious. For as soon as one State encreases what it calls its troops, instantly other States encrease theirs also, by which means no one gains any thing any farther than that the ruin becomes general. Every Monarch keeps standing as great Armys, as he could raise if his People were in immediate danger of being exterminated, and this constant Effort of all against all is call'd *Peace*. Therefore Europe is in so ruinous a condition, that if Private Persons were in the same situation with the three most oppulent Powers of this Part of the World, they would not have where

[4] From Book 3, chapter 7.　[5] From Book 6, chapter 2.
[6] From Book 6, chapter 12.　[7] From Book 9, chapter 6.
[8] From Book 13, chapter 17.

with all to support themselves. We are poor, with all the riches and all the Commerce of the Universe and soon from having such a number of Soldiers, none but Soldiers will remain, and we shall be in the same condition with the Tartar.

The great Princes not satisfyed with hyering troops of the little ones, seek on every side to pay for Allyances, or in other words are finding out the most effectual means of throwing away their Mony.

The Consequence of such a Situation is the perpetual encrease of Taxes, and that which anticipates all future Remedys, we no longer depend on the annual Produce, but carry on the war by means of the Principal. It is no unheard of measure for States to morgage their funds even in time of Peace, and to take methods to ruin themselves which they call extraordinary ones, and which indeed are so extraordinary, that even the imagination of the most extravagant Men can hardly conceive them.

Effect of the Climate in England.[9] Slavery allways begins by a kind of drowsyness, but a People that can find Rest in no Situation, who is continualy feeling itself, and who finds Pain in every Part cannot easily fall a sleep.

Politicks is an imperceptible File, that wears by degrees, and moves slowly to its end. The Men we have mention'd can never bear the slowness the detail, the coolness necessary in negotiations, they will often succeed worse than any other nation whatsoever, and they will loose by their Treatys that which they have gain'd by their Arms.

Pride and Vanity.[10] Vanity is as useful a Spring to Government as Pride is a dangerous one, to prove which we need only consider on one side the many advantages that have their rise in Vanity, from thence luxury, Industry, Arts, Fashions, Politeness, Taste, and on the other side the many evils that proceed from the Pride of some Nations, Idleness, Pouverty, every thing abandon'd, the destruction of those Nations that Chance has t[h]rown into their Hands, and of their own also. Lazyness is the effect of Pride, industry the attendant of Vanity, the pride of a Spaniard will induce him not to work at all, the Vanity of a French Man will excite him to work better than other People.

Of England.[11] This nation may have great influence in the affairs of its neighbours, for as it will not use its Power to make Conquests, its friendship will be more saught after and its anger more dreaded, than either the inconstancy of its Government or its inward agitation seem to allow of.

Therefore it will be the fate of the executive Power to be allmost always desturb'd at home and Respected abroad.

[9] From Book 14, chapter 13. [10] From Book 19, chapter 9.
[11] From Book 19, chapter 27.

Of Publick Debts.[12] Some People have thought that it was well for a State to owe to itself, they thought that it increas'd the Richess by increasing the circulation.

I think they confounded a circulating Paper that represents Specie, or a circulating Paper which is the sign of the profit that a Company makes or will make by Trade, with a Paper that represents a Debt. The two first are of great advantage to the State, the last cannot, and all that can be expected from it is that it should be a good security to private People for what the Nation owes, that is to say that it should procure the Payment; but here are the inconveniencys that result from it.

If foreigners are in possession of a great part of that Paper that represents the Debt they draw anualy from the Nation a considerable Sum for the Interest. 2ly in a nation that is allways in Debt Change must be very low. 3dly the taxes rais'd for the payment of the interest is hurtful to Manufactures by making workmanship dear, 4thly it is taking away the Revenus of the State from the active and industrious to bestow them on those who are in a state of Idleness, that is to say they give the conveniencys for working to those who never work at all, and the difficultys only remain for those who do work. That which may occasion the Mistake is that a paper which represents a National Debt is certainly a sign of Richess for none but a rich State can support it with out falling into decay, its not falling into decay being a Proof that the State is very Rich in other respects. They pretend that there is no evil because there are remedys to the evil. They pretend the evil is an advantage because the remedys are stronger tham the Evil.

Of the Order of Succession in Monarchys.[13] It is not for the sake of the reigning family that the order of succession is establish'd in Monarchys but because the interest of the State requires that there should be a reigning Family.

The Law that settles the Succession of private Persons is a Civil Law, whose Object is the interest of private Persons, that which settles the Succession to a Monarchy is a political Law whose object is the good and preservation of the State.

It follows from thence that when a Political Law has oblig'd any Family to give up its Right of Succession, it is absurd to draw reason for a Restitution taken from the Civil Law, for Restitution is in the Law and may be good against those who live under the Protection of the Law, but they cannot be good for those who were establish'd, and who only exist for the sake of the Law.

It is ridiculous to pretend to decide of the Rights of Kingdoms, nations, and the Universe by the same maxims by which they decide in cases of Private Persons the Right to a Gutter, to use an expression of Cicero's.

---

[12] From Book 22, chapter 17.   [13] From Book 26, chapter 16.

Lending Mony on Interest.[14] They ['the schoolmen'] confounded the lending mony on Interest with Usury and condemn'd it as such. by which means trade that before was the profession only of low People became the busyness of dishonest Men, for when ever a thing is forbid which in itself is necessary or might be allow'd it only serves to render those who practice it dishonest Persons.

We begin to be cur'd of *Machiavelisme*, and the disease will decrease every day, More moderate councils are now become necessary, that which was formerly call'd a bold stroak of Politicks would at present, abstracted from the Horror of the thing be nothing more than great imprudence.

The Spanish West Indies.[15] I have often heard People lament the blindness of the Council of Francois Ier who gave no encouragement to Christopher Columbus when he propos'd the discovery of the West Indies, it is very possible they did thro imprudence a very wise action. Spain has acted like that mad Prince who ask'd that every thing he touch'd should turn to Gold, and who afterwards was oblig'd to beg of the Gods to put an end to his Misery.

An accidental Profit that does not depend on the Industry of the Nation, the number of its inhabitants, nor the cultivating its Lands, is a bad kind of Richess.

The King of Spain who receives great Sums from his Customhouse at Cadiz is in this respect nothing more than a Private Person exceeding rich, in a State that is exceeding poor, almost every thing passes between him and Foreigners so that his Subjects have little or no concern in it, which renders this Trade entirely independent of the good or bad fortune of this Kingdom.

Unnecessary laws.[16] The Laws that would make things appear necessary which in reality are of no consequence, only tend to make things of real Consequence appear unnecessary.

Of new Religions.[17] This is the fundamental Principal of Political Laws relating to Religion, when we have it in our Power in any State to receive a new Religion or not to receive it, we should not suffer it to be establish'd, but when once it is establish'd, it must be tollerated.

Under a despotick government[18] People strive more to keep what they have allready got than to make new acquisitions, in a Free Country, they are rather intent on getting more than in keeping what they have.

[14] From Book 21, chapter 20.
[15] From Book 21, chapter 22.
[16] From Book 29, chapter 16.
[17] From Book 25, chapter 10.
[18] From Book 20, chapter 4.

12

NOTES ON CONSTITUTIONAL LAW

Printed from Add MSS 51380 ff. 234–40.

John. The foundation of English Libertys, not to go so far back as the Saxon Government, may be dated from *Magna Charta* and the *Charta de Foresta*.

Most of the Benefits of Magna Charta are comprehended in ye 29th Chap:

No Freeman shall be taken or imprisoned, or disseised of his Freehold, or Liberties, or free Customs, or be outlaw'd, or exiled, or any other ways destroy'd. Nor will we pass upon him, or condemn him. But by the lawful Judgement of his Peers. Or by the Law of the Land. We will sell to no Man. We will deny to no Man. We will defer to no Man Justice or Right.

Before the Charta de Foresta the Norman Kings where ever they chose to have a Forest, order the Ground to be mark'd out, a Sort of Fence to be made, not regarding any Mans Property. And then punished with the greatest Severity and in the most arbitrary Manner, all those who transgress'd what they call'd the Forrest Laws.

Historians of those Times tell us that to make New Forest in Hampshire. Twenty two Parish Churches, besides Villages, Manors &ra were destroy'd. Besides New Forest it is said there were sixty eight other Forrests at that time in England.

That People began to recover there Liberties may be collected from what Bracton says, a famous Judge, and Lawyer in Henry ye 3d Time, *The King of England hath two superiors God and the Law*.

Edward ye 1st. The next is the Statute *de Tallagio non concedendo* where by no Aid or Tallage can be levied without the assent of Parliament.

Edward ye 3d. Statute of Treasons. Before this Statute, Treasons were extended to so many different Branches that it was difficult to know what was Treason, what not. But by this Act it is declar'd nothing shall be

Treason but what is therein particularly specifyed, except that which shall hereafter be particularly declared so by Parliament.

Charles ye 1st. The Petition of Right. Whereas the Contents of Magna Charta, Charta de Foresta, the Statute de Tallagio non concedendo are fully comprehended. And the Power and Independence of Parliament are more fully ascertain'd.

The Star Chamber abolished, which had been settled in the reign of Henry the 7th. This was a Court of Equity in criminal cases which were not capital. The Court was composed of some of the great Officers, Bishops, Chief Justices without a Jury. The[y] Punished by Fine, Imprisonment, and some corporal Punishments. And very arbitrary uses were made of this Court. And most Crimes against the Administration were by some means or other brought into this Court.

The Power of the Privy Council was restrain'd at the same time, by hindering them to take cognisance of civil Affairs between man and man, and other things which they had taken to themselves which were properly cognisable at Common Law.

The High Commission Court, established by Queen Elizabeth, relating to affairs of Religion, was also abolished about the same time.

Charles ye 2.

The *Habeas Corpus* Act. Before the passing of this Act there was a Writ of Habeas Corpus, a remedy at Common Law for those who were unjustly detain'd in Custody.

But it was often render'd useless, by the Judges, Sherifs, or even Gaolers who could occasion Delay, and sometimes entirely erode the Intention of these Writs.

By this Act every Prisoner is entitled to have from the Gaoler a copy of his *Mittimus*.

If Treason or Felony be not expressly charg'd, the Chancellor or any of the Judges must grant a Habeas Corpus, if demanded.

If upon return of the Habeas Corpus the Prisoner be not charged with Treason Felony or such crimes as are not bailable by Law, the Judge must discharge the Prisoner. Bail being given.

If Treason or Felony are Specially express'd then the Prisoner cannot have his Habeas Corpus, till he has petition'd in open Court in the first Week of Term, to be brought to Tryal. Then if he be not brought to Tryal the next Term he shall be bail'd and if not indicted the second term shall be discharged.

Charles ye 2. An Act passd soon after the Restoration for taking away the Court of Wards. Also the *Tenure in Capite K[n]ights Service*, and *Purveyances*. And for settling a Revenue on the King in lieu therof.

William and Mary. The Lords and Commons in Parliament assembled after having specified the Oppression and Tyranny of James ye 2d, his Abdication, and the Throne being Vacant. Make the following declaration,

That the pretended Power of suspending Laws or execution of Laws without Consent of Parliament is illegal.

That the Commission for erecting the late Court for Commissioners for Eclesiastical Causes was illegal. And all other Commissions of the like Nature are illegal also.

That levying Money without Consent of Parliament is illegal.

That a Standing Army in time of Peace without consent of Parliament is illegal.

That Subjects being Protestants may have arms for their own Defence suitable to their Condition.

That Elections for Members of Parliament ought to be free.

That the Freedom of Speech, and Debates and Proceedings in Parliament ought not to be question'd in any Court or Place out of Parliament.

That excessive Bail ought not to be required, nor excessive Fines imposed, nor cruel or unusual Punishments inflicted.

That Jurors ought to be duly impanel'd and return'd. and that in cases of Treason they should be Freeholders.

That Grants and Promises of Forfeitures before Conviction are void and illegal.

That for redress of Grievances, for amending, strengthening, and preserving the Laws, Parliaments ought to be frequently held.

That it is the Right of Subjects to Petition the King and that all Commitments, and Prosecutions for such petitioning are illegal.

13

NOTES ON THE CONSTITUTION

These pages evidently form part of the material prepared by Waldegrave for use in teaching Prince George during his years as Governor to the Prince, 1752–6. Printed from Add MSS 51380 ff. 238–40.

As to the other Branches of the Legislature, the Peers and the Representatives of the People. What are their seperate Rights and Privileges, how far they are dependant or independant of each other. Is a Subject of a more doubtful and delicate Nature, which however in general is easily understood.

But above all he who is to be entrusted with the executive Power, should know what are the Dutys of that Trust and how far that Power extends.

He should know that the Prerogative of the Crown is a discretionary Power for the more speedy Execution of certain necessary Acts of Government, with which he is entrusted for the public Good. And whether a Prince extends this Power beyond its proper Lymits. Or whether he fear or neglect to use it in those particular Cases where it ought to be exerted. He shews himself equaly unfit to govern, the Constitution is equaly betray'd.

The various Changes which our Constitution has suffer'd at different Periods, and under different Princes, should also be thoroughly understood. what Causes have produced those Changes, and the Effects which have followd them.

But more particularly it is necessary to be acquainted with that great Revolution of our Government in the Year 88, whereby we were not only preserved from the immediate Dangers of Popery and Arbitrary Power, but every thing being then ascertained, Points formerly problematical, and which Force alone could decide, are now made clear, by which a Foundation is laid for our lasting Security.

Besides this general Knowlege their are many particular Points which require a very nice Examination.

A Prince should be thoroughly acquainted with the Disposition and

Temper of the People he is to govern, with their Vices as well as with their good Qualities. He should know their Faults not to turn them to any particular Purposes of his own, but that he may use all lawful means to reclame and amend them. And their good Qualities being known and meeting with proper Encouragement, must naturaly be turned to the public Utility.

A Prince also should have a competent Knowlege of the Laws by which his People are governed. I do not mean that he should be qualified for a Lawyer, or to be his own Chief Justice, but that he should be acquainted with the Genius and the Spirit of the Law, which by our Constitution, must be executed in his Name and under his Authority.

Whether some Method might not be found out of reducing the Body of our Laws into one entire System, of rendering them so far intelligible to men of common Understanding that at least we might be able to judge for ourselves in the most common Actions of Life.

Whether in proceedings at Law, too great Advantage may not some times be taken upon very slight Errors in Point of Form.

Whether many of those Forms might not be entirely taken away without any great Inconvenience, or at least so far alter'd, that Suits at Law might be render'd less expensive, and be brought to a much shorter Issue; Are Questions of very great Importance worthy the Attention of the whole Legislature.

The next Branch I shall touch upon is in relation to our commercial Interest. The great Source of the Riches and consequently of the Strength of this Country.

Trade must be supported by great, extensive, and rational Measures. By giving proper Encouragement to Arts, Industry, Manufacturs, and Navigation. Not by jobs which may be hurtful to thousands, whilst Favor is only shewn to a particular Person, a Particular Company, or a Particular Set of Men.

It is right therefore for a Prince on many occasion[s] to advise with considerable Merchants, Men of Knowledge in their Profession, and of fair Character. He should hear what they have to propose, and ought to give them proper Assistance when ever it appears reasonable and necessary.

But never suffer them to dictate, should never be directed by them.

A Prince also should know that as Trade gives us Wealth, our Maritime Force gives us Security, and consequently demands his very serious attention.

Riches, Defence, and Power, flowing from the same Source, clearly point out the natural Strength of this Country.

A Man may have Inheritance in title of Nobility and Dignity three Ways. By Creation, by Descent, and by Prescription.

By Creation two ways. by Writ, and by Letters Patents. The first Creation by Patent was by Richard ye 2d AR II to John Beauchamp de Holt Baron of Kedminster. It is to be observed that if any Man is call'd to Parliament by Writ, he hath a fee simple in the Barony, tho there be no Words of Inheritance.

But if he be created by Patent, the State of Inheritance must be limited by apt Words, or else the Grant is void.

If a Man be call'd by Writ to Parliament and the Writ be deliver'd to him, and he dieth before he sits in Parliament, Quere whether he was a Baron or no. Answer he was no Baron, for the Direction and Delivery of the Writ to him, maketh not him noble, and the Writ hath no Operation until he sit in Parliament and thereby his Blood is ennobled to him and his Heirs lineal. Lord Coke concludes that tho the Creation by Writ be the ancienter, the Creation by Patent is the surer. For a Man may be sufficiently created by patent, and made Noble, tho he never sit in Parliament.

14

NOTES ON ENGLISH HISTORY

Probably as part of his duties at Leicester House, Waldegrave drew up a simple abridgement of European history, A.D. 307 to 1725 (Add MSS 51380 ff. 191–202) and an outline of the constitutions of a number of European states (*ibid.*, ff. 202–12), the latter possibly abstracted from a handbook like John Campbell's *The Present State of Europe* (4th edn., London, 1753). Neither section reveals much of Waldegrave's own attitudes. More useful in this respect is his abridgement of English history from the reign of William the Conqueror (*ibid.*, ff. 213–32), again presumably prepared for the instruction of the two princes. The section from 1603 is printed here.

1603 Queen Elisabeth dyes at Richmond. Elisabeth carried things to the greatest height whereever her Prerogative was concern'd. imprison'd Members, deny'd freedom of Speech, under pretence of restraining licentiousness of Speech. Would not allow Matters of State or Religion to be debated. Suffer'd great abuses to the Hurt of Trade, in Relation to Monopolies. But all this was suffer'd as she certainly had great Abilities, was saving of her Subjects Money and in very difficult times kept the Nation safe and quiet at Home. And she was fear'd and respected abroad.

On the conterary her Successor James the first, who did not in reality carry the Prerogative higher than Queen Elisabeth. Yet by squandering the Nation['s] Wealth amongst unworthy Favorites, talking ridiculously about his Prerogative. Making himself contemptible both at home and abroad. Did not meet with the same Obedience as was paid to the Superior Abilities of Elisabeth. His arbitrary Acts mett with greater Opposition. And his son Charles the First pursuing the same Measures, using arbitrary means of raising Money without the Consent of Parliament. Not calling Parliament, which he found he could not govern. At last when he could not carry on Affairs without them, they in their Turns, and in their own Defence, carried things to Extremity. Which ended in the King's Ruin.

As Parliaments would not do for James and Charles what they had done for Elisabeth and others of their Predecessors who they fear'd and esteem'd. Charles and James attempted to do without Parliaments.

There was another essential Difference in the Conduct of Elisabeth, from that of James and Charles. She often refused subsidies which Parliament granted. They wanted more than what the Parliament chose to grant and not being supply'd according to their expectations, they raised money without Consent of Parliament. An Oppression which at all times the Nation never could bare patiently. Charles took Tonage and Poundage, which indeed had been granted to other Kings for their Lives before it was granted to him. Ship Money he also rais'd, and forced Loans, and Benevolences.

1661 Soon after the Restoration the Militia vested in the Crown. Act of Uniformity.

1662 A Conference between both Houses on a Road Bill. The Commons object to Amendments made by the Lords because they related to assessing the Commons. The Lords quote Precedents in a Bill for the assessment of Horse and Arms in P[hilip] and Mary, another for repairing Dover Pier in Queen Elisabeth, and another for rating the Poor. All which bills began in the House of Peers. The Commons object as they are only single Instances.

The Peers agree with the Commons in the Money Clauses, and adhere to a Clause of the Number of Horses.[1]

William and Mary 1689. Bill of Rights pass'd, being an Act declaring the Rights and Liberties of the Subject, and settling the Succession of the Crown.

At the third reading of this Bill in the House of Lords, a Rider was offer'd, that all Pardons on an Impeachment of the House of Commons should be null and void, unless with the Consent of both Houses of Parliament. The Rider was rejected.

1689 The Act of Toleration pass'd. Tho the repealing of the Sacramental Test, for the Admission of Protestant Dissenters into Places and Employments had not succeeded. This Act of Toleration was carried. Whereby all penal Laws for not coming to Church &ra were repeal'd.

1701. Lord Somers impeach'd on Account of the Partition Treaty.

George 1st. 1719 An Act pass'd entitled an Act for the better securing the Dependancy of Ireland on the Crown of Great Britain. In this Act the House of Lords in Ireland are restrain'd from all Judicature. And it is also declared in the Act that the Kingdom of Ireland hath been, is, and of right ought to be subordinate unto, and dependant upon the Crown of Great

---

[1] For Waldegrave's defence of the constitutional prerogatives of the House of Lords, see above, speeches 16, 21, 36–8.

Britain and that Acts of Parliament made in England are binding to the People and Kingdom of Ireland.

Anne 1703–4. Ashby and White and the Aylesbury Men. Differences between the two Houses of Parliament upon the great Question, Whether an Action lyes at common Law for an Elector who is denied his Vote for Members of Parliament.

In this dispute, the Right was evidently on the side of the House of Lords, and the Queen in her Answer to the Address of the House of Lords tells them that she certainly would have granted the Writ of Error, but that it was necessary to putt an end to the Session of Parliament. The Parliament was accordinly prorogued soon after which ended the Dispute.

A writ of Error is clearly not a Writ of Grace, but a Writ of Right.

Upon Ashby's having carryed his Cause against White before the House of Lords, other Aylesbury Men attempted the same method of Proceeding, were imprison'd for Contempt by the House of Commons. Sued out their Habeas Corpus but three Judges of the Kings Bench sent them back to Prison conterary to the Opinion of Chief Justice Holt. These Men on being remanded back Petition the Queen for a Writ of Error to bring the Affair before the Lords.

All Suits are begun and carried on by the Kings Writs.

INDEX

acts: Papist Registration (1714), 22–3; Heritable Jurisdictions (1747), 39, 246–9; Buckingham Assizes (1748), 39n, 249–52; Regency (1751), 49, 156, 162, 252–3; Forfeited Estates (1752), 54, 58; Clandestine Marriage (1753), 156; Jewish Naturalisation, repeal (1753), 19; Sheriff Depute (1755), 247; Paddington Road (1756), 275–6; Seamen's Wages (1758), 86, 290–2
Addison, Joseph (1672–1719), 14
Adolphus, John, historian, 112n, 130
Ailesbury, Thomas Bruce (1656–1741), 2nd Earl of, 7
Aix la Chapelle, conference of (1748), 35, 48, 65
Albemarle, William Anne Keppel (1702–54), 2nd Earl of, 42, 48, 137, 139
Albemarle, George Keppel (1724–72), 3rd Earl of, 43, 89, 94, 139–40
Albemarle, George Thomas (1799–1885), 6th Earl of, 130, 132
Alcide, 68
Allen, John (1771–1843), polemicist, 119–27
Almon, John, journalist, 242
Amelia, Princess, daughter of George II (1711–86), 54
America, 61, 67–72, 158–9, 189–90, 259, 270–1, 280–4, 298
Anne, Queen, 2, 64
Anson, 1st Baron (1697–1762), Admiral, 33, 43, 85, 140, 168–9, 173, 185, 208, 244n, 303
Argyll, Archibald Campbell (1682–1761), 3rd Duke of, 33, 216, 247n, 275
Argyll, John Campbell (c. 1693–1770), 4th Duke of, 43
Arthur's, *see* White's

Asburnham, John (1724–1812), 2nd Earl of, 42, 47–8, 56
Ashby v. White, 331
Astley, Thomas, journalist, 242n
Atterbury, Francis (1662–1732), Bishop, 27
The Auditor, 238 and n
Audley, James Touchet (1723–69), Lord, 24
Augusta, Dowager Princess of Wales (1719–72), 14, 50, 53–6, 58, 64n, 72–3, 76–9, 90, 111, 113–15, 124–6, 129n, 130, 133, 135, 140, 144, 149, 156, 159–60, 162–4, 170, 176–83; as 'Penelope', 228–37; 238, 252, 262, 274
Austria, 65–71, 166–7, 172, 212, 283n, 294n, 305
Austrian Succession, war of, 26, 42, 65
Ayscough, Rev. Francis (1700–63), 52

Bagehot, Walter, 2, 6
Barré, Isaac (1726–1802), MP, 239 and n
Barrington, William Wildman (1717–93), 2nd Viscount, 43, 47, 171, 221, 240n, 303
Bath, William Pulteney (1684–1764), 1st Earl of, 33, 42, 47, 156n, 278
Bathhurst, Allen (1684–1775), 1st Baron, 52, 56
Bavaria, 65, 166
Bedford, John Russell (1710–71), 4th Duke of, 17, 35, 41, 48–9, 51, 54, 58–9, 83, 90, 130, 156n, 187, 199, 204–5, 254, 275, 295–301
Bellfield, Robert Rochfort (1708–74), Baron, later 1st Earl of Belvidere, 46
Bentley, Richard, 108
Berington, Fr Joseph, 23n, 29
Berkeley of Stratton, John (c. 1697–1773), 5th Baron, 37
Berwick, James Fitzjames (1670–1734), Duke of, 22, 27, 31–2, 318

Bohemia, 65, 283
Bolingbroke, Henry St John (1678–1751), 1st Viscount, 13, 52, 55–6, 125, 128, 132–3
Borley, Essex, 21n, 23n
Boscawen, Admiral Edward (1711–61), 68–9, 159, 173, 294n
Boswell, James, 77–8
Bourgogne, Duc de (d. 1712), 13n
Braddock, Major General Edward (1695–1755), 66–7, 158, 189
Breda, conference of (1746), 35
British Critic, 21, 76, 113, 163n
British Review, 113, 116n
The Briton, 238 and n
Brodie, George, 120
Brougham, Henry (1778–1868), 1st Baron, 123, 130
Brunswick, *see* Hanover
Bryant, Jacob (1715–1804), on Bute, 164n
Buckingham, John Hobart (1723–93), 2nd Earl of, 292
Buckingham, Lady Catherine Darnley (?1682–1743), Duchess of, 31–2
Buckinghamshire, politics of, 249–52
Burke, Edmund (1729–97), MP, 49, 94, 117, 128, 130
Burnet, Gilbert (1643–1715), Bishop, 124
Bussy, François de, 27
Bute, John Stuart (1713–92), 3rd Earl of, 4, 13, 18, 32, 43, 53, 62, 64 and n., 72–3, 75–9, 87–91, 93–8, 111, 113, 128, 129n, 130, 133, 140, 149, 163–4, 170, 176–8, 182–3, 193, 197–8, 214–17, 219–20; as 'Bombastus Vigorosus', 229–37; 238, 240n–241, 253, 262, 286, 295–7, 303–4, 308, 310–11
Butler, Joseph (1692–1752), Bishop of Durham, 50
Butterfield, Sir Herbert, 1, 21, 112n
Byng, Admiral John (1704–56), 116, 173, 188–90
Byron, George, Lord (1788–1824), 107, 133–4

Cameron, Dr Archibald, 60
Cardigan, George Montagu (1712–90), 4th Earl of, 24, 43n, 56
Cardigan, Elizabeth Waldegrave (1758–1823), Countess of, 109
Caroline, Queen (1683–1737), 5, 31, 40
Caroline, Queen, trial of (1820), 104, 109n
Carteret, Lord, *see* Granville
Catholicism, Roman, 11, 15, 21–4, 27–32, 58, 244–5, 254–8, 264–7
Cave, Edward, journalist, 242n

Cavendish, Lord Frederic (1729–1803), MP, 94
Charles I, King, 21, 249, 324, 330
Charles II, King, 4, 31–2, 86, 279, 324
Charles Edward Stuart, Prince, 40, 245
Chesterfield, Philip Dormer Stanhope (1694–1773), 4th Earl of, 9–10, 12, 42, 47, 74, 197–8, 261, 318
Chewton, Somerset, 21, 23, 25–6, 108
Cholmondeley, George (1703–70), 3rd Earl of, 208
Churchill, Col. Charles (c. 1720–1815), 46n, 87, 250n
Cider Tax, 95, 310–14
Civil War, 121–2
Clarendon, Edward Hyde (1609–74), 1st Earl of, 2, 124
Clément, Pierre, 30n, 46–7, 256
Cobham, Richard Temple (1711–79), Viscount, 54
Coke, Edward (1719–53), Viscount, 44
Coke, Lady Mary (1727–1811), 87
Colburn, Henry, 108
Cologne, 65
Conway, General Henry Seymour (1719–95), 43, 96, 103n
Cornwall, 50–2, 97
Cosimo III, Grand Duke, 22
Court, culture of, 1–21, 49–50, 52–9, 147–8, 179, 199, 208–9, 211, 213
Coxe, Archdeacon William (1747–1828), historian, 25–6, 110
Craggs, James (1686–1721), 23
Cresset, James (d. 1775), 55 and n, 72, 124–5, 143–4, 159
Croker, John Wilson (1780–1857), MP, 3–4, 113–17, 119, 126
Cumberland, William Augustus (1721–65), Duke of, 25, 38–40, 42, 47–8, 51, 54–5, 59, 66n, 69–70, 72, 74, 80, 82–5, 88, 90–2, 94, 99, 114, 126, 140, 155–6, 159–60, 162, 164, 168, 192–3, 214, 216, as 'Cambrianus', 226–37; 252–3, 276, 296, 304

Damer, Mrs Anne Seymour, 103
Dashwood, Sir Francis (1708–81), MP, 303, 310
Debrett, John, 242
Defoe, Daniel (?1661–1731), 13n
Delafaye, Charles, 29–30
Delawar, John West (1693–1766), 7th Baron, 35–6
Denbigh, Basil Feilding (1719–1800), 6th Earl of, 95, 296
Descartes, René, 22n

Index

Devonshire, William Cavendish (1698–1755), 3rd Duke of, 33, 42, 50, 157, 162
Devonshire, William Cavendish (1720–64), 4th Duke of, 5, 42, 47, 49, 79–85, 91–4, 154, 186–7, 192–3, 199–201, 204, 208, 210–11, 303–4
Digby, Edward (1730–57), 6th Baron, 43, 74
Dissenters, 265–6
Doddridge, Philip, 43
Dodington, George Bubb (c. 1691–1762), 1st Baron Melcombe, 42–3, 58, 72, 108, 112, 115–16, 129–30, 132, 186, 194–5, 254n, 296
Dorset, Lionel Sackville (1688–1765), 1st Duke of, 42, 47, 81, 208, 210
Douai, Benedictine college, 21n, 28–9
Downe, Henry Dawnay (1727–60), 3rd Viscount, 45, 47, 89
Drax, Harriet, 41, 87
Dupplin, Thomas Hay (1710–87), Viscount, 196

Echard, Laurence, historian, 56
Edinburgh Review, 11–12, 76n, 77, 113, 119–27
Edward, Prince (1739–67), 13, 53, 56, 126, 183n
Egmont, John Perceval (1711–70), 2nd Earl of, 43, 50, 72–3, 88, 185, 194–5, 304
Egremont, Charles Wyndham (1710–63), 2nd Earl of, 42, 139n, 201
Elias, Norbert, 2, 19n
Elibank, Patrick Murray (1703–78), 5th Baron, 11, 60
Elizabeth, Queen, 329–30
Elliot, Gilbert (1722–77), MP, 97
Ellis, Welbore (1713–1802), MP, 241
Erskine, Sir Harry (1710–65), MP, 89
Erskine May, Sir Thomas (1815–86), 130–2
Escobar y Mendoza, Antonio, Jesuit, 232
Eton, 29–30, 32, 97, 110, 164n, 229n, 241n, 255
Etough, Henry, 12n

Fane, Charles (1707–66), 2nd Viscount, 47
Fauconberg, Thomas Belasyse (1699–1774), 4th Baron, 24 and n
Fawcett, Christopher, 59, 62, 125
Fazackerley, Nicholas (?1685–1767), MP, 44, 243
Fénélon, François de Salignac de la Mothe (1651–1715), Archbishop, 13, 19
Fitzjames, Henrietta (c. 1667–1730), 22, 31, 245n

FitzWalter, Benjamin Mildmay (1672–1756), 19th Baron, 38
Fleury, Cardinal (1653–1743), 26–7
Fox, Henry (1705–74), MP, 26, 33, 42, 60, 63–4, 66n, 67, 70, 72, 74, 78, 80–1, 83, 85, 89–96, 99, 108, 112–15, 120, 126, 129, 153–7, 160–2, 168, 170–1, 183–4, 186–7, 192–4, 198, 201–4, 208, 213n, 261, 275–6, 284n, 296, 304
France, 2, 5–7, 9, 13, 22, 25–7, 40, 61, 64–72, 166, 172, 246, 259, 272, 281, 294, 305–6
Frederick, Prince of Wales (1707–51), 2, 5, 12, 34–5, 39–40, 43, 49–52, 54, 64, 74, 78, 88, 148n, 155, 158, 162, 164, 183n, 227n, 243, 248n, 249–52, 278
Freeman, E.A., historian, 121
Froude, J.A., historian, 121

Galmoye, Piers Butler, 3rd Viscount, 22n
Gardiner, S.R., historian, 121
Gentleman's Magazine, 44, 238n, 242n, 293n
George I, King (1660–1727), coronation, 2; court of, 4–5; treatment of son, 12n; and 1st Earl, 24; will of, 25; 330
George II, King (1683–1760): accession, 8; coronation, 2; court of, 3–5; and Prince Frederick, 12; and 1st Earl Waldegrave, 24; suppresses father's will, 25; and diplomacy, 26; favours 2nd Earl Waldegrave, 37, 48–50, 253; and Hanover, 46, 162–3, 175, 222, 245–6, 261; and Leicester House, 54–9, 143–5, 163–70, 176–83; conciliates Fox, 63, 161–2; foreign policy, 64–72; plans for 2nd Earl, 74–6; uses 2nd Earl as negotiator, 79–82; controversies over 1750s, 112–33; 2nd Earl's character of, 146–8; and politics of 1757, 186–211; on British constitution, 206–7; as 'Augustus', 226–37; death, 213
George III, King (1738–1820): court of, 4; on kingship, 10–11; as Prince of Wales, 52–9; as 'Telemachus', 226–37; his education, 13–14, 52–3, 73, 140, 176, 253–8, 262–7; problems at Leicester House, 52–9; political opposition, 72–84, 170, 176–83, 277–80; aversion to 2nd Earl Waldegrave, 53, 78–9, 99; brother's marriage, 87; accession, 88, 213–17; marriage, 89, 164–5, 170; and Peace of Paris, 90–6; attacks on, 107, 133–4; historical controversies concerning, 112–34; 2nd Earl's character of, 148–9, 176–7
Gifford, William, 105

336 Index

Glorious Revolution, 1688, 21n, 22–3, 56, 118, 121, 132, 256, 258, 264, 326
Gloucester, Duke of (1743–1805), 87
Glover, Richard (?1712–85), MP, 112n
Godfrey, Mrs (Arabella Churchill) (1648–1730), 31–2
Goodall, Dr J., 110
Gower, John Leveson (1694–1754), 1st Earl, 41, 43, 88–90, 95, 204, 208, 296
Grafton, Charles Fitzroy (1683–1757), 2nd Duke of, 33, 42, 47, 50, 103, 135, 183, 199, 275
Grafton, Augustus Henry (1735–1811), 3rd Duke of, 135–6, 308
Grafton, Henry (1790–1863), 5th Duke of, 134–5
Granby, John Manners (1721–70), Marquess of, 93
Granville, John Carteret (1690–1763), 1st Earl, 33, 37, 49, 150, 168, 176, 178, 185, 196, 199, 202, 204, 278, 311
Grenville, George (1712–70), MP, 43, 62, 73, 103, 157, 174n, 186, 250, 290–1, 303
Grenville, James (1715–83), MP, 157
Grenville, Richard (1711–79), MP, 157, 249
Grosvenor, Sir Richard (1731–1802), 1st Baron, 308

Halifax, George Montagu Dunk (1716–71), 2nd Earl of, 34–6, 44, 194–5, 203, 209, 303, 309
Hallam, Henry (1777–1859), historian, 118–19
Hamilton, Lady Archibald (d. 1752), 54
Hamilton, William Gerard (1729–96), MP, 94
Hanover, Electorate of, 10, 25, 46, 48, 52, 55, 65–72, 126, 143, 159, 162–3, 165–7, 169n, 170–1, 173, 175, 188, 192, 196, 206–7, 209, 222–3, 245–6, 252, 261–2, 269, 277, 280, 284–6, 298, 300
Hanover, House of, 4–5, 11–12, 23, 26, 32, 39, 124–5, 147, 154, 252, 256, 260
Harcourt, Simon (1714–77), 2nd Viscount, 1st Earl, 42, 52–9, 97, 114, 124–5, 143–4, 163, 176, 253–4
Harcourt, Lady, 41
Hardwicke, Philip Yorke (1690–1764), 1st Earl of, 33, 38–9, 78n, 154, 156, 167–9, 178, 185, 194, 198, 207, 239–40, 247–8, 275, 287, 304, 308, 310
Hartington, Marquis of, see Devonshire, Wiliam Cavendish, 4th Duke of
Hawke, Admiral Sir Edward (1710–81), 69–70, 85, 168–9, 294n

Hawley, General Henry (c. 1679–1759), 59
Hayter, Thomas (1702–62), Bishop of Norwich, 13–16, 52–3 and n., 54–6, 58–9, 62–3, 73, 114, 124–5, 143–4, 163
Henley, Sir Robert (c. 1708–72), MP, 208, 292, 308
Hertford, Francis Seymour Conway (1718–94), 1st Earl of, 56
Hervey, John (1696–1743), Lord, 2, 4, 6–8, 20
Hesse Cassel, 70, 165n, 166, 267–71, 298, 300
Hessian troops, 74, 173, 271–3, 277, 280
Hever, 23–4
Hill, Dr John, 238 and n
Hillsborough, Wills Hill (1718–93), 2nd Viscount, 47
Holburne, Admiral Francis (1704–71), 68, 189
Holdernesse, Robert Darcy (1718–78), 4th Earl of, 42, 47, 49, 82, 84, 90, 194, 202–3, 219–20, 271, 295
Holland, 65–7, 271, 294, 296, 305
Holland, Henry Richard Vassall Fox (1773–1840), 3rd Baron, 3, 12, 27n, 101–12, 119–20, 123n, 129, 164n
Holland, Henry Edward Fox, 4th Baron, 119
Home, Rev. John (1722–1808), 238 and n
House of Lords, 5, 17, 24, 34–7, 61, 242–315
Hume, David (1711–76), historian, 22n, 120
Hunt, John, 107
Huntingdon, Francis Hastings (1729–89), 10th Earl of, 88–9

Ilchester, Stephen Fox (1704–76), 1st Earl of, 42
Irby, Sir William (1707–75), 88–9
Irwin, Henry Ingram (1691–1761), 7th Viscount, 274–5

Jacobitism, 10–13, 14n, 15, 17, 21n, 22–3, 26–9, 35, 38–40, 50n, 51n, 55–6, 59–60, 62–3, 116, 119, 124–5, 128, 132–3, 144, 158, 175n, 176, 206, 224, 243–5, 247–9, 252, 254–8, 262–7, 272–3, 321
James I, King, 329
James II, King, 2, 21–2, 24, 31, 56, 58, 86, 132n, 245n, 249, 279, 325
James III, King (1688–1766), 33, 243–5, 257–8, 266
Jeffrey, Francis (1773–1850), journalist, 119n, 120n, 122

Index

Jesuits, 22 and n, 28–9, 32 and n, 52, 232, 255
Johnson, James (1705–74), Bishop of Gloucester, 56, 59, 125
Johnson, Samuel, 129n

Keene, Sir Benjamin, 67
Keppel, Augustus (1725–86), MP, 139–40
Keppel, Rev. Frederick (1729–77), 86, 100, 137–40, 176n, 189n, 191n, 194n, 198n, 203n, 209n, 211n, 218, 238
Kildare, James Fitzgerald (1722–73), 20th Earl of, 43
Klosterseven, Convention of (1757), 85

La Bruyère, Jean de (1645–96), 6–7, 9
La Flèche, Jesuit college, 22 and n, 29
La Rochefoucauld, François, Duc de, 9
Lauderdale, James Maitland (1759–1839), 1st Baron, 104
Lecky, W.E.H. (1838–1903), historian, 132–3
Lee, Sir George (c. 1708–58), MP, 197–8
Leeds, Thomas Osborne (1713–89), 4th Duke of, 56
Legge, Henry Bilson (1708–64), MP, 43, 73, 153, 174–5, 186, 196, 205, 207, 221, 291
Leicester, Thomas Coke (1697–1759), 22nd Earl of, 47
Leicester House, 13–14, 39, 52–9, 62, 64, 68, 71–84, 112n, 113–5, 119, 128–33, 135, 159, 162, 164, 167, 169, 171, 176–83, 189, 193, 194, 197–8, 210, 226–37, 250–1, 262, 272, 278, 280, 286, 290
Leveson-Gower, Lady Elizabeth (Lady Elizabeth Waldegrave) (1724–84), 41–2, 85–6, 98
The Liberal, 107n
Lichfield, George Henry Lee (1718–72), 3rd Earl of, 239 and n
Lincoln, Henry Clinton (1720–94), 9th Earl of, 44, 47
Literary Gazette, 106, 109, 112
Lockman, John, 238
London Chronicle, 293n
London Gazette, 293n, 294n
London Magazine, 242n, 277
Loudoun, John Campbell (1705–82), 4th Earl of, 189
Louis XIV, King, 2, 12–13
Louisa, Princess (1692–1712), 31
Lys, 68
Lyttelton, Sir George (1709–73), MP, 43, 47, 157, 174, 186, 252

Lyttelton, Col. Sir Richard (1718–70), MP, 46

Macaulay, Mrs Catharine, 19
Macaulay, Thomas Babington (1800–59), Whig writer, 118–21
Mackintosh, Sir James (1765–1832), MP, 103, 120–1, 123n
Magna Charta, 323
Mahon, Lord (1805–75), later 5th Earl Stanhope, historian, 118–19
Mainz, 65
Mann, Sir Horace, 57, 73, 98
Marlborough, Charles Spencer (1706–58), 3rd Duke of, 42, 47, 85, 93
Marwood, Thomas, 22n
Mary of Modena (1658–1718), Queen, 21n, 31
Mauduit, Israel, 295
Militia, 74, 187, 276–7, 280, 286–90, 301–3
Minorca, 70, 172–5, 186, 210, 280–1, 283, 286
Mirepoix, Duc de, 67
Molina, Luis de, Jesuit, 232
Monarchy, 1–21, 37, 40, 112–34, 146–8, 195, 248–9, 252–3, 256, 258, 262–3, 272, 290, 303, 313, 319, 321, 326–7
Money Bills, 247, 276, 288, 310–14, 330
The Monitor, 238n
Montagu, George Brudenell (1712–90), 3rd Duke, 24
Montaigne, Michel de (1533–92), 292n, 316–17
Montesquieu, Charles de Secondat, Baron de (1689–1755), 2, 6, 8–10, 47, 272n, 318–22
Monthly Review, 129n, 318–19
Mountstuart, John Stuart (1744–1800), Baron, 88–9
Münchhausen, Philip Adolf, Baron von, 159, 223
Murphy, Arthur, journalist, 94–5, 238n
Murray, John (1778–1843), publisher, 104–8, 110–11, 112n, 134
Murray, William (1705–93), Lord Mansfield, 28, 50, 54–6, 59, 62, 75, 81, 116, 119, 125, 133, 144, 160–1, 171, 174–5, 183–4, 205, 207, 240, 254, 257, 308

Navestock, Essex, 21–2, 24, 28, 31, 33, 38, 47, 60, 87–8, 100, 102, 109–10
New Edinburgh Review, 21, 117 and n, 118
New Monthly Magazine, 112–13
Newcastle, Thomas Pelham–Holles (1693–1768), 1st Duke of, 26, 29, 33, 37,

Index

Newcastle, Thomas Pelham (*cont.*)
40, 42, 47–9, 51–2, 57n, 59–76, 79–85, 88–90, 93–4, 108, 113, 115, 125, 138, 144, 150–1, 153–5, 158, 160–3, 167–71, 175, 177–80, 183–7, 191–9, 201–3, 205–7, 209–10, 212, 214, 216–20, 252, 258, 273n, 275, 278, 280, 287, 295–6, 301, 303–4, 308
Nicholls, John (?1745–1832), MP, 20, 40, 128n, 129
Norfolk, Thomas Howard (1683–1732), 23rd Duke of, 23
North, Francis (1704–90), 7th Baron North, 1st Earl of Guilford, 52, 99
The North Briton, 238n
Nugent, Thomas, translator, 9n, 319

Onslow, Arthur (1691–1768), MP, 38
d'Orléans, Father F.J., historian, 56
Oxford, University of, 11, 62, 110, 144, 258

Parsons, Alderman Humphrey, Jacobite, 27–8
Pelham, Henry (1695–1754), MP, 19, 38–40, 42, 49, 51–2, 54, 59–60, 63, 65, 145, 150, 153, 158, 250, 260
Pelham, Thomas, Jr. (*c.* 1705–43), 29–32
Péréfixe, Hardouin de Beaumont de (1605–70), Archbishop of Paris, 13, 56n
Physiocrats, 6
Pitt, Thomas (*c.* 1705–61), MP, 50–1
Pitt, William (1708–78), 1st Earl of Chatham, 11, 17–18, 26, 32–3, 43, 47, 62, 64, 72–3, 79, 82–4, 88, 90, 94, 113, 115–17, 135, 152–3, 160–1, 163–4, 167–8, 171, 174–5, 184, 186–98, 201, 205–7, 209–10, 212, 214–17, 220–1, 240n, 252, 271, 276, 280, 285n, 286, 291, 295–6, 303–4, 309–10
Plutarch, 315
Pomfret, George Fermor (1722–85), 2nd Earl of, 95, 296
Popery, *see* Catholicism, Roman
Portsmouth, Louise de Kerouaille, Duchess of, 32
Potter, Thomas (1718–59), MP, 208
Poulett, John (1708–64), 2nd Earl, 245, 261
Pratt, Charles (1714–94), MP, 208
Pringle, Sir John, physician, 77–8
Prussia, 65–72, 167, 171–2, 212, 261, 280, 283, 293, 295, 298–300, 309
public opinion, 17–18, 175, 189, 242, 273, 285, 288–90, 292, 316–17
Pulteney, William (?1731–1763), Viscount, MP, 47

Quarterly Review, 3, 76n, 104, 106, 113–18, 126

Radstock, William, 1st Baron (1753–1825), 109
Ramsay, Andrew Michael (1686–1743), 13
Ravensworth, Henry Liddell (1708–84), 1st Baron, 59, 95
Rebellion of 1715, 22–3, 257
Rebellion of 1745, 15, 27, 38–9, 54–5, 60, 155, 176, 246–9
Retz, Cardinal de, 9
Rigby, Richard (1722–88), MP, 46, 51, 60, 84–5, 95, 275
Robinson, Sir Thomas (1695–1770), MP, 47, 154, 160–1, 168, 171, 184, 196
Rochefort expedition, 85–6
Rockingham, Charles Watson Wentworth (1730–82), 2nd Marquis of, 43, 74, 93, 130, 311
Rodney, George Bridges (1719–92), Admiral, 43
Roebuck, John Arthur (1801–79), MP, 17
Rose, George (1744–1818), MP, 52–3, 122n
Roxborough, Robert Ker (*c.* 1709–55), 2nd Duke of, 37
Russell, Lord John (1792–1878), 1st Earl Russell, 120, 123, 127–30
Russia, 70–1, 166, 171–2, 267–71, 293, 295
Rutland, John Manners (1696–1779), 3rd Duke of, 93
Ruville, A. von, 1
Ryder, Sir Dudley (1691–1756), MP, 174

Sackville, Lord George (1716–85), MP, 42, 85, 194, 239 and n
St Germain-en-Laye, 22, 31
St Leger, Matthew, 44–6
St Omer, Jesuit college, 21n, 28–9, 32, 238n, 255–6
Saint–Simon, Louis de Rouvroy, Duc de (1675–1755), 2, 6, 7, 19
Sanchez, Thomas, Jesuit, 232
Sandwich, John Montagu (1718–92), 4th Earl of, 34–6, 40–1, 43, 48–9, 51, 139n, 239 and n, 304
Sardinia, King of, 305
Savile House, 183 and n, 214–15
Saxony, 65, 71, 166, 172, 283n
Scott, George Lewis (1708–80), 52–3 and n., 55–6, 60, 125, 143, 149
Secker, Thomas (1693–1768), Bishop, 242–3
Seven Years' War: outbreak, 64–72, 158–9, 166–9, 171–4, 258–62, 267–73, 280–90;

Index

successes of, 292–5; end of, 215, 223, 238–41, 294–301, 303–10
Shelburne, William Petty (1737–1805), 2nd Earl of, 17–18, 20, 54, 95, 296, 308–9, 311
Sherlock, Thomas (1678–1761), Bishop, 252
smallpox, 32n, 96–101
Smollett, Tobias (1721–71), 238n
Somerset, Lord Charles Noel (1709–56), 4th Duke of Beaufort, 245
Southey, Robert (1774–1843), 107n
Spain, 67, 90, 133, 259, 293, 295, 297, 300, 305
Stanhope, James (1673–1721), 1st Earl, 5
Stanhope, Philip (1714–86), 2nd Earl, 9–10, 47
Stanhope, Sir William (1702–72), MP, 44, 250
Stannaries, Wardenship of, 50–2, 60, 190, 252
Stone, Andrew (1703–73), MP, 42, 52, 53n, 55–6, 58–9, 72–3, 76, 116, 119, 125, 133, 143–4, 149, 183, 254, 257–8
Stone, George (1708–64), Archbishop of Armagh, 42
Strange, James Smith Stanley (1717–71), Lord, 194–5
Suffolk, Henry Howard (1739–79), 22nd Earl of, 308
Suffolk, Lady, 54
Sunderland, Charles Spencer (c. 1674–1722), 3rd Earl of, 5
Sussex, George Yelverton (1727–58), 2nd Earl of, 45

Talbot, William (1710–82), 2nd Baron, 35–6, 53n, 95, 240 and n., 241n, 252, 296
Telemachus, 13, 226–37
Temple, Richard (1711–79), 2nd Earl, 47, 80, 90, 186, 188–96, 199, 205, 207, 209, 240n, 267, 284n, 296, 308
Teynham, Henry Roper (1734–86), 11th Baron, 24
Thomas, Dr John (1696–1781), successively Bishop of Peterborough, Salisbury and Winchester, 52–3, 136, 149
Thompson, Rev. Antony, 255n
Timberland, Ebenezer, 242
Tory Party, Tories, Toryism, 11–12, 39, 54–5, 63–4, 83, 118 and n, 119–20, 128, 132–3, 144, 158, 224, 239n, 243n, 245, 248, 264, 271–2, 318
Townshend, Charles (1674–1738), 2nd Viscount, 20, 24, 26

Townshend, Charles (1725–67), MP, 43, 89–90, 186–7, 194–5
Townshend, Hon. George (1724–1807), MP, 43, 74, 240, 276–7, 286
Townshend, Miss, 41
Trier, 65
Tweeddale, John Hay (c. 1695–1762), 4th Marquess of, 17

Wake, William (1657–1737), Archbishop, 25
Waldegrave family, 21–33
Waldegrave, Arabella, 31
Waldegrave, Sir Charles (d. 1684), 3rd Bt., 29
Waldegrave, Lady Charlotte Maria (Lady Euston), 134–5
Waldegrave, Lady Elizabeth Laura, 108 and n
Waldegrave, Sir Henry (1661–89/90), 4th Bt., 1st Baron, 22, 29, 31, 245n
Waldegrave, James (1684–1741), 2nd Baron, 1st Earl, 21n, 22–33, 35, 43, 100, 110, 243–5, 254–5, 287n, 318
Waldegrave, James (1715–63), 2nd Earl: *Memoirs*, 11–12, 76, 100–40, 213n; and media, 18; and Jacobitism, 23; and father, 25, 243–5; education, 29–32, 232; and Navestock, 31; as courtier, 7–8; begins career, 33 ff; Lord of Bedchamber, 37; and '45, 38; social life, 41–8, 60, 88; and Montesquieu, 9–10, 318–22; marriage, 86, 139; family, 87; H. Pelham's opinion of, 49; a Regent, 50, 253; Warden of Stannaries, 50–2; George III's opinion of, 53, 79; and Leicester House, 55–60, 72–84, 143–5, 176–83, 251, 253–8, 262–7, 326; moves Address (1754), 61–2; intermediary with Fox, 63–4, 161–2; moves Address (1756), 79; foreign policy, 64–72, 153, 166, 209, 267–71, 280–6, 294–301, 303–10; politics in 1757, 79–84, 187–211; attempts to form ministry, 81–2; KG, 84; defends Cumberland 85; on peace, 90–6; satires against Bute and Princess of Wales, 13, 64n, 76–9, 111, 137, 140, 159n, 164, 170–1, 181, 226–37, 258n; death, 96–101
Waldegrave, John (1718–84), 3rd Earl, 30–2, 37, 41–8, 59–60, 85–6, 94, 109n
Waldegrave, John, 6th Earl, 27n, 102–11
Waldegrave, Maria Countess, marriage, 86–7; background, 87; widowed, 97–101; and *Memoirs*, 136–40, 212–13
Waldegrave, Philip, 23n

Waldegrave, Sir William (1618–?), physician, 21n, 22n
Walpole, Sir Edward (1708–84), MP, 87, 139
Walpole, Horace (1717–97), MP, 5, 6, 11–12, 17, 19, 25, 27, 31–2, 41–2, 52–3, 55–9, 62, 64, 72n, 73, 78, 81, 84–8, 94, 96–109, 113–14, 116, 118–24, 129–30, 132–3, 139–40, 164n, 212n, 213n, 243–4, 250–1, 254, 257, 267, 292, 304, 310, 318
Walpole, Horatio (1678–1757), Lord Walpole of Wolterton, 42, 76, 190, 243
Walpole, Lady Maria (c. 1725–1801), 46n, 86–7, 250n
Walpole, Sir Robert (1676–1745), MP, 5, 8, 20, 24, 26, 35, 37–8, 42, 46n, 116, 150, 243–5, 250, 252n
Warburton, William (1698–1779), Bishop, 265n
Washington, Major George, 66
Webb, Sir John, Bt., 22–3, 32
Webb, Mary, 22–3
West, James, 43

Westminster, Convention of (1756), 71, 171n, 172n
Westminster school, 32, 137, 255, 257
Weymouth, Thomas Thynne (1734–96), 3rd Viscount, 296, 304
Whig Party, Whigs, Whiggism, 11–12, 17, 54, 56, 58, 63, 118, 120–34, 154–5, 157, 191, 224, 246–9, 264, 318
White's Club, 42–8, 50, 60, 62n, 85, 88–9, 96, 154n
Wicquefort, Abraham von, 26
Wildman's Club, 62
Willes, Edward, MP, 249–50
Willes, Sir John (1685–1761), 186, 249–50
William III, King, 2, 324, 330
Winchelsea, Daniel Finch (1689–1769), 8th Earl of, 195–6, 198, 201–2, 204, 209
Wolfenbüttel: Duke of, 25; Duchess of, and daughters, 164–5
Wraxall, Sir Nathaniel (1751–1831), 20, 76
Wyndham, Henry Penruddocke, 112n

Yarmouth, Lady (1704–65), 135, 159, 261